The floating pound and the sterling area
1931–1939

THE FLOATING POUND AND
THE STERLING AREA
1931-1939

IAN M. DRUMMOND

University of Toronto

CAMBRIDGE UNIVERSITY PRESS

Cambridge

London   New York   New Rochelle
Melbourne   Sydney

Published by the Press Syndicate of the University of Cambridge
The Pitt Building, Trumpington Street, Cambridge CB2 1 RP
32 East 57th Street, New York, NY 10022, USA
296 Beaconsfield Parade, Middle Park, Melbourne 3206, Australia

First published 1981

Printed in the United States of America
Typeset and printed by Heritage Printers, Inc., Charlotte, N. C.

Library of Congress Cataloging in Publication Data
Drummond, Ian M
The floating pound and the sterling area, 1931–1939.
Includes bibliographical references and index.
1. Sterling area—History. 2. Foreign exchange problem – Great Britain.
I. Title.
HG255.D68   332.4′560941   80–14539
ISBN 0 521 23165 5

Contents

Preface

In 1971, when working on Empire trade and migration between 1917 and 1939, I collected the first of the archival materials that I later worked into the fabric of this book. Other materials were added as time permitted. My researches were assisted by two Canada Council travel grants, a Canada Council Leave Fellowship, a visiting professorship in the University of Edinburgh, and a year's association with the Institute of Commonwealth Studies, University of London. All this assistance is most gratefully acknowledged. I must also thank archivists and librarians in the Public Record Office (London), the Public Archives of Canada (Ottawa), the Roosevelt Library (Hyde Park), and the South African State Archives (Pretoria), as well as university librarians at Toronto, London, Cambridge, Edinburgh, Birmingham, Cape Town, and the Witwatersrand. Among those who have helped by commenting or discussing, or who have read sections of the manuscript, I must mention in particular Robert Boyce, David Dilks, Malcolm Knight, Donald Moggridge, Susan Howson, Leslie Pressnell, Brian Tomlinson, and G. H. de Kock. Sections of the book have been presented, usually in draft or preliminary form, to the Economic History Workshop in the University of Toronto, to the Monetary History Group in London, and to university seminars in Edinburgh, Hull, Exeter, Swansea, Leeds, Cape Town, and the Witwatersrand. I have learned a great deal from the comments, questions, and suggestions of the participants in these gatherings.

Special thanks go to Derek Chisholm, who conducted research on my behalf at Queens University (Kingston) and the Public Archives of Nova Scotia and whose work on other Canadian archival materials has been a most valuable check on my own, to Katherine Munro and Marcelle Kooy for hospitality and kindness in South Africa, and to Mrs. May Simpson and Murielle La Brie for typing so much of the manuscript with such admirable speed and precision.

I.M.D.

Toronto
September 1980

1

Introduction: the sterling area
in the 1930s

This opening chapter sketches the structure of the sterling area from the collapse of the gold standard in 1931 to the outbreak of war in 1939. It describes the chief institutions and their interactions and presents some archival evidence about attitudes and policies in the United Kingdom during the critical months of 1931–2 and at the Ottawa Conference in the summer of 1932. The material serves as an introduction to the more detailed discussion in Chapters 2 through 10.

Chapters 2 through 5 examine the routes by which India, South Africa, and Canada did or did not adhere to sterling after September 1931 and trace some aspects of the relationship between sterling and the economies of Australia and New Zealand. These chapters are meant to provide a survey of the relationship between sterling and the more important Empire currencies. In Chapters 6 and 7 we turn to the World Monetary and Economic Conference of 1933 – the London Conference that was called by the League of Nations in response to Anglo-American initiatives. Concentrating on the monetary side of the meeting, we first survey the formulation of policy in London and the defense of that policy in various international arenas, then treat the discussions with France and America before and during the conference, and finally examine the role of the Empire governments with respect to Britain's private initiatives and her public stance. Chapters 8 through 10 concentrate upon international financial diplomacy from the conference until the outbreak of war. Although they contain some material on the actual movement of rates and reserves, they are chiefly concerned with intergovernmental discussions about exchange management and exchange policy. The sterling area and the Empire retreat into the background, though from time to time they are summoned out of the wings. The final chapter is a sort of extended meditation on the significance of sterling and the sterling area during this troubled decade.

I began to study the history of sterling for several reasons. First, for any economist who was professionally active in the 1950s and 1960s it is interesting to learn why and how the sterling area emerged during the decade when it might be said to have taken shape. Second, because in the 1970s the world has embarked on a general float of exchange rates I thought it might be interesting to know more about the last period when most exchange rates were unpegged. Third, my earlier work on Empire trade and migration had revealed the existence of an arcane subject called "empire money" and had sparked my interest in this matter. Finally, though the literature on the 1930s has been transformed in the past seven years or so, when my researches began I found it diffuse and incomplete.

At first I had seven questions in mind. Why did various countries inside and outside the British Commonwealth adhere to sterling in and after 1931? What did adherence involve? What attitude did Britain's officials take toward the emergence of a sterling area after the pound had departed from gold? What was the importance of sterling balances for the management of exchange rates and reserves? Did Britain's authorities try to manage the balances and, if so, how? Was there any sense in which the sterling area or the Empire component thereof could be said to have had a common monetary policy and, if so, what was the policy and how was it devised and kept in being? Finally, what sorts of consultations occurred within the sterling area? As I worked with the documents and the secondary literature I had to add questions. What was the intellectual basis for Britain's exchange policies and for her international monetary initiatives? To what extent can one detect "monetary interpretations" of the depression in the documents of the period itself; and how did such interpretations influence policy? Did Britain discuss or defend her own float or the sterling system in negotiations with non-sterling countries – in particular, with France and the United States? Did such negotiations have personal or political dimensions and, if so, what were they and how important were they?

At no time did I plan to explain the actual movement of the sterling exchange rate except insofar as some of the things in which I was interested were relevant to the management of that rate. Nor did I plan a heavily quantitative exercise, though I hoped to marshal such numbers as might exist. For the sorts of questions with which I was concerned rather simple approaches can extract answers from the few available numbers. For econometric exercises readers will have to look elsewhere. To master the qualitative material, I expected, would be a sufficient task. So it has proved to be. Whether the results are proportionate to the labors the reader must judge for himself.

1. *What was the sterling area?*

When we talk of a sterling area in the 1930s, what do we mean? In 1939 and for more than two decades thereafter the term has a reasonably precise meaning. The sterling area contained those countries whose foreign exchange reserves consisted wholly or chiefly of sterling. Generally they owned short-dated United Kingdom government securities or treasury bills. Their exchange rates were pegged to the pound so that the sterling area moved up and down as a single unit whenever sterling itself appreciated or depreciated. With respect to the rest of the world the sterling area maintained a common though not uniform fence of exchange controls, although within the area such controls were relatively lax or altogether absent. Foreign exchange earnings were largely pooled and held by the United Kingdom on behalf of the members. Only South Africa maintained significant gold reserves outside of the pool. There were consultations about controls, imports, capital movement, and drawings on the pool; these discussions naturally centered on the exchange control.

Before the outbreak of war in 1939 things were less tidy, and they are therefore harder to describe. There was no formal pooling of reserves, and exchange controls were almost unknown in Britain, the Empire, and the foreign countries that had adhered to sterling. Yet it was generally understood that soon after Britain had abandoned the gold standard in September 1931 a sterling area or sterling group had somehow come into existence. It included India, the Dependent Empire, some semiindependent territories such as Egypt and Iraq, a varying cast of foreign countries, and all the Dominions except Canada. As the area was not fenced about with exchange controls its members had relatively little to confer about, and it appears that they seldom did so. We may define the sterling area most precisely by asking two questions. How were exchange rates fixed? Where were reserves held?

Most of the sterling countries kept their official reserves, wholly or in part, in the form of sterling claims. Such arrangements were of very long standing. Peter Lindert has estimated that in 1913 Britain's short-term obligations to governments and central banks were at least £80 million – 250 percent of her gold reserves at that time.[1] He also claims that since before 1900 such obligations had been growing faster than reserves. Among the holders who could then be identified, much the largest were India and Japan. They pointly accounted for 75 percent of all the identifiable obligations to external governments and central banks. But 19 other holders can also be identified. Among them were Australia, New

3

Zealand, South Africa, Canada, and various Latin American and European states and banks. Besides these identifiable claims, Lindert reports a much larger total of unspecified claims, largely though not entirely private.

Besides these official balances commercial banks and private traders had long held working balances in the London market. Many payments had been through London banks and much finance had been raised there, while every quarter large sums were transfered from overseas debtors to British owners of overseas bonds and shares. Through the highly developed London financial market sterling could be lent out for short periods at attractive rates of interest and with little or no risk of default. As long as sterling was firmly attached to gold such sterling assets also bore no exchange risk. The transactions balances in sterling were especially important for the "imperial banks" that provided commercial and exchange banking services throughout so much of the Empire, the Far and Middle East, and Latin America; but European and American banks also maintained transactions balances in London, and so did many private traders and governments.[2]

During the First World War and in the 1920s, London no longer enjoyed the same unquestioned centrality in world finance. As the United States became a more important buyer, supplier, and financier, the world found it more important to hold relatively large transactions balances of dollars in New York. Nevertheless, the imperial banks and the Empire trading and financial system continued to rely chiefly on London. Further, the Empire monetary authorities were increasingly likely to hold sterling as official reserves. This tendency was increased by the growth of the currency boards, which provided most of the colonial Empire and the Middle East with currency and coin.

In the 1920s the Indian authorities continued to hold sterling along with gold and silver. The currency boards built up their holdings. So did the new South African Reserve Bank, though it still relied more on gold than on sterling. In New Zealand and Canada the monetary authorities held only gold, and the Canadian banks held only small working balances in London, relying chiefly on New York funds as secondary reserves. The New Zealand banks, however, like the Australians, operated a sterling standard whereby they held London funds, buying and selling claims on London at exchange rates agreed among themselves.[3] In Australia the monetary authorities were prepared to hold sterling, although they were not always eager to do so. Outside the Empire altogether, there was a considerable buildup of official sterling balances among the Continental countries. Encouraged by the Brussels Conference of 1920 and then again by the Genoa Conference of 1922 to economize on gold by holding foreign exchange instead, some countries built up considerable sterling holdings. The largest and most inconvenient belonged to France.

The Macmillan Committee estimated that in December 1928 Britain's net short-term sterling obligations were at least £300 million – more than four times her gold reserves.[4] Such obligations continued to increase through 1928, but then they fell substantially in 1929–30 and disastrously in 1931. In three years the total reduction was £403 million; of this, £293 million went across the exchanges in 1931 alone.

As long as sterling was freely convertible into gold at a fixed price, sterling obligations were "as good as gold." But with the collapse of the gold standard in summer 1931, culminating with Britain's departure from gold on 21 September, this was no longer so. Sterling balances would still buy gold; sterling had not become inconvertible into other currencies; but the gold value of reserves and their international purchasing power fluctuated with the value of sterling. With the floating of the pound countries had to choose what exchange regime to adopt. Each country in principle could stay with gold, float, or stay with the pound.

A currency could be related to sterling in three ways. First and simplest was the currency board system of the colonial Empire, Egypt, Iraq, and some mandated territories such as Palestine, in which an overseas monetary authority maintained an automatic relationship between its money and sterling, mechanically issuing local currency in exchange for sterling and vice versa. Second and considerably more complex was the system of semiindependence, in which local monetary developments were not linked simply or mechanically with sterling, though the monetary authorities had pegged their moneys rigidly to sterling and held large sterling balances. This was the system of India, Australia, New Zealand, South Africa, and Portugal. Third was the autonomous system, in which the monetary authorities simply tried to maintain a reasonably steady sterling exchange rate without necessarily concentrating their reserve assets in sterling or committing themselves absolutely with respect to that rate. This was the system after 1931 in Scandinavia and after September 1936 in France.

For the currency board areas there were no questions of policy when Britain left gold. For the areas of monetary semiindependence it was necessary to decide whether to follow sterling, gold, or something else. For other countries, especially those that left gold soon after Britain, it was necessary to decide whether to follow sterling, return to gold, or follow some independent course.

In Canada the government had stumbled in 1929 to a floating dollar.

It was now to ask itself whether, for the sake of Empire solidarity, a predictably protective tariff, or both, it should peg to the pound. For India and in South Africa also, decisions had to be taken. In later chapters we examine the appropriate vacillations and uncertainties.

In Australia and New Zealand the governments did not yet control the fixing of exchange rates. At the Bank of England Governor Montagu Norman believed that the Australian treasurer had to approve the exchange rates that the banks fixed,[5] but it is very far from clear that this was so; only after a considerable battle among the banks did the Commonwealth Bank impose an exchange rate in December 1931. As the banks had always quoted an exchange rate on sterling and sterling alone, the Commonwealth Bank did the same. It may be argued that Australia stayed with sterling due to absence of mind. According to the Commonwealth Bank's historian, it imposed its rate without the concurrence of the other banks and without consulting the government, with whom its relations were not good. Thereafter, though the Australian trading banks continued to hold London funds of their own, the Commonwealth Bank managed the rate by allowing its own London funds to rise and fall. The Bank had more or less accidentally become the holder of Australia's basic exchange reserves, both gold and sterling.[6] In 1922–4 the Australian currency authority had considered returning to gold in advance of the United Kingdom; in 1931 its successor, the Commonwealth Bank, seemed not to have considered the matter at all.

Similarly, in New Zealand the banks had managed the exchange rate among themselves for many years. In New Zealand as in Australia and South Africa, exchange rates had long been quoted as premiums or discounts on London funds – a technique that perpetuated the illusion that a pound was a pound regardless of its location. But in 1930 the premium had begun to rise – that is, the Australian and New Zealand pounds had depreciated markedly vis-à-vis sterling. At length the New Zealand government, hoping to revive the domestic economy, imposed an exchange rate on the banks while indemnifying them against loss. This rate too was in terms of sterling; like the Australian, it endured without change for many years.[7]

Why choose sterling? India, as we shall see, was not allowed to choose anything else. For colonial currency authorities, the question could hardly have arisen. For Australia and New Zealand, in retrospect the choice seems natural enough. Britain was the chief market and the chief industrial competitor; if the exchange rate was a sterling rate, banks would not have to learn anything new and their London funds would not suffer windfall loss, whereas it would be easy to forecast the local price that any external price would imply – no small matter for governments facing a collapse of world market prices for their products. In South Africa, unlike Australia or New Zealand, there was a genuine attempt to stay with gold, and therefore the question of exchange regime was debated openly. The discussion was much influenced by the fact that Britain was South Africa's chief export market.[8] Similar considerations must have swayed the smaller countries in Europe and Latin America that sooner or later pegged to sterling. For Canada and South Africa both situation and debate are complicated by Anglophobia.

For some parts of the Empire pegging to sterling was not a novelty. Most colonial currencies had been stabilized in this way for a very long time. Nor was it at all novel to keep one's external reserves in London. Britain's overseas banks had always done this. Their exchange transactions operated almost entirely through London, and they could not employ idle balances in the overseas territories where they operated because these territories did not have active money markets. Empire governments regularly held sterling balances because they regularly spent large amounts of sterling, especially to service their external debt. Colonial monetary authorities held sterling assets as cover for their currency issues and to manage the exchanges. As central banks were set up in the Dominions and India these new institutions also carried sterling balances for the same reasons. In the 1920s and 1930s there was some shift of sterling balances from "unofficial holders" – chiefly the overseas banks – to "official holders" – monetary authorities and central banks inside the Empire and outside it. But the sterling balances were not created in 1931. They had been there for decades. Indeed, their prior presence made it more natural for so much of the world to opearte a sterling standard after 1931.

When Britain left gold Portugal at once pegged the escudo to sterling at the rate of 110 to the pound. For some time the country had been deliberately accumulating sterling reserves. On 26 September the government told the U.K. embassy, "It is certain that the majority of Portuguese interests abroad are bound to English currency and the stability of the financial reorganisation which had been undertaken in Portugal closely depends on the stability of the pound." The embassy reported that the government had £50 million in London and that there were also large private balances; hence Portugal could not regard the depreciation of sterling with equanimity. By December Montagu Norman told the Foreign Office that though he had no official information on Portuguese exchange policy he believed that Portugal was "content to stabilise on sterling as long as the pound does not depreciate beyond a certain point, which for the time being has been fixed at $3.32."[9] That is, if sterling were to fall below $3.32 the Portuguese would think again. If Norman is to be believed, the Bank of England was not in close contact with the Portuguese monetary authorities, and there is nothing in the Foreign Office records to suggest any sort of liaison. It appears, therefore, that Portugal stabilized on sterling because it was trapped; its sterling balances were so large that it could not bear the capital loss that any other policy would have entailed.

In Scandinavia the development was more complex. Denmark, Sweden, Norway, and Finland all followed sterling off gold. But none pegged to sterling at once, and both Finland and Denmark experimented with exchange controls both before and after their departure from gold.

On 6 October 1931 the Bank of Finland acquired a monopoly of dealings in foreign exchange, fixing a daily rate for transactions in sterling. Exchange control was introduced, and the country tried unsuccessfully to borrow abroad. These efforts were not sufficient, and confidence was not restored. Hence on 12 October the Bank of Finland announced that it would apply for permission to end the gold convertibility of its paper currency. Thereafter there was a severe "valuta crisis" – restrictions and prohibitions on the delivery of foreign exchange. British traders complained that they could not get payment for exports; the Foreign Office transmitted these complaints to the Finnish government. By 31 November the Bank of Finland was following sterling, but to do so it was employing a stringent exchange control. A black market quickly appeared. On 17 December the embassy learned that the Bank of England had offered its Finnish counterpart a credit of £500,000 for four months; almost at once the finnmark was freed to find its own level as the exchange controls were dismantled.[10]

Among the Scandinavian countries things were somewhat confused. Denmark left gold in a sort of two-stage shuffle. On 23 September the export of gold was banned, but it was still possible to convert notes into gold bars. At once the public began to present notes for conversion; at the same time the agricultural interests wanted the country to leave gold altogether. In Sweden the authorities were trying without success to raise a French loan for the defense of the gold standard. In Norway too the central bank was most reluctant to leave gold, but when the Bank of Sweden learned that it could not raise a loan on acceptable terms, on 27 September it convened a meeting with central bankers from Denmark and Norway. Immediately thereafter Sweden banned gold export and ended gold convertibility, Denmark also ended the convertibility of notes into gold, and the Norwegian central bank, with deep misgivings, followed Sweden's example.[11] Both in Sweden and in Norway there were strong reasons for depreciation; many export contracts were denominated in sterling, and these were often long-term obligations. Denmark found its principal export market in the United Kingdom. Hence the British debacle had at once generated speculative pressures that the three central banks could not withstand unaided. The Danes had been obliged to introduce exchange controls. Even after leaving gold they could not at once dismantle them. In all three countries the process of adhering to sterling was an extremely gradual and imperfect one. Although central banks would quote sterling exchange rates, these rates were by no means stable; during the winter of 1931–2 it was said in Whitehall that Scandinavia followed sterling "as far as possible." By January 1932 Venezuela, Bolivia, and Japan had joined the group of independent countries that were basing themselves on sterling or gravitating that way.[12]

In the documents there is remarkably little sign of intergovernmental discussion with respect to these currency developments. The Treasury was actively opposed to any such discussion, and when the Foreign Office accidentally suggested to the Danish, Swedish, and Norwegian governments that they should cooperate with His Majesty's government the Treasury insisted on a retraction. The central banks could and should cooperate with the Bank of England; the governments could not cooperate and should not. In 1935 S. D. Waley of the Treasury wrote to F. Ashton Gwatkin of the Foreign Office, remarking that His Majesty's representatives "should hold studiously aloof from any devaluation controversy so that no country can later claim they stayed on gold or left gold as a result of suggestions from this side." Nor could Britain safely urge countries to join the sterling area either by pegging to sterling or by holding sterling balances. Countries were welcome to peg to sterling, but the decision had to be theirs. As a Bank official later wrote, "We here do not encourage any country to join the sterling bloc or indeed to devalue in any way; our attitude has always been that each country must decide this question for itself."[13] The Treasury view had long been the same, as the Foreign Office was told when from time to time it asked for guidance. The reasons are not clearly explained, but one can easily guess at them. If the Bank or the Treasury were to urge an overseas government to peg to sterling, they could hardly avoid some responsibility for the security and convertibility of the results. Further, exchange policy was political dynamite inside the Empire and outside it. The U.K. authorities could hardly appear to take sides in such controversies. For India and the Dependent Empire, of course, the case was different. As London was ultimately responsible for their good government, they could not be allowed to pursue incorrect policies. As we shall see in Chapter 2, India's officials had to be taught this lesson in 1931. On the other hand, this experience had itself taught a lesson to Bank and

Treasury. If a dependency could demand a £100 million credit to support its exchange position, what might not a Dominion or a foreign state expect?

There were, however, certain encouragements that Britain could give. In December 1931 the central banks of Denmark and Finland applied "urgently" for credit from the Bank of England. Denmark wanted £250,000, and Finland £500,000. These were needed to increase resources so as "to maintain the sterling basis." The Bank would not grant the credit without governmental approval. In the Treasury Sir Richard Hopkins was very much in favor of such credits. He wrote:

One of the leading objectives that we ought to have in mind as soon as we can keep sterling steady at a reasonable level, is to make it easy for as many as possible of the unstable currencies to base themselves on sterling so that we may become the leaders of a sterling block which, pending our restabilisation on gold, would have the best opportunities of mutual trade and would give sterling a new force in the world. The natural leading components of such a sterling block are first of all the various parts of the Empire and secondly the Scandinavian countries. If we have this sort of objective in view I think the Bank of England ought to be ready to give assistance to countries which are following us when the assistance asked is within our compass. . . . This may perhaps be regarded as a first step upon a long road, the end of which cannot be foreseen. On the other hand we need go no further down it than we wish, as it seems to me, the road leads in the right direction.[14]

Neville Chamberlain, the chancellor of the exchequer, approved, and the loans were extended. The sums were small relative to the amount that Britain had committed and would commit to Australia and New Zealand. But they were enough to dissolve some of the exchange controls in the Nordic zone and to ensure that Nordic currencies would float less wildly than in the autumn of 1931.

Already in 1930 the Bank had provided sterling so that the New Zealand government could meet its external obligations.[15] Australia too was allowed a credit in 1930 when its overseas funds were alarmingly insufficient but before the Commonwealth Bank had undertaken to manage the Australian exchanges.[16] Later drawing rights were arranged from time to time. As Professor Giblin has explained,[17] each such drawing right was connected with Australian nervousness about London balances and with an Australian commitment that the Australian pound would not be further depreciated. The Commonwealth Bank took over the management of the exchange in December 1931 when it imposed a rate on the other trading banks. Thereafter it was obligated to buy and sell sterling freely at a price of £1.25 Australian. By mid-1932 it doubted if it had enough sterling to maintain that rate through the year. Accordingly, in July it sought help from the Bank of England, asking and obtaining a drawing credit of £3 million. In July 1936 the Bank was asked for another such credit of up to £5 million so as to stave off a further depreciation. In 1937 another credit of £3 million was arranged in London, largely for defense needs. In mid-1939 the directors of the Commonwealth Bank were considering a further approach to the Bank. In fact, none of these credits was actually used, but their extension shows how anxious Norman was to maintain stable exchange rates within the sterling area.

In managing Britain's long-term lending the authorities did not ignore the effect of lending an exchange stability. Believing that in the 1920s Britain had overdone both her long-term lending and her short-term borrowing, they wanted to control the volume of new long-term overseas lending. Informal controls had existed before September 1931; they then became more systematic. The controls of the 1920s had treated the Empire preferentially, and in the new regime Empire borrowers were soon largely exempted. Norman, we know, hoped that Britain would continue to provide the Dominions with new long-term capital,[18] and he spent an immense amount of time on Empire flotations.[19] Such new loans could be raised and old loans converted only with the authorities' permission and in accordance with their scheduling. The Treasury described the position as follows:

Under the Chancellor of the Exchequer's request of 1 October 1932 no issue ranking as a trustee security can be made in London without prior agreement with the Bank of England regarding the amount and date of issue . . . Further, under the same request the optional replacement of existing issues by new issues involving new underwriting or an invitation of the public to subscribe new cash is made dependent upon the express approval of the Chancellor. The object of these requests is to co-ordinate the requests of intending borrowers and so to prevent possible congestion and depression of the market, and their value has been abundantly proved by recent experience.[20]

But in giving permission it was necessary to consider the position of the would-be borrowers. In the early 1930s there was real risk of Australian default, and Norman wanted Britain to be a patient creditor. Hence, in due course Australia was allowed and helped to convert overseas debt to the lower interest rates that ruled in the 1930s. In 1939 Norman arranged for the refinancing of a large New Zealand maturity. The terms were stiff, but the alternative was either default or depreciation.[21]

It was hard to ensure a rationally metered flow of new sterling when subordinate governments could borrow in London or when conversion loans might be floated in London for the repayment of nonsterling obligations, especially in the United States. As Australasian trade and debt were so firmly based on Britain, there was little risk that credits would at once lead into a demand for dollars or other foreign moneys. In Australia the Commonwealth government coordinated the borrowing of the states and floated loans on their behalf. But Canada was extremely worrying. The senior Dominion had nothing like the Australian Loan Council; its provinces could and did borrow as and when they liked. Further, its great cities floated loans of their own. By 1930 its provinces and cities were as indebted to American financiers as to British. Hence there was a considerable risk that they would try to borrow in London at the low interest rates of the 1930s so as to repay old and more expensive credits in the United States. Also, if any Canadian entity were to borrow heavily in London the dollar-sterling exchanges could at once be disturbed. Canada was not a member of the sterling area; neither government nor banks held significant sterling balances; in the absence of special arrangements a sterling loan would at once be transferred into dollars, depressing the exchanges or depleting Britain's reserves. Finally, the Treasury believed correctly that many Canadian municipalities and some Canadian provinces were bad risks, and it also suspected that some American firms might try to borrow in London through their Canadian subsidiaries.[22] Hence there was some effort at informal control. In 1933, when in London for the World Monetary and Economic Conference, Prime Minister R. B. Bennett promised the Bank that the Dominion would be the only Canadian borrower on the London market;[23] but this was a gentlemen's agreement only, and when Bennett left office in 1935 it lapsed. In 1936 Norman and the Treasury pressed for a new understanding that would exclude the provinces and the municipalities while admitting the smaller mining and industrial issuers. The new Canadian cabinet would not make any such promise, but the minister of finance told Norman that if the Bank refused permission Canada would not object.[24]

With respect to Empire demands for long-term finance, Sir Henry Clay tells us that Norman "exercised a banker's right to criticise."[25] At times he may have done more. To support the exchanges and to get sterling for their home charges the Indian authorities could and did borrow at large in the City, where short-term India bonds were well known and understood. But during its troubles of 1931–2 the South African government had not found it easy to borrow at large either in London or elsewhere. Further, when New Zealand's reserves were dwindling rapidly in 1938–9 neither Norman nor the City was at first inclined to be helpful. From time to time, as in mid-1931, even India could find the market unreceptive. At such times would-be borrowers were inclined to suspect that the Bank had told the market to be unreceptive. It is impossible to prove that such things never happened and tempting to believe that they sometimes did. A further difficulty was that Norman himself was often the intermediary between the would-be Empire borrower and the market. The governor could and did say that some issue was impossible because the market would not provide the funds. In Chapter 5 we shall see examples. But how did he know? Was he always right? Could he always give technical advice only, ignoring his feelings about the borrower's policies?

By managing Britain's lending, both long-term and short, the U.K. authorities could do a good deal to foster exchange stability within the sterling area and to discourage exchange controls. In principle they might also have done something by cooperating with other central banks. As far as Europe was concerned this was possible; in the Empire it was much more difficult.

When sterling left gold in September 1931, the Empire was not well endowed with monetary expertise or even with central banks. As the outer Empire countries equipped themselves with central banks and as those new institutions were staffed so extensively from London, it was natural to suspect that Britain was equipping the Empire with monetary institutions that the Bank of England could somehow control. The Reserve Bank of South Africa had been set up in 1921. Its first governor came from the Bank of England. Only in 1934–5 were central banks established in Canada, India, and New Zealand. The Bank of England provided a deputy governor for the Bank of Canada and a governor for the Reserve Bank of New Zealand; Montagu Norman selected the first governor of the Reserve Bank of India. In 1930 the Bank's advice had been sought on the Australian financial crisis and on New Zealand banking law. Sir Otto Niemeyer made an expedition to the Antipodes. New Zealand's reserve bank law was largely based on his recommendations. Lord Macmillan presided over the Canadian Royal Commission that recommended a central bank for the senior Dominion. All these new central banks were "shareholder institutions," modeled more or less closely on the Bank of England itself. In Australia the suggestions of Sir Ernest Harvey had helped the Commonwealth Bank to evolve into a proper central bank.

Norman's biographer has explained that though the governor took an active interest in the development of Empire central banks he did not want to run them or try to do so. Nevertheless, through correspondence and visiting he made a determined effort to keep in touch with their governors. Professor Sayers has given us more information about Norman's efforts and concerns with respect to Empire central banking.[26] Norman's activity reflected several interests. In the Empire as on the

European continent he wanted to spread the gospel of central banking, and he hoped that the new banks would stand in proper independence of government – hence his labors to disseminate a code of central banking practice. This labor was not inappropriate. Everywhere in the overseas Empire there was confusion about what central banks were, were for, or could achieve. Norman also wanted to make sure that the new banks were properly run. Finally, his concern with these matters cannot have been divorced from his hopes with respect to sterling after September 1931. The better managed the Empire monetary and currency regime, the greater the chance that exchange rates would remain reasonably stable at least within the Empire, and the larger the likelihood that sterling and the sterling bill would retain their importance in world trade and finance.

2. *Empire money and the sterling bloc*

The idea of a sterling bloc could easily become entangled with the idea of an Empire bloc. Indeed, in the winter of 1931–2 it was hard to keep the two ideas distinct, even though Canada and Hong Kong were not on sterling and Egypt, Iraq, Portugal, and the four Nordic countries were – at least, more or less. During the autumn of 1931 the City contained a good deal of sentiment in favor of some sort of sterling bloc, and the Empire money enthusiasts, knowing that an Imperial Economic Conference would soon convene at Ottawa, elaborated their schemes with increasing fervor. Inevitably therefore, the Bank and the Treasury officials had to concern themselves about the sterling area while worrying about a sterling policy, war debts, reparations, and all the manifold perplexities of that complicated and discouraging winter. It is now well known that the authorities began to manage sterling and to worry about the correct sterling-dollar exchange rate almost as soon as they had abandoned gold. Professor Sayers and Dr. Howson have traced the adventures of Bank and Treasury from September 1931 through summer 1932. The authorities quickly convinced themselves that they could not at once peg the pound or return at once to gold. They also came to believe that the pound should be kept below the old par of $4.86 2/3, but for some time they were skeptical about their power to peg sterling at any particular level. London's external liabilities were still immense and her gold reserves still exiguous.[1]

The Dominions and India were intensely interested in the price of sterling because it directly affected the prices in domestic currency of the things they bought and sold outside the sterling area. When South Africa and India inquired about exchange policy they were rebuffed.

14

To J. H. Thomas, the Dominions secretary, and his staff the question was of importance. They would have to deal with the Dominions' importunities, and they recognized the interconnections between exchange rates and tariff bargaining. They could less easily be ignored. In the Treasury, though perhaps not in the Bank, the authorities were at one with the Empire on one question: wholesale prices were clearly too low, and recovery depended on a reversal of the price decline that had pushed some debtors, private and governmental, to the brink of default or over that precipice. The authorities certainly did not and could not place Empire questions in the foreground, but in formulating exchange policy they could not ignore and did not ignore the question of the sterling area. To them it was closely connected with the question of confidence. If sterling were rationally managed people would have confidence in it and adhere to it. Further, and equally important, they would hold sterling balances. But confidence also depended on the avoidance of inflation and therefore on the balance of the government budget. Sterling therefore was still dependent on fiscal rectitude, and so was the sterling area. Later in the decade the authorities would read similar sermons to the French. For the time being it was most important to read them to one another and to their political masters. The outside world, too, should be reassured by emollient pronouncements.

In October 1931, from the Treasury, a senior official explained,

The countries that have been driven off the gold standard with us may become the nucleus of a new block. If we can manage our devaluation in an orderly fashion – and only on that condition – then leadership of the block will be ours and we may be able to maintain to a large extent the prestige of sterling and the vital commercial business which it carries with it. In that case force of circumstances must bring some accommodation with the gold standard countries. But the key to that future is less a present study of future policy than a resolute handling of the problems of today.[2]

Soon thereafter the Treasury officials were set to work on the question of Empire money. The Federation of British Industries and the Empire Economic Union had produced a joint report that advocated among other things stabilization of intraimperial exchange rates and a common Empire currency. Eventually, early in March 1932 the Cabinet received a Treasury memorandum on the subject. Though this memorandum seems to have been lost, its contents can be reconstructed from the surviving drafts. The principal authors seem to have been Sir Richard Hopkins and Sir Frederick Phillips of the Treasury.[3] One official explained, "The object to be aimed at is an Imperial Sterling standard, which . . . should include as many foreign countries as possible." But sterling could be a satisfactory standard only if Britain itself had "some definite monetary policy ... an intention of stabilizing the internal purchasing power of the pound." Another official explained that a sterling standard, preferably at par, would be highly desirable for the Empire:

There is no reason why the British Government should not definitely adopt a sterling basis for the currencies of the Empire as an object of policy and invite the Dominions to concur in it. A very large part of the business of London as a financial centre consists of the business of the British Empire, and the employment of sterling as the basis of all the currencies of the Empire would be a long step towards making sterling an effective rival of gold.[4]

At the time another official, S. D. Waley, was reminding himself that the Dominions were independent monetary authorities for which the currency board system was not appropriate. However, in 1923 the Imperial Economic Conference had recommended that the various Empire countries should set up central banks and hold sterling reserves for stabilizing the exchanges. These things were still appropriate. Further,

It would clearly be desirable from many points of view that the Dominion currencies should be linked with sterling during the period that must elapse before we can return to the gold standard. This depends of course upon the decision of the various Dominion governments. If we can succeed, as we hope to do, in maintaining the pound at a relatively stable level, and in avoiding further depreciation, it may be hoped that Canada and South Africa will recognise that it is in their interests to relink their currencies to sterling.[5]

By spring 1932 the Treasury had concluded:

The object to be aimed at should be an Empire Sterling Standard which would be as nearly as possible universal within the Empire. It involves on the part of each participating Dominion or Colony the acceptance of the policy of keeping its currency at par with sterling. It does not entitle the Dominion or Colony to claim to participate in the decisions upon which the level of sterling is varied or maintained, for the moment that claim is made the proposal passes into the realm of an Empire Federal System and therefore into the realm of impracticability. The Mother Country cannot do more, nor can she do less, than to agree in general principle that subject to her own overriding necessities the interests of the Empire would at all times be borne in mind in the framing of general policy. Within these limits there is room for fruitful discussion at Ottawa ... The Treasury suggest that after discussion at Ottawa in which the objective would be declared, and its general colour defined, the block would be best left to grow. A sane management of sterling would do more than many conferences to secure the object in view.[6]

Meanwhile, in September 1931 Prime Minister Ramsay MacDonald had convened his own Advisory Committee on Financial Questions. Originally this committee had six members – R. H. Brand, Sir Walter Layton, Reginald McKenna, Lord Macmillan, Sir Josiah Stamp, and

H. D. Henderson. Later in the autumn John Maynard Keynes and Sir Arthur Salter joined the group. In its own work the Treasury was aware of the committee's preliminary suggestions. In March 1932, now a committee on the Economic Advisory Council, the group produced a report whose conclusions were much like the Treasury's. The members thought it would be "very desirable" if the countries that had left gold could be encouraged to link themselves closely to sterling. "By this means," they wrote, "trade secures the advantage of stable foreign exchange within the sterling area; the utility of the sterling bill as an instrument of international commerce is enhanced; and sterling itself acquires a greater measure of stability relative to gold standard countries." However, there could be no real centralization of control on an international basis because no one wanted an international central bank either for the Empire or for the world sterling area. "There remains only one form which the pursuits of a common policy can take, namely, that the Bank of England should control the value of sterling independently by the same means that it employs today; and that the other countries should so regulate their monetary systems as to maintain their exchanges at a fixed parity with sterling. This, however, is the practice that prevails today, in so far as other countries adhere at all closely to sterling." Britain could consolidate a sterling group only by convincing other countries, inside or outside the Empire, that "the closest and most definite adherence to sterling is likely to be in their best interests." This adherence depended on confidence, which in turn depended partly on international consultation. British authorities should keep in touch informally and naturally with the authorities of the other sterling countries. But little could be expected from a formal discussion, at the coming Ottawa Conference or elsewhere. Meanwhile, it would be useful if Britain could again lend overseas as long as the borrowers would spend the proceeds in the United Kingdom.[7]

This committee reported because the prime minister asked them to think about the sterling area and the Empire; the Treasury worried about these matters partly because in response to the suggestions of industrialists and Empire visionaries Chamberlain asked them to do so,[8] partly because such ideas were in the air, and partly because J. H. Thomas, the Dominions secretary, was pressing the chancellor. Early in January 1932 he asked Chamberlain about monetary policy at Ottawa. He or his officials wrote:

I am of course well aware of the danger and difficulties of any proposals for anything like a common monetary policy within the Empire. On the other hand, disparities between exchange . . . may obviously be of even greater significance . . . than tariffs. The question, difficult as it is, can hardly be avoided.[9]

17

He feared Canada would raise the question of silver and asked what Britain should now do to define its policy in case any of the other Ottawa participants want to talk about money, credit, and the exchange.

Partly because his officials were at work on the question already, Chamberlain did not answer in haste; on 3 March Thomas was obliged to write again. Rather plaintively he asked, "Are you yet in a position to say anything further regarding the question of monetary policy (including silver) at the Ottawa Conference, about which I wrote you on January 4?" Chamberlain responded, "I hope to be in a position to let you have something about monetary policy and the Ottawa Conference fairly soon." Thomas hoped that the Cabinet Committee on Ottawa would discuss the matter, but its records do not reveal if it ever did so. It is known that the Treasury view was circulated, however; presumably the Treasury argument disposed of the question.[10]

Governor Norman was eager for "real, effective, and permanent monetary cooperation" within the Empire, but he did not think Ottawa would be the right place to discuss monetary questions. The Bank had little interest in a new form of "empire currency." It looked to the gold standard in the end, and for the time being it hoped "by all possible means [to] defend the continued validity of sterling and the sterling bill as an instrument of international exchange."[11]

In essentials the Bank and Treasury positions were identical. It was desirable to have sterling used as a means of exchange, a unit of account, and a store of value, in international trade and finance, both inside the Empire and outside. If managed sensibly it would be used in this way. If we are to judge from his actions Norman was willing to go a step further. Once a country had decided to stabilize on sterling the Bank would extend modest credits to prevent any adventitious change in an exchange rate. As long as a government was managing its domestic affairs with circumspection the Bank would provide temporary sterling finance for that government's London obligations. But if domestic budgets were unbalanced deliberately, or if domestic credit expanded recklessly, the erring government could not count on help from London – as the New Zealand authorities discovered to their cost in 1938–9.

Outside Whitehall there was considerable interest in the expansion of the sterling area, and in the fixing of exchange rates within it. There was still a tendency to think that a pound was a pound whether it was a New Zealand or a South African pound or a United Kingdom one. Hence it seemed unnatural for the Australian and New Zealand pounds to be worth less than a United Kingdom pound. And it seemed even more unnatural to change the exchange rates within the sterling area. Because of these assumptions and because before 1931 many financial arrangements had been made in terms of "pounds" *simpliciter*, intra-imperial changes could be inconvenient to traders, pensioners, creditors, and debtors. Furthermore, there was a widespread assumption that a big sterling area was somehow a good thing for Britain. The visionaries of imperialism were inclined to see the sterling area as a symbol of Britain's predominance and of Empire unity. It was divisive to increase intra-imperial tariffs; it was also divisive to change intraimperial exchange rates.

Leo Amery was out of office, but he had considerable influence with the Empire Economic Union (EEU) and the Federation of British Industries (FBI). It appears that it was Amery who inspired the EEU and FBI to propose an imperial currency system. He also presided over the Iraq Currency Board, and to the would-be welder of monetary unity the currency board was an ideal device. Foreign exchange reserves were held not in gold or foreign moneys but in sterling; the local supply of currency was determined automatically on the basis of these sterling reserves; because one could not change the exchange rate without at once altering the domestic currency supply, that exchange rate was almost immutable. In 1932 Amery urged R. B. Bennett to give Canada this excellent British invention; in 1933 he urged Chamberlain to do something similar for the whole Empire.

The chancellor was not impressed. He responded:

With regard to the Imperial Sterling area, I cannot see what advantage you think would accrue by your proposal even if it were practicable . . . the interests of the Dominions and of the Mother Country might not exactly harmonize on all occasions. If, therefore, New Zealand had been tied to a value of the pound fixed by Great Britain in the interests of Great Britain surely this would have led to friction and not to unity with New Zealand. I think it is much better to go on as we are doing, gradually building up world confidence in sterling, which, by degrees, is bringing one country after another into line, without any compulsion. There is another thing, which I don't think you quite appreciate at its true value, and that is the psychology of the European countries with respect to gold. If they thought that we had decided permanently to divorce ourselves from gold, I doubt very much whether they would approve, as gold still seems to them the one stable and satisfactory measure of value, though, of course, they realize that something has gone wrong with the use of it. The more I see of this difficult and complicated question, the more I am convinced that it would be wrong to lay down rigid rules in conformity with theoretical considerations. There are too many factors in the case which do not lend themselves to theory.[12]

With respect to the attitudes of the gold countries the events of summer 1933 had confirmed the chancellor in his beliefs; with respect to the size of the sterling area and Britain's place in it the events of 1933–6 did nothing to change his mind.

At times the authorities and advisers worried about the future of the sterling bill.[13] It was feared that if sterling floated financial business would leave London because the sterling bill of exchange, which still financed so much of world trade, would be an unstable instrument relative to other moneys. Overseas importers and exporters would be reluctant or altogether unwilling to invoice or finance in sterling because final costs and payoffs would, in terms of their own currencies, be uncertain. In the City there were discount houses and acceptance firms whose livelihood seemed to depend on the continued existence and activity of the sterling bill; if the value of sterling finance were to fall substantially these firms might starve to death. Further, there was known to be a connection between the bill market and the sterling balances. Overseas firms held sterling for placement in the market and as transactions balances to finance and support their own activities as borrowers and lenders in that market. If the market were to contract one might suppose that these balances would fall, and fall sharply. Thus the capital account of the nation would suffer no less than the profit and loss accounts of the City.

In the event, these worries proved excessive. Certainly the bill market did contract, and the specialist firms did have trouble.[14] For this there were many reasons; among the more important were changes in the pattern of international payment and the fall in the volume and value of world trade. But the sterling bill and the sterling balances linked therewith did not vanish from the scene. Even when the pound was at its most unstable, as in the winter of 1931–2, many foreigners found that there was still no substitute for London. The market in forward sterling, which had existed before September 1931, developed much more quickly than some observers had expected. Through the market, therefore, exchange risks could be reduced, shifted, or altogether avoided. From late 1933 until mid-1938 sterling did not fluctuate very much, and so the actual risks were smaller than had been foreseen in the winter of 1931–2. Finally the sterling area itself, where exchange rates changed seldom or not at all, covered a very large proportion of the external trade that had financed itself through London before September 1931.

In the Foreign Office the sterling area was always regarded with unease. Until January 1932 the FO contained no specialist on economic affairs and so the unease was muted. Thereafter it was somewhat easier for the unease to be expressed, and presumably through informal channels it reached the Treasury and the Bank. However, the monetary authorities did not ask the opinion of the Foreign Office, which spluttered along by itself. Naturally it was concerned about the way in which a sterling bloc might affect international relations. France and the United States were especially worrying to the Foreign Office, but from time to time Germany also attracted its nervous glances.

Early in 1933 Sir William Selby and F. Ashton Gwatkin of the Foreign Office prepared a memorandum on the future of a sterling group. They discussed the suggestion for stabilizing exchange rates within the bloc and then reflating so as to raise sterling prices. Such ideas had often been canvassed, and they were especially noticeable in the winter of 1932–3. Britain and the Empire were preparing for the World Monetary and Economic Conference; the Scandinavian states had asked to be informed and perhaps consulted about Britain's plan for the conference. Selby and Gwatkin thought that it would be unsafe to reflate the sterling bloc in isolation because the gold bloc would not tolerate the forcing of Britain's exports through currency depreciation. Therefore the United Kingdom would shortly be unable to import except from within the sterling bloc. They also feared that Britain might lose the bill business of the nonsterling world. Further, they thought it politically unsatisfactory to envisage any such solution without France and the United States. They wrote,

Politically, every consideration points to our not attempting to move towards a sterling bloc as an end and aim of our policy, while economically there may equally be reasons – and strong reasons – why we should not push our position as the centre of a sterling bloc too far . . . both our political and our economic interests lead in the direction of an international rather than a sectional solution.[15]

Another official minuted his agreement: "Even if such a sterling policy would work, which is uncertain, it would be 'disastrous politically'."[16] Summarizing these and other comments, Sir Robert Vansittart, the permanent undersecretary of the Foreign Office, observed that if the World Conference were to fail Britain might be driven into a sterling bloc but more likely would have to rearm and form an alliance with France so as to control Germany, while conciliating the United States. He asked, "How would that square with a sterling bloc? Ill, I should say." Nevertheless, "the question anyhow seems to be at present rather a remote one. If matters begin to mend we shall not come to that pass; and if all goes amiss events are not likely to work out in that direction but in an opposite and worse one."[17]

On the other hand, even in the Foreign Office it was sometimes suggested that the sterling bloc might be a good weapon with which to frighten the gold countries into reasonableness, especially in relation to the maldistribution of the world's gold.[18] It was also suggested that if

Europe were to collapse and crash into financial chaos a sterling bloc might "prove an invaluable rock to which not only we and the Dominions and other countries might cling, but at which the remaining gold standard countries, which are largely responsible for existing conditions, might also catch and thereby save themselves from destruction." [19] Exactly how this salvation would be effected the writer of the minute did not explain. To Keynes the case for a sterling bloc was largely of this sort. He hoped that such a bloc would manage its currency in a rational way, first raising and then stabilizing the price level so as to assist the economic recovery not only of Britain and the Empire but of the world. Keynes assumed that the Bank of England and bloc would operate whatever monetary policy he thought sensible at the moment.

The trouble was that the sterling area generated expectations either excessively optimistic or positively dangerous.

In the early 1930s monetary nostrums were legion. Some but not all had been brewed by Keynes. To influential public men in India, Australia, and New Zealand, as in the United States, monetary expansion was to bring salvation. And imperial visionaries yearned for some visible articulation of imperial unity in the monetary sphere. These themes and pressures interacted. Politically and diplomatically they were important. Even if its monetary authorities had been minded to experiment Britain could not safely have done anything too terribly visionary: foreigners held very large sterling balances, and from late 1931 the Bank kept itself regularly informed about these alarming obligations. The balances generated a fear that was the main obstacle to Keynes's more visionary schemes for commodity money and managed currency. It was bad enough to be off gold; if the balances were not to drain away and depreciate the pound to an unacceptable extent it was essential to be orthodox and especially noninflationary, no matter how much one might want prices to rise. Credit could become easy and cheap so long as the new credit did not finance government deficits, and so long as the budget stayed balanced. Thus foreign confidence could be retained and the sterling balances kept in London.

From the winter of 1931–2 until the end of the decade the Treasury was constantly on guard lest the overseas sterling countries, especially the Empire countries, should undermine confidence in sterling by foisting or trying to foist experimental programs – deliberate credit expansion, deficit budgeting, public works programs – onto the United Kingdom. The Treasury officials also guarded against the idea that the administration of sterling might somehow be internationalized. In an Age of Conferences such an idea was natural enough, and it was sometimes suggested by those who should have known better, such as Keynes.

In November 1931 Keynes circulated a paper proposing an Empire Monetary Conference that would decide how sterling should be managed in future. By fixing "broad outlines of an Empire Sterling Standard" the United Kingdom "could then approach other countries in a vastly stronger position," and "South America, Central America, and Scandinavia might eventually go in a sterling standard, managed by the Bank of England and pivoted on London."[20] There were, Keynes observed, three ways to manage sterling, and the conference ought to consider all of them. The pound might go back to gold at some new, presumably lower, but definitive parity. It might simply be managed by the Bank with no definite commitments. It might be managed so as to stabilize sterling prices – the alternative that Keynes himself favored.[21] Fortunately for everyone this suggestion died almost at once. But when MacDonald's committee of worthies reported early in March 1932 Keynes's suggestions had been discarded, consigned to the same wastepaper basket that was to receive so many schemes for Empire monetary solidarity.[22]

3. *Empire money at the Ottawa Conference*

Meanwhile, Leo Amery was doing his best to excite trouble on the monetary front. For years he had been concerned about Empire money. In the early twenties he had espoused schemes of Empire exchange and credit, which had won him nothing but the contempt of the Treasury officials. Late in January 1932, Amery wrote to Prime Minister R. B. Bennett of Canada, "I trust you will not let the Treasury here veto the fullest discussion at Ottawa of the currency question."[1]

Late in February the Canadian House of Commons resolved that the Canadian government should "initiate and support measures for the stabilisation of the currencies of all British countries." Hence nobody was surprised when Bennett told Sir William Clark, the U.K. high commissioner, that the conference should emphasize currency as well as trade.[2]

Chamberlain decided that he wanted to know in what form the Canadians would raise the question of currency.[3] Clark thought that the Canadians had nothing concrete in mind, but Thomas asked him to find out for certain.[4]

For more than two months there was no word from Ottawa. In mid-April Bennett told Chamberlain he expected the United Kingdom delegation would make the most important contribution.[5] At the same time the government of India weighed into the lists. Delhi supported Canada's idea of a discussion of "fundamental issues of whether there could be a concerted currency policy among the Empire countries." It hoped Britain would accept "the principle that sterling policy shall be regulated with the deliberate purpose of producing a certain level of prices," taking account of Empire countries' interests.[6]

This was more than the Treasury could stand. Later that month its officials wrote that it was impracticable for Britain to admit the Dominions to the management of sterling. The coming conference was not likely to say anything definite about sterling management, and so "the outcome of the discussion on currency policy at Ottawa is likely to be somewhat negative."[7]

At long last, late in May the Canadian prime minister cabled his draft conference agenda to London. He said:

The Canadian Government . . . are convinced that measures for the development of inter-Imperial trade must, to a considerable degree, be dependent upon the stabilization at appropriate levels of our several currencies. It is recognised that in some respects these questions will not admit of satisfactory settlement on exclusively Imperial lines. The Canadian Government accordingly, feel it would be premature to proceed with detailed plans for concerted action in this field until it is clear as to the policy which will be adopted at the forthcoming conference in Lausanne.[8]

In the agenda, under "Monetary-Financial Questions" he included: "Consideration of desirability and feasibility of taking steps to restore the general price level and to stabilize exchange, including consideration of monetary standards." The Canadian authorities thought it vital to stabilize exchange rates, though as yet they had nothing special to propose.[9]

Following the usual practice for imperial conferences, Bennett repeated his telegram to the other Dominions. In response the New Zealand government urged that the agenda papers should include "currency and price level, central banks, and kindred problems." It feared that the United Kingdom would omit or ignore these matters.[10]

Whitehall was not happy with the Canadian suggestion for the agenda. It replied that it would prefer the following words: "consideration of existing interrelationships of various currencies and monetary standards of the Empire and of means to be taken to promote secure exchange conditions most favourable to mutual trade." And it commented: "We . . . are of opinion that favourable conditions for framing any definite plan of stabilisation may be found not yet to exist."[11] The Canadians insisted that they wanted to fix "wider terms" than the British wording would allow. They demanded and got the following: "Consideration of existing interrelationships of the various currencies and monetary standards of the Empire, and of the desirability and feasibility of taking steps to restore and stabilise the general price level and to stabilise exchange."[12]

Once the agenda was settled the Treasury prepared another memorandum that was in effect a comment upon it. The arguments were the same as before. It would be a good thing if prices were to rise. But monetary manipulation alone would not raise them. It would be premature to restore the gold standard or peg the pound because the underlying disequilibriums still remained. Interest rates however had fallen and should remain low, whereas credit should be sufficiently easy to be "adequate to meet the requirements of expanding trade and industry provided that no speculative movements occur." With respect to the conference itself a penciled Treasury note said the interrelationship of Empire currencies was a "minor" question. The author urged that there should be no discussion of the price level and stabilization. "All the economic and currency experts will want to propose every kind of scheme. If the matter is referred to them we shall have nearly as many recommendations as there are experts, with a very unsettling effect on sterling and on confidence."[13]

At Ottawa in summer 1932 Chamberlain hewed to the Treasury line and got his own way to a large extent. With him in Ottawa were Sir Frederick Phillips from the Treasury and R. N. Kershaw, the Bank's expert on Empire monetary matters. As Hopkins and the Bank had urged, he was able to avoid any commitment to the gold standard, exchange stabilization, or inflationary finance. Yet he was able to convince the Dominions and India that the United Kingdom was conveniently committed to cheap money and to credit expansion for legitimate commercial purposes. Finally he was able to convert the Dominions concerned with low agricultural prices into acquiescence in his own projects of commodity control.

The conference delegated monetary and financial questions to a special committee. On July 29 Chamberlain explained what the United Kingdom would and would not do. Prices should rise, he said. But disequilibriums between production and consumption were as much to blame for the existing situation as any monetary policy. Reparations had caused further problems, as had the drying up of investment capital. He announced: "it cannot be contended that the world can be put right or even that prices can be restored merely by an alteration of the monetary factor." The conferees could do nothing for the prices of commodities in which there was a world market. When Britain was the principal buyer, Chamberlain urged, the delegates should consider regulating their exports. As for stabilization, there was no point in discussing it. The flows of hot money were so great that even Britain's Exchange Equalisation Account could not be sure of stabilizing the exchanges, much less pegging them permanently at some definite level. Britain would continue to keep credit plentiful and cheap. But there should be no "rash experiments in monetary policy." [14] In response to pressure from Dominion delegates, especially from S. M. Bruce of Australia, Chamberlain later went so far as to say his government was "confident that the efforts which have successfully brought about the present favourable monetary conditions can and will, unless unforeseen difficulties arise, be continued." [15] Later he told his own delegation that 'it was unlikely that any very startling recommendations would result from the deliberations of the Committee . . . As the Delegations were not agreed on the major issues, their report would contain no controversial matters, and would in all probability be unanimous." [16]

It has been said that the Ottawa Conference committee on monetary questions was meaningless.[17] In the context of the conference proceedings that adjective is certainly appropriate; the conference was not about money, and it took no binding decisions on exchange rates. Nevertheless, though at the time the committee report was little more than Chamberlain's device to head off the wilder inflationary proposals and to keep the Empire quiet, once embedded in the conference conclusions the report acquired a very considerable importance. On the one hand Britain could and did use it as a public statement of its own policies with respect to cheap money, low interest rates, and easy credit for legitimate commercial purposes; on the other hand it could and did serve to define Britain's policy with respect to gold and the gold standard.

Neither the committee nor the conference said anything about the desirability of stabilizing sterling relative to gold. It was merely observed that the United Kingdom would try to offset speculative movements in the price of sterling, and that it would be valuable if Empire countries could maintain stable exchange rates on a sterling basis. Nor was anything said about exchange reserves, London credits, or exchange controls. It was higher prices, Chamberlain and the delegates agreed, that would help to stabilize intraimperial exchange rates. Indeed, Chamberlain made every effort to convert the monetary discussion into a program for price raising through production control.

With respect to the gold standard itself, Chamberlain recognized that Canada and South Africa were in favor of gold. But he explained, "We must make it clear that we have no intention of returning to the gold standard unless we can be thoroughly assured that a remedy has been found for the maladjustments which led to the breakdown of that standard last year . . . Before we change our present basis we must be sure

26

that the change can be maintained and that we shall not have to do our work all over again in a few years' time."[18] The committee report followed the same course. Ultimately, it declared, there should be a "satisfactory international standard." This should not only keep exchange rates stable but should ensure that finance and trade would work smoothly. Such a standard could exist only if there were agreement among the "great trading nations of the world" and only after "several conditions precedent" had been attained: higher commodity prices and an "adjustment of the factors political, economic, financial, and monetary which have caused the breakdown of the gold standard in many countries, and which, if not adjusted, would inevitably lead to another breakdown of whatever international standard may be adopted." Furthermore, the new arrangements, when and if they were introduced, should be designed to avoid "wide fluctuations in the standard of value."[19]

With respect to gold and the stabilization of exchanges Britain and the Empire had now defined a policy. But it was still really Britain's policy; South Africa still clung to the full gold standard, and Canada was operating a somewhat unclean float with her eyes fixed not on sterling but on the U.S. dollar. As for the rupee, though the Indian currency was stabilized on sterling both Indian opinion and Indian officials wished it were not. In the next three chapters we follow developments in these three great Empire countries.

2

Sterling and the rupee

In the historiography of Indian nationalism, the "question of rupee ratio" regularly obtrudes itself. By the "ratio" is meant the exchange rate between the rupee and sterling. Should the rupee have been worth one shilling and fourpence, as before 1914; two shillings, as briefly in 1920; or one shilling and sixpence, as from October 1924 until long after 1939? Should it have been pegged to gold, to sterling, or to nothing in particular? Because a cheaper rupee implied a more protected domestic market for Indian producers, neither industrial opinion nor the Congress Party was prepared to ignore the question. In the 1920s Congress pressed for devaluation at least to the prewar level of 1/4. London was adamant in its determination to keep the rupee at one shilling and sixpence. Expatriate officials, as we shall see, often disagreed with Whitehall policy. But as B. R. Tomlinson has recently shown, Whitehall prevailed.[1]

In this chapter we first trace the arguments that lay behind the Whitehall position and the expatriate officials' efforts to change that position in 1931. Our discussion parallels Tomlinson's work and relies on most of the same materials, but the emphasis is perhaps somewhat different. We then turn to some later developments, where we shall see that the rupee exchange rate and the management of the sterling-rupee exchange were closely intertwined with the movement of India toward responsible self-government. Finally we glance at the links between Indian gold exports and British gold imports in the later years of the 1930s.

1. The crisis of 1931

Indian currency history is complex enough to have discouraged even Oscar Wilde.[1] From January 1898 until late 1916 the government of India rather absentmindedly operated a sterling exchange standard. In India there were paper rupees, which the Indian government issued. There were also silver rupees whose bullion value was far less than their face value. They were often described as "notes printed on silver." With

28

some reluctance at first, the government of India maintained the rupee at or very near to 1/4; it held gold, silver, and sterling securities, and it normally was a seller of rupees for sterling in the London market. Occasionally it supplied sterling in exchange for rupees.[2] During the war the system broke down and the rupee appreciated dramatically. In 1920 the government of India, following the recommendation of the Babington Smith Committee, tried vainly to stabilize the rupee first at 2/– gold and then at 2/– sterling. The rupee had appreciated in response to temporary pressure, which ceased to operate just as the government tried for a 2/– rupee. The currency then floated relative to gold and sterling, which, of course, was also floating relative to gold. By October 1924 the rupee, having fallen to 1/3 sterling early in 1921, had risen to 1/6 sterling. This level Government maintained. When sterling returned to gold in April 1925, 1/6 sterling became 1/6 gold.[3] In 1926 the Hilton Young Commission on Indian monetary affairs recommended a gold bullion standard. Government should commit itself to buy and sell unlimited amounts of gold bullion at a fixed price that yielded an exchange rate of 1/6. In 1927 Government introduced and passed a currency bill that established the exchange value of the rupee as 1/6. The measures committed Government to buy gold at a fixed parity, though it was allowed to exchange rupees either for gold or for sterling. The Hilton Young Commission had also strongly urged Government to set up a reserve bank, which could rediscount paper and control the currency and exchanges. In 1927–8 Government attempted to do so, but after discouraging encounters with the legislature it desisted[4] and did not resume its labors until 1933. The Reserve Bank of India began to function only in January 1935. In the early 1930s, therefore, Government was directly responsible for maintaining the convertibility of the rupee and its external value.

Exchange arrangements were as complex as the currency system. India had several kinds of banks – indigenous banks of various sorts; the Imperial Bank of India, which had been formed as a commercial bank and a bank of rediscount in 1919; and the British-based "exchange banks" such as Chartered and Grindlay's. The Imperial Bank was a merger of the three long-established Presidency Banks of Calcutta, Bombay, and Madras and a successor to them. It was not allowed to undertake exchange business, which was reserved for the exchange banks and for Government.

Under normal conditions India's commodity trade produced an excess supply of sterling, which the exchange banks and others would offer for sale. As the government of India normally required some £30 million sterling per year for its "home charges" – pensions, interest on debt, procurement, some defense outlays, and miscellaneous administrative costs – Government bought the sterling that the commodity trade supplied. Much of this sterling was earned through India's trade with third countries, where India typically ran very large export surpluses.[5] Until 1923 Government bought the sterling by selling "council bills" in London, whereby it received sterling in London and delivered rupees in India. Thereafter it bought sterling in India, again giving rupees locally and receiving sterling in London.[6] The form had changed but not the substance.

Of course there was no guarantee that everything would balance conveniently. Government's attention was concentrated first on its own finances. For smoothing purposes government held rupee balances in India and sterling balances in London. It could and did borrow in both places on various terms. The London market was familiar with long-term flotations and with short-term "India bills," which were denominated in sterling. In addition Government had long maintained two separate kinds of monetary reserves. One, the Paper Currency Reserve, had originally been meant to ensure the convertibility of paper rupees into silver. The other, the Gold Standard Reserve, had originally been devised to help the authorities move toward a pure gold standard.

The Gold Standard Reserve was fixed at £40 million, and it could contain gold and securities. In our period all its assets were in London until late 1930, when it began to accumulate gold in India, giving up sterling in London to support the exchanges. Its London gold holding remained fixed at £2.2 million from 1928 until 1933. The idea of a fixed maximum Gold Standard Reserve strikes one as odd. It had begun before 1914, when the Reserve had been built up from seigniorage on the silver rupee currency and from interest on Reserve securities. The point about the maximum was that once it had been reached such revenues could be used for Government's general purposes.

In 1932–3 the Reserve partially rebuilt its holdings of London securities at the expense of its Indian gold holdings. It did not, however, ship gold. The authorities were supposed to divide the security holding between different maturities so as to achieve a reasonable mixture of yield and liquidity. During 1931 the Reserve had to sell or run off most of its short-dated securities, so that by mid-June 1931 it was dangerously illiquid.

As for the Paper Currency Reserve, it was also divided between India and London. In our period, some securities were in London and all other assets were in India. World attention was inclined to focus on the Paper Currency Reserve because it contained such immense quantities of silver. There had once been silver in the Gold Standard Reserve as well, but this had been sold off. As India had moved to a gold bullion standard in 1927 this silver seemed to represent a threat to the world silver price. Indeed, by shedding silver from the Gold Standard Reserve, Government may have contributed to the collapse of silver in the late 1920s. By 1930 the Paper Currency Reserve contained gold, silver, securities, and advances to the Imperial Bank of India. There were statutory limits that controlled the Reserve's holdings of certain rupee securities and its advances to the Imperial Bank.

In principle both Reserves could have provided metallic assets so as to support the rupee exchange. The mechanics would have been different, depending on the choice of Reserve, but the external effect would have been the same. In practice, however, the expatriate officials, for two main reasons, were most reluctant to draw gold from either. First, they suspected that the Indian populace was too unsophisticated to accept or hold a paper currency that was not visibly backed by large metallic reserves. Second, they were sure that the Congress Party would make immense political capital out of any plans to "denude India of gold for Britain's benefit."

At the British end, the accountant general of the India Office (Sidney Turner in 1930 and thereafter) was much concerned with the management of the Gold Standard Reserve, and he cooperated with the Office's Finance Department and with the financial secretary, Sir Cecil Kisch. At the Indian end, responsibility for both Reserves and for the general management of the paper circulation rested with the controller of the currency in Calcutta; meanwhile, Sir George Schuster was the finance member in Delhi.

The Depression dealt severe blows not only to Indian prosperity but to Indian Government finance. The fall in primary-product prices created great difficulty in the collection of rent revenue and land tax, some of which, like irrigation charges, had to be deferred. Customs duties also yielded less as the volume and value of imports declined. Hence the Indian government began to run sizable deficits – at least after providing for sinking fund. In any event, both in London and in India the government borrowed heavily – in India largely on treasury bills, creating an enormous floating debt that was a continual worry both in Delhi and in London. In spring 1931 a large India loan in London "failed," having been left almost entirely with the underwriters.

Meanwhile, both in India and in London it was by no means clear who could control Indian finance, currency, and exchange policy in the new constitutional dispensation. Both Indian and British financiers were nervous about the prospect of full responsible government in which an Indian finance minister would run such matters, subject to the nor-

mal parliamentary checks of responsible government. It was widely believed that in such circumstances the rupee would be either devalued to
1/4 or floated. In the longer term it was feared that an Indian ministry
might continue the large budget deficits, default on sterling loans, issue
large quantities of paper money to finance its internal deficits, and otherwise engage in "reckless practices of unsound finance." Unfortunately,
among the Indian Congress supporters there were many who advocated
such practices, and there was little of the "sound financial opinion"
that might be expected to support a policy of fiscal responsibility.

In this situation the Indian government faced several difficult tasks.
It must finance its own domestic deficit and roll over its domestic debts.
It must somehow acquire enough sterling to meet its standing home
charges, both for administration and for debt service. It must generate
sufficient confidence in the fixity of the 1/6 exchange rate to encourage
Indian holders of rupees to stick with the rupee. And it must do all these
things in an environment of constitutional uncertainty in which all
holders of rupees and all holders of sterling-denominated Indian liabilities were justifiably nervous about the future value of such things. At
bottom it was Britain's Labour government, having started the process
of constitutional discussions, that was largely responsible for the uncertainty.

It is hardly surprising that rupee holders began to buy sterling in some
quantity during the autumn of 1930. The export of capital funds, a most
unusual phenomenon for India, appeared to be causing a steady and
painful drain throughout at least the first eight months of 1931. The fall
in the world prices of primary products had so reduced India's current
earnings of foreign exchange that the current-account balance must
have worsened also. Thus the fall in prices plus the capital export made
it impossible for the Indian government to find its home charges in the
usual way – by purchasing sterling in the foreign exchange market. From
early 1930 the Indian government was unable to buy much sterling for
remittance; thereafter all the home charges were paid by new sterling
borrowing and by reduction in the reserves. The Indian budgetary position, though bad, was not as bad as one would think if one looked at
these accumulating new sterling liabilities and at this reduction of sterling assets. But the rupee exchange had moved to the gold export point
and, given the organization of the Indian exchange market, this fact
expressed itself partly in the "nonavailability of exchange" and partly
in the reduction of India's external balances.

As the winter of 1930–1 gradually passed into spring, with respect to
the exchange matters grew steadily worse. The government of India
reported that the outflow of capital would probably continue until the

political future had become clearer and that for some months it did not expect to be able to purchase any sterling for remittance. Home charges, it suggested, should still be covered by gold sales. It was buying gold in India, it reported, and could therefore sell gold from London holdings without shipping any. Indeed, it suggested, there should be a sizable substitution of securities for gold so as to increase interest earnings in sterling.[7]

The India Office, however, wanted India to ship gold from India so as to replenish the Gold Standard Reserve at home. And the Bank of England was extremely uneasy about India's financial prospects. Montagu Norman was urging a severe contraction of the rupee circulation so as to force the exchange above the gold export point. If the exchange could be raised, India might be able to float a £10 million loan for a term of two or three years. But if the rupee stayed weak, Norman told Wedgewood Benn, the secretary of state, even a short loan would be impossible. Hence the India Office urged the government of India and especially its finance member, Sir George Schuster, to "push contraction hard now."[8]

From India both Schuster and the controller of the currency responded that more monetary contraction would be neither helpful nor possible. They had already "maintained a steady continuous course maintaining fundamentals of the position sound." They had deflated so vigorously that Indian interest rates were now much higher than world rates. Only the political situation thus prevented an inflow of capital funds. But the situation was an insuperable barrier to any improvement in the present exchange position. It would be possible to engineer a monetary squeeze, but such a squeeze would increase the depression, cause a collapse of the market for government securities, destroy the demand for treasury bills, and enormously embarrass the Indian government in the management of its floating debt, while increasing the government deficit through its impact on debt charges.[9]

What could be done? The basic problem was political. It originated with His Majesty's government in the United Kingdom. Hence, Schuster argued, only a unilateral action by that government could improve matters. They must "show clearly that they are prepared to back India financially while constitutional changes are being considered." Britain could do so by arranging a guaranteed line of credit at the Bank of England; £50 million would suffice, Schuster thought, and he urged Benn to try to arrange one.[10]

At first his proposal was not well received at the Council of India – the London body that advised the secretary of state. But before long the Council had been convinced, and so Benn, who favored the proposal strongly, carried it to his colleagues in the Cabinet Committee on the India Round Table Conference. On 19 May he asked the prime minister to set up a financial subcommittee to discuss urgent matters of finance, and MacDonald did so. On the subcommittee were Lord Sankey and Benn from the India Office, H. B. Lees-Smith, and F. W. Pethick-Lawrence, the parliamentary undersecretary of the Treasury. Many officials also attended and took part. The group might have been designed as a cockpit for a battle between the Treasury and everyone else; such it soon became.

The Treasury officials and ministers were seriously worried about the general financial implications of India constitutional reform. They feared that the United Kingdom might become responsible for the service of India's sterling debt, which totaled well over £350 million, and for military and civil pensions. They also had little confidence in the Indians' ability to manage their own finances. And they were more than a little alarmed about the current financial practice of the British officials in India. Nor were they convinced that £50 million would be enough. Indeed, Schuster had already proposed £100 million.[11] Further, the liability was indefinitely extensible. As the chancellor of the exchequer, Philip Snowden, wrote: "It would inevitably have to be extended to all the Government of India's obligations and . . . it could not be confined to India . . . His Majesty's Government . . . would be absolutely compelled to do the same for Australia," lest that Dominion repudiate her overseas debts. To guarantee a loan would actually weaken India's credit because the action would be proof that India could no longer borrow on that credit alone and because Indian leaders would immediately announce their intention of repudiating any external loan that had been floated to protect the 1/6 rupee. Anyway, nothing could be done merely by credit because India could not enforce sufficient monetary stringency to protect the exchange rate. Hence, Snowden concluded, "the cause of the trouble is lack of confidence in the political situation and so long as that remains the case it cannot be altered by merely technical operation." India still had £50 million it could use to support the exchange; it must put its own house in order without asking for help; if the British government were to make a proper declaration on financial safeguards under responsible government, all would be well. If this could not be provided, better a fall in the rupee than a British guarantee.[12]

But the India Office would not hear of a fall in the rupee.

Later in the summer of 1931, Kisch examined the effect of such a collapse at length. If the peg were removed, he wrote, "all holders of rupees would try to get rid of them as soon as possible," and the Gold Standard

Reserve was not large enough to support any particular level of the rupee. Hence there was no reason to expect that the "headlong fall" would stop short of the bullion value of the rupee's silver content – that is, the rupee would fall to about four and a half pence. But the Indian government had sterling outlays of £30 million per year. Hence it would have to raise taxes sharply and might very well have to default. Unless their rupee salaries were raised British officials would suffer severely, and rupee savers would suffer serious loss in terms of sterling; government might have to rescue some of these, especially the Europeans. Wage earners would suffer from the resulting sharp rise in the internal price level – at least until money wages had adjusted. Peasants would gain from falling real tax levels but suffer from the higher rupee prices of imports. Traders would tend to export more and import less until internal prices and money wages had adjusted to the new exchange rate. Until these adjustments had occurred the importers might repudiate their external debts. British exports would lose the Indian market for a time, India would lose all credit in the London market, and the home government would have to intervene to pay home charges and service India's sterling debt. Meanwhile, within India the disruption of established relations might well cause serious disturbances up and down the country.[13]

In June Kisch and his colleagues argued in less detail but along similar lines. They wrote:

The Government of India do not overstate the case when they observe that if stability of exchange is not maintained there is little hope of proceeding with constitutional reforms until the finances of India are rehabilitated. There has arisen in India a lack of confidence in the future financial stability of government, and in particular a lack of confidence in the stability of the rupee exchange . . . the present tendency is to press for the removal of all currency control and for the rupee to be left completely unstable. Many people fear that the new Federal Government will be unable or unwilling to maintain the existing ratio. The natural result is a flight from the rupee . . . [hence] the surplus sterling which would normally be available for purchase by Government is acquired instead by private parties and Government is able to make little or no remittance.[14]

India had depleted her overseas gold and sterling reserves and had borrowed abnormally in London, so that now no one wanted her bonds. Thus, because of the political situation and the capital flight that this situation had caused, the secretary of state might have to default – unless the guaranteed credit were secured.

The cabinet subcommittee discussed India's financial situation with officials – experts from the Treasury, the India Office, and the Council of India. Sir Henry Strakosch, eminent monetarist and member of the Council, explained that it was not safe to use the Paper Currency Reserve. It was only £55 million in gold and sterling, while the paper and silver circulation was nearly £300 million. These were "very slender resources" given the primitive nature of the Indian monetary environment. Sir Frederick Leith-Ross explained that he thought Snowden believed no amount of credit would reassure investors so long as there were no firm and definite decisions about the exchange rate and financial safeguards. Snowden may have been correct, but the real problem was different. Admittedly, for the moment India could not raise any more sterling in London. But it was not the sterling bondholders who were switching from rupees to sterling. Nor need one hold India obligations – whether rupee bonds or sterling bonds – to speculate against the rupee when devaluation was in prospect. F. W. Pethick-Lawrence, transmitting Treasury opinion, argued that, if India could not stop the flight from the rupee without spending £155 million to support it, "the time had come when the Government of India must seriously reconsider the maintenance of the existing rate." It is odd to find this opinion emanating from Treasury members in early summer 1931! Benn argued differently. He claimed that because it had forced the 1/6 rate on India in the first place the United Kingdom government should pay enough to maintain that rate. Snowden later objected to this thought. The Treasury officials argued desperately for the refusal of credit. It was unsound, they wrote, to bolster a weak exchange while the underlying causes of instability are untreated; the United Kingdom taxpayer ought not to bolster Indian credit because other parts of the Empire, such as Australia, would immediately ask the chancellor to do the same for them; as Parliament would have to approve the credit, the parliamentary debates would so expose the weakness of Indian credit and the basic instability of the situation that the confidence building would become confidence destroying. Nevertheless, over Pethick-Lawrence's objection the subcommittee agreed with Benn, the India Office officials, and the Council of India: *something* must be done, and the only effective action was to grant the £50 million drawing credit.[15]

In the Cabinet Committee itself,[16] as Kisch had expected,[17] Snowden was able to defeat Benn and his subcommittee. Asking for £100 million instead of £50 million, Schuster had said that the situation was "a crisis for which there had been no parallel in the history of India."[18] Constitutional uncertainty plus low agricultural prices plus the coming period of heavy rupee and sterling loan maturities led to the crisis. The round table conference had made matters worse because it had ended with no clear understanding about financial policy or safeguards.[19] At the next conference there would have to be a definite understanding; otherwise the United Kingdom would have to delay responsible government or take over India's sterling obligations itself. Strakosch and Kisch pleaded for the credit, which, Kisch said, would be almost essential to prevent the rupee from falling to eight pence or thereabouts. Strakosch considered that India was "within measurable distance of being driven off the gold standard and of being swept into the vicious spiral of inflation. This might well lead to serious social unrest . . . The remedy for which the Government of India asked was an earnest that British credit stood behind the Government of India, in the shape of a guaranteed drawing credit of £50,000,000."

Snowden, however, found Kisch and Strakosch no more convincing than Schuster. He saw no reason to believe that a mere £50 million would suffice, observing that Schuster had already raised his request to £100 million. If asked for authority Parliament would, he thought, demand exactly the sort of safeguards that everyone agreed would imperil the round table conference. India should emulate Australia and put its own house in order; it could restore the position "if she put her back into it." By this time, it is true, Australia had begun to reduce government outlays. But it had also accepted a sizable devaluation, reduced more wage rates, and cut home interest rates as well. Did Snowden really want India to adopt the entire Australian package? As for credit or guarantee, Snowden believed "it would be fatal for the British Government to commit itself to the financial support of India." He was prepared to accept with only minor modifications a statement "which would imply a contingent promise to ask Parliament for a guarantee if and when the situation required it."

It was agreed to accept Snowden's modifications of the India Office draft; to obviate any parliamentary discussion, MacDonald was to consult the leaders of the other parties and then to make a statement in Parliament forthwith. On 26 June he stated:

The financial strain on the resources of the Government of India, already great owing to the world economic depression, has been accentuated by uncertainties which have attended the discussion of constitutional changes and more particularly the discussion of the provisions to be embodied in the new Constitution to ensure financial stability. It will not be possible to introduce the proposed constitutional changes if financial stability is not assured. His Majesty's Government are determined not to allow a state of affairs to arise which might jeopardise the financial stability *and good government* of India *for which the Secretary of State is at present responsible*. They have therefore decided that, should the need arise, they will apply to Parliament for the authority necessary for them to give financial support *under suitable conditions*.[20]

As far as I have been able to discover, this remarkable commitment was not discussed in the full Cabinet or even reported formally to it. However, it was elaborately examined both in the India Office and in the Treasury, where officials worked to make it more precise. On 4 July, after the usual interchange of unofficial letters, Hopkins wrote officially to Kershaw. His purpose was to spell out the conditions under which the Treasury accepted MacDonald's statement. These were: (1) "The Government of India will use its sterling reserves freely to maintain the exchange . . . Parliament cannot be approached unless and until there is serious danger of these reserves being exhausted"; (2) "The Government of India will take firm and effective action with a view to restoring and maintaining a sound financial and monetary position in India both as regards making good the budget deficiencies . . . and as regards contracting the currency to such extent as may be proved necessary." Benn accepted the conditions, and notified the government of India.[21]

Almost immediately London began to press India to ship gold and to contract the money supply. Kisch wanted Schuster to send £4 or 5 million worth of gold. Schuster replied that he had already decided to contract the money supply by three crores of rupees (30 million rupees), but he was most unwilling to ship any gold to Britain or sell any of the gold that was already there. The controller of the currency and the managements of the banks agreed, he said. Any such action "would destroy confidence, weaken all markets, very seriously militate against success of rupee loan, and might lead to renewal of [government] sales of sterling. Hence no gold transactions should be contemplated until further drawings on our sterling reserve made it imperative." If the exchange should strengthen by late August, when the rupee loan would have closed, the question could be considered again. But the Finance Department thought it might do better to buy sterling in India and make remittance through the market, and not ship gold at all.[22]

Sir George Schuster must have been disappointed: though he shipped no gold, the government of India was soon obliged to sell sterling once more. Was he hoping to husband his gold while so depleting his sterling that MacDonald's guarantee would have to be invoked? For six weeks or more, the India Office allowed him to continue on his chosen path. On 26 August an official brought the matter to the attention of the Finance Committee of the Council. Surely, he wrote, the government of India has recently sold so much sterling to the market that it should ship gold to London and thereby replenish its holdings of sterling. The Finance Committee agreed that India should explain why it was selling so much sterling and should ship home all the gold it had recently bought.[23] Two days later a telegram was sent. It contained no request for explanation, but it asked India to ship £6.3 million in gold.[24]

Schuster, however, was no more willing to ship gold in August than he had been in July. Because in London the government of India still held £18.5 million in gold and securities, because there was fear about the exchange rate, and because of the rupee loan, the moment was "particularly inopportune . . . we urge at least postponement for further consideration end September, unless meanwhile sterling sales seriously deplete your reserves or exchange strengthens sufficiently to offset anticipated sentimental effect."[25]

In London this response was not well received; but once more Sir George got his way. An official minuted, "It is very important that the rupee loan should be a success, and I suppose that we must accept the Government of India's assurance that gold shipments would deter subscriptions."[26] The same official drafted a telegram that withdrew the request for immediate gold shipments, noting that London might "feel obligated to ask you at short notice to begin shipment" because India's London reserves were no longer sufficiently liquid in the face of India's continuing sales of sterling. On 18 September London asked New Delhi "yet again to reconsider idea of immediate shipment of gold."[27]

London may have wanted Indian gold to help with its own problems, though I have found no documentary evidence of such a wish. The documents talk only of Indian credit and Indian needs. In any event, weeks or months would have passed before Indian gold could reach Europe.

Meanwhile, Schuster had been pressing with respect to the guarantee. What would happen, he asked, if assistance were needed while Parliament was not in session? He asked for "definite announcement . . . that His Majesty's Government proposed to lay before Parliament as soon as it reassembled legislation enabling the Treasury to guarantee a very substantial credit to the Government of India. As you know, we consider figure for this should be £100 million."[28] Kisch thought this request silly. After October aid might be needed. But for the time being the government of India and almost £30 million in gold in India and, in London, £2 million in gold and £20 million in securities. Hence there was no immediate danger; reserves were large, and balances were sufficient for three months.[29] On August 15 Schuster was sent the bad news: as balances were sufficient for the moment there was no need for action at once, and the question of credit was closed: it had been "rejected, and cannot now be re-opened."[30]

Moreover, the Indian government was reluctant to pursue the policy of even more forceful monetary contraction that Norman and the India

Office had urged on it. In May it had explained its position, and its opinion remained unchanged. Schuster agreed with Norman that the situation was serious, but he maintained that India had done the best it could. It had systematically deflated by supplying the market with treasury bills against rupees to the maximum safe extent; it had maintained high money rates in the face of universal cheapness abroad. But Norman and the India Office wanted "something much more vigorous." Exactly what, Schuster asked, did they have in mind? And how could it be done? Political uncertainty had generated capital exports; therefore the rupee was weak. There was no point in trying to frighten bear speculators because speculation, in the usual sense, was not the problem. Because the floating rupee debt was so immense, the government of India would be at the mercy of the market if it attempted to squeeze too hard. The market would simply let its treasury bills run off, forcing the government to replace the bills with paper currency. The government's budgetary position was so bad that it would be reluctant to pay the higher interest cost of a tighter money policy. Because the Imperial Bank automatically advanced against government securities at Indian Bank Rate, it was difficult or impossible to force a contraction without changing this practice; yet any change would certainly cause panic. So would the "disastrous depreciation" of government securities that would certainly follow any more severe credit squeeze. Of course, the government would then be unable to float a rupee loan. So far, the government had tried to keep interest rates sufficiently high to attract foreign *short* money to India. But to go further and to create a "drastic increase" in interest rates and "money famine" would not stem *long-term* capital exports because the flow was responding to politics, not to differential interest rates.[31]

To observers of more recent British economic history, Sir George's plaint has a melancholy familiarity. The Authorities must maintain orderly conditions in the government securities markets; the government borrowing requirement dominates the Authorities' thinking; politics, not economic costs and returns, control the flows of capital funds.

India's budgetary position continued to frighten London. On 17 September, Sir Samuel Hoare, the new secretary of state, told the Cabinet that the India Office staff was at work on budget-balancing proposals; the government of India had been urged to close its prospective deficit but as yet had not done so: "to introduce a budget of this character would be disastrous," as there would be a gigantic financial crash in India; meanwhile, the flight from the rupee had begun. The Cabinet discussed these complicated questions for some time and approved Hoare's plan to send a telegram pressing for a "true balance over two years."[32]

This was the background against which the officials and politicians were to fix the course of the rupee after Britain left gold. On 21 September Hoare told the Cabinet's India Committee that the rupee would stay pegged to sterling at 1/6. There was no discussion.[33] The previous day he had told the Indian government that sterling would leave gold and had argued for maintaining the 1/6 ratio. To float the rupee would "precipitate a crash." It would absolve the United Kingdom from the obligation to aid India in case of need. As for pegging at 1/4 gold or sterling, it was "unthinkable that we should change the ratio in present crisis." The United Kingdom would "be prepared should the need arise to request parliament to assist India in fulfilling her obligations provided that every effort is made to maintain the rupee at 1/6 sterling. Above understanding should in no circumstances be disclosed." The Indian government should prepare a scheme of exchange control just in case. This should provide for the compulsory acquisition of all foreign exchange, whether from commercial or financial transactions, and should limit sales to the financing of genuine commercial purposes. New Delhi was authorized to impose exchange control without consulting Whitehall. Finally, the Indian government was asked to raise its bank rate "to the extent that will at least maintain the existing difference" between London and India.[34]

Unfortunately, the Indian authorities learned of sterling's fall before they received the official telegram. The viceroy signed an ordinance that suspended rupee convertibility into gold or sterling. This was done, the Finance Department reported, to conserve India's reserves.[35] Having received the official signal, Sir George Schuster hastened to defend the course he had followed. The position, he said, had recently been

one of complete lack of confidence, both in India and in London, in our ability to maintain the exchange rate of 1/6. We have been selling large and growing quantities of sterling; foreign money was being withdrawn from India as rapidly as possible, capital was being exported in large amounts, and in Bombay there have been heavily speculative purchases of gold. At the beginning of last week it looked as if a crisis was approaching, and, but for the restriction of credit by the Imperial Bank, strong announcements in India and the Prime Minister's statement in Parliament, the crisis would probably have materialised.

But now that the United Kingdom had left gold, "no verbal assurances will be believed." If India were to simply repeg to gold, "we shall, when we re-open for business, be overwhelmed with demands for sterling which no mere bluff credit could stop." Exchange control was a good idea and Schuster would at once elaborate a scheme. Nevertheless, India could peg to sterling only if a credit for at least £50 million were given, only if it could use this credit before drawing on its own reserves, and

41

only if it could tell the nation it had received the credit.[36] The whole Council, he reported, supported this course.

The Treasury thought the United Kingdom could properly renew its contingent obligations to assist if needed. But Hopkins thought that the £50 million credit was, "of course, out of the question," and he told the India Office so. He also believed, with the India Office, that the rupee should stay at 1/6.[37] In this he was at one with Sir Cecil Kisch.[38]

In his tale of woe, Kisch does mention the impact on Britain, but he does not stress it. And in Cabinet discussion this matter was hardly touched upon. Hoare explained that the experts were agreed the rupee must stay tied to sterling; he mentioned that India's controller of the currency, currently visiting the heart of the Empire, agreed. The Cabinet decided that the rupee should stay tied to the pound and that the prime minister's undertaking of 26 June should be confirmed. The Treasury was willing to agree as long as the rupee remained pegged at 1/6 but not otherwise. Hoare at once telegraphed India, saying that the rupee must stay at 1/6, that the Indian government could state publicly that the June undertaking would stand, and that the Treasury would help in liquidating any sterling investments that might have to be sold; the Treasury would also arrange for advances against gold in transit.[39]

The Treasury and the India Office were braced for the worst. Hoare thought that the government of India would resign if more definite promise of support were not given. He asked for a credit to be used when the reserves of £12 million had been used up. S. D. Waley thought that any such arrangement could only cause a new demand for £50 million; "if the 1/6 rupee can only be saved by huge credits then the lesser evil is to let it go." On the same day a Treasury official wrote that Schuster was being "unreasonable." India still had plenty of reserves to hold the rupee at 1/6 "for a long time, especially if (as is proposed) they institute a system of exchange control to stop speculative transactions. There is no justification for His Majesty's Government to be called in at the moment; and I take it that there will be no question of acceding to the latest demand."[40] A little later Leith-Ross wrote, "Sir George Schuster is really becoming impossible." Ever since the prime minister made his June statement about helping India the Treasury had stipulated that India must be willing to use its sterling reserves freely to protect the exchange. But Schuster was now saying that India must neither use her London reserves nor ship gold. The India Office and the Treasury were agreed that, once the sterling reserves had all been spent, India could and should ship gold.[41]

Sir George Schuster, however, would not go down without a fight. On 23 September the government of India telegraphed, "We cannot accept your plans . . . unless you can meet us it will be impossible for us to carry on as a government." Hoare was obliged to ask the Cabinet to reaffirm its determination: the rupee would stay at 1/6.[42] In a long telegram the India Office first rehearsed the familiar objections to a rupee float; it then laid down the law. A floating rupee would disorganize the internal Indian economy and, by further unbalancing the budget, lead inevitably to default. "Such a policy would be disastrous to the interests of India and cannot be entertained by His Majesty's Government." Britain would help India to meet its sterling obligations if necessary, but "if policy of maintaining the rupee at 1/6 is abandoned His Majesty's Government will regard themselves as free to refuse to help, and will not renew their promise. Reason for this is obvious as the burden on His Majesty's Government would be immeasurably increased owing to the various reactions of an inflationary regime."[43]

At this point the government of India gave in. It reported, "Statement is being made in Assembly this afternoon on lines of your policy." The rupee would stay at 1/6; exchange control would prevent any speculative flight of capital. Schuster continued to wonder what would be done in London if trouble occurred, as legislation would be needed before Britain could advance or guarantee a credit. What if the trouble arose after a parliamentary dissolution that was now expected on all sides? On 28 September the Cabinet agreed that there could be no legislation before dissolution and that there was still no need to anticipate any need for credits. The policy, Hoare reported, was working well.[44]

2. Later developments

In the event, things turned out much better than the government of India had hoped. Admittedly, late in 1931 Indian officials again proposed that the rupee should drop to 1/4 sterling. Norman, however, still believed that the United Kingdom should simply enforce the 1/6 ratio and take measures to ensure that it was effective. Once more the question expired without trace as far as London was concerned. India's political future remained cloudy, but it appeared that MacDonald's June statement plus the Cabinet actions of late September convinced the Indian public that the exchange rate would not quickly be changed. Gradually it became clear that London would not concede any Indian government enough financial power to damage India's credit. There was no longer so strong an incentive to sell rupee securities and move the proceeds to London. In the City, too, India's credit improved as the U.K. government's financial intentions became clearer. Therefore, the India Office was much less likely to run out of sterling: if its own reserves were depleted it could now borrow sterling on the market, in the same semi-automatic way as before 1930. In India itself the government, pressed by the Treasury and the India Office, quickly balanced its rupee budget and began the process of reestablishing control over its domestic monetary system.[1]

All these developments explain why the flight from the rupee did not continue after the end of September 1931. However, they did nothing to improve India's current-account balance. India's export trade did not revive. Indeed, from mid-1931 to mid-1933 the prices of India's exportables continued downward. Throughout these years, at the Ottawa Conference and again at the World Monetary and Economic Conference, India's financial representatives begged Britain and the world to do something about the price level. The depreciation of sterling did help India a good deal, especially in 1931–3. Sterling items predominated in India's invisibles account and made up almost all the home charges. With the rupee pegged to sterling and with sterling falling relative to the dollar and the other gold standard currencies, some rupee prices rose and others fell less than they would have done if Britain had not left the gold standard. At the time no one thought that this change could have produced enough extra sterling to meet the Indian government's home charges; yet soon after the pound was floated the Indian government was able to buy sterling once more. The "remittance problem" vanished. Without shipping its own gold, without depleting its London reserves of gold and sterling, and without new London borrowing, the government of India was once more able to buy enough sterling to meet its home charges. How was this done?

The answer surprised everyone at the time, and even today it is surprising. For the first time in many decades, India became a gold exporter. For this utterly unexpected and unforeseen development there were several reasons.

For many decades all classes of Indian society had hoarded gold. Indeed, the subcontinent was famous as a sink into which gold vanished without trace. The depression, however, seems to have forced many people to dishoard. Already in spring 1931 government was buying gold in India. During March and April 1931 it bought £3 million for the paper currency reserves. By late August, an India Office official noted that since mid-March government had bought £6.5 million in gold, though it had begun to sell sterling for London delivery in July and August.[2] It appears that in summer 1931 gold purchases accounted for some though by no means all of these sales.

We have seen that in summer 1931 the officials believed capital was fleeing India because of uncertainty about Indian budgets, monetary policy, and exchange rates. The evidence was a large demand for sterling and, as the summer progressed, a large offer of gold in India. Certainly funds were fleeing from the rupee. But they may well have been fleeing from the sterling area itself – from the rupee into sterling and then onward into dollars or francs. Given the working of the exchanges, the Indian officials could not possibly have detected any such movement. As far as the surviving correspondence can tell us they did not pay much attention to monetary developments in the larger world. Probably they could not conceive that sterling could leave gold, fall, or float. But the private citizen may not have been so confident. Whether or not he believed that the rupee would fall relative to sterling, he might very well suspect that the pound would fall relative to the dollar. If so, he would surely sell rupees and buy something else. This hypothesis is doubly attractive because the observable capital flight ended with *Britain's* departure from gold. On the other hand, it is equally possible that after 21 September anxious Indians simply changed the *mechanics* of the transfer. Still worried about India's future, they may have begun to export capital in the form of gold. Indeed, given the controls on capital export that Sir George Schuster introduced after 21 September, for some time they could not have exported capital in any other way. For the Indian authorities the results would have been a happy coincidence. Unwilling to export their own monetary gold, by forbidding capital export through official channels they forced nervous Indians to export nonmonetary gold and then they purchased the sterling proceeds. If this hypothesis is true, it helps to explain why India's position quickly became so much more comfortable after 21 September. Further, if some Indians were nervous not about Indian politics but about sterling they may very well have repatriated funds after 21 September. We know that soon after Britain left gold, short-term funds flowed back to London. If any Indian funds then moved on to the subcontinent they would pass through the exchange mechanism in the usual way. Government would buy sterling and sell rupees; Indians would not have to import gold.

Thanks to Britain's devaluation, after 21 September the rupee price of gold at once rose by 20 percent. Thereafter it fluctuated, but it never returned to the old levels of 1924–31. Further, relative to commodities gold remained much more valuable for the rest of the decade. The economist observes a sort of Pigou Effect: in India the real value of gold had risen while real incomes had fallen, and the change induced people to sell gold so as to enjoy a larger flow of real consumption. In the subcontinent production, consumption, and importation were all larger than they would otherwise have been. That is, they were larger than they could have been if there had been no hoards, and also if relative prices had not changed so conveniently.

The gold flow rapidly became a torrent. By February 1932 Sir Frederick Phillips was observing that it was "the single most powerful force working to produce a general rise in world prices," which was the Treasury's "most desired objective."[3] Little of the gold passed through government hands. It was large exports of gold on *private* account that allowed the Indian government to resume its purchases of sterling and make remittance in the traditional way.[4] In March 1932 Phillips, arguing with Leith-Ross and Hopkins about an appropriate value for the pound, noticed that a relatively cheap pound was advantageous inter alia because it would bring forth more Indian gold, thus helping to raise the world price level.[5] And these gold flows were not unsubstantial. From September 1931 to September 1933, India exported £115.750 million sterling on private account; the government of India was able to remit £35.733 million to the secretary of state, of which £13.750 million was actually added to India's gold standard reserve in London.[6] In January 1932 the Indian government, noting that gold exports had greatly improved its sterling position, proposed to end the exchange control that it had installed at London's prompting in September 1931.[7] At the end of that month it did so.

These happy developments did not satisfy Sir George Schuster, the viceroy's finance member. We have already noted his demand for a sterling credit, but that was not the end of his demands. On 1 October 1931 he asked London to let him have a rupee that was pegged not to the pound but directly to gold, at a rate not higher than a gold 1/4 and "preferably lower than, say 1/3." He went on to say, "It would be a fatal error not to take this providential opportunity to escape from a position which has been the main cause of the most bitter anti-British policy of the past few years."[8] He meant, of course, the policy of the 1/6 rupee, which Congress and the Indian millowners so disliked. Leith-Ross observed that the rupee would have to be linked to sterling or to nothing; in mid-October, the India Office sent Schuster the bad news.[9] The rupee could not be pegged to gold; as yet nothing could be said about "policy as regards sterling."

If the rupee could not move vis-à-vis sterling, might the pound not move conveniently vis-à-vis gold? Early in 1932 Sir George suggested that it could and should. India, he announced, needed higher agricultural prices and therefore wanted a still larger depreciation of the gold value of the rupee. "We press now for . . . regulating sterling and rupee so as to bring about an appreciable rise in wholesale prices of commodities in which we are interested." What did Britain propose to do about sterling?[10]

The Treasury and India Office officials thought this a very strange idea. They agreed it would be "disastrous" deliberately to depreciate the pound or to unhitch the rupee from the pound. Leith-Ross minuted that Schuster was "inspired by Strakosch and his ideas of a commodity basis of sterling stability." India must either stay pegged to the pound or "let the rupee go to pieces," but "the tail can't be expected to wag the bulldog." After telling the chancellor that the officials had prearranged a correspondence "to put a stopper on Schuster," Hopkins wrote formally to the India Office:

A policy of deliberate depreciation, such as that apparently contemplated by the Government of India, would . . . be disastrous to this country and so far as They [Treasury lords] could judge would be fraught with great peril to India. But if, at any time, the monetary policy adopted by this country appeared to the Secretary of State to conflict with the interests of India, They would be glad to consult with him as to whether the difficulty should be met by a modification of the monetary policy of this country or of India . . . in any case the ultimate responsibility for the monetary policy of this country rests with His Majesty's Government.[11]

Schuster would not stay stoppered. When sterling rose sharply in early March 1932, he quickly expressed his dismay. The rise would reduce the gold premium on which so much depended; he hoped the United Kingdom would keep all this in mind when determining the sterling policy. After sarcastic discussion in the Treasury and after Chamberlain's approval, Schuster was told that the sudden rise in sterling exchange was "due to special circumstances and in no way represented any alternation in the policy of the authorities in this country."[12] He does not seem to have been told that the Treasury officials were themselves seriously worried by sterling's rise. They were in disarray as to the right exchange rate, but they were already devising the Exchange Equalisation Account to prevent any further rises if such should prove inconvenient.

The Treasury officials did not forget about Indian gold. In 1933 we find Phillips arguing again that British depreciation had probably helped raise the world price level because it had caused India to disgorge such enormous amounts of gold.[13] In May 1937, when he feared a deluge of gold, Phillips said that Indian gold contributed part of the 37.6 million ounces of gold that became "available for money" in 1936.[14] By then, of course, the Americans had raised the dollar price of gold, more than offsetting the upward float in the pound vis-à-vis the dollar. Even when the exchange rate was five dollars to the pound, at $35 per ounce Indian gold was still far more valuable in terms of rupees than it had been in mid-1931. When the pound was worth $4.86 and gold cost $20.67 per ounce, an ounce of gold was worth 56.65 rupees. When the pound fell to $3.50 and gold was still $20.67, that same ounce was worth 78.72 rupees. Further, because the general price level had fallen so dramatically between 1929 and 1932, in terms of purchasing power the gold was worth well over 100 rupees of 1929 purchasing power. By mid-1936 gold was $35 per ounce, and the exchange rate hovered just below $5 per pound. But an ounce of Indian gold was now worth 93.33 rupees. Although the price level was higher than in 1932, it had not risen enough to prevent the substitution of goods for gold in India.

In 1937, when he agreed that it would be useful to have a general discussion about gold prices with Henry Morgenthau, Chamberlain thought the South Africans should be told.[15] He did not mention India. One wonders if the Treasury told the India Office or P. J. Grigg, the new Finance member, or the governor of the new Reserve Bank, Sir Osborne Smith.

From the troubles of 1931 there were other reverberations. The Indian importunities formed part of the background to the evolution of the Treasury's monetary policy that Chamberlain reluctantly unveiled at Ottawa, where Sir George Schuster spoke in terms that his earlier correspondence had made painfully familiar. At least to some extent the "Ottawa monetary policy" must have been devised – and announced – to keep him quiet. Equally important, the events of 1931 had deepened the distrust with which the Treasury officials regarded Indian finance in general and Sir George in particular. This distrust must have helped to confirm them in their resolve to exclude the Empire countries from the management of sterling. It must also have deepened their determination with respect to India's constitutional problem. India's financial administration was not to be trusted. Sir George had embraced all the heresies – unbalanced budgets, floating exchange rates, deliberate depreciation, management of the price level via the money supply. He had been willing to gamble India's credit and to risk a sterling default by unbalancing his budget and by floating his rupee. If an expatriate administration could fall into such error, what was to be expected of a "responsible" Indian finance minister?

In the discussions of Indian constitutional reform that had begun in 1929 and that culminated with the Government of India Act of 1935, questions of financial responsibility were deeply intertwined with questions of external debt, the rupee exchange rate, and the management of the monetary and credit systems. I cannot pursue all the complications here.[16] It must suffice to report Chamberlain's comments on the prospect of Indian financial autonomy. In December 1932 he expressed a vigorous distrust of Indian financial management. "The Indians," he said, "are not really capable of handling this question." They might destroy India's credit in a very short time. The City would refuse to handle any Indian loan "if a whisper or rumour of transfer of responsibility to India at any particular date was heard." Once it was realized that India could not command loans without confidence its leaders would ask for British guarantees, "a liability that he, as Chancellor of the Exchequer, could not contemplate." If a reserve bank were to be set up it would need a British governor. He doubted whether any Indian legislature would ever create such a bank.[17]

With the Government of India Act came the Reserve Bank of India.[18] Its own statute defined its functions more or less as Whitehall wanted. The Reserve Bank was to issue paper currency, serve as banker to government and to other banks, and keep reserves and maintain the exchange rate at 1/6 sterling. It was endowed with all the gold that government had held, plus enough sterling securities to provide a currency cover of 50 percent. It was also given the right to draw up 500 million rupees (50 crores) in silver coin. Its first governor was Sir Osborne Arkell Smith, an Australian who had worked in banking for fifty years, most recently as one of the managing directors at the Imperial Bank of India, which he had joined at Norman's suggestion in 1926. Norman indeed recommended Smith to the secretary of state in 1934.[19] Smith appears to have had to promise that he would respect and defend the "ratio," but he was at odds with P. J. Grigg, Schuster's successor as finance member. Grigg was rigidly devoted to the ratio and to fiscal rectitude;[20] Smith soon came to believe that interest rates should be lowered and the rupee devalued.[21] Hence Smith resigned in October 1936. In India and even on the Reserve Bank board, there was still agitation about the ratio.[22] But government was not prepared to give way.

The Reserve Bank's official historians report the "three-day float" of September 1931 but not Shuster's struggles to devalue the rupee or to float it permanently. Asking why the government of India clung to a 1/6 rupee when Indian opinion favored 1/4 but lacking access to London documentation, they deduce four answers – prestige, the home charges, the interest of expatriates in India, and the interests of U.K. exporters.[23] All these considerations were certainly present. But the evidence of this chapter reveals that New Delhi was not swayed by them. With respect to diagnosis and prescription alike Schuster was at one with the Reserve Bank historians. As for Whitehall, certainly it was concerned about trade and about expatriates, but neither matter was mentioned very often. Budgetary balance and inflationary possibilities worried Whitehall much more. When they worried about a falling depreciating rupee, India Office officials must have recalled the troubles of the early 1920s and of earlier times, when a weak rupee had disorganized government finances greatly. As for the Treasury, it did not care about trade or about expatriates. It simply did not want to shoulder any contingent liability with respect to India's *sterling* obligations. Therefore it scrutinized all questions, especially credit, exchange rates, and fiscal autonomy, with this concern in mind.

It is sometimes suggested that the gold outflow should have been garnered by the Indian government to strengthen reserves. In fact, government repaid £16.9 million in external debt, and its improved position allowed it to refund £11.9 million more on attractive terms.[24] Also, government did increase its holdings of sterling securities from late 1931 until the end of 1937. Such adjustments certainly improved the external position much as extra gold reserves would have done. More telling is the criticism that if the government of India had pursued policies of Keynesian reflation at home, the extra gold would have financed the extra imports that extra production would have sucked in. But of course it would then have been impossible to strengthen the external position to the extent actually managed while simultaneously paying all the home charges in sterling.

Indian opinion naturally believed that the gold "contributed to a substantial extent to the strengthening of the Bank of England reserve."[25] In a sense the statement is true, but the connections are more roundabout than one might suppose at first thought. Indian gold plus South African gold allowed the world to increase gold reserves from 1931 until the outbreak of war. If the Indian authorities had been allowed to fix a lower exchange rate, India would have exported still more gold because the rupee payoff would have been even larger. To the world monetary system there was no difference between the gold that South Africa was mining and the gold that India was dishoarding. From the winter of 1931–2 to the spring of 1938 much of this extra gold – both Indian and South African – did end up in the British Exchange Equalisation Account. Even more flowed to the United States, which continued to absorb gold after Britain began to lose it in 1938. Because India was shedding gold and South Africa was mining gold, Britain and the United States were able to accumulate gold rapidly without creating stronger deflationary pressures or protectionist developments elsewhere in the world economy. But Britain was not able to draw gold into its reserves merely because Indians were dishoarding. It could retain gold only because its balance of payments allowed it to do so. And it was Britain's capital account, not its current account, that was responsible. From

1931 through 1938 Britain cumulated a current-account deficit of £375 million. Only in 1935 did it run a current-account surplus, and that was very small compared with the surpluses of the 1920s. Further, Britain was undertaking overseas direct investments on a considerable scale. Therefore, it was only because old debtors were repaying old loans and because new creditors were moving funds to London on a sufficient scale that the Bank of England and the Exchange Equalisation Account could heap up gold. As we shall see in Chapter 10, when the sterling balances began to flow out in spring 1938 the gold went too.[26] What mattered, therefore, was not India's gold sales but the unexpected and rather eccentric strength of Britain's capital account.

Britain did not scheme to acquire Indian gold. Dr. Tomlinson has rightly observed that in autumn 1931 no one expected any such disgorging of private hoards.[27] When they urged Sir George Schuster to export gold from government hoards, the Treasury and the Indian Office were thinking more narrowly: they simply wanted India to increase its London balances, which the difficulties of 1930–1 had so severely depleted. They were especially concerned that India should have enough sterling to meet its home charges. I have not detected any evidence that in 1931 they concerned themselves with the implications for sterling itself.

3

The Canadian debate over money
and exchanges, 1930-1934

In Chapter 2 we saw how India moved from gold bullion to sterling standard at Whitehall's behest, over the protests of its expatriate administrators. We also saw that with Britain's departure from gold India's payments moved almost at once from extreme difficulty to extreme ease. The Indian authorities were not free to choose exchange regime or exchange rate. They would manage the composition of their external assets and indirectly they could affect the size of these assets, but they could not have kept their assets anywhere but in London.

The Canadian situation was very different. The "senior Dominion" had complete control over its monetary and financial affairs. The commercial banks – "chartered banks" in Canadian usage – were locally owned and managed. As an external asset the government held only gold, and the chartered banks held their external assets as claims on New York, not on London. Lacking a central bank until 1935 and served in London by an unimpressive high commissioner, between 1930 and 1935 Canada was not exposed to informal influences from the Bank of England, nor was there anything to parallel the close connection between Treasury and India Office. Canada and its provinces had borrowed heavily in London, but because the United Kingdom could not be held responsible for these debts the Dominion's financial problems did not worry the Treasury very much. Already by 1930 Canadian trade and finance looked as much to "the States" as to the United Kingdom. After September 1931 Canada did not join the sterling area: it neither pegged its currency to the pound nor held sterling in its official monetary reserves. It has been often assumed that Canada's abstinence was natural or inevitable – a simple reflection of the links with the United States. But in 1931–2 the question of Empire versus America was very much alive. Publicists and legislators assumed that Canada could choose to align itself with one monetary system or the other. As we shall see, so did the government's advisers.

Regrettably, we cannot discuss the question of sterlng without treating the other dimensions of monetary debate. R. B. Bennett, the Conservative prime minister who held office from mid-1930 to mid-1935, received advice from many quarters inside government circles and outside. For the advisers, the various questions were intertwined. Prices should go up. Would a sterling standard help to raise them? Lacking a central bank, could the Dominion itself raise its own price level and, if so, how? What monetary policy should be followed, and how could it be worked?

Prime Minister Bennett was a powerful personality who liked advice but did not like to delegate power. He was his own minister for external affairs, and for almost two years he was his own finance minister. His Cabinet colleagues could seldom act of their own volition. Further, Bennett was a lawyer and a millionaire. In financial and industrial circles he was well known and generally respected though often not well liked. His work with public utilities, like his party work, had given him especially close connections with financial interests in Canada's great cities and in New York. In a peculiar sense the policies of the Bennett government are Bennett's own policies – especially in matters of finance.

Supporting the Canadian government was an exiguous civil service that Bennett did a good deal to strengthen. By Whitehall standards all the departments were tiny and badly staffed. Dr. O. D. Skelton, an Anglophobe political scientist, headed the Department of External Affairs. He was its deputy minister, the equivalent of permanent secretary. In this department also were Norman Robertson and a few other senior officials. All were polymaths who gave advice on the large questions of international politics and economics. In the Department of Finance, which managed the Dominion's own note issue, Bennett found several officials of dubious worth; in 1932 he strengthened that department by installing W. C. Clark as deputy minister. Clark was a financial economist who had worked in the United States; before his appointment he had taught commerce at Queen's University of Kingston, Ontario, where Skelton had also once professed political science. Thanks to Clark, and under the pressure of events, the Department of Finance soon raised its eyes to the large issues.

Because Canada was a small society in which patronage was all-important, very small financial questions were generally considered by full Cabinet or at least by the Treasury Board, its financial subcommittee. Regrettably, there were no Cabinet minutes, and Cabinet papers, when circulated, have survived only by accident and without much indication of their provenance. The Treasury Board minutes were so formal as to help the historian little. Departmental records are invaluable but chaotic. As Britain's high commissioner later remarked, "In the administrative system of Ottawa anything is possible." In any event, it appears that Bennett did not always bring the important questions to Cabinet lest his conclusions or opinions might be disputed. Hence, in Canada the historian of economic policy relies chiefly on politicians' private papers.

1. *The financial system*

Before turning to the archival materials we must first learn a little about the monetary regime that Bennett inherited and within which he found himself constrained to work.[1] Some Canadian economists and historians are well informed about this regime, which has often been described in the secondary literature; but even in Canada many specialists know little of it, and outside the Dominion few scholars have an inkling of its oddities.

In Canada there were two kinds of paper currency – bank notes and Dominion notes. Each chartered bank could issue its own bank notes in an amount up to its paid-in capital plus reserves. It could exceed this amount if it would deposit gold in the "central gold reserves," which existed only for the purpose of accommodating the banks in this way. A dollar-for-dollar backing was required. The minimum denomination for chartered-bank notes was five dollars. The numerous "near banks" – the trust and mortgage companies and the various savings institutions that operated under Dominion or provincial charters – could not issue paper currency.

Dominion notes were issued by the government under three very different arrangements but the notes, once issued, were indistinguishable one from another. The basic Dominion notes legislation dated from confederation. Throughout the period 1914–34 it provided for a fiduciary component of $50 million, issued against a 25 percent reserve requirement of gold and guaranteed debentures, and a nonfiduciary component, issued against 100 percent gold reserves. If this had been the only source of the Dominion note issue, the issue would have expanded and contracted in response to gold movements more or less in accordance with the British model of 1844. However, on 3 August 1914 the Dominion took power to issue Dominion notes against approved security whenever the chartered banks wished to borrow notes from the Dominion. The approved securities might be government bonds, treasury bills, or the mere promises of the banks. Originally introduced by order-in-council to protect the banks against the risk of an internal drain, this "rediscounting" arrangement was embodied in the Finance Act of 1914 and took final form in the Finance Act of 1923. As the Dominion Department of Finance was then willing to function as a lender of last resort the chartered banks saw no need for a central bank, whose only purpose they conceived to be to act as such a lender. Finally, during the First World War the Dominion issued several million dollars in fiduciary Dominion notes, partly against the security of U.K. treasury bills. With the retirement of some securities this issue was later reduced but never completely canceled. All one-dollar and two-dollar notes were Dominion paper, but the Dominion circulation also included very-large-denomination notes, which the chartered banks held and passed among themselves for clearing purposes.

From the creation of the Dominion until the outbreak of war in 1914, bank notes and Dominion notes were convertible into gold on demand at a price of $20.67 per fine ounce of gold. As gold could move overnight from New York to Toronto or Montreal, the gold points were closely set, and the Canadian-American exchange rate could not move any distance from par. On 3 August 1914 the Dominion ended the free sale of gold, thus leaving the gold standard. Bank notes and Dominion notes were no longer convertible into gold, and gold export was allowed only when licensed. The government did not introduce exchange controls. The Canadian dollar promptly depreciated relative to the American. Stimulated by the issues against imperial treasury bills and railway securities and by rediscounting, the Dominion note issue expanded greatly during the war, contracting rapidly in the recession of 1920–2, which was specially severe in Canada.

In the Finance Act of 1923, which made the rediscount scheme part of the Dominion's financial system, Parliament stated that on 1 July 1926 the export of gold would once more be permitted and the paper currency would once more become convertible into gold at the same price as in prewar years – that is to say, the American and Canadian dollars would once more be at par. Canada's Parliament had thus created the same situation as Britain's: unless there was new legislation the gold standard would return automatically. In 1924 and 1925 there was some discussion about the timing of the return. Was Canada moving precipitously? Certainly on the more obvious criteria there was little to fear. The Department of Finance held excess reserves of gold; that is, it held more than it was obliged to hold to support the "basic" issue of Dominion notes. It could if necessary sell gold without contracting its circulation. The Canadian dollar had floated very near to par. Canada's trading position seemed to be strong. Indeed, we now know that the country was running a current-account surplus, something it had never managed to do in the prewar boom years. Capital was flowing in, partly for direct investment and partly as a reflection of external borrowing by junior governments and corporations. The Dominion government was running a budget surplus. And the world was rapidly moving back toward gold.

Canada's exiguous bureaucracy was not aware of these developments, but the Finance Department records suggest that it gave little thought to them. In January 1925 the officials noted that for some time they had been wondering whether Canada should return to gold. Because the Dominion held more gold than the notes legislation required, for a year the government had been freely licensing gold exports. The Department favored return to gold, but it had observed that financial men did not agree "as to the wisdom of returning to a gold basis before the pound is again at par or thereabouts ... it would be better to wait a while than to take action against the judgment of some of our most outstanding financiers." By April 1925 the officials thought "there is little if any doubt of the advisability of our returning to the gold standard, say, on the 31st December next."[2]

Early in 1926 the banks appear to have raised the question with James Robb, the minister of finance. He told the president of the Bank of Montreal that he agreed Canada should return at the earliest possible moment but promised to consult the financial institutions before taking any definite steps. This consultation seems to have occurred in March; near the end of that month the president of the Canadian Bankers' Association reported that only the Royal Bank of Canada wanted to return at once; all the other banks wanted to wait until 1 July 1927.[3] The Finance Department papers do not reveal their reasons. Can they have noticed that 1 July would be the Dominion's diamond jubilee?

On 22 March Robb sought the advice of Gilbert Jackson, an economist at the University of Toronto. He asked for a memorandum on the gold standard, and Jackson reported a month later, suggesting a return to gold on 1 July 1926. He also provided a long memorandum on the "restoration of the gold standard in Canada."[4]

Unimpressed by the arguments for a managed currency, Jackson preferred monetary automaticity, but he pointed out that there were risks if Canada went back to gold while the Department of Finance stood ready to print Dominion notes at any chartered bank's request. It was all very well to use rediscounting in times of crisis, but the Finance Act provisions could be used in a very different way: the banks would expand their activities, creating bank money and drawing new Dominion notes ad lib whenever their own expansion created a new demand for circulation. Further, there was nothing to prevent them from rediscounting, obtaining new Dominion notes, and promptly converting the new notes into gold, which they could add to their own gold hoards or even export. Jackson's counsel was therefore simple. Rediscounting might be useful in emergencies, and it could and should be kept for such occasions. In more normal times, however, it could cause inflation, it would disturb the automatic self-regulating mechanism of the price-specie flow system, and it would not be needed, as the banks could always borrow in London. A gold standard might not be perfect, but with Britain and the United States on gold Canada's dollar must be kept at par if only to avoid exchange risk. There was no reason to fear a gold drain: Canada's price level was relatively low, and the paper notes would stay in circulation because they were needed for that purpose.

Late in May 1926 a senior official reminded Robb of the legal position:

My chief object in submitting this memorandum is to make sure that in the turmoil of your sessional work the fact that we automatically go on the gold standard on the 1st July if legislation to the contrary is not introduced will not escape your notice. . . If it is your intention to revert to the gold standard, no action need be taken, but on the other hand, if you desire to extend the present conditions, additional legislation will be required.

The official went on to argue that there was no reason not to return as the pound was now at par, the Canadian dollar was and would remain at par in New York, the trade balance was favorable, and Canada was a sizable gold producer. Jackson's memorandum he thought sound. Should one tell the chartered banks what one proposed to do?[5]

In the event, Canada did return to gold on 1 July, and Parliament did not repeal the objectionable clauses of the Finance Act. Furthermore, as we shall see, the gold standard quickly fell victim to the inconsistency that Jackson had noticed. By spring 1929 at the latest Canada had made an early and unadmitted departure from gold,[6] and she has never returned. Having discovered in autumn 1928 that there was a risk of a gold drain, the Dominion Department of Finance made appropriate private arrangements with the chartered banks; in January 1929 the government simply ceased to pay gold on demand, though on occasion it would agree to do so. The Mackenzie King government did not admit that it had left the gold standard. After all, the Canadian dollar was still supposed to have the same gold value as before, and the Dominion currency legislation had not been changed. Nevertheless, the world at large was not deceived, and for much of 1929 the Canadian dollar stood outside the gold export point. When R. B. Bennett took office after the Conservative victory of 1930 he inherited a floating currency – and a frightening financial tangle.

The "economic blizzard" had already begun to afflict the Dominion. Federal revenues, heavily dependent on commodity taxation and customs duties, were falling sharply with the volume and value of the national import trade. Provinces faced similar difficulties, and municipalities were already having trouble in collecting the property taxes on which they depended. The collapse of agricultural prices threatened to bankrupt the cooperative wheat pools, the banks that had lent to the pools on the security of wheat inventories, and the provinces that had guaranteed the loans. Though the chartered banks were not allowed to lend on mortgage, the prospects for the near banks, many of which had specialized almost entirely on mortgage lending, were grim indeed. Many farm families would shortly need relief in some form or other. There was no unemployment insurance, and poor relief was the responsibility of the municipalities, whose tax base was collapsing as these needs expanded. Also, both provinces and municipalities were heavily indebted, and much of this debt was external. Canada's corporations, too, had borrowed abroad in the 1920s. Direct foreign investment was not particularly worrying: if profits vanished there would be nothing to remit abroad. But debt was another matter. In addition, the Dominion government was directly responsible for the debts and deficits of the Canadian National Railways. Bennett's predecessors had assembled this system most unwillingly, in 1916 and thereafter, as private railways followed one another into bankruptcy. With American financiers, state enterprise was no less unpopular simply because its origin had been accidental or inadvertent. New York and Chicago watched with interest as Canadian National operating deficits rose ever higher. The Dominion had to pay the railway's deficits; it would shortly have to do something to save the wheat farmers and the financial institutions that depended on them; it could not long defer some sort of relief as the junior governments tottered toward financial collapse.

Where might funds be found? Unless it was willing to amend the Dominion Notes Act the government could not print paper money for its own purposes in any straightforward way. There was no central bank. The chartered banks were not accustomed to finance the Dominion government. Though the domestic bond market was well developed the government was uncertain how much new debt it could absorb. Taxes – especially tariffs – could be increased, but when the volume and value of Canada's trade were shrinking so fast no one could be sure that tariff increases would really pull in enough revenue. As for other taxes, in the depth of the slump the prospective revenues could not be anything but depressing. It is hardly surprising, therefore, that Bennett and his officials were forced to seek emergency sources of finance. In the first place the Dominion began to float short-term loans in the United States. By doing so it gave hostages to fortune; if New York financiers were to become even more nervous about the Dominion's policies and prospects, it might not be possible to roll the loans over when they fell due. Second, the Dominion began to print Dominion notes for its own use by a covert means, the "Finance Act rediscounting."

Although the chartered banks were not eager to finance the Dominion, they did not mind taking up treasury bills as long as the Department of Finance would promise to take the bills for rediscount, issuing new Dominion notes against the bills. The mechanics were cumbersome. The Department of Finance had to estimate its requirements quarter by quarter. The Canadian Bankers' Association then assigned a quota to each of the ten chartered banks. The Dominion retired the bills and canceled the notes as and when it could.

External loans were arranged through the New York banks that had long been the Dominion's fiscal agents in the United States. The Department of Finance records show how the financing was arranged and how close was the relationship between Bennett and his senior officials on the one hand and the American bankers on the other. For an example we may glance at the sale of a $60 million issue of one-year notes.[7] The issue was denominated in American gold dollars. It was sold in toto to the Chase Harris Forbes Company, a subsidiary of the Chase National Bank, for $59,608 million. Forty million dollars were needed to roll over two-year treasury notes maturing on 1 December 1932. Another $13 million was required to roll over another issue of treasury notes maturing in mid-December. In 1933 these notes were again rolled over for 15 months.[8]

In New York the arrangements were handled by Charles Batchelder, the executive vice-president of Chase Harris Forbes. He made occasional trips to Ottawa, and he was on a first-name basis with Watson Sellars, the comptroller of the Treasury. Having distributed Canada's securities on the American market, Batchelder was obliged to handle many inquiries from worried purchasers whenever the Dominion did anything peculiar or puzzling with its money or its finances.[9]

At first the Dominion seems to have enjoyed a good credit rating on the American scene, but once American bankers held sizable quantities of short-term Dominion securities they became more interested in Ottawa events – and nervous about them. Terrified of "unsound finance" abroad as at home, they watched the evolution of Bennett's policy toward the Canadian railway's deficit, the overall government deficit, and the Dominion notes issue. They must also have worried about new and disquieting voices in the Dominion Parliament: the new recruits to the parliamentary forces of "funny money." The apostles of cheap credit, easy money, and currency expansion were no longer drawn only from the agrarian Progressive group; they now had adherents among western Liberals and Conservatives as well.

Bankers in Canada, like those in other countries, did not favor any monetary experiments. The Dominion's banks were sound, they said. American financial collapse would not be repeated in Canada, where banks eschewed mortgages and where the nationwide branch system successfully spread risks. Nurtured on the real-bills doctrine and uninterested in speculative or theoretical propositions, the Canadian bankers were generally unhelpful.

There was, however, one exception. Compared with other banks, the Royal Bank of Canada was a positive fountainhead of innovation and creativity. Its assistant general manager, S. R. Noble, was interested in monetary questions; he seems to have followed British and European controversies about monetary policy. In 1917–21 his bank had been the only Canadian institution to advocate the immediate establishment of a central bank. He was interested in the use of monetary policy to stabilize the price level. He employed a bright young man, Graham Towers, whom he actually encouraged to think about monetary policy. In private memorandums he and his bank urged Bennett to make more creative use of monetary weapons. He also did his best to spread such ideas among the business community of Montreal.

Thanks to these efforts, Bennett first heard of Noble's proposals from T. B. Macaulay of Montreal's Sun Life Insurance Company. In August 1931, following a conversation with Noble, Macaulay wrote to Bennett, urging the prime minister to

give most earnest thought to the advantages which would accrue to Canada from temporarily suspending the convertibility of Canadian currency into gold, and of then allowing American exchange to rise to a premium of say 20% or perhaps better still, 25%. The basic cause of our trouble is the great drop which has taken place in all countries which are on the so-called gold standard.[10]

Canada need not wait for the United States, Macaulay argued; it could devalue, thereby reflating at once and unilaterally. Such a move would help farmers, paper producers, and import-competing manufacturers, some of whom might become exporters to Europe, Asia, or South Africa. Unemployment would fall. The government should act at once so as to alleviate unemployment and misery during the coming winter. In Argentina a 30 percent devaluation had reduced hardship; why should Canada not do the same? Sir Herbert Holt, president of the Royal Bank, was in agreement, Macaulay reported.

Bennett, however, had long been preoccupied by the domestic-currency cost of servicing Canada's external debt. Just after Britain left gold he wrote, "I feel sure that those who recommend this country to go off [the] gold standard do so without any recognition of the obligations payable by this country in New York, to say nothing of the obligations of private industries and corporations."[11] In Parliament and in public Bennett argued in the same fashion.

2. *The departure from gold and a policy for the dollar*

When Britain left gold on 21 September Bennett insisted that Canada would never follow the British example. But it had already done so. During the summer of 1931, Canada's dollar was not freely convertible into gold, at $20.67 Canadian, and its depreciation relative to the American dollar, which had been arrested and reversed during 1930, was resumed. Following Britain's action the Canadian dollar fell sharply. What should be done? Should Canada try to follow sterling, float freely, or return to parity with the dollar? What were the costs and advantages of the various courses the Dominion might follow, and how would Ottawa carry out any particular policy?

At once S. R. Noble resumed the attack that Macaulay had begun in August. Writing to Bennett on 26 September, he repeated Macaulay's argument for a 25 percent devaluation, and in an attached memorandum he tried to deal with the debt question that so concerned the prime minister. The taxpayers, he wrote, would be so much better off after devaluation that they could easily pay higher taxes or subscribe to new loans to handle these matters. In any event the Dominion government would automatically collect more sales and income taxes, and relief outlays would go down: "this objection is pure illusion." Devaluation would counter pessimism and low turnover, help avert panic and hoarding of currency, and thereby obviate the threat to the banking system that was already apparent in the United States. "The World has been wrecked by mismanagement of the gold standard, principally by the United States . . . the cause of world stability has been enormously advanced by Great Britain suspending gold payments."[1]

Noble's memorandum provoked a comment, probably the work of a senior official. "It is really difficult to say at the present moment whether we are on the gold standard or off . . . the 10 per cent discount on Canadian funds in New York reflects the actual practice," but because the balance of payments had not moved sharply against Canada this should not be interpreted to mean that Canada was "in reality . . . off the gold basis." The official blamed the discount on "confusion" caused by Britain's action, "the tendency to link us up with London, and also the suspicion of weakness engendered by our practical ban on withdrawal and export of gold . . . If in the next few weeks it is found impossible to stay on or to persuade the financiers that we are on, it may be necessary to get off before our reserves are exhausted." The writer accepted Noble's argument for the advantages of a "depreciated or *depreciating* currency" but thought that "no single remedy applied in one country can affect such great results as Mr. Noble assumes." In any event, if Canada were to leave the gold standard and deliberately depreciate,

will there not be a tendency, a demand, to increase the dose? . . . Mr. Noble, I think, attributes to the gold standard, or to its mismanagement by Paris and New York, too much responsibility for the depression. I agree with him that the failure of the world's monetary mechanism to adjust to changing industrial and commercial needs was an essential and underestimated factor in the catastrophe . . . The recent price declines are, in brief, a phase of a violent international readjustment, the accumulated total of the postponed readjustments of the past decade.

Canada might seek a seat on the Bank for International Settlements or set up a central bank so as to help in the *international* cooperation that was essential to any solution of Canada's problem, but the solution "cannot be worked out by ourselves alone, whether on a gold basis or on a depreciated currency."[2]

These comments were examined in another anonymous memorandum. Its author argued that the advantages of devaluation, though real, would be temporary. Other countries might retaliate with currency surcharges of the sort that Canada herself had imposed on British goods. Devaluation would be dangerous, provoking a further weakening of confidence and generating severe difficulties of control: "There is no reason to believe that it will be much easier to maintain the dollar at a 25% discount than to maintain it at par." Canada therefore should admit that it had left the gold standard but should let the market determine the level of depreciation; it should not borrow to support the rate.[3]

From Montreal Noble continued to press the case for devaluation. A premium of 25 percent should be attained, he later argued, by deliberate expansion of the Canadian money supply. This could be managed either by purchasing gold with new Dominion notes or by increasing the fiduciary issue. After referring to Keynes and McKenna, Noble wrote, "what this memorandum suggests is a managed currency." As the pound was now a managed currency, Noble remarked, Canada "would probably run much less risk of wide swings from boom to depression if we hitched up with sterling." However, Noble drew back from actually urging Bennett to link the dollar to the pound.[4]

Early in October 1931 another eminent banker, Sir Thomas White, urged Bennett to end the convertibility of notes into gold and to prohibit the unlicensed export of gold.[5]

Bennett continued to resist such counsel, which seems to have been unsought, but he certainly knew that all was not well. The newspapers were rude about his contention that Canada was still on gold. The Currency Branch reported that the note issue was rising while gold reserves were falling, and by 5 October there was almost no excess gold.[6] Bennett responded by asking yet more advice. Professor T. E. Gregory was asked whether Canada was on the gold standard. His advice was disquieting: the Dominion was not and should not be.

"Canada is not on the gold standard in the full sense of the term," Gregory wrote, because gold could not be freely exported and because the Canadian dollar had depreciated. There was no reason to believe that the price-specie-flow mechanism would restore balance-of-payment equilibrium if Canada were to allow gold export. Hence, Gregory counseled, there was no point in trying to return to parity by allowing gold to flow. It would be better to save gold for some future return, prohibiting its export for the present. "Administrative pressure has its attractions, but it becomes known, and is thus politically inexpedient." A depreciated currency would be advantageous so long as it was not accompanied by destabilizing speculation, did not increase the troubles of financing in New York, or "destroy confidence in the future of the currency or the country."[7]

How could the Canadian government increase the premium or peg the exchange in a more undervalued position? Gregory had several suggestions. The government might lend to the chartered banks, establish an exchange fund to buy and sell foreign exchange, run a budget surplus, or float a funding loan. There should be a loan council to coordinate Dominion and provincial borrowings. Whatever premium might be aimed at, Gregory thought it should not exceed 20 percent because more might upset the public; however, a lesser premium would be otiose because it would not do enough to reduce the burden of fixed charges.

While the officials and advisors debated the Canadian dollar moved away from "parity." Britain's high commissioner reported that Canada's press and public now regarded the statement that Canada was on the gold standard as a "polite fiction." The banks would not demand gold from the Department of Finance for export except in cases that the government had approved. Citizens were actively discouraged from demanding gold.[8] Late in October 1931 Bennett was obliged to admit the obvious. In the Finance Act there was a provision by which the Finance Department might refuse to pay gold on demand "in case of any real or apprehended financial crisis." Presumably that was the authority under which the department had refused to pay gold in 1929. On 19 October 1931, doubtless to establish the legal position more firmly, the government issued a new order-in-council: henceforth gold export would be prohibited except under licence. At once, using the Canadian Bankers' Association and the associations of investment, mortgage, and grain dealers, the government acted to control capital exports.[9] In 1932 Parliament passed a Gold Export Act that made permanent Canada's departure from gold. But the 1931 order-in-council marked the definite public break from the old forms.

Both the pound and the dollar had departed publicly from gold just at the time that people began to think about Empire solidarity in relation to the coming Ottawa Conference. In Canada as in Britain, the run-up to the conference encouraged people to meditate upon Empire money. We have already seen that the Royal Bank, believing sterling to be a managed currency, thought Canada should peg her dollar to sterling. John Ford Darling and his Empire Currency Notes were neither dead nor forgotten. In 1917 Lord Milner had asked Darling, who had extensive banking experience both in Britain and in India, to devise a scheme for an Empire currency. Darling obliged at once and continued to work out new plans throughout the twenties and early thirties. He was especially active before the Imperial Conferences of 1923 and 1930. The details of the plans changed from time to time, but every scheme included some large and flamboyant institutitonal novelty – Empire currency bills, a Bank of the Empire, or whatever. Darling was anxious to stabilize the gold-silver ratio so as to help India, and he thought it would be useful to centralize the Empire's gold reserves in London; whenever sterling was afloat, as before 1925 and after September 1931, he also worried about the stability of intraimperial exchange rates. In the Treasury, and apparently in the Bank, he was thought an impractical visionary; in the world of politics and affairs, however, he had a certain following. So long as exchange rates floated, manufacturers worried about fluctuating exchanges. Until the sterling-dollar rate had been fixed they were not willing to discuss the preferential tariff rates that everyone knew would be at the center of the Ottawa Conference.[10] Perhaps some Canadians hearkened to Leo Amery's proposals for Empire monetary union. Certainly Amery himself brought them to Bennett's attention as he had brought them to Chamberlain's.

For Canada Amery offered a definite prescription that was a mixture of the sensible and the odd. He urged Bennett to peg the Canadian dollar to the pound either at the original parity of $4.86 or, to simplify calculation, at $5.00. The action, Amery said, would protect Canadian producers from price declines on world markets, and the devaluation would stimulate Canadian domestic production, making it easier to repay the higher carrying charges on the American debt. The pegging would be easy: the government could simply fix a rate and announce that it would freely accept, at that rate, exchange both ways. "Of course the new rate must be a reasonable one, and the government must be determined to see it through." If the rate undervalued the dollar Canada could simply accumulate external balances, repay old debts, or undertake domestic credit expansion. It would be best to have a central bank to run the scheme, but one could get by with an office of the Treasury or with a Currency Board like the Iraq Board that would manage the necessary London funds. The currency reserves would be held in sterling; the note issue would rise or fall with the movement of the board's London funds.[11]

Long before he received Amery's proposal, Bennett had had to concern himself with the question of Empire currency. In February 1932 the Canadian House of Commons resolved that the government should "initiate and support measures for the stabilisation of the currencies of all British countries." Bennett asked a committee of Conservatives to examine the currency question, and in April 1932 he must have asked W. C. Clark, then still a professor at Queen's University, to treat it in his memorandums on monetary matters.[12] Further, the Canadian officials, O. D. Skelton and Norman Robertson, did not ignore the matter when preparing for the Ottawa Conference. Graham Towers also prepared a memorandum, apparently at Bennett's request.

Towers urged that to avoid being dragged down by the American deflation Canada should either manage its own currency or peg to sterling. "But we lack the experience to do the former, and there is no reason to believe that we could manage our own currency any better than sterling will be managed." The extra cost of the American debt "can easily be overemphasized." The Dominion could buy sterling through the banks, gradually work the rate up to $4.60 or $4.70, and then make a suitable announcement, introducing legislation for an extra $75 million in fiduciary issue, so as to bring the exchange back to $4.86.[13]

Having read Towers's suggestion, Bennett wrote: "Mr. Towers' final memorandum . . . just leaves the matter where it then was. The question is not a simple one; it is: would the benefits accruing to Canada in conditions of inflation compensate for the loss sustained in the purchase of exchange to meet our foreign obligations, private, public, and corporate?"[14] Clark explained that Bennett was right in believing that, *if* Britain would agree to "endeavour to stabilise the price level on, say, approximately the present basis," Canada *could* peg to the pound at roughly four dollars to the pound. Presumably, Clark wrote, the Scandinavian countries and the Empire countries would then form a "sterling block." Canada would have to arrange to buy and sell sterling securities, and as to note issue it would have to close the Finance Act loophole, but it need not make any "drastic changes" in its monetary and banking arrangements, "though it is obvious that it would be somewhat easier to work if we had a central bank." Clark then went on to ask whether Canada should peg to the pound. "In view of our trade and debt relationship with the United States, would it be wiser national policy for Canada to tie up with gold standard New York than with London? Do we want to be dependent on any other country in so far as a monetary standard goes, or does wisdom lie rather in complete independence and flexibility – freedom to change our minds and adjust ourselves to changing conditions as they arise?" Also, there was a risk that Britain might not be able to maintain internal price stability.[15]

Clark did not answer these questions or express any judgment, but the structure of the letter makes it obvious that he did not favor pegging to the pound. In his memorandum on monetary and financial questions, he developed these arguments at greater length, and in terms that closely resemble Whitehall's. It was, he said, desirable that as many Empire countries as possible should peg to sterling. Eventually there should be a return to gold, and in the meantime there should be monetary "experimentation" to stop the decline in prices. At no point did Clark mention monetary expansion as such; though he talked about stabilizing prices and exchange rates he did not suggest how this might be done. For the time being Canada should not peg to anything, because to do so would produce "intolerable" deflationary pressure. Canada could act on its own to reflate its own price level by buying sterling or New York funds with newly issued Dominion notes. If prices did not soon begin to rise in terms of gold, Canada should consider a unilateral stabilization on sterling; the rate, however, should be chosen by Canada alone.[16]

Bennett passed the Clark memorandum to several university economists. A.F.W. Plumptre wanted the dollar pegged to sterling, but only if Britain's monetary policy became more expansionary. Professors Mackintosh, Monpetit, Balcom, Knox, and Angus agreed with Clark as to the undesirability of any immediate stabilization. Professor Kierstead wanted Bennett to peg the dollar to the pound at once. All agreed with Clark that monetary policy should be used to stabilize exchange and to raise prices. They shared his conviction that nonmonetary factors had been as important as monetary disturbances in causing the depression and, like him, they hoped for an eventual but not immediate return to a "managed" gold standard.[17]

Watson Sellars, the comptroller of the Treasury, was equally reluctant to link the Canadian dollar and the pound and much more reluctant to manipulate the money supply. There would, he wrote, be a loss of confidence, and this might cause an expensive flight from Canadian money. The pound might be pegged at 90 percent of par, and this would not be enough depreciation to help Canadian producers. It would be politically harmful and detrimental to Canadian industry if currency control were transferred to London. If Canada were to expand the currency by, say, $300 million, no good would be done: the effect would merely be to "drive over 300 millions of real credit out of the country, and leave us much worse off than we are today." World prices would rise if only tax burdens were lightened, international balances were freely settled by delivery of goods, and creditor nations were freely assisting debtor nations.[18]

In the Department of External Affairs the officials opposed any pegging to sterling because so much of Canada's trade and financial relations involved the United States and because one could not be sure that the United Kingdom would operate its monetary policy to attain "the essential aims of monetary policy, namely the immediate cessation of price decline, then reflation of prices, and thereafter stability of prices." Canada should consider reflation through the purchase of external balances with newly issued Dominion notes, and in six months or more Ottawa might want to link its dollar with some other money. If gold prices continued to fall and if British monetary policy were sufficiently expansionary, there would then be a case for pegging to the pound as the lesser of two evils.[19] The troubles would be ended, however, only through international and not Commonwealth action, through the Bank for International Settlements, the coming Monetary and Economic Conference, and "otherwise." The Bank should be allowed to discount the treasury bills of gold-standard countries, to purchase their gold balances, and perhaps to deal in commercial paper. It should also establish a "new currency unit and money of account for international payment" to which governments could adopt or peg their own moneys. The gold contents of standard moneys could properly be reduced. However, although a managed paper currency would be the "ideal solution of monetary difficulties," it was "impracticable at least for the present."[20]

Such memorandums would have brought little joy to the hearts of the Empire-money fanatics. The Canadian officials agreed that it was a good thing to stabilize as many Empire currencies as possible, and they admitted that eventually Canada might peg to sterling, but not just yet.

What Bennett made of it all is harder to say. In July 1932, before the opening of the Ottawa Conference, he told the Liberal journalist J. J. Dafoe, "I believe it is possible to establish a certain measure of stability within the Empire in currency matters."[21] In May Skelton had reported to W. C. Clark that Bennett had said he would have been prepared to take "powers to amend the Dominion Notes Act . . . if it could have been done without discussion but enquiries indicated that this was not feasible. Further, there had been strong representations made by timorous financiers from Montreal and Toronto."[22] Just before the conference opened the minister of railways received a letter that reveals the nature and force of such representations. The secretary of the Canadian Bankers' Association wrote:

> It has occurred to us that you, as the intermediary between the conference and the press, should take the greatest possible care with any reference which may be made to our currency system and the possibility that Canada may adopt any one of half dozen faddist notions with regard to our monetary system which are now mooted. If the press made a mere suggestion that there was likely to be a change in our currency system, the immediate result which bankers foresee would follow would be that New York exchange would at once jump out of sight, with great loss in many directions.[23]

Once the Ottawa Conference assembled, Bennett showed considerable interest in the discussions of price raising and credit cheapening. But at the conference neither Bennett nor anyone else appears to have proposed a sterling standard for Canada. And in early 1933 we find Bennett writing: "I find it difficult to understand how men of intelligence, knowing the extent of our financial obligations to the United States, can even suggest the possibility of our coming within the sterling area until we have paid off these obligations. Leading bankers in Great Britain regard such talk as fantastic."[24]

The Ottawa conferees had resolved that the Empire countries were determined to avoid government deficits but to make credit cheap and easily obtainable for legitimate trading purposes. The Canadian officials thought well of such ideas. Now that Clark was inside the Department of Finance his voice was added to Robertson's and Skelton's. All three men favored a modest monetary expansion. They were not optimistic about its effects. Robertson believed that Canada's monetary contraction had been a consequence, not a cause, of declining prices and outputs.[25] Skelton thought a "20% rise in prices would do more to lift us out of the present slough of despond than all the trade agreements and tariff preferences that could be negotiated with Empire and foreign countries in a decade"; unfortunately, he observed, tariffs were easier to manage than prices. "International action . . . is safest and most effective, but it is difficult. National action would be less effective as regards our export trade, and more open to possibilities or suspicions of unchecked inflation, but it is within the power of governments and banks to effect." Skelton, like Clark, went on to point out, "in either case, strengthening of the facilities for control and direction of credit policy and exchange movements appears a necessary first step."[26]

Skelton and Clark recognized that there was not much point talking about exchange policy until one had a central bank or something like a central bank that could manage the domestic money supply and the foreign exchanges. As yet Canada had no such thing, and most of its commercial bankers were still convinced that it did not need one and should not have one. Bennett and E. N. Rhodes, his finance minister, must have heard about these bankers' worries from many quarters. Among the more vociferous was the voice of Sir Thomas White, doyen of Canadian bankers and eminent Conservative. Sir Thomas had been finance minister in Sir Robert Borden's Conservative government during the First World War. It was thought that he had run the Dominion's finances with conspicuous success. His counsel was bound to be heard with respect.

Sir Thomas was extremely worried about the dangers of currency inflation and extremely skeptical about Canada's power to manage its exchange rate without causing a wave of inflation, a collapse of foreign confidence, or both. He feared that any monetary management or any discussion of such management would destroy public confidence, thereby provoking a flight from the Canadian dollar. He was especially worried about the suggestion that Canada might peg to sterling because sterling had already depreciated so far. He suspected that the public would perceive that Canada could stabilize on sterling only by expanding her own money supply and by piling up unstable sterling reserves instead of gold. Supported only by sterling assets, the paper dollar would look less attractive to the nervous public. Sir Thomas was prepared to tolerate a depreciation of the Canadian dollar as long as this occurred automatically, without any deliberate government manipulation. But if the dollar were to fall as much as sterling or even lower, the nation's credit would suffer, and Canada would not be able to roll over its external debt. In any event, other wheat-producing countries would retaliate by depreciating their currencies. Hence, Canada should abstain from any deliberate manipulation or management of the exchanges. Indeed, it should work for international action to stabilize currencies and for other pacifying actions such as tariff reduction and the renegotiation of reparations and war debts.[27]

In spring 1932 Sir Thomas had made some representations with an eye to the coming Ottawa Conference; in the autumn of 1932 and winter of 1932–3 he was worried by the renewed plaints of the inflationists and by the parliamentary resolution, which the Liberal opposition had supported, that seemed to imply that the government should peg its dollar to sterling. He need not have worried. Within the government his views were already shared by the prime minister, by E. N. Rhodes, the finance minister, and by W. C. Clark, now deputy minister of finance. Commenting on White's memorandum, Clark disagreed only with inessentials. He too feared competitive depreciation. Australia, he said, could get away with depreciation; Canada could not. Like White, Clark was desperately afraid that monetary expansion would destroy Canada's credit. He wrote:

Perhaps if inflation had been started some time ago (as in the case of Australia and New Zealand) and had been carried on gradually and quietly, it might have been possible to keep it in check and to avoid undue public reactions. However, with the financial markets of the world so panicky as they are today, with the credit of Canadian public bodies so much in the limelight, and with inflation the chief topic of newspaper discussion and definitely sponsored by important or highly vocal groups in Parliament and across the country, Sir Thomas is justified in fearing that deliberate inflation by the Government would lead to the re-sale of Canadian securities held abroad, the withdrawal of foreign bank deposits, and even a flight from the dollar on the part of certain Canadians . . . the New York market would be closed to all Canadian issues, and it would be exceedingly difficult to float securities in the domestic market. Anyone who has any responsibility for Canada's public finances at the present moment cannot afford to contemplate lightly such a prospect.[28]

As to Sir Thomas's remedy – international cooperation – Clark agreed completely. One could not peg to sterling without engendering a monetary expansion that would be thought inflationist. How fortunate that a World Monetary and Economic Conference was shortly to convene! In the interim the government would not try to "manipulate or manage" the exchange rate, though perhaps it would have to smooth out any "unnecessarily wide and panicky short-time speculative fluctuations."[29]

Perhaps because he found currency, exchange, and credit "bewildering,"[30] Rhodes was not inclined to disagree with Sir Thomas or with his own deputy minister. He saw no advantage in currency depreciation. If one country were to depreciate, so could others: "While there might be monetary advantage, it would immediately be nullified by similar action in another country, and in the final analysis there would be no benefit." For Canada there would be the additional "danger of instability, probable panic, and the more real danger of a flight of capital." The only solution to the exchange problem, he wrote, was "international action; we can but hope that at the forthcoming world conference this action may be taken."[31]

Rhodes did not want a sterling peg for the dollar because as long as sterling was depreciated relative to the American dollar a sterling peg for Canada would imply much higher domestic-currency costs of servicing the Dominion's immense external debts, so many of which were payable in New York. Although he was aware of the argument that a monetary expansion would so stimulate domestic revenues as to obviate the budgetary problem that a depreciation seemed to pose, he was not convinced. He was far from sure that the extra payoff would be sufficiently large and sufficiently well distributed to ease the burdens of the debtors. He also thought that inflation, if once begun for the purposes of deliberate depreciation, would rage out of control. Inflationist hysteria was abroad, and Rhodes feared the worst.[32] It was better by far to "remain firm and stable in the matter of . . . credit and . . . currency."[33]

3. Later developments

By the beginning of 1933, Bennett and his advisers seem to have pinned their hopes on the coming World Monetary and Economic Conference. They had learned that American financiers and even Japanese journalists became nervous when Ottawa made the slightest gesture of financial innovation. They approved of cheap and abundant credit. Early in 1933, officials told Bennett that Britain's cheap-money policy had created "confidence that improvement was on the way." When Chamberlain urged cheap and easy credit of the World Economic Conference an official noted, "Canada should associate herself wholeheartedly with the Chancellor of the Exchequer."[1] Bennett appears to have heeded those words. In Chapter 7 we shall see that when Britain seemed to be associating itself too closely with the gold countries at the London Conference, Bennett joined with J. C. Smuts in urging a contrary policy. He wanted stable exchange rates. Indeed he said so, at a conference plenary session. But if stable rates were to be bought at the cost of tight money and falling prices, as the gold bloc seemed to want, the Canadian prime minister thought the cost too high.

To the Canadian government and its advisers the collapse of the World Economic Conference must have been a heavy disappointment. Nevertheless the conference was not useless to Canada. It had done something for silver producers. Moreover, it had passed a resolution regarding metallic reserves. It had recommended that no country should hold more than 25 percent metallic reserves in support of its paper currency. Devised by British officials and aimed at France, this resolution allowed Bennett to modify the Dominion notes legislation in a completely respectable way. If a world conference had recommended a reduction in metallic cover no sensible person could criticize any Dominion legislation that would effect this end. Although his own party was far from united, Bennett introduced new legislation in just these terms. Canada would not gratuitously print more money; the dollar would remain sound; on the other hand, cheap credit was important, and the London Conference had thought that reserve ratios should be lowered. By changing its own law Canada could contribute to world recovery.[2] Within a year Bennett had issued $53 million in new Dominion notes. The funds were spent on public works. Inevitably bank cash increased.[3]

While at the World Economic Conference Bennett had arranged for Lord Macmillan to come to Canada and head a Royal Commission on Banking. Canada's bank charters expire every ten years; decennial review was a long-established custom; with luck, a royal commission would recommend the establishment of the central bank that Bennett's advisers had been urging on him since 1932. Not only could a central bank manage money and credit; it could work in a relatively invisible way that would not attract public notice or attention within Canada or abroad.

Early in 1934 Bennett sent a remarkable cable to London: "I should be glad to have your view as to practicability of stabilising exchange between Empire countries and outlook as to stabilisation of sterling."[4] The documents provide no background for this cable. It may reflect Bennett's unease about the Roosevelt depreciation, then drawing near its end. Alternatively, it may reflect the fact that Bennett was about to invent a central bank.

In London, the telegram was received with amusement. Nobody seems to have thought that Bennett himself proposed to join sterling. The Treasury had long settled that nobody should ever be *advised* to join the sterling area, lest Britain later be obliged to support another currency. Dismayed by French intransigence and Rooseveltian experimentation, with respect to any general stabilization Whitehall was at its most pessimistic. In due course the chancellor told Bennett,

Stabilisation of sterling on the United States dollar would expose us to risk attaching to hazardous experiment and one result might very probably be to compel abandonment of gold by present gold bloc, opening fresh era of currency instability and reducing world trade still further. As regards attaching sterling to gold bloc you are well aware of conditions laid down at Ottawa and clearly these conditions are not near fulfilment. Prospects for tripartite stabilisation between the United States dollar, sterling, and gold bloc appear to me poor and I do not believe this will become serious world politics until the United States experiment has gone considerably further.

As for Empire rates, Chamberlain observed that these *had* been stable within the Empire for twelve months except for the Canadian dollar. Did Canada want Chamberlain to consider "questions which would arise in the event of the Canadian government deciding to stabilise Canadian currency on sterling"? Chamberlain was not sure that Bennett wanted him to do so, but if asked he would give the question "close consideration."[5]

Nothing more was heard from Bennett. This is hardly surprising. We have already seen that Bennett and his officials were not eager to link the Canadian dollar with sterling. With respect to the larger question of tripartite stabilization, Whitehall's pessimism must have reinforced Ottawa's. Perhaps, too, Roosevelt's return to gold in February 1934 assuaged Bennett's fears for the future. In any event, other monetary matters were soon to exercise his attention. Soon the prime minister would have to approve the necessary central banking bill and help pilot it through Parliament. Soon, facing a general election in 1935 at latest, he would have to devise and present other legislation that might keep him and his party in power. In that effort he was unsuccessful. Nevertheless, his party and his government did endow Canada with a central bank.[6] In that achievement he should have taken some pride.

In his invaluable survey of Canadian financial development, R. C. McIvor says, "The most fundamental criticism of Canadian monetary policy during the depression is that none existed."[7] The evidence of this chapter suggests that McIvor's statement is at best half true. Admittedly there was no central bank, no vigorous pursuit of monetary expansion, no clear-cut public decision as to the management of the exchange rate. Admittedly the government was not instant in institutional innovation. But perhaps its timidity was justified. Surely Bennett was right to worry about foreign reaction to domestic monetary experiment. We now know that in percentage terms the Canadian money and credit base contracted no more than the British and far less than the American. Although the banks did not work to a fixed reserve or liquidity ratio it is reasonably clear that they had excess reserves throughout the period 1930–4; the Dominion would have manufactured more reserves through the Finance Act mechanism if the banks had requested them.

Looking back on the period 1931–3, an official summed up Bennett's monetary policy as follows:

We have retained our monetary independence . . . refusing to tie up either to the pound sterling or to the US dollar . . . in view of our important commercial and financial relations with both the US and Great Britain this compromise seems to have been a not undesirable one . . . Moreover, if we desire to do so, we might also make the claim that under the limitations of our machinery and our conditions we have been following during the last two or three years the same kind of managed currency policy as Great Britain. Like England, we have actually been on a paper standard; like England also, we have actively pursued an easy money policy (by sponsoring a reduction of interest on savings deposits, by our loan conversion programme, and by the $35 million loan sold to the banks in October 1932); and we have handled our gold purchases and sales in such a way as to smooth out to some extent fluctuations in our external balances and in our exchanges . . . what is required is cooperation of the US and Great Britain in an effort to raise the world price level. That has been clearly seen by Canada for some time, and it has been a fundamental of our policy to promote that cooperation. It is true that if Canadian currency had been inflated to the point where the London-Montreal exchange rate ruled at $5 instead of say $4, the Canadian exporter would have secured 5 Canadian dollars . . . but this would merely represent a redistribution of the national income in favour of the exporting industries . . . at the time of the Ottawa Conference I felt that . . . it would have been possible to embark on a certain measure of inflation without causing a lack of confidence or an outflow of capital. A few months later it became impossible because of the condition of the investment markets. Today with recent developments in the US, the danger of an outflow of capital to that country has probably been removed and it may again be desirable to consider whether some expansionist policy aimed to keep the Canadian dollar depreciating at least as rapidly as the US dollar might not be in order.[8]

It is with respect to the exchange rate, not the domestic money supply, that the Bennett regime can most readily be criticized. If the Canadian dollar had been deliberately devalued and held at a lower valuation relative to the American, Canada's recovery would surely have been more rapid and more complete than it actually was. Contrasting Canadian recovery with Australian, or South African, one is inclined to suggest that Canada almost deliberately chose a relatively high value for its money and thereby delayed its recovery, whereas the Australian and South African governments had to accept substantial devaluations and thereby were able to recover relatively fast. Though Bennett was prepared to consider attaching Canada's money to sterling he was persuaded, partly by Clark and his other official advisers and partly by outside influences, that this was not a good idea. Although the persuaders used arguments that historians and economists might think unsound, they managed to convince the prime minister, and in the Bennett government no more was required.

4

South Africa, sterling, and
the gold standard, 1931 and thereafter

1. *The confusions of 1931*

When Britain left gold, South Africa did not follow at once. Its government said it would never follow. Unlike R. B. Bennett, Prime Minister J. B. M. Hertzog and Nicholaas Havenga, his finance minister, were serious in their determination to retain the gold standard. Their policies were controversial both in London and in South Africa. In October 1931 Charles te Water, the South African high commissioner in London, told his diary:

The gold standard – depreciated sterling – to remain or not to remain– this is the only topic of conversation. It has been an intensely interesting crisis. No two opinions alike. I have had long and intricate discussions with men of such divergent views as J. H. Thomas, Runciman, Sir Robert Horne, Sir H. Strakosch, Ernest Oppenheimer, and a host of others . . . To do what suits us best.[1]

For fifteen months the controversy ebbed and flowed. What *was* best for South Africa? What, if anything, did the United Kingdom want or expect of the South African government? What pressures were applied? What arguments were marshaled by the government, and by the opposition in Parliament and outside? How was the gold standard finally abandoned, and what followed from that abandonment? Finally, why did South Africa adhere to sterling at all? These are the questions with which this chapter is concerned.

The South African debate was very public, and highly politicized. It therefore claimed the attention of the South African public in a way that the Canadian debate never managed to do. Indeed, even today one meets ordinary South Africans who know about the controversy at least in a general way. Because the arguments were conducted in the public arena and because the government took some pains to document its opinions and to marshal support for them, this chapter can rely largely on published materials. Nevertheless, as far as possible we have drawn on documentary evidence, partly to discover whether people meant what they said and partly to explore the question of British interference. Before turning to the evidence, however, we must learn a little about financial organization in South Africa.

Banking was dominated by two great firms, Barclay's and Standard. Both maintained extensive branch networks, and both had their head offices in London. In addition, there was a small bank, the Netherlands Bank of South Africa. Its share capital had been taken up in Europe, but its head office was in Pretoria. Since 1921 there had also been a South African Reserve Bank. This institution had a monopoly of the note issue, and the three commercial banks were obliged to maintain reserves with it. The required reserve ratios were defined in relation to deposit liabilities, as in the United States. The Reserve Bank was also a bank of rediscount, though in this respect its powers were as limited as those of the Federal Reserve had originally been. As the commercial banks had trouble obtaining the kind of assets that the Reserve Bank would accept for rediscount, they could not rely upon the Reserve Bank and consequently had to maintain excess reserves of gold and paper currency. Standard and Barclay's leaned heavily on the London market where they kept liquid funds and also some long-term placements. Within South Africa there was no money market and only the most limited of new-issue markets as far as the banks were concerned: they could not deal on the Johannesburg stock exchange, where the major counters were mining shares, and the government bond market was both small and thin. The commercial bill was almost unknown, and so was the treasury bill. The banks lent principally on mortgage and on open advance. Since spring 1925 the country had been on a pure gold standard. Gold sovereigns circulated, and anyone could buy gold coin or bullion in exchange for paper currency. Anyone could import or export gold. The mines sold their gold to the Reserve Bank, which exported it to London and sold it for sterling. As gold exports dominated the South African balance of payments, within South Africa the Reserve Bank was almost always a net seller of sterling. There was no foreign exchange market, and transactions in forward exchange were almost unknown. The commercial banks bought both gold bullion and sovereigns in South Africa for export to the Far East, especially to India. After Britain left gold the South African gold standard was from time to time less "pure" in fact than in form: exchange restrictions, varying in rigor, were in force for greater or lesser periods. Nevertheless gold export was never restricted, and until 28 December 1932 the Reserve Bank's paper currency remained freely convertible into gold. It was by ending this convertibility that the South African authorities at last left the gold standard. For some weeks the South African pound then floated. Early in February 1933 it was pegged to sterling.[2]

When Britain left gold the South African commercial banks found themselves in an unenviable position. In London Barclay's and Standard held sizable investments. These reflected shareholders' equity, and they were regarded by the banks as a sort of secondary guarantee to the depositors in South Africa. In addition, at any time the banks might be net borrowers in the London market or net lenders to it. They had long been accustomed to watch this short-term position when managing their overseas activities. On the other hand, they did not think of their London investments as a "supply of sterling" on which South Africa could "draw in emergency." If questioned about their power to support the exchange they typically answered in terms of assets in South Africa relative to liabilities there. If such assets exceeded such liabilities, South Africa borrowed from Britain through the banks, which would find themselves "oversold" in terms of sterling; that is, their short-term sterling obligations would exceed their short-term sterling claims. They could then cover themselves in any or all of three ways: they might sell sterling investments, borrow in the London market, or buy sterling from the South African Reserve Bank. As the Reserve Bank bought all the gold that the Rand produced, it was normally willing and able to be a net seller of sterling, which it obtained by exporting the gold. When other exports were doing well and when South African exporters were eager to sell foreign money and buy South African, the commercial banks could be relatively independent of the Reserve Bank because their purchases and sales of sterling would be more nearly in balance. An inflow of overseas private capital would have the same effect, as the remittance would almost always be effected through the banks. But if export prices or volumes fell, if South Africans kept export proceeds in sterling form, or if the country began to export capital funds in other forms, the banks would quickly find themselves oversold in terms of sterling. All these things were happening in the autumn of 1931 and, perhaps to a lesser extent, through much of 1932.

In certain circumstances one supposes that the banks would not object to an oversold position. They might expect that the relevant flows would quickly be reversed, so that the position would be temporary. So long as they could borrow freely in London, or liquidate investments at satisfactory prices, and so long as they did not expect the exchange rate to change, they would presumably have maintained an oversold position with equanimity. But in 1931–2 these conditions were not satisfied. The banks knew that the capital flows and the exporters' difficulties, which produced the excess supply of South African money and the excess demand for sterling, were directly related to the government's policy about the exchanges. They can have seen no reason to expect that the situation would change, as long as that policy was continued.

Every month, therefore, the banks might expect new demands for extra sterling. But they could not indefinitely increase their London borrowings or deplete their overseas investments without serious risk. Further, the longer they pursued any such policy, the larger their holdings of South African assets relative to their holdings of sterling assets and the greater the capital loss in sterling terms if the South African pound should eventually fall relative to the British. In effect, the banks' sterling assets would be gradually liquidated in step with their South African liabilities, though their South African assets would not change.

The banks were understandably reluctant to let such things happen, if only because their day-to-day operations were telling them that the business community believed the exchange rate would change. The banks could maintain a balanced position only with the cooperation of the Reserve Bank. Here, however, there were difficulties both technical and personal. The law allowed the Reserve Bank to rediscount only certain sorts of very short-term obligations. Such paper had never been plentiful in South Africa, and the banks were not at all sure they had sufficient to go on buying the sterling they needed. Of course the banks were not obliged to deal in exchange, and if they could not supply enough sterling to their customers they could simply divert those customers to the Reserve Bank itself. Obliged to maintain the convertibility of paper currency into gold at a fixed price, the Reserve Bank could not legally refuse to meet such demands. But for the two big British banks there were political dangers in following such a course. Their relations with the governor-elect, Johannes Postmus, were less than happy. With the Nationalist government their relations were distinctly unpleasant. Neither the prime minister nor the finance minister understood the banks' position. Both were worried by the troubles of the Reserve Bank, which had experienced severe capital losses in terms of South African pounds: when Britain left gold the Reserve Bank held some £9.5 million sterling. Both resented the fact that Standard and Barclay's dominated South African banking; both believed that the banks' *total* assets should somehow be at the disposal of the South African economy; neither understood the banks' desire to avoid capital loss for the sake of their South African depositors.

When the government asked the banks to ration foreign exchange soon after 21 September the bankers cooperated. Efforts were made to ensure that sterling would be supplied only for legitimate commercial and personal purposes. Nevertheless, the banks could buy little sterling, and the sterling assets of the Reserve Bank were steadily depleted. Though the Reserve Bank could and did buy current gold production it could not export much of its own gold reserves, as the currency law linked these rigidly with the note issue. Hence the Reserve Bank's position was not as strong as it looked. In a sense, therefore, South Africa was really forced off gold in the autumn of 1931. As the parliamentary opposition was quick to point out, if one has to restrict the sale of exchange one is not really on gold. N. C. Havenga, the finance minister, denied that there were restrictions. Indeed, he claimed that the Reserve Bank stood ready to sell sterling freely to all comers. But even if the claim had been true there would have been risks in trying to exercise it. Already the Reserve Bank was pressing Standard and Barclay's for the names of persons who bought sterling in large quantities. The banks would not oblige the governor, but the demand can hardly have remained a secret, and it would have made a prudent person pause before approaching the Reserve Bank itself.

By mid-October Havenga was pressing the banks to provide sterling in London. They responded that they could do little by themselves. Their South African advances were still rising rapidly while their local deposits were falling, and they were running out of suitable assets for local rediscount. They would be prepared to borrow South African treasury bills against the security of sterling securities that they would deposit with the high commissioner in London; they could then rediscount the new treasury bills with the Reserve Bank. The Treasury rejected the idea, and it did not appear to understand the banks' concern to avoid an uncovered position. It thought that the banks could provide sterling support in the amount of £10 million to £15 million and that they should use their sterling assets irrespective of any loss that the sale of these assets might entail. But it was not that sort of loss that was worrying the banks.

Late in October the Reserve Bank, doubtless acting for the Treasury, proposed an "exchange pool." The government would find £5 million and the two commercial banks another £5 million. The banks disliked the idea, but early in November they agreed. It remained to be seen, however, where the government would find £5 million in gold or foreign exchange. It first tried New York; rebuffed there, it explored Paris and Amsterdam, where it met with no greater success.

The South African government does not seem to have realized that in autumn 1931 the conditions were hardly propitious, either in the United States or in Europe, for a substantial international loan. American bankers were worried not just about their domestic assets but about their overseas activities, and in Europe the system was still reverberating with the Austro-German financial collapse of the summer. Further, South Africa's own troubles were not exactly unknown overseas. Indeed, the London press doubtless exaggerated these troubles from time to time. But the South African authorities believed that London had somehow intervened to obstruct or prevent these loans. London's motive, they thought, was to force South Africa off gold. From London the high commissioner wrote to the prime minister:

My deduction then is that though the British Government undoubtedly has not been guilty of the crass stupidity of direct intervention in the question of the South African gold standard, I have in my own mind little doubt that it has used every indirect means to achieve its ultimate object: namely, to force South Africa off gold . . . On the point of South Africa remaining on the gold standard, J. H. Thomas is clearly embarrassed by our Government's decision . . . Imperial solidarity is a point on which he continually harps, while discussing this problem, and though on this and on another occasion, when I discussed the question with him, he was careful in his choice of words, I feel sure he would welcome our abandonment of the gold standard.[3]

When he learned that the South African Treasury had proposed an approach to J. P. Morgan, Charles te Water thought this a great mistake, because the firm is "so notorious an anglophile. . . . Much malicious satisfaction is being expressed among Morgan's friends in London, who happen to be the South African Government's enemies. Thomas, I judge, would have been delighted, as he, I know, is intensely annoyed, for he told me so himself, at the news of our activities in Amsterdam."[4]

In Johannesburg and London it was reported that J. P. Morgan had insisted on a United Kingdom guarantee for any new South African loan. Believing this rumor, te Water reported, "The Morgan incident . . . in itself, was to my mind full of significance. The 'British guarantee' condition was, I feel confident, inspired, for Morgan would not act without at least consulting the Bank of England."[5] From Washington, however, the South African minister quickly denied that any guarantee had been demanded. Eric Louw wrote:

Terms were never even discussed at this end – and as I conducted all the negotiations after my arrival – and Botha before that – I ought to know! I feel sure that the despatch from the Johannesburg correspondent was a deliberate attempt to embarrass the Union Government, and that the correspondent (or the people who gave him the news) knew that the statement was false . . . So far from asking for a British "guarantee" . . . people expressed themselves very frankly about Great Britain's credit and her muddled economic and financial situation . . . I think it would be well if you took occasion to tell Thomas that I have branded the report as a deliberate falsehood.[6]

Sir H. Stanley, Britain's high commissioner in South Africa, had already reported that he thought the Union was really not on the gold standard at all. Exchange was rationed to limit the amount of capital flight, and though Reserve Bank notes were theoretically convertible into gold, "a Director of a commercial bank states that persons requiring such exchange are subjected to a 3d Degree examination which must be passed successfully before obtaining gold."[7] Early in November Stanley reported that "the cover of the Reserve Bank is shown in today's statement as £50 which means that henceforth it must rely on weekly shipments of gold to cover public transactions through commercial banks and this sum is insufficient."[8] The point was that though the Reserve Bank still held massive reserves of gold, the currency law prevented it from freely using these reserves in support of exchange.

Such reports must have increased the suspicion, already present in Whitehall and Threadneedle Street, that South Africa would not be able to stay with gold. Late in September Sir Frederick Leith-Ross had asked R. N. Kershaw what the Bank of England expected. After explaining that the Bank "had made no attempt to influence the Reserve Bank in any way," Kershaw said that because of pressure from its agricultural interests South Africa would be forced off gold within a year.[9] This question arose because on 29 September the South African government had asked, "If British Government had decided point below which it will not allow sterling to fall that is figure at which sterling will be stabilised in relation to gold." Leith-Ross observed that nothing could be said about the future of sterling.[10] As for the future of the South African pound, when J. H. Thomas met te Water on 30 September he told the South African high commissioner, "it was, of course, entirely a matter for the Union government to decide what policy they would pursue," but it was desirable to keep in touch and to "cooperate as much as possible." Though te Water concurred,[11] it seems to have been this interview that first fueled his suspicions about British government intentions, activities, and desires. These suspicions he quite properly transmitted to Pretoria.

In due course Stanley reported that South African ministers now had suspicions. He had heard that some ministers believed the Bank of England had influenced Morgan's to refuse the South African request and that the Bank also manipulated Standard and Barclay's, which were still reluctant to use their sterling assets to assist the Reserve Bank in its struggle to stay on gold.[12] Hearing of this suggestion, Leith-Ross expressed himself with his customary vigor. The Bank of England had not been consulted about the negotiations with Morgan's, and so it had not commented on them. As for the commercial banks, the Bank was "in no way responsible" for the attitude they had taken.[13] When South African newspapers reported that the U.K. government had told the French government to discourage South African attempts to raise a Paris loan, the Dominions Office at once told Stanley that any such attitude would be "wholly contrary to [U.K.] policy, and indeed unthinkable."[14]

Though te Water knew of such disclaimers, he did not find them convincing. For this conclusion there appear to have been two reasons. First was a natural Nationalist suspicion of the United Kingdom. Second was the fact that te Water confronted Whitehall, the Bank, and the government of the United Kingdom chiefly through the mediation of J. H. Thomas, the Dominions secretary. Regrettably, te Water took Thomas's imperialist bluster seriously. If we are to judge from his correspondence, he also believed that Thomas was really privy to the innermost thoughts of Bank, City, and Treasury. Thus te Water wrote, "It must not be forgotten that Thomas keeps in the very closest touch with the City in all matters of high finance."[15] And te Water appears to have credited Thomas with great intellectual powers. He certainly overestimated Thomas's capacities as dissimulator, manipulator, and negotiator. He therefore subjected Thomas's utterances to a close textual analysis that they did not deserve.

In Paris and Amsterdam the loan discussions were no more fruitful than in New York. By mid-November the original pool lapsed, as the government could not raise £5 million. On 20 November the Reserve Bank proposed a new pool, itself offering to gradually provide £5 million from its purchases of current gold production. The banks would provide another £5 million. The pool would last until the end of January 1932, and the Reserve Bank would provide exchange cover without demanding any more contributions from the banks. Thus, when the South African Parliament assembled late in November, Havenga was able to tell the House of Assembly that the banks had become more cooperative. Exchange rationing, however, would continue though the Reserve Bank would continue to sell gold for notes on demand: those who wish to speculate must take the trouble of buying gold and shipping it.[16]

The government believed that South Africa could stay on gold. Both the finance minister and the governor of the Reserve Bank argued that all was well because the current account was balanced and the budget in good order. Taking together the holdings of the Bank and the banks, there were plenty of external assets.[17] Why, then, were there exchange difficulties? The causes, they said, were various – speculation; fear; confusion; mindless Anglophilia; the evil counsel and disreputable practices of the commercial banks, whose managements thought there could be only one kind of pound. So that the government could act to protect the standard, it was decided that there would have to be a financial emergency regulations measure, which would give immense discretion to the finance minister. Late in November 1931 Parliament was assembled in special session to pass this bill and to provide an export subsidy and a general "primage" on imports. Though long opposed to agricultural subsidies, Havenga decided to provide them temporarily so as to ease the burden his exchange policy had placed on farmers. The subsidy could be temporary, he believed, because the problem was temporary. In a few months he expected prices would rise in the United Kingdom. This would happen because sterling had fallen. World prices were determined in gold terms, and so a depreciated pound must imply a higher sterling price. Hence, in terms of South African money, receipts would soon be as high as if sterling had not been depreciated. Similarly, Britain's manufactures would no longer provide "unfair competition" within South Africa.

On the question of sterling prices versus gold prices, there was, as we shall see, a good deal of confusion, both in Parliament and in the proceedings before the Select Committee that Havenga set up early in 1932. We shall shortly pursue these confusions. But first we ask why Havenga thought prices would adjust quickly. He may well have been basing himself on the Kemmerer-Vissering report of 1925. In 1924 Professor E. W. Kemmerer came from Princeton University and Dr. Gerard Vissering came from the Netherlands Bank to tell South Africa whether it should return to gold without waiting for the United Kingdom.[18] They wrote about price flexibility in extremely optimistic terms. Kemmerer and Vissering argued that the advantages of a depreciation of currency were temporary because prices and wages would usually adjust "within a few months' time."[19] This view was not shared by W. H. Clegg, the governor of the South African Reserve Bank.[20] But Clegg's opinion was buried in the voluminous minutes of evidence, whereas the visitors' was prominently displayed in the summary conclusions that were all that most members of Parliament could possibly have read.

More fundamentally, the price question was confusing and the discussion was confused because people had different reference points in mind. The gold-mining industry attracted a great deal of attention, but remarkably little of this attention was directed to the price of gold in South African currency. Obviously, as long as South Africa and the United States were on the gold standard at the par values of 1931 the dollar price of gold was fixed, and so was the South African price. If the South African pound were to be devalued relative to the American dollar, the local price of gold would rise. One must suppose that such considerations caused the Chamber of Mines to change its policy. Immediately after Britain left gold, the Chamber thought that South Africa should stay with gold at the old parity. By the end of November 1931 it thought the South African pound should leave gold and adhere to sterling. At first the Chamber and many of those who later thought it wrong to leave gold were more concerned about the cost of gold production than about the price of the gold itself. In 1920–2, it was argued, the South African economy had been put through a deflationary wringer. When the mines had tried to reduce money wages and to "dilute" the labor force by using more blacks in the relatively skilled jobs, the white workers had rebelled. The deflation, however, had followed the inflation of the years just before 1920, when the South African pound had been off the gold standard. The country could not afford to run the risk that if it left the gold standard once more it would again pass through a cycle of inflation and deflation that might once more produce a rebellion among the white miners.

But why should there be price inflation merely because the South African pound had left gold? To this question there were various answers.

One answer was in terms of world prices. If the world price level of each commodity were fixed in terms of gold, the local price level would necessarily rise whenever its currency was devalued relative to its gold value, because the conversion factor – the exchange rate – had changed. In terms of local currency both importables and exportables would become more expensive. Because both entered into the local cost of living, that cost would necessarily rise; the result would be wage demands throughout the economy, and these would force up costs and prices in the sheltered activities also. For the opposition South African Party, this line of thought was both an opportunity and an embarrassment. General Smuts, the party leader, originally based his party's attack on the prostration of the exporting agricultural interest.[21] As sterling fell relative to the dollar, in terms of local currency the South African farmer suffered from a special price decline that was added to the general decline from which he was already suffering. Leave the gold standard, Smuts argued, and the South African pound will depreciate relative to the dollar, raising the returns to the South African farmer. Some of his followers argued that by pegging to sterling the returns could be both raised and stabilized. But to the Nationalists, who were inclined to think in terms of gold prices, it was not at all obvious that sterling prices would be more stable than gold prices, though in terms of local currency they would temporarily be higher. Everything would depend on the way that sterling would move relative to the gold-standard countries. In autumn 1931 the South African government had asked J. H. Thomas what would happen to sterling. Would it continue to fall? Would it rise? Or would it be stabilized, and if so, at what level? They got a dusty answer: no one could tell.[22]

In any event, there was much controversy about the relevant price base. Where was the price of exportables genuinely determined? Britain, the opposition said, was South Africa's largest market. But many of the nation's exports were reexported from British ports. Some exports, such as wool, were sold basically on a world market where the final buyer was as likely to be a German or an American as a Yorkshire spinner, but other exports, like wine and fruit, were exported almost entirely to the United Kingdom. For those who produced the latter goods Smuts's arguments were telling. Perhaps their sterling receipts might rise, but there would be nothing speedy or automatic about the process. For those who produced the goods that were sold throughout the world, it must have been hard to separate two developments: gold prices were still falling, and the channels of trade were increasingly clogged. Perhaps the gold standard had not worsened the situation for them. But it coexisted with a worsening, and if it were abandoned they would be no worse off.

But there were other routes for inflation to attack a country whose currency floated. Whatever these were, they had caused inflation in 1918–20, when the South African pound had not been on gold. They would do so again, many people thought.

In terms of gold, prices had fallen by nearly one-third since 1928. There is something unreal about inflationary fears when prices are falling so far and so fast. The charitable might suppose that the Nationalists were thinking of a "natural level of prices," which would exist in the absence of interference. The evidence does not support this supposition. One might also suppose that someone was worried about the link between an undervalued currency and inflation. Both Havenga and Postmus argued that as long as the South African pound was on the gold standard at the old par the exchange rate was an equilibrium one in the sense that demands for foreign exchange should roughly equal supplies. If the South African pound were to be pitched lower relative to sterling and the gold currencies, it would be undervalued. Any such undervalued rate could be held only if the South African Reserve Bank were to accumulate gold and foreign exchange reserves. Indeed, we are told that when the South African money was pegged to sterling in February 1933 the Bank expected that it would have to build up its sterling balances once more. This was the reason, presumably, for the exchange guarantee that the government then gave the Bank. Never again would the Bank shareholders have to face a disaster like that of September

1931. But the Bank could not accumulate such balances and gold reserves without adding to the local reserve base; that is, the commercial banks would inevitably acquire larger holdings of currency, larger deposits at the Reserve Bank, or both. The Bank could not hope to offset these additions through open market operations. It did not hold enough government securities; there was, in any event, virtually no open market. Extra reserves therefore would imply extra credit and extra bank money for the South African economy. After December 1932 these connections were certainly at work. As G. H. de Kock explains, at no time thereafter could the Reserve Bank control credit or money: the commercial banks simply had too much high-powered money to play with.[23] To those who like the quantity theory of money, this extra money would seem bound to raise prices, and we may suppose that to some extent it did so. We may also suppose that the extra reserves came directly from the devaluation of winter 1932–3, because this devaluation stimulated gold mining and the other export industries, attracted a sizable inflow of new foreign capital, and led to the repatriation of the capital outflows that had occurred since September 1931. In 1933 the Reserve Bank increased its holdings of gold and sterling dramatically. The reserve base of the commercial banking system as measured by commercial bank deposits with the Reserve Bank also increased. Though in later years the percentage increases were less dramatic, such growth continued until the outbreak of war. Only in 1937–8 was there a drop in gold and sterling balances. Even then, within South Africa monetary expansion continued. To the economists of today such interconnections are not exactly surprising or subtle; but in the South African debates of 1931–2 they do not appear to have been mentioned, nor should the historian be surprised by this fact or critical of it.

When Britain left gold, General Smuts, the leader of the opposition South African Party, was in Britain. During his absence Sir Patrick Duncan, a Johannesburg lawyer, led the party. At first Duncan and most of the opposition agreed with the government that South Africa should stay on the gold standard. It was natural to suspect that they had got their cue from the Johannesburg Chamber of Mines, which at first took the same view. But party notables could also be men of principle, and such, it appears, was Duncan. In mid-October he wrote to a personal friend:

A great controversy is raging here over the gold standard. The farmers, coal owners, sugar planters are all clamouring for an abandonment of the gold standard. The government say they will die in the last ditch before they go off it. Of course it is a very tempting prospect for them to be able to get what appears to be enhanced prices for their products and to pay off their creditors

86

in depreciated money. What is happening now of course is that they are being paid in depreciated money a price that is no more in pounds than it used to be when paid in good money and they are very vocal on the subject. It is quite possible that between their pressure and the rush of speculators to buy British money we may be forced off – which I think would be a great misfortune. It is a pity politically that we can't fight the government on this point. It would really be an excellent stick to beat them with and some of us have already succumbed to the temptation. But unfortunately I think they are right. The calamity for us would be if the nations found some other way of settling trade balances than by gold. Then our gold mines would go the way of the silver mines . . . in practice the Banks are putting every possible difficulty about allowing people to remit money to England. The farmers and others who export produce to the English market and who now find their London cheques subject to a 20% discount are in great distress and demanding that the government shall follow the English currency. I think for once the government is right but whether they will be able to hold out very long is doubtful.[24]

At the same time Duncan wrote in similar terms to a party associate who thought South Africa should leave gold:

it is of vital importance for South Africa that gold should continue to be the basis of the world's currencies and the balancing factor as between the different nations . . . it does seem that if we, the chief producers of gold in the world, were of our own free will and not by actual compulsion as was the case in England, to abandon the gold standard it would have a great moral effect in the direction of some new method of trade balancing being found . . . prices would inevitably begin to rise . . . and things would adjust themselves to the new levels, that is on the assumption that the British pound can be held at something like its present parity and does not go even lower. At present it seems impossible to say what is going to happen about that. For these reasons, the vital interest to us of gold being retained as the monetary basis of the world and the uncertainty of the present position with regard to British currency, I and others of us here have taken the view that we should for the present adhere to the gold standard unless the drain of gold from us is such as to make it impossible to continue.[25]

In London Sir Henry Strakosch at first took a similar line. The financier had long been interested in South African mining, and he was known to the politicians of both parties. On 21 September he had sent a telegram to the South African authorities, urging that because of the outstanding national interest in gold mining the country should not follow sterling.[26] By 24 November, however, he believed that South Africa should leave gold and follow the pound.[27] Strakosch's opinions are important because it is reasonable to suspect that General Smuts consulted Strakosch before announcing that South Africa should leave gold.[28]

On 2 November Smuts cabled Duncan saying that he was sending a statement on the gold question. He asked Duncan to correct it for publication; Smuts would then give it to Reuter's.[29] Duncan did so, and after thanking him Smuts wrote:

I feel very strongly that it is a mistaken policy for us to be and remain on the gold standard when Great Britain is off. The South African houses in London as well as the officials at South Africa House (apart from te Water) think that the position is becoming quite untenable and that South Africa will be *forced* off the gold standard in spite of what the Government may do. The position will probably become worse because I believe that the pound will drop a good deal lower than it is at present. Before September wholesale prices were 40% below 1929 wholesale prices, which means that to get even back to the 1929 price basis £1 will have to fall to the neighbourhood of 12/–. Our farmers could not stand a loss of that magnitude on their English market.[30]

Such arguments appear to have helped change Duncan's mind and other minds within the South African Party. Further arguments were doubtless supplied by the increasing difficulty of remittance and the increasing pressure from agricultural interests in October and November of 1931. Furthermore, the Chamber of Mines had changed its view. The Chamber had noticed that if wage rates did not rise too much a devaluation would serve both the industry's interest and the nation's. In terms of South African money, profits would obviously rise. Further, an enormous mass of low-grade gold ore would become usable. In effect, devaluation would "manufacture" a new and much larger base for the mining industry, which could thereby prolong its own life. For more than a decade the industry and the government had been worried about low-grade ore. The mines were a wasting asset whose end was believed to be in sight. The longer they could operate, the more remote the painful national adjustments that would follow their exhaustion.[31]

Thus, when the South African Parliament assembled on 20 November to debate the Financial Emergency Regulations Bill, the government faced a reasonably united opposition. Nevertheless, a few South African Party members were still attached to gold. One such person was J. H. Hofmeyr, who, early in 1932, explained his position in a private letter that was later published. First, he wrote,

I find it quite impossible to accept the proposition that any country should make so radical a change in the basis of its currency as is implied by departure from the gold standard, unless it finds itself virtually without any alternative . . . where a country goes off the gold standard, it does, actually or potentially, affect the relations between creditors and debtors, and also between employers and employed, to such an extent, that its conduct is not free from reproach, unless it can produce adequate proof of substantial constraint.

Furthermore, in two respects it would be dangerous to go off gold, convenient though the action might seem in the short run. Because the South

African pound would inevitably link with sterling, there was the risk that sterling might fall further, especially if there were a German default. There was a certainty also that in South Africa costs would eventually rise. "I believe," Hofmeyr wrote, "that it will in the long run be a considerable rise." Thereafter, because Britain would certainly go back to gold at the old parity when she could, "that will mean the disappearance of the gold premium, and the necessity of forcing down wages. The difficulties which were experienced in this regard on a previous occasion are such as not readily to be forgotten."[32]

Hofmeyr's concerns have close parallels in the arguments that N. C. Havenga placed before the House of Assembly in November 1931 and again in January and February 1932. The gold standard, Havenga said, ensured a stability of prices and exchanges. If South Africa were to leave gold she would almost inevitably have to adhere to sterling, "a standard over which we have no control." No one knew how sterling might move, and therefore the sterling price level was indeterminate. The pound could move for all sorts of reasons that had nothing to do with South Africa. The gold standard, admittedly, might require some wage cuts, but a sterling standard would produce inflation, which would cause strikes and industrial disagreements. Further, the gold standard helped to attract foreign capital. If the government adhered firmly to gold the speculators would be defeated and speculation would cease. The troubles of the South African farmers would pass once sterling prices adjusted to the depreciation of sterling vis-à-vis gold. In the long run South Africa would lose if the world ceased to use gold as a monetary standard. Meanwhile, the national position was sound. The budget was balanced. There was a surplus on commodity trade, and there was plenty of sterling in the commercial banks. To go off gold would be "repudiation." "We can remain on the gold standard and we shall remain on the gold standard."[33]

Of course there was good reason to worry about the movement of sterling. Who could tell how far it might fall or how it might fluctuate? As the United Kingdom still had no policy about sterling, it could hardly have communicated its policy to any Dominion even if it had cared to do so. Hence, as we have already seen, it said nothing. Havenga's words in the House of Assembly were strictly accurate, but perhaps a little disingenuous: "The policy so far as we know still is to go back to the old parity but will it be possible? . . . We have never had a single word from the British Government that it is not possibly their policy eventually to revert to 20s. in the pound."[34]

Having passed the government measures, the House adjourned on 27 November, to reassemble two months later. The debates, like most parliamentary proceedings, had been prolix and often beside the point, but they were revealing. The prime minister disliked the thought of abandoning the gold standard partly because there would then be *no* standard – just "paper which is worth nothing."[35] Much of the Nationalist Party connected the gold standard with economic independence, and this, of course, was linked with political autonomy. By having its own money, the Nationalists thought, South Africa could demonstrate its economic independence. If it were to leave gold because Britain did it would be telling the world that it was still a dependency – and so much the more if the South African pound were to be linked with sterling. As for the advice of the gold-mining industry, that could not be accepted, because the Nationalists, still largely an agrarian party, had always disliked the Rand magnates and their works, from which they thought so many evil things had followed. Similarly, because the two great commercial banks were run from Britain their advice and their activities were suspect. The Nationalists claimed that the South African Party was the party of the English, whose interests and affections were not wholly rooted in the Union. That was why the opposition wanted to follow sterling off gold, and that was why so many of Smuts's followers wanted to link the good South African pound to the weak and unpredictable sterling.[36]

2. The Select Committee

The House reassembled on 27 January 1932. In the preceding eight weeks Smuts had returned to South Africa and had commenced a tour in which he spoke strongly against the gold standard. To offset his propaganda the government resolved that there should be a parliamentary select committee on the gold standard, which could enlighten the public as to the immorality and evil effects that would follow from Smuts's policy. Indeed, according to the finance minister, it was because of Smuts's interference that the government could not raise funds overseas. Further, it was only because of South African Party agitation that South Africans were still speculating against their own currency; that speculation arose only from those who had divided loyalties. According to Havenga, "South Africa is the only country in the world where such a thing can take place." The Afrikaners proper could not and would not behave thus. "The responsibility," he announced, "for this increase in our difficulties will have to be borne by the opposite side."[1]

Before the Select Committee began its work the House of Assembly debated long and hard. Sir Patrick Duncan later wrote:

We are still labouring at the gold standard controversy, covering acres of Hansard with our words . . . meanwhile business is becoming more and more stagnant. The farmers all over the country are at the end of their resources, and there is in practice though not yet in law a moratorium so far as regards their debts to mortgagees and others. The result is that all the investment and trust companies cannot get money in and the banks are restricting credit in every way they can.[2]

Smuts himself tried to convince the House that the gold standard was purely a matter of business, not a party matter and not a question of national independence. "To my mind," he said, "the dominant crucial fact has been that our principal market . . . has gone off the gold standard." If Britain had not done so, "the case would have been different with us . . . But . . . our exports had this handicap of the exchange of 25 or 30 percent, and it became clear that it was not in the interests of South Africa to remain on the gold standard." Thus, besides the low prices that were already a serious problem, "We are now losing on the exchange as well." The export subsidies had followed inevitably; how long would they go on?[3]

Sir Ernest Oppenheimer, in one of his rare parliamentary interventions, tried to convince the government that a gold standard was no more independent than a sterling standard. At first, he said, he had thought that South Africa should stay on gold, but he now thought otherwise: "by adhering to gold we are tying ourselves to the deflationary policy of France and the United States . . . Today gold brings with it a policy of deflation. We are tying ourselves to an international gold currency controlled by the United States . . . We control neither sterling nor the international gold currency." The United States and France were absorbing gold and sterilizing it. The choice was between one managed currency – sterling – and another – the gold dollar. The former would mean better prices for primary producers; the latter would mean deflation and a heavy burden on debtors. Sir Ernest proceeded: "There is no such thing as financial independence, and there is no such thing as a natural currency system. At the present time we have to choose between two systems, both of them artificial, and both of them outside our control."[4]

At the shareholders' general meeting of the South African Reserve Bank on 7 July 1931, Governor W. H. Clegg had expressed extreme uneasiness about the maldistribution and sterilization of gold. By December 1931, the U.K. high commissioner reported, Clegg had urged the South African government to leave gold.[5] Both Clegg and Oppenheimer were aware that in the world as it was the gold standard could not be expected to work well. The government was not prepared to hear such advice. For the Cabinet the gold standard had become a matter of independence, morality, and fairness as between debtors and creditors.

Though the opposition would not cooperate in the work of a Select Committee whose only purpose was to support the predetermined government policy, the committee nonetheless labored long and hard. As expected, the Cabinet members, especially Havenga, treated the committee room as a mixture of court and inquisition chamber. The representatives of Barclay's and Standard, the English-based banks, were grilled with especial rigor. Jakobus Dommisse, the general manager of the Netherlands Bank of South Africa, received kinder treatment.

Dommisse thought that everyone was too well off. All over the western world people had been living too well ever since the war. People must get back to "reality" – that is, to prewar real incomes. This end could be attained by a program of "gradual sobering, a policy of deflation, a reduction of the incomes of the people, and a tremendous cutback of expenditure by all Governments." There had been far too much credit, both for production and consumption.[6] Dommisse did not say and was not asked how debtors were to pay off creditors in the steadily deflationary world for which he hoped. Nor did he consider whether the resulting distribution of wealth would be attractive. Nevertheless, he was strongly against the "cheating" and "mulcting" of creditors by abandoning gold – "default and repudiation."[7]

The committee consulted South Africa's university economists. Seven appeared before it, and as might be expected, their advice varied. Three professors thought that South Africa should stay with gold at the present parity. One lecturer thought it should align with sterling. Three thought that it should leave gold and let its currency depreciate as a preliminary to a new pegging at a more appropriate level. As the committee's report was predetermined, the academic advice and the professorial disagreements did not affect the outcome. It is interesting to observe, however, that when Havenga was choosing his advisers for the World Monetary and Economic Conference of 1933 he selected two of the professors who had thought he was right to stick with gold.[8]

The Standard and Barclay's bank officials gave testimony that tells us something about developments after sterling had left gold. James Shorrey Shiel spoke for Standard and Harry Judson for Barclay's. Both men thought that South Africa should link its money with sterling. Judson explained, "continued adherence to the gold standard is exercising a very heavy strain on the country . . . the strain has not been arrested . . . The country is being carried on its gold production . . . a very heavy blow has been struck at our agricultural and industrial development."[9]

On 28 September, Shiel told the committee, the Standard directors had advised the South African government that the disadvantages of the gold standard, especially the strain on farming, local industries, and the export trade, outweighed its advantages. A sterling standard involved some risks, but at least capital flight would stop and a reflux would begin.[10] Between £13 million and £17 million had left the country since 21 September. Judson insisted that Barclay's was not restricting its advances: "as long as money is safe we are prepared to lend it . . . It is the distressed borrower who is pressing us now."[11] Shiel, however, confessed that there was a restriction of credit. This followed, he said, from the contraction of deposits: "Yes, we have got to do it. Our deposits have fallen, therefore advances must come down."[12] Indeed, he claimed, relative to its deposits Standard's local advances were already dangerously high. Barclay's had contributed £2.25 million to the exchange pool, and Standard had contributed £2.75 million while exposing a further £850,000. Havenga pressed Shiel, asking, "Is it not a fact that the difficulty we have had so far has been due to the fact that the commercial banks were reluctant to face a so-called loss on exchange by transferring the balances they had in London to South Africa?" Shiel responded, "No. Not the crux . . . We made our London balances available to assist the position when the Reserve Bank had no more sterling." In any case, Shiel explained, if South Africa were to leave gold the Standard Bank would have an exchange loss of roughly £3.6 million because this was the extent of its uncovered commitments in sterling.[13] In advocating a sterling standard, therefore, he was arguing against his own bank's interest.

If the government had not already chosen its policy, Governor Postmus's testimony might have been called decisive. It had long been known that Postmus, who succeeded Clegg at the end of 1931, favored gold. Before the committee the new governor argued that, because at the existing exchange rate the national payments were roughly balanced, if South Africa were to leave gold its pound would naturally settle above sterling. No more than £10 million could possibly have left the country, and for legitimate business there was no shortage of capital. The trouble was that there were so few good propositions on which the banks could safely lend. Naturally, he observed, the banks found it impolitic to say so. Thus one should not blame the gold standard for the constriction of domestic credit. Regrettably, the commercial banks, interested in their deposits/advances ratio, were most unwisely squeezing advances because the export of funds was reducing local deposits. They need not do this, but they were doing so. Further, they were reluctant to draw on their London balances because they thought Britain would go back to gold at par or that South Africa might leave the gold standard. But South Africa, Postmus argued, should certainly not do this. If it did, it would be interfering with the measure of value and creating bad money, which would never create better business. Indeed, the bad money would cause the nation to relax its effort. Thrift would be discouraged, and the overseas debt would be a heavier burden in domestic currency. Contracts between debtors and creditors would become less reliable. Capital would flow less readily to South Africa. "It does not seem justifiable to alter the basis of all contracts just to render assistance to a no doubt comparatively small number of mortgagors." To leave gold deliberately "would be mere robbery, mere theft and nothing else . . . No decent country that can pay its debts should refuse to pay . . . What I am concerned with is that the intrinsic value of our currency should remain the same." [14]

The Select Committee recommended that the gold standard was a Good Thing that should be encouraged. By 31 March the Reserve Bank's London funds had fallen to £194,000, of which £107,000 was the working balance at the Bank of England. At the end of March 1931 these working balances had been £253,000, and in the London market the Reserve Bank had held sterling balances of £8.553 million. [15] In a single year sterling assets had fallen by £8,612 million, and gold reserves had declined also, falling by £810,000. In one year the Reserve Bank had lost 58 percent of its external reserves – gold and sterling. Almost all these losses had occurred since 21 September 1931, and the Committee knew about them.

In February 1932 the South African government tried to borrow in London. Both Norman and Chamberlain were strongly opposed, largely because they thought Britain's balance of payments was still too weak. Hopkins observed that matters might look different if and when "money is easily obtained for the needs of all Dominions." [16] But long before the committee presented its *Report* the exchange position had become easier. Gradually the authorities were able to reduce and withdraw the restrictions on the sale of exchange. The antigold agitation did not cease, nor did the capital flight, but both subsided. In July 1932 Governor Postmus believed that the storm had passed. In August 1932 Havenga was able to borrow £8 million in London on his way back from the Ottawa Conference, [17] where he had strenuously defended the gold standard. In London, both Standard and Barclay's were lending sterling to the South African government.

Smuts remained despondent. Writing to Leo Amery, he had said:

The government, in its insane obsession with the idea of economic independence, has tied this country with the gold standard, which is killing our exporting industries and reducing business to a standstill. The next move will be our own currency which will divide us still further from the British system . . . I fear we are going to pay a very heavy price for Nationalist folly . . . The gold standard to which the Government stands pledged is strangling all industry and I am afraid we shall soon be without the necessary cash to carry on the business of the country . . . South Africa is paying dearly for its Nationalism, and I hope it will in the end profit from its experience.[18]

Clearly he did not think it would.

3. A forced devaluation

Late in December 1932 N. Teilman Roos left the Supreme Court bench to campaign for a coalition and for devaluation. His action precipitated an internal crisis that forced the government to change its course. Roos had been an eminent Nationalist politician. Many people believed that his action would soon split the Nationalist Party, quickly forcing a change in policy. Paper money flowed into the banks; gold coin flowed out. Britain's high commissioner reported that funds were again moving to England on a really large scale and that the Cabinet had discussed the question of the standard.[1] The government was not at once prepared to change its policy. On 27 December Havenga summoned Governor Postmus and bank representatives and reluctantly agreed to consider the financiers' views. The banks explained that the exchange drain and the gold drain were so great that the position would soon be untenable. Between £2 million and £3 million had left the country in three days. On 28 December the Reserve Bank notes became inconvertible.[2] As Sir Patrick Duncan explained:

The government has been driven to relieve the Reserve Bank of its obligation to pay gold for its notes so that in fact we are off gold. But they have put such stringent restrictions on exchange transactions that the effect cannot be felt . . . The political and financial fog still shrouds us. We are off the gold standard but no one seems to know from day to day what the rate of exchange is to be. That however is a condition under which greater communities than ours are labouring today.[3]

The government had not embargoed gold exports or exchange transactions.[4] By December 30, however, the Reserve Bank had ceased to quote exchange rates, though it was still prepared to sell exchange. The gold producers could now sell their gold as and where they liked, though it appears that they continued to market much of their output through the Reserve Bank. The exchange position was now extremely peculiar, however: by controlling the volume of their gold sales the gold producers were really in control of the rate, though Standard and Barclay's had met on 29 December to fix it. On 29 December the high commissioner reported: "Exchange transactions are today at complete standstill as Commercial Banks are unable and Reserve Bank refuses to quote rates . . . Bank director . . . stated that conversations are now proceeding at Pretoria with view to fixing exchange rate probably approximating to parity with sterling."[5]

The mining industry wanted sterling parity as soon as possible. The banks were more reluctant. At least one bank was still heavily oversold in sterling. It hoped for time to adjust this position. The Chamber of Mines was supplying the commercial banks with the sterling they needed, obtaining the funds by gold export. In the event, the exchange rate did move gradually. Nevertheless, the Standard Bank lost £664,000 from its published reserves because of the change in the exchange regime.[6] The government meantime refused to fix the rate definitively. When Parliament assembled early in February 1933 the exchange was still floating in theory, but in practice it had reached parity with sterling, and until 21 January 1932 it was held there by the joint action of the mining industry and the commercial banks. On that date the Reserve Bank re-entered the market. Protected by government guarantee against exchange loss, it resumed its practice of fixing the exchange rate.[7] There was now little doubt that the government would opt for sterling parity. It could have acted under the emergency legislation of November 1931 – the measure under which it had abandoned gold. In January 1933 it said it would do so,[8] but it preferred to wait until Parliament could meet, discuss the question, and pass new legislation.

Early in February 1933 Parliament considered a Currency and Exchange Bill that would allow the Reserve Bank to hold more of its reserve outside the Union and less of its reserve in the form of metal, while stabilizing the South African pound relative to sterling by buying and selling gold and foreign bills.[9] Introducing the measure, Havenga explained that South Africa had left gold only when circumstances had compelled it to do so. The pressure, he said, arose from speculation, and its origin was inside the Union. The government knew it would have to manage its depreciated currency; as South Africa was too small to have an independent standard it would link up with sterling. There could be no "isolated scheme of stabilisation" until the government knew what the World Economic Conference would bring forth. It was "not the policy of the government, however, to follow sterling wherever it goes." The inconvenience of a floating currency could be minimized by a sterling peg, but if sterling fell more, or fell too far, the government might or might not change its policy. The Reserve Bank would manage the rate of exchange at the government's risk. The course was "not an ideal course . . . only a second-best course, but it is the best available to a small country with an unstable currency."[10]

4. *Later developments, 1933–1939*

In the event, the South African pound was held at parity with sterling until the outbreak of war and, indeed, until long thereafter. To maintain this rate the Reserve Bank was obliged to build up very large hoards of gold and foreign exchange. Between 1 April 1932 and 1 April 1936 its gold reserves rose from £6.5 million to £29.4 million, and from 1 April 1932 to 1 April 1934 its sterling assets rose from £53,000 to £22.424 million.[1] To control the sterling balances the government repaid £8 million of overseas debt in 1934 and another £24 million in 1936–7. With respect to sterling assets the most dramatic year was 1933. As capital funds flowed back to South Africa, the Reserve Bank added £18.6 million to its sterling bills, and the commercial banks added £3.1 million to their liquid assets outside the Union.[2] Thereafter, as de Kock explains, in their attempt to maintain a balanced position the commercial banks sold any excess sterling to the Reserve Bank.[3] Between 31 December 1933 and 31 December 1938 the commercial banks raised their sterling balances by only £3 million; if the South African government had not retired £2 million in sterling debt, Reserve Bank sterling balances would have risen by £21 million in the same period. As the Reserve Bank was again buying the newly produced gold it was normally a seller of foreign exchange. The Bank accumulated gold at home because it did not usually need to export all the mines produced. Thus gold holdings rose from £6.5 million on 31 March 1931 to £29.3 million in 1936; after a decline in 1937–8 the hoard rose once more to £26.8 million on 31 March 1939, when sterling balances stood at £7.5 million – almost as large as in March 1931.[4]

Though South Africa adhered firmly to sterling after January 1933, its leaders had not forgotten that their commitment had originally been a tentative one. Until the outbreak of war Nicholas Havenga continued as finance minister; his senior official was Dr. J. E. Holloway, who since 1924 at least had favored a gold standard. In 1925 he had told the Kemmerer-Vissering Commission that if one pegged to sterling one would be exposed to fluctuations in prices and wages that a gold standard would obviate.[5] In March 1935 there was concern that sterling had recently fallen. There was some suggestion that Parliament should review exchange policy. Havenga then told the House that though the government still adhered to his statement of February 1933 the government was watching the circumstances carefully, though for the present it did not want to change the system.[6] Early in 1937 Havenga told Sir William Clark, the new high commissioner, that the position was already difficult. The country had a 97 percent specie reserve, and its gold production continued to rise. In 1936 the country had contained the position by paying off the sterling debt, but that expedient was no longer open. However, according to Sir William Clark, the government had in mind "some other jugglery which he [Havenga] did not clearly define but which would relieve the strain this year." Nevertheless, at this point, according to Clark, the South African government thought that it might not be able to keep the South African pound at par with sterling.[7]

It is very hard to imagine what Havenga had in mind. Regrettably, if the relevant South African Treasury records survive they are not yet open to researchers. Admittedly, the 1933 statute controlled the quantity of *sterling* assets that the Reserve Bank might hold in its currency reserves. But it would accumulate gold without limit, and it could pay for the gold by creating its own deposit liabilities. Even the Bank of England found the matter perplexing. R. N. Kershaw, the Bank expert on Dominion money, told a Treasury official, "I cannot understand why there should be any doubt of South Africa's ability – given the will – to keep her pound from rising in value." South Africa could always increase the local money supply, thus raising prices. If "what Havenga really wants is to keep the South African pound where it is and at the same time avoid inflation, this indeed may be difficult to do if there is not sufficient external debt to pay off."[8]

Havenga was probably concerned not with exchange rates but with tariffs. In the same conversation he had told Sir William Clark that Britain must remember his country was not really protectionist. In 1936 he had given notice that South Africa would want to reexamine the Ottawa Agreements.[9] Sir William had implied that if South Africa wanted to stay at par with sterling it would have to encourage imports by reducing its tariffs; Havenga may have been telling Sir William that this argument was not relevant. The government was not immutably attached to sterling parity; in any case, if South Africa had to let its money rise British goods would gain an advantage at the same old tariff rates.

However this interchange may have originated, it did not lead to anything. Indeed it could not: in 1937 and 1938 South Africa's reserve assets were falling, not rising. Total reserve assets declined by £200,000 from March 1936 to March 1937 and by nearly £5 million from March 1937 to March 1938.[10] Thereafter they increased once more, but in March 1939 they were still somewhat smaller than they had been in

March 1936.[11] Whatever rigidities Havenga and his advisers may perhaps have feared, in the world recession of 1937–8 South Africa's current and capital accounts moved in a way that was convenient for the Reserve Bank, however painful it may have been for the national economy.

South Africa had in very truth been forced to leave gold. In origin the pressure had been political and psychological, and the visible signs had been capital flight and internal drain. In Australia during 1930–2 the local pound had fallen because the current account was weak. In New Zealand during 1938 exchange controls had become necessary for the same reason, though a capital flight had made the problem worse. If the South African current account showed any sign of weakness during 1931–2 the effect was completely masked by the capital movements that followed directly from expectations about the exchange rate. Governor Postmus may well have been right in believing that at the old exchange rate South Africa's payments were roughly balanced. Nevertheless, for the South African economy the devaluation, though forced, was a godsend. Once the drought of 1933 had passed the agricultural industries benefited from higher prices in terms of local currency than they could otherwise have commanded. The gold mines boomed, and they received a further impetus from American policy once President Roosevelt began to raise the gold price later in 1933. Within South Africa the money supply rose rapidly in 1933 and thereafter. The Reserve Bank could not prevent this increase. The domestic economy, however, like the world economy, was grossly underemployed; hence monetary expansion chiefly raised the volumes of output and imports, not prices.

Because the South African devaluation raised gold production the devaluation reduced the strain on the whole world economy. If Havenga and Hertzog had clung to gold much longer, both Britain and the United States would have had much more difficulty in adding to their gold reserves. Given the other elements in world trade and payments, there would have been heavier pressure on payments, prices, and gold reserves elsewhere. Exchange controls would have become even more widespread; trade barriers would have risen even farther and faster. South African production, like Indian dishoarding, did much to turn the wheels of the world economy. When Tielman Roos left the bench he had no such high ends in view. Nevertheless, the citizens of many countries would have cause to be grateful to him.

5

Australia and New Zealand, 1930-1939

In Australia and New Zealand a few great banks provided local banking services, and in September 1931 they were still managing the exchanges as they had done for decades past. In New Zealand, until 1934 the banks also provided the paper currency. Gold could freely enter the country, but without official permission it could not leave. Hence the New Zealand pound could never rise above gold import point though in principle it might fall indefinitely. In Australia the banks had lost the right to issue their own paper money in 1910, when the government introduced its own treasury notes. In 1920 control was transferred to a local Notes Board and in 1924 to the Commonwealth Bank, a government-owned institution that had also been set up as a trading bank in 1910. Although the legislation of 1924 was meant to encourage the evolution of the Commonwealth Bank into a central bank, neither then nor for several years thereafter was it more than a trading and savings bank that happened to have a monopoly of the note issue. In 1934, when New Zealand established its Reserve Bank, the New Zealand note issue was transferred from the trading banks to the Reserve Bank.

To a large extent the same trading banks operated in Australia and in New Zealand. Their London funds, therefore, were originally a support for all their Australasian business, and in 1930 they were still unable or unwilling to segregate their Australian business from their New Zealand affairs. In Australia and in New Zealand the only exchange rate was the rate on London, and this had normally been quoted as a premium or discount on London funds. Thus, in Australia and New Zealand, as in South Africa, people tended to assume that a pound was a pound wherever it had been issued or whatever it said on its face. Before Britain's return to gold in 1925 the premiums and discounts had sometimes been sizable, but this had appeared unnatural. The exchange rate was settled by agreement among the trading banks; in Australia the Commonwealth Bank took part because it was a trading bank like the others, but in the 1920s it was not in control of the exchange market, though it held sizable London funds.

In the later 1920s capital inflows kept the Australian pound at par with sterling. The current account was weak. External reserves varied little, and although the trading banks naturally watched their London funds, L. F. Giblin reports that before 1930 the Commonwealth Bank was remarkably uninterested in the size or management of Australia's London funds. "Reserves," he writes, "without qualification, meant only cash and gold in Australia."[1] However, early in 1929 the inflow of external capital dried up. Export prices, too, began to slide. The result was a major balance-of-payments crisis. Long before sterling itself left gold the Australian pound had departed and had fallen to a discount against sterling. As the banks did not segregate their external reserves New Zealand was also affected, though its payments position did not worsen as fast or as far.[2]

In 1928, Giblin explains, Australia's international reserves of sterling and gold were about £95 million. Of this total £12 million was required by law as "support" for the note issue. Another £20 million was an irreducible minimum transactions balance. In June 1931 reserves fell to this figure, and the government was obliged to use the Notes Reserve in support of the exchanges.[3] Matters were complicated because the Australian government had extremely heavy home charges, chiefly for debt service.

Thus the Australian adjustments began for reasons peculiar to the region and had been largely completed before September 1931. From December 1929 sterling was at a premium that exceeded the gold export point. One hundred pounds sterling cost £101.15 Australian. But gold could not be freely exported. In August 1930 the Commonwealth Bank and the trading banks agreed to "mobilize" their London funds so as to ensure the service of overseas debt. From September 1930 the Commonwealth treasurer was authorized to requisition the trading banks' gold, giving paper currency in exchange. Thereafter the trading banks held little or no gold. They continued, however, to own their London funds. Furthermore, the trading banks still jointly controlled the price of sterling.

In 1930 the banks rationed sterling and allowed its price to rise above par. From March 1930 £100 sterling cost £106.10 Australian; from October 1930, £109 Australian; from mid-January 1931, first £118 Australian and then £125 Australian; from 29 January 1931, £130.10 Australian. On 2 December 1931, after much heated discussion with the trading banks, the Commonwealth Bank took control of the sterling exchange rate. That rate, it announced, would be £125 Australian; henceforth the Bank would freely buy and sell sterling exchange at a rate to be fixed each week by itself.[4] In the event, the exchange rate remained unchanged for the rest of the decade and for many years thereafter, though not without occasional support from the Bank of England.[5]

In New Zealand much the same thing happened. Between October 1928 and late January 1931 the banks raised the price of sterling from just over par to £1.10 New Zealand. In January 1933 the government, anxious to revivify agriculture by raising domestic prices, told the banks that henceforth the price of sterling would be £1.25 New Zealand. It would indemnify the banks against any loss. When the Reserve Bank began to function it maintained this rate and took over responsibility for it.[6]

The premium on sterling was widely thought to be unnatural, and from time to time politicians would suggest that it should be erased. But the depreciation was a godsend to the prostrate and debt-burdened farmers: in terms of domestic currency it raised their receipts. Further, depreciation provided shelter for import-replacing manufacturers. Especially in Australia, the later 1930s saw a very considerable industrial revival. As tariffs were falling at the same time, it is hard to explain this revival without taking some note of the currency depreciation. In New Zealand, where the domestic market was tiny and where tariffs were lower, there was relatively little by way of spontaneous import replacement. When a Labour government took office in 1935 it was pledged to erase unemployment by the promotion of local manufacture. It hoped to do this partly through planning and partly through import controls. But as yet no Empire country had resorted to any permanent system of exchange controls or to any general quota system. In Australia and South Africa there had been exchange rationing for a few months. India, and the United Kingdom itself, had controlled certain kinds of capital movement for greater or lesser periods of time. In Whitehall and Threadneedle Street controls were deplored and, when possible, resisted. New Zealand's efforts would therefore involve a confrontation with London – a dispute at least as serious as the Anglo-Indian disagreement of 1931.

Before turning to New Zealand's problems in the later 1930s, we pause to comment on the above developments of 1930–1. First, to several Pacific colonies they caused distress. In Fiji the colonial government had to choose between sterling and the New Zealand pound. In 1934, it chose sterling at an exchange rate of £111 Fiji = £100. The Solomon Islands, the Gilbert and Ellice islands, and Tonga all followed the Australian pound instead of sterling. In these islands the principal commercial and financial ties were with Australia and New Zealand. Thus their choice reproduces in small the choosing of sterling elsewhere in the Empire. Second, in Australia the Commonwealth Bank was able to preserve its independence. In 1930–1, when the Scullin Labour regime badly needed financial support, the Bank first limited its accommodation, then refused any extra, and finally made its support contingent on financial reform that would first control government deficits and then eliminate them. In certain respects Montagu Norman must have disapproved of the Commonwealth Bank. To an important degree it did not accord with his canons of central banking – not only did it have a large commercial business; even worse, it was state owned – but its financial policy had a rigor that must have pleased him. Hence, presumably, the Old Lady's willingness to help her Australian daughter when credit was needed to protect the exchange. Norman and his staff had tried to ensure that in New Zealand the Reserve Bank would be properly independent. Under Labour, however, the Reserve Bank was steadily converted into a mere arm of government – a manufacturer of money for government projects. This development must have contributed to New Zealand's later difficulties when its prime minister came to Norman for aid.

In Australia and New Zealand the exchange rates were adjusted in the early 1930s with relative ease; in South Africa the rate was changed only with great difficulty. In explaining the difference, it is not quite enough to observe that South Africa had a pure gold standard, a central bank, and a government that was determined to preserve the standard "at par." The three economies were similar in many respects. They all contained primary producers whom the price fall had impoverished. South Africa, in addition, contained a large gold-mining industry for whom a devaluation would generate immense profits. Australia too produced some gold. Though Australia and South Africa sold substantial amounts outside the Empire, all three countries found their primary export markets in the United Kingdom, and all were heavily dependent on British capital funds. In all three economies banking was run by "imperial banks" that had extremely close connections with London, even though some of the larger Australasian banks were managed in the Antipodes.

In all these countries ordinary people and even financiers were inclined to believe that a pound is a pound regardless of provenance. In New Zealand and especially in Australia this belief was stabilizing; in South Africa it was destabilizing. When the Australasian banks were obliged to raise the price of sterling, their customers perceived a "loss" from shifting into the currency of the motherland, and they must have been reluctant to do so. When sterling floated down relative to the South African pound the residents of South Africa perceived a "profit" from the purchase of sterling, which they eagerly tried to buy. Expectations also played a part. Australians and New Zealanders knew their moneys were weak, but they had no particular reason to expect further declines, whereas from September 1931 to December 1932 South Africans had every reason to believe that sooner or later their pound would be devalued relative to sterling.

In all three countries the trading banks – that is the commercial or joint stock banks – believed that the local money *should* depreciate relative to sterling. The reason was in their own transactions and in their own books – an excess demand for sterling and depletion of the London funds that were their secondary reserves. Whatever they might think about the "natural" parity of the several pounds, the Australian and New Zealand banks could adjust the exchange rates in the right direction because they controlled these rates. Though in a sense there was no market in foreign exchange, the rate cartel adjusted the price in the right direction. They knew that if they made a serious mistake "outside transactions" would begin; the banks would be bypassed, and they would lose both business and revenue. In South Africa, however, the commercial banks did not control the exchange rate. Paper money was freely convertible into gold, and gold could be freely imported and exported. The largest export earnings accrued to the Reserve Bank because it bought all the newly minted gold; normally a seller of sterling to the commercial banks, it could bring them to heel by refusing to supply sterling, while the mechanism of the gold standard kept the exchange rate at the gold export point.

Might the Australasian banks have decided to follow gold instead of sterling in September 1931? The question answers itself. In New Zealand they held large reserves of gold that they could not export; in Australia the government had already sequestered their gold. Their London funds were already under severe pressure. If their managements had considered the question, they would have thought it madness to contrive an appreciation of local money relative to sterling, creating considerable capital losses in terms of local money at a time when reserves were already dwindling fast. In effect, the question could never have arisen.

1. *New Zealand's troubles*

Once Australasian banks had surrendered control of the exchange, London funds were increasingly centralized in the hands of the official agencies – in Australia by the Commonwealth Bank and in New Zealand after August 1934 by the Reserve Bank. The Australian authorities allowed their sterling balances to rise and fall while they maintained a stable exchange rate on sterling. From time to time, nervous about their external reserves, they requested and obtained a line of credit at the Bank of England. It appears, however, that these credits remained unused. Through 1936 New Zealand also managed reasonably well, partly because its domestic economy was so deflated that import values were extremely low. Though the six trading banks continued to hold London funds, they surrendered their gold to the Reserve Bank, which also began to accumulate London funds of its own, partly by selling this gold. For the rest of the decade Australia's adventures need not be scrutinized here. In New Zealand, however, the late 1930s brought traumatic developments. Because they help us to understand what and how London thought about the sterling system, we shall examine them at some length.

In 1932–5, before Labour came to power, New Zealand was occasionally agitated over the question of the exchange rate. At the Ottawa Conference the New Zealand delegation circulated a memorandum stating that the country was on a sterling exchange standard and would remain so.[1] But at what rate? In November 1932 the governor-general reported on the situation.[2] He wrote: "Acute depression among farmers has resulted in strong agitation for increasing artificially New Zealand exchange rate on London to 25%. Government divided on matter, majority apparently favoured such a course. Decision left to Dominion Banks. Have confidentially expressed to Prime Minister and Chairman of associated banks my earnest hope that no hasty decision be taken."[3] As we have seen, the devaluation in fact occurred, and Downie Stewart, the finance minister, left the government over that decision. In 1935 he still hoped for par but by then recognized that as everything had adjusted to the new arrangement it would be unwise to change.[4] The New Zealand Labour Party proposed to revalue the New Zealand pound, returning to par. In Britain the Treasury, when asked by the Dominions Office, refused to say what New Zealand should do. "The British Government," Sir Frederick Phillips wrote, "do not regard the New Zealand exchange as any business of theirs, and under no conditions would they be prepared to intervene by suggestions or otherwise with the free choice of the New Zealand Government."[5] New Zealand was different from India not because it was small but because it could be trusted not to default. At least, so it appeared in 1933.

The New Zealand Reserve Bank as originally designed had limited powers. Its governor, who came from the Bank of England, was reluctant to innovate.[6] But the New Zealand polity was not immune to the "funny money" ideas that we have already observed in Canada. The social credit movement and the Labour opposition that contained so many of these "credit reformers" had not welcomed the original proposals for a reserve bank; the Douglasite movement wanted to print more paper money, and the Labourites hoped for a state bank and a great deal of credit creation. There was also a suspicion that the Bank and its governor had been forced on New Zealand by overseas financiers. The historian of the Reserve Bank has successfully dispatched these beliefs,[7] but in 1935 they must have helped to provide some support for the Labour campaign program – a plan that included credit expansion, trade agreements, social security, and guaranteed prices for the chief export products.[8]

Having won the election, Labour took office late in 1935. The new prime minister was M. J. Savage, and the finance minister was Walter Nash. Both men were imbued with hostility toward the traditional gold standard, whose wickedness had figured largely in their campaign. Nevertheless, at first they hoped to restore the New Zealand pound to par with sterling. The governor-general agreed with his chief minister that the end was highly desirable, but he took the occasion to observe that it could not be accomplished without financial stability. Meanwhile, the governor of the Reserve Bank told the governor-general that the goal would be most difficult to attain: "it is like trying to make water run uphill," Leslie Lefeaux explained.[9]

At once the new government introduced a bill to nationalize the Reserve Bank and give it new powers: the Bank would receive all the foreign exchange from the bulk selling of exports; it could create credit to finance the domestic purchases of dairy products at guaranteed prices; it could grant much larger overdrafts to the national treasury. The government did not at once make large use of these new provisions. According to G. R. Hawke, "The credit-creation programme of the Labour Government was not really established until 1937–38."[10] Nevertheless, the legal changes, quickly noticed in Treasury and Colonial Office, were not attractive. There must also have been some unease about the new provision by which the bank was "to give effect as far as may be to the monetary policy communicated to it from time to time by the Minister of Finance . . . the bank shall regulate and control credit and currency in New Zealand, the transfer of moneys to and from New Zealand and the disposal of moneys that are derived from the sale of any of New Zealand's produce and for the time being are held overseas."[11] Sir Otto Neimeyer had proposed an independent central bank, and the legislation of 1933 had appeared to provide for one; just what did the new administration intend?

In October 1936 Walter Nash set out for London, where he planned to negotiate a trade and payments agreement.[12] Before his departure he met R. B. Bennett, who, having lost office in 1935, had embarked on a world tour. Bennett thought Nash's views so alarming that he wrote privately to Chamberlain. The New Zealander, Bennett found, was strongly attached to exchange control and to bilateral balancing. Given Britain's large investments in New Zealand, Bennett suggested, London should try to wean Nash away from these ideas.[13]

Chamberlain minuted this letter, "See if Dominions Office know anything of Mr. Nash." From Wellington the governor-general shortly reported his fear that Nash should introduce exchange control, and asked Malcolm MacDonald to devise "any influences of a moderating kind which can be brought to bear on Mr. Nash while he is in England."[14] Hence, when Nash met MacDonald on 9 November, MacDonald suggested that the talks begin with the specific problem of the meat quota. He did so quite deliberately, so as to defer discussion of the more general proposal until Nash had "had time to meet various people in London and to discover that his ideas here are regarded as retrograde and barbarous."[15]

Both Treasury and Bank joined in this campaign. In December Sir Richard Hopkins wrote: "The Governor has already seen Mr. Nash and has tried to make the best job he could of it but he told me Mr. Nash is hopelessly wedded to his theories."[16]

Nash wanted to sell Britain much more meat and dairy products. This was bad enough – such sales would disrupt the fabric of agrarian protectionism that Walter Elliot and Chamberlain were rapidly erecting – but he also wanted to erect a general system of bilaterally balanced trade arrangements, which he would enforce with foreign exchange controls. Such arrangements, he thought, would serve the general good. As New Zealand would export more food, the British would eat better; as the sterling New Zealand earned would all be spent in Britain, British exports and employment would also grow.

In December, Phillips summed up the Treasury objections:

Our real reason for objecting to Mr. Nash's proposals is that they involve a degree of government control and of regimentation of industry which is intolerable except in a totalitarian state. It is extremely dubious if the scheme could be worked in New Zealand and at this end it would be doubly difficult as every step would bring us into conflict with third parties.[17]

In January S. D. Waley added a further gravamen. Everyone was familiar with the sort of thing Nash wanted – it had been done all over the world – but Nash was unique in that he wished to introduce a system of exchange control and bilateral balancing when he had *no* transfer difficulties. Other countries had done so only under duress, and most or all aimed to abolish such controls as soon as possible. Waley concluded: "If the United Kingdom were to enter into an agreement with another member of the British Commonwealth on the lines proposed by Mr. Nash, the policy which we have consistently advocated on both sides of the Atlantic would be stultified."[18] That is, Britain would be visibly acquiescing in a permanent and unnecessary set of restrictions on transfer.

On 9 January MacDonald told Nash that Britain could not accept his proposals. This rejection led to a series of trade discussions that do not concern us here. Nash still wanted a unilateral exchange control, but he was obliged to recognize that Britain would not cooperate. Early in July he went home.

By autumn 1937 the government of New Zealand was nervous about the possibility of a capital flight. It announced that though for the present there would be no exchange control all foreign exchange receipts were to be paid into the Reserve Bank.[19] Waley minuted:

New Zealand is proposing to institute the machinery for exchange control as a protectionist measure. This will presumably lead to a flight of capital to London and then exchange restriction will be imposed in good earnest, and we may then have to propose the bilateral clearing we refused to contemplate as part of a Trade Agreement.[20]

In fact, nothing happened for some time. For eleven months the Dominion abstained from exchange controls. Hawke and Keith Sinclair have traced the lengthy debate, inside the Labour government and outside it, that occurred in 1936–8.[21] Leslie Lefeaux, the governor of the Reserve Bank, consistently opposed exchange controls. He and his staff produced numerous memorandums listing the disadvantages. But some Labour politicians and some advisers, though apparently not Nash himself, certainly favored exchange control as part of a long-run policy of full employment and protected industrialization. By the Industrial Efficiency Act of 1936 they had taken power to protect and license particular industries; it is hard to see how these powers could be made fully effective if importation remained easy, controlled only by tariffs. Nevertheless, as Hawke explains,

Exchange control was eventually introduced not as part of a coherent policy but as a crisis measure. The trend of overseas assets of the banking system was clearly downward between 1936 and 1938 and by late 1938 the Reserve Bank was having difficulty in satisfying the statutory requirement of a 25 percent reserve of gold and sterling for its note issue and demand liabilities. It was becoming apparent that there was a real danger that some commitments of New Zealand to overseas creditors could not be met from the resources of overseas exchange. It was in this sort of crisis situation that exchange control was introduced.[22]

Although the government had known for 18 months that it was losing foreign exchange, Sinclair argues that Nash had two main reasons for his inactivity. At first, he had not wished to annoy Lefeaux and the British government. Later, he had not wished to act before the election of 1938.[23]

From June to November 1938 the Reserve Bank advanced £8 million to the Dominion government, and in the autumn it began to lose reserves rapidly. New Zealand was now running a current-account deficit at an annual rate of £7 million, and capital was leaving as well.[24] Hence, no one at the Bank of England was surprised to receive a cry for help early in November 1938.

The governor of the Reserve Bank approached Britain's trade commissioner in Wellington, asking how the United Kingdom would react to a "quota system aimed at reducing the value of imports from the United Kingdom by say £5 million per year."[25]

Phillips wrote:

This is a dreadful business. Of course there is no remedy except for the New Zealand Government to lower the price paid to the New Zealand farmer, to stop extravagant public works, and generally to abandon the policy on which they have just secured re-election. I think we can only hear what if anything the governor [Norman] has to suggest.[26]

Might not New Zealand be asked to devalue? Waley thought so but remarked that devaluation had "disadvantages." Norman thought a devaluation would be "disastrous" because it could spread, especially to India,[27] where devaluation sentiment had revived with the 1938 recession. In any case, the real problem was perceived to be the internal policy of the New Zealand government. Like France, New Zealand had embarked on a reckless program of public expenditure. Further, it had guaranteed an uneconomic price to its dairy farmers and was providing their funds from domestic credit creation. Waley thought that "the obvious reply is that we *do* deprecate import control: we are convinced that salvation can only come from slowing down Mr. Savage's policy, but we do not wish to say so, for it is his business and responsibility not ours."[28]

On 19 November the governor-general reported that his government proposed to introduce foreign exchange control and import quotas. Earnings would be allocated "to bring about a reduction of trade with other countries so far as practicable, and extension of purchases from the United Kingdom. It is desired to commence regulations forthwith, but action will be deferred" until after London could reply.

On 25 November Whitehall officials met to consider their response. Depreciation, they concluded, was not the answer because it would spread to India and because the real problem was the internal policy of the New Zealand government. The representative of the Department of Overseas Trade thought that Nash was simply using the situation to force a British acquiescence in exchange control. The officials agreed to draft a telegram, which was dispatched on 2 December. It counseled against exchange control and suggested that as the main export season was approaching the New Zealand government might perhaps find it possible to "postpone for a time the measures which they have in mind."[29] At the same time Whitehall cabled the trade commissioner in Wellington, with a message for informal transmission to the Reserve Bank and the ministry. The real trouble, it said, was New Zealand's deficit financing, and the trade commissioner "should take every opportunity to stress this."[30]

On 6 December Wellington informed London that export licensing would begin the next day. The governor of the Reserve Bank later told the British trade commissioner that the control regulations had been drafted two years before. Hopkins wrote, "The above . . . indicates that the New Zealand Government have considered . . . our views and have paid no attention to them."[31]

In 1936, during the tripartite discussions with France and the United States, Chamberlain and the Treasury officials insisted that sterling must be free to float and that domestic monetary policy must be run in the interest of recovery, not of the foreign exchanges. In 1938, the New Zealand government pursued a policy of domestic credit expansion for the sake of fuller employment. The Treasury officials and the Bank of England deplored this policy and deplored the thought that by devaluation New Zealand could handle the payments crisis that her monetary expansion had caused. Hence they acquiesced reluctantly in a regime of "temporary" foreign exchange control that is still in force. Why did they not see the New Zealand position and the British position in similar terms? The documents do not directly answer the question, but they help us to construct a reasonable opinion.

First of all, Whitehall certainly knew that New Zealand was most unlikely to devalue. Indeed, the Savage-Nash government had earlier intended to *revalue* the New Zealand pound, bringing it back to par with sterling.[32] Though this commitment had slipped into limbo, the government could not readily have moved in the reverse direction.

We have already seen that in 1930–1 Whitehall feared an Indian devaluation because it would push the Indian budget further into deficit, leading to further tariff increases, more money creation, or a collapse of India's credit at home and overseas. In 1938 New Zealand's position was the same in many respects and in one respect much more precarious. There was reason to fear that its budgetary position would worsen, and its overseas indebtedness was substantial. Further, its Labour administration had brought the Reserve Bank of New Zealand directly under government control. In India the Reserve Bank had been devised as an emphatically autonomous institution. In New Zealand the Reserve Bank had begun on such lines, but the Savage-Nash administration had transformed it. That administration was already committed to a heavy program of spending, and it relied on the Reserve Bank to create enough money to finance its outlays for housing and price support. If it devalued it might simply require the Bank to create the extra local currency with which to service the sterling debt. But monetary expansion, Whitehall officials believed, had caused the foreign exchange crisis in the first place. How could they encourage such events or even acquiesce in them? The only alternative, a tariff increase, would have been equally unattractive though for different and more obvious reasons.

Finally we must consider the nature or source of the New Zealand credit expansion. The Reserve Bank was creating money for two purposes: to finance a government public works and housing program and to buy up New Zealand's exportable dairy produce at "fair prices" that had no necessary relation to probable receipts. For neither end would the British authorities tolerate credit expansion within the United Kingdom. Easy money was meant to meet the needs of trade and to encourage private investment; it was not meant to pay for government investment programs or to subsidize farmers. Credit expansion, Whitehall thought, should not be used as a means by which government could evade the canons of sound finance. In Britain it had not been thus used and would not be; in New Zealand its only role was to permit such evasion. No wonder the Treasury deplored it.

The New Zealand exchange control gave government and local bodies first claim on the national earnings of foreign exchange – chiefly for overseas debt service. Then came raw materials and essential imports of goods not produced in the Dominion. There was bound to be a fall in other sorts of import, but it was hoped that there would be more direct British investment for the sake of import replacement; the control would be operated to favor British goods as far as possible.[33] The New Zealand government appeared to be aware of its obligations under the Ottawa Agreement though many Labourites were not; perhaps it had heeded the warnings that had been informally transmitted through the trade commissioner, or perhaps Nash had profited from his London adventures of 1936–7. Nevertheless Whitehall later had occasion to complain. Nash admitted that his government was contravening Article 8 of the Ottawa Agreement but pleaded dire necessity.[34]

In May 1939 Nash made another pilgrimage to London. His principal task was to negotiate the renewal or refunding of a £17 million loan that fell due on 1 January 1940. In addition, New Zealand local authorities owed £2.3 million in the United Kingdom.[35] Further, Nash wanted to raise at least £20 million in new money. Of this £10 million was meant for defense, and £10 million, though nominally for public works, was really meant to pay for New Zealand's ordinary imports during 1939. The national exchange reserves had fallen to disastrous levels. Too many imports had been licensed. The New Zealand trading banks had contributed £2 million sterling to pay for current imports, but this sum was dwindling fast.[36] The situation was desperate, and Whitehall knew it.

Before Nash reached London officials began to confer about his plans. He had already asked for a £5 million defense loan, and it was known that he would want at least £10 million more, plus help with his £17 million maturity. Regrettably, the Treasury reported, New Zealand credit was not strong. The City would not provide any new money for the time being, and the government could not. If New Zealand were to get government money for defense there would be less to defend Europe; if New Zealand made a public issue there would be less money for Britain's own defense loans. The Treasury insisted that Nash could not even hope to roll over any of his maturing loan unless he repaid some of it. Norman and Kershaw of the Bank agreed. In any event, New Zealand's difficulties were its government's own fault. Many times it had been warned that it was carrying public works and social outlays too far. As Waley explained, "The method for New Zealand to get out of her difficulties was to follow the example of France and reverse the direction of her internal policy. The United Kingdom taxpayer ought not to be called upon to help the social policy of New Zealand or any other Dominion government."[37] Britain itself had cut back on non-military outlays so as to make room for defense; New Zealand should be ready to do the same. But as the Savage-Nash government had always ignored good advice, this time it might default. This action would provoke complex actions under the Colonial Stock Acts, which would allow bondholders to proceed by petition of right or even sequester the proceeds from the New Zealand government's butter trade. Or New Zealand might devalue her currency, with unsettling reactions in Denmark, Australia, and even India.[38] Meanwhile, besides repaying some debts, Nash would have to cut back on public works and reduce his country's imports. Only then might the City gradually recover its confidence and provide money.[39] And City opinion was essential; the government of the United Kingdom would neither provide a loan itself nor guarantee any public flotation.

Early in June Nash reached London. At once he began a complex round of meetings with officials and ministers. He maintained that his country was short of sterling only because it had recently been repaying debt, whereas in the 1920s it had been a consistent borrower. If it had continued to borrow throughout the 1930s it would not now be in trouble. Just for the moment, however, its trouble was desperate: The government had overordered, and it had overissued import licenses. If new money could not be raised at once, the country would have to default on its commercial obligations and on government accounts, whatever might happen to the £17 million obligation that fell due on 1 January. Norman and Scrimgeours, his financial advisers, quickly told him that he would probably be unable to raise any new loan or to roll over any of the old loan unless he repaid part of it. He was prepared to contribute a few million in gold, which he could mobilize by revaluing the Reserve Bank hoard and exporting part of it. He was told firmly that the government would not lend for defense or provide a guarantee. If Governor Norman said the market would not be receptive, he knew best. The U.K. authorities were not acting out of political malice; the Dominions secretary and Sir Frederick Phillips carefully explained that they had very little room for maneuver.[40] New Zealand should bend all its efforts toward meeting that £17 million maturity; Nash could once more seek counsel from Montagu Norman.[41]

In fact Norman had already devised a medicine that, in the end, Nash was obliged to take. Explaining matters to the Dominions secretary, Sir Thomas Inskip, Norman made gloomy noises about New Zealand's credit. The country was at the end of its resources, and the City knew it. As matters stood the City would not even agree to refinance the £17 million. Something might be done if Nash would agree to repay £1 million at once and £16 million over four years, the repayments to be secured against his country's export earnings. But the governor did not want to make so stringent a proposal until he knew what the government would approve. Inskip admitted that in the last analysis the United Kingdom would not stand by and see New Zealand default; the general credit of the Empire would have to be preserved, if only because a default would have extremely serious effects on the international situation. Norman should see the chancellor and the prime minister; if they approved he should put his stringent suggestion to Nash.[42]

At a cabinet meeting on 21 June it was decided that New Zealand should be given some help and that this should be provided through the Export Credits Guarantee Department (ECGD). The refunding scheme was not discussed, but presumably Sir John Simon, now the chancellor of the exchequer, and Chamberlain spoke to Norman about it. On 22 June Norman then offered the plan to Nash, who was most reluctant to accept it. Expostulating to Inskip the next day, he said that he thought the City was motivated by political prejudice. It was unprecedented that he should have to pay off £17 million on stiff terms just so that at a more distant date he might be able to raise the new money he needed at once. He still demanded that His Majesty's government should lend him £10 million. Later, when he realized that Norman proposed to sequester a definite part of the butter proceeds, Nash was even more incensed. This proposal, he complained, seemed to imply a distrust of New Zealand, whose credit would not recover for a long time to come. The terms were "quite unprecedented and unfair."[43]

Whitehall, however, had begun to propose as a sweetener the guaranteed credit under the Export Credits Guarantees Department, whose powers would shortly be increased. Inskip first made the suggestion on 23 June; Nash ignored it. Three days later he repeated his demand for a £10 million intergovernmental loan;[44] but Norman was in favor of an export credit as long as Nash would accept the Bank proposals with respect to the refinancing and repayment of the £17 million maturity. On 27 June it was agreed that on this condition the Treasury could prepare a proposal for Nash to consider.[45] By 5 July Nash had received this scheme, which, if anything, made him angrier still. The ECGD credits would have to be repaid within five years and would bear interest at 4½ percent. They could be used in part for defense purchases and in part for ordinary commercial transactions. In accordance with ordinary ECGD practice, however, every transaction would have to be separately approved, and New Zealand bills would circulate in London with ECGD endorsement. These credits would be available for twelve months. There were two conditions. First, Nash must agree to a four-year conversion secured upon a "specific charge on the sterling arising from the exports of New Zealand dairy produce." Second, he must give "satisfactory assurances regarding the operation of the import restriction in New Zealand."

It would be hard to say which part of the package Nash disliked most. He still longed for a "global credit . . . placed at the disposal of the New Zealand Government for use as and when they needed it." He did not like the thought of New Zealand bills on the London market, with endorsement.[46] He still thought Norman's terms unjust. As for the import restrictions, he still wanted to be able to set up local monopolies without consulting Britain's industrialists who would, he said, give no advice against their interest; he would not say that the import controls were temporary. But even though the export credits were less ample than he had first hoped, they did provide the bridging finance he so desperately needed; and so at length he agreed to make commitments about uneconomic industries and about the eventual removal of the more drastic restrictions. By 12 July these commitments were sufficiently definite for Nash to agree on a publishable form of words. By 17 July he had accepted Norman's terms for the refinancing loan.

Because it was known in New Zealand and in Britain that Nash was in London, he could not leave without some sort of public statement. The announcement of 12 July, however, was almost entirely concerned with trade.[47] The closest of readings would not disclose that Britain had made certain commitments about credit. Only by knowing the background could one know how deeply the discussions had been affected by the Treasury abhorrence of reckless public spending and dislike of exchange control. Nash of course had got a good proportion of what he had wanted. In the end Norman and the bankers agreed to a refinancing of the 1940 maturity. New Zealand was to pay off the £2.3 million in local authority loans and £1.2 million of its own obligation at once; the balance was to be repaid, as Norman had prefigured, over the period 1940–4.

Norman then intervened to ensure that the issue would be floated successfully and cheaply. At his urging the six New Zealand banks took £6 million; as the public took only £3.5 million the Bank of England, as underwriter, had to absorb £6.5 million itself.[48]

By imposing exchange control Nash had removed his country from the relatively liberal monetary regime that British policy had been so concerned to preserve. He had also abandoned the "Ottawa monetary policy" because he was expanding credit for the wrong ends and trying to suppress the inflationary result. Whitehall saw no particular reason why Britain should underwrite his experiments in price support and deficit financing, having run its own monetary and fiscal systems on much more stringent lines for eight years. Partly because Nash's adviser later took pen in hand, the episode had acquired a place in the myth and demonology of New Zealand Labour.[49] It is hard to see, though, why Whitehall should be expected to have acted differently. Indeed, New Zealand now exemplified the results of the monetary heresies that Chamberlain had feared in 1932 and that Phillips had deplored in 1933 and 1934: if by creating money one tries to absorb unemployment and create prosperity one will get in trouble. In the Treasury New Zealand was seen to be reaping a whirlwind it had sown itself.

2. *Australia's adventures with the London capital market*

Compared with New Zealand's adventures, Australia followed a relatively tranquil course once the Commonwealth Bank had taken over the exchanges and the national government, pressed by the Bank, had begun to manage its financial affairs and those of the states more parsimoniously. Nevertheless, for Whitehall Australia could still generate moments of drama. As we shall see in Chapter 7, its leaders were among those who pressed most strongly and consistently for a policy of Empire price raising. Furthermore, Australia had borrowed enormous amounts in Britain. London could not ignore the various dreary possibilities that these debts created. At home the Australian authorities had forced a reduction in interest rates as part of their plan to balance budgets and to distribute burdens fairly. What of the interest on their overseas debt? Within Australia there were strong pressures for a simple default or for a writing-down of interest. By summer 1932 the cost of capital funds was far lower than it had been in the 1920s and earlier, when most of these debts had been incurred.

The Australian authorities had noticed with interest the successful British conversion of 1932. In spring 1933, when its London debt was over £550 million, Australia wanted to convert some £84 million from 6 percent or over to 4 percent or less; it could not simply be refused. For such conversions the chancellor's permission was needed, and the Bank of England would necessarily be involved in the scheduling of the issues and the grooming of the market. The question was whether Australia would accept the gradual conversion that both chancellor and governor proposed or whether, as Sir Richard Hopkins feared, it might "run amok."[1]

The London negotiations were run by Australia's resident minister and former prime minister S. M. Bruce. Believing that he could not expect to convert 100 percent of so large an amount, Bruce asked for support from the Bank, the Treasury, or both. In the correspondence between Bruce and Prime Minister J. A. Lyons that Bruce supplied to the Treasury, there was a strong hint that Australia would default if it were not given both permission to convert all £84 million and help to do so. Was this bluff, the Treasury wondered? Sir Edward Harding of the Dominions Office thought it probably was. He told Hopkins that "there was no substantial body of opinion anywhere in Australia that wished to go back to the methods of Mr. Lang," the premier of New South Wales who had defaulted deliberately in 1930.[2] The Treasury also took legal advice. In spite of the Statute of Westminster, the imperial government could still disallow financial legislation if such measures infringed the security of bonds issued under the Colonial Stock Act of 1900. Had the Australian loans been so issued? The answer was far from clear, but it did appear that the act applied. The Treasury does not seem to have warned Bruce, but the advice doubtless strengthened its own resolve.

There could be no question of help on the scale that Bruce envisaged. By 28 March Phillips thought that Bruce might be allowed to convert £26 million. The United Kingdom authorities might then have to take up as much as £10 million, for the time being.[3] Such support would be needed, one supposes, because Australia could not safely draw down its London funds or borrow short in the market to handle any shortfalls.

The Treasury proposal went to Chamberlain and Norman, who put it to Bruce. The resident minister told Norman he thought £26 million was not good enough and he would not recommend it to his home government. Despite all the blandishments and arguments that Norman could devise Bruce would propose a flotation of £40 million. For the unconverted balance he would issue treasury bills or convert by force. Norman maintained that it would be quite impossible to get the market to digest the relevant volume of Australian treasury bills. He told the Treasury officials that he would explore with the banks the question of the bills. "This is only an off chance," Hopkins wrote, "and the only remaining possibility to explore."[4]

By mid-May 1933 Bruce reported that the Australian authorities had decided to wait until after the World Economic Conference. Norman arranged for an Australian issue of £11 million at 5 percent. Early in July, however, Bruce wanted to deal with £32 million at 6 percent. Hopkins wrote, "We always had in mind that we should have to help him at one stage in his operations."[5] Norman was prepared to subscribe on a 50–50 basis to cover any deficiency up to a maximum of £7.5 million. Chamberlain agreed that Norman could negotiate with Bruce on this basis.

After various demurrals Bruce agreed to an underwriting issue of £17 million at once and another £15 million in September. The Treasury and the Bank had got their way: the Australian conversion was proceeding gradually, without compulsion, and with only limited help from the U.K. authorities. In 1934–5 further conversions followed.

We have examined this Australian adventure for two reasons. First of all, one would not want to suggest that New Zealand was the only Dominion to worry the U.K. authorities. Secondly, the Australian problems, like the New Zealand difficulties, show how complicated and multidimensioned were the connections between monetary authorities in Britain and those in the overseas sterling area. Loans, like pricing policies and monetary management, could keep the Dominions cheerful and stave off the defaults that in the 1930s were always possible and often extremely likely. It was the sterling area that in the 1920s had borrowed so massively in Britain. By managing the flow of new credit, in the 1930s the U.K. authorities could help to ensure that these old obligations would be honored until they could be refinanced at the new and lower interest rates that directly reflected Britain's own cheap-money policy. In managing the sterling bloc, long-term debt mattered as much as sterling balances.

In the event, Australia was able to convert very large sums once the new low interest rates had arrived. In 1933 alone it converted £75.9 million, and in 1932–6 inclusive, £198.5 million,[6] or 61 percent of all overseas refunding and conversion loans. For Australia, at least, there was something to be said for the sterling area, and for the chancellor's control of conversion and refunding operations.

6

Monetary preparations for the World Economic Conference

In June 1933 a World Monetary and Economic Conference was assembled in London. In July the conference collapsed in disorder and failure. At the time the world believed correctly that President Roosevelt had been responsible. Therefore the conference has often been examined in American historical writings, in the memoirs of American participants, and, to a lesser extent, in the memoirs of delegates from France and from other lands. It was widely believed that the conference had broken up over a dispute about exchange rates. France and its Continental associates wanted to fix a relationship between their currencies and the pound and the dollar, both of which were then floating vis-à-vis gold; when the American president refused to tolerate any such linkage, the conference collapsed in disorder and was soon adjourned, its work largely undone.

We shall not try to offer a full account of this remarkable and almost certainly foredoomed effort of world economic diplomacy. We are interested in the conference because of its relationship to the management of sterling and because in the end it provided an unexpected opportunity for a display of Empire monetary solidarity. Our principal purpose, therefore, is to explore the process by which Chamberlain and the Treasury defined and defended their policies with respect to cheap credit and the floating pound. We shall also see how the U.K. authorities tried to define and to propagate schemes for world monetary reconstruction that would help the United Kingdom while avoiding almost all commitments to other powers. We concentrate on the monetary side of the conference, ignoring other aspects of its work – commodity control, support for silver, and tariff reduction. Though the question of commodity control was very important to the Empire countries that attended the conference, it was not connected with the question of Empire monetary policy – a question that surfaced, much to Chamberlain's chagrin, only when President Roosevelt had already torpedoed the proceedings.

The chapter has five sections. The first traces the administrative and diplomatic background to the conference itself. The second presents some of the intellectual background against which Chamberlain and the Treasury prepared for it. The third treats the activities within the Preparatory Commission of Experts, where the U.K. authorities had first to define and present their opinions. In the fourth section we examine the discussions with the United States and France. These conversations followed the work of the commission, and preceded the conference itself. They helped to dispose of the monetary initiative in which the Treasury had had most confidence, while raising an awkward question as to the kind of monetary commitments the American president might have in mind. Finally, the fifth section surveys the preliminary contacts between Britain and the Empire governments. We shall see that though Chamberlain wanted to talk about commodity control he did not want to discuss money with his overseas Empire brethren.

1. *Why a world conference?*

In retrospect it seems not unreasonable to convene a world conference on economic reconstruction when the world is sunk in depression. By 1933 the nations had had some experience with such gatherings. In 1927 the League of Nations had sponsored a World Economic Conference, and this conference had proposed a "tariff truce." In 1920 and 1922 the Brussels and Genoa conferences had brooded on monetary reconstruction and on reparations. Nevertheless, in the deepening Depression the nations did not at once rush to meet in solemn conclave. Indeed, a world meeting was first proposed, in a spirit of confusion, not by the League but by Britain and America. Further, though in a sense preparations began in June 1932, for months thereafter no one could be sure the gathering would occur or, if it did, when it would happen or where. The experts who met in the winter of 1932–3 were supposed to settle these matters but did not. Further confusions arose when President Herbert Hoover lost the autumn election to Franklin Roosevelt in 1932. In accordance with immemorial custom the president-elect took office months later, early in March 1933. Only when he and Ramsay MacDonald met at Washington in April of that year was it decided to go ahead. Only then, too, were the location and opening date finally decided.

In 1930–1, Leith-Ross and his co-workers did what they could to promote the idea of a world conference on credit and gold. Though the eventual conference did not grow out of these efforts they form a necessary part of the background because they help to explain why the Treasury welcomed the conference and how it prepared for the gathering.

By December 1930 the Treasury was prepared to consider an international conference on money, credit, and gold. In Britain there was popular pressure for some such gathering. Leith-Ross envisaged something like the Brussels Conference of 1920, at which discussion of reparations and war debts would not be allowed.[1] Because French gold and credit policies were more reprehensible than American, discussion began with the French. Neither Treasury nor Foreign Office then knew what the United States might think, but everyone agreed that there was no point in calling a conference unless the Americans and the French would cooperate.[2]

France and the United States were both attracting gold, but Whitehall thought that the pull to France was more artificial: It reflected the undervaluation of the franc and the refusal of the French authorities to increase the supply of francs via open market operations. Indeed, the French Treasury had made matters worse because from time to time it chronically heaped up paper francs and sat upon them. The Bank of France would issue currency only against gold or commercial paper. The French banks, however, held little commercial paper. Hence they could get more Bank notes only by importing gold and selling it to the Bank of France.

In several directions the Treasury hoped to improve French financial management. First, the Bank of France should expand the credit base via open market operations. To do so it would need new legal powers. Second, the French Treasury should stop sequestering large heaps of francs. Third, the French capital market should become much more open to capital export. Finally, France should gradually convert its sterling balances into some sort of long-term investments.[3]

Early in January 1931 Leith-Ross discussed these desiderata and the question of a conference with French officials. The results were discouraging. On credit expansion the French were unhelpful, and on capital export they were willing to talk but not to act. They took the point about their own balances and promised to do something, but they rejected the British analysis of their gold receipts.

The French view was simple; gold flowed to Paris because the French balance of payments was strong and because compared with the pound the franc was generally trusted. The British diagnosis tried to look behind this simplicity; it asked why France's payments were strong and what could be done to make them less so. Understandably the French were not happy with this diagnosis. They were inclined instead to insist that the British should contract credit. The Treasury admitted that by so doing they could attract gold to London, but the gold would come from the rest of the world, where prices would therefore fall and where depression would deepen.

In effect the United Kingdom was trying to engage the French in a program of world reflation. The French would not cooperate. Nor did they want an international conference. It would, they thought, merely give Germany an excuse to default on reparations and other debts; also, it could not hope to solve the economic problems that faced the world.[4]

In January and February 1931 there were further conversations. British arguments did not impress the French officials, who sat firmly upon their gold while declining to confer about it. Leith-Ross continued to hope that they might change their ways.[5] Foreign Office officials were less hopeful.

Soon after Britain left gold, Philip Snowden mentioned a possible conference when speaking in the House. At once the French ambassador called on Lord Reading, the foreign secretary. He explained that while MM. Laval, Briand, and Flandin would themselves be favourably disposed, French public opinion would not, especially if the conference were explicitly about gold. He also said the Americans would have to acquiesce, and Reading explained that no one would try to force a conference over French objections.[6]

M. de Fleuriau, the French ambassador, had already discussed the conference idea with Charles G. Dawes, the American ambassador, who also called on Lord Reading. He had no news from Washington, but he himself was "against any action at once." He also doubted whether the U.S. government would like the idea, though he would at once inquire informally. From Washington Sir Ronald Lindsay reported that he thought President Hoover "would decidedly not welcome a conference on gold and silver." If he did happen to want one, the American president "will have no difficulty in allowing his views to become known."[7]

By 2 October Leith-Ross was advising ministers that if an international conference tried to treat gold debts and credit policy it would certainly fail because the United States and France would refuse to consider a proper reflationist policy or to give up gold. But he was still prepared to urge a gold conference on the French. Britain had now left gold, and the French wanted it to return as soon as possible. Perhaps they would now be more cooperative. In early October he asked them. If anything, in October 1931 they liked the idea even less than in January. Such a conference, they thought, would do no good and might do harm, for it would ventilate the dangerous inflationist theories that were abroad in the United Kingdom. There would be disagreement about these theories, and the disagreement would further weaken confidence, especially in sterling. The conference could not occur.[8]

France's monetary policies, of course, were still deplorable to Whitehall. In December Leith-Ross told a French official:

it seemed to us that the monetary policy pursued by France was largely responsible for the world crisis which had led to the reparations difficulty and to the abandonment of the gold standard, and we could not be expected to stabilise till we had some assurance that gold prices would remain stable in future. Further, we had to take account of the fact that there were large foreign balances which could be withdrawn.

The official was sympathetic but unhelpful. Certainly there could be no conference; further, he said, because of "personal difficulties" there was little to be expected from a conversation among the three central banks. Leith-Ross agreed and observed that among the three sets of Treasury officials there would be similar tensions. Informal conversations and contacts, therefore, could not be expected to do the job for which a conference might properly be designed.[9]

From Paris the British ambassador had already sounded a note of ultimate pessimism. "It would," he wrote, "be well not to lay too much stress on idea of conference for distribution of gold until it is possible to explain more fully what is intended, and so prevent French public from regarding it, as they do at present, as little more than an attempt to pilfer the Bank of France." What was needed, he thought, was a quiet interchange of views between London and Paris.[10] When tried, however, these had come to nothing.

Thus, by year-end the way seemed to be blocked. In response to a parliamentary question Chamberlain told the House early in February 1932 that he believed an international monetary conference would not achieve any practical results at that time. It seemed that the idea was dead. Nevertheless it sprang back to life once more in the spring of that year.

On 10 May 1932, during the second reading of the finance bill, Churchill called for international cooperation to arrest the decline in prices. Replying for the government, the minister of agriculture said, "Any attempt to work more and more along parallel lines and bring us more and more into relationship with men of good will by proposing a policy similar to ours would be welcomed . . . anything that we can do in that connexion with friendly nations both inside and outside the circle of the British Empire will always be one of the most keenly sought after ends of the present administration." He added that this was an official declaration on behalf of the government. Next morning the Exchange Telegraph carried a cable that said that the United States, though dubious about the value of a conference, would be willing to take part so long as the meeting did not discuss war debts or tend toward a high-inflation monetary policy for the United States. This purported to be the opinion of a high American official. At once the Foreign Office cabled

Sir Ronald Lindsay, the ambassador. Could he discover whether this really was the American attitude? Also, he was to tell the Americans that if anything occured France must be a party. Further, he was to suggest that the United States might attend the second section of the Lausanne Conference, already scheduled for June 1932. Though principally about war debts, at French insistence the conference was also to discuss "the measures necessary to solve the other economic and financial difficulties which are responsible for, and may prolong, the present world crisis."[11]

Lindsay learned that the report originated with a misquotation of a remark by a high official in the State Department; Washington had not considered the matter, the official told Lindsay. He was skeptical about the value of a conference, but if invited, he thought, the United States would have to attend. Having consulted President Hoover, on 14 May Lindsay was told that though Hoover would not favor an abortive conference he would be interested if Britain would convene a gathering with a definite agenda, which must not include war debts and tariffs and must include silver.[12]

In London the Foreign Office officials did not like the idea of convening another conference that would simply overlap with Lausanne. They thought that some useful work might be done on monetary affairs even if debts and tariffs were excluded. The foreign secretary minuted, "I don't think that much will come of it . . . the fundamental fact is that the USA is no good for conferences until after November,"[13] when the presidential election would occur. Sir Robert Vansittart observed:

let us remember that we only threw in the second half [of the Lausanne agenda] to save the French face. We regarded it as verbiage and hoped for little result . . . Personally, I would not . . . pursue Mr. Churchill's hare any further at present. It may give us a run later; at present it is likely only to squat.[14]

Lindsay was instructed to ask if the Americans would attend the second part of the Lausanne Conference, but before he had done so, the American secretary of state telephoned Ramsay MacDonald, who was resting at Lossiemouth.

Meanwhile, in parallel with these developments, the American embassy had been making very informal inquiries about a silver conference. The price of silver was falling, with results that seemed inconvenient for the silver-standard countries, especially China and Hong Kong, as well as for the silver producers, especially the United States and Canada, not to mention the holders of silver, especially India. The United Kingdom had just inquired into the question of Hong Kong currency.[15] India held large stocks of monetary silver that it seemed to want to shed.[16] The United States produced silver, and the silver interests were articulate. Would Britain be interested in joining a silver conference? Neither the Foreign Office nor the State Department believed that the new proposal descended from these American inquiries. Nor was silver on the Lausanne agenda. But London can hardly have been surprised when Washington spliced the silver question onto the others.

President Hoover, Herbert Feis tells us, liked the conference idea for its psychological possibilities and as a way of pacifying the silver senators.[17] He may or may not have thought that such a conference could achieve anything, and he insisted that it should not be allowed to discuss reparations or war debts. Henry Stimson, the secretary of state, tried to convince Hoover that these bounds were too restrictive. Herbert Feis, then senior economic adviser in the State Department, pressed for a general devaluation on gold. Neither Feis nor Stimson prevailed. On 25 May, therefore, Stimson telephoned Ramsay MacDonald to propose that Britain should convene a conference on monetary and economic matters. Hoover, he reported, wanted to raise prices by easy credit and to lower interest rates. We now know that in summer 1932 the American authorities did take steps to increase the money supply.[18] Stimson told MacDonald that he and Hoover thought there was scope for joint monetary action to raise commodity prices.[19] On 30 May Andrew Mellon and Ray Atherton, American diplomats, called on Sir John Simon, the foreign secretary, so as to carry the conversations further.

At this time no one had any clear idea of the possible issue from such a grand international gathering. Nevertheless, both in London and in Washington the conference was imagined to be chiefly concerned with price raising. Although trade and exchange might be discussed, neither was at the center of the stage. Certainly the Americans wanted to exclude not merely war debts and reparations but also any discussion of specific tariff rates.[20] With such exclusions, one might suppose that the conference was doomed to failure from the start. Nor could the Americans attend at Lausanne, because in American minds that conference was "inseparably linked to reparations." But by June 1932 the Bank of England and the Treasury were already hoping to stimulate recovery through cheap money and easy credit.[21] At this stage, however, neither Treasury nor Bank seems to have been formally consulted.

When Mellon and Atherton had explained that the United States could not come to Lausanne, Simon proposed that the Lausanne Conference might deal with the second part of its agenda simply by setting up expert committees. These would gather information. If there were later a discussion in which the United States could join, this material would be available. Mellon agreed that this was a good idea and said he would consult his government.[22] To the immense surprise and consternation of the Foreign Office, Washington at once announced that Britain had initiated conversations on the convening of an "international conference . . . to stabilize world commodity prices."

The announcement distressed Whitehall because it seemed to imply that Britain had been negotiating with the Americans behind everyone else's backs. Simon was then obliged to explain matters not only to the French and Italian ambassadors but to the Belgian, German, and Japanese authorities and also to the Dominions, who were given the news but no details. No one, it was explained, should expect anything to happen until after the Lausanne and Ottawa conferences had done their work. The conference, Simon told Atherton and Mellon, could not be summoned forthwith; indeed, it could not meet for several months.[23]

The Lausanne Conference on reparations, war debts, and economic reconstruction had been adumbrated for many months. Because of its subject, and because the League had sponsored it, the United States could not attend it. But as Simon wrote, the second part of the Lausanne agenda would really cover much the same ground as the new conference was likely to treat. The ideal course would be to detach this part from the reparations issue, so that the Americans could join the conversations.[24]

At Lausanne things worked out much as Simon had hoped. The delegates assembled on 16 June and dispersed on 9 July. They agreed to end reparations contingent on a "satisfactory settlement" of inter-Allied debts. The delegates had no time or inclination to do more. Hence they decided that the League should be asked to convene a World Economic and Financial Conference. This would treat "Financial Questions – monetary and credit policy, exchange difficulties, the level of prices, the movement of capital" – and "Economic questions – improved conditions of production and trade interchanges, with particular attention to tariff policy, prohibitions and restrictions of importation and exportation, quotas, and other barriers to trade, [and] producers' agreements."[25] The United States would be asked to attend. Expecting that the League, in turn, would propose that the new conference should meet in London, on 4 August the Cabinet agreed to accept such a proposal.[26] The League was to convene a Commission of Experts, which would draft an agenda and fix a date for the gathering.

In September Simon told the French ambassador that he hoped the new conference would assemble in November – after the American elections but well before Christmas.[27] In August the Cabinet had expressed the same hope. However, as the Preparatory Commission wrangled over the agenda the conference itself receded farther and farther into the distance. On 7 November the experts adjourned in disagreement, proposing to reassemble in the New Year.

As we shall see, the U.K. representatives then thought that the disagreements were so great as to preclude any agreement even on the agenda itself. Admittedly some observers were optimistic. The Canadian government, for instance, was receiving cheerful reports on the prospects. On 8 November its Geneva representative wrote, "Members of the Commission seemed to be fairly optimistic as to the outcome of the Conference, providing that there can be careful political as well as technical preparation." In January 1933, after the experts had completed their work, he reported, "Sir Fredrick Leith-Ross said that in order to give satisfaction to everybody their work was rather a hodge podge, but nevertheless it showed the way to recovery."[28] Among themselves, however, the Treasury officials were much less hopeful.

2. *Some of the background*

In the early 1930s it was widely believed that price declines had caused the Depression, either wholly or in part. More or less sophisticated arguments were used to support this belief; economists, publicists, financiers, and politicians all took part in its dissemination. Long before the World Economic Conference opened in June 1933, Chamberlain and the Treasury officials were persuaded of its truth. Their comments and their proposals reflected their conviction and were influenced by some of the diagnoses that connected price decline with the malfunctioning of the gold standard – in particular, with the accumulation and sterilization of gold by France and the United States. Scholars have never quite forgotten the possibility that depressions might be connected with low prices. Professors Arthur Lewis and C. P. Kindleberger, in particular, organize their account of the Great Depression around the relative decline of primary-product prices.[1] Nevertheless, the more recent literature very seldom puts the problem in the way that contemporaries were accustomed to see it. We cannot understand why Britain's officials and its politicians did what they did without knowing something of this particular piece of intellectual history. This section is meant to provide that knowledge.

It is convenient to center our summary on the figure of Sir Henry Strakosch, whom we met in Chapter 4. Financier, author, chairman of the *Economist*, member of the Council of India, perennial delegate to League and Empire meetings on monetary affairs, Strakosch would belong on any list of the "good and great." He had been involved for many years with the gold-mining industry of South Africa, and he had been a visitor to the Union where, indeed, he had helped to devise the statutes for its Reserve Bank. Rich, articulate, and endowed with enthusiasm and zeal, Strakosch used his newspaper and his public activities with vigor.

Like many other observers Strakosch believed that a profit squeeze had caused the slump. Prices had fallen relative to wages. It was hard to reduce money wages, influenced as they were by trade unions and by other forces that rendered them more or less rigid. Prices, however, were anything but rigid. If the supply of money did not behave properly, wholesale prices would behave improperly. The prices of primary products – foods and raw materials – might suffer first and most seriously, but the prices of manufactures would not be immune. Because prices in general had fallen since the late 1920s the cause of the decline must also be general; that is, one could not hope to find the explanation simply in the relative overproduction of certain goods, however important such a thing might be in particular cases. The only general cause, Strakosch thought, must be an inadequate supply of money in the world economy. If the quantity of money were disproportionate to the quantity of goods, prices would fall. But why was there not enough money? Under gold-standard conditions, one would be inclined to blame a shortage of gold. However, in the 1920s world gold reserves were growing almost as fast as world production. Prices collapsed in 1929 and thereafter because gold was increasingly *maldistributed*. Gold flowed from the world at large into the vaults of France, Belgium, Switzerland, Holland, and the United States. For these flows there were various reasons. Among the most important was the system of protective tariffs; this was especially important in restraining French and American imports. Another cause was the undervaluation of the French franc. Yet another was the continuation of reparations and war debt payments after the United States had ceased to be a large international lender. Finally, one must record French policy in switching out of sterling balances and into gold after the end of 1927.

If the recipients of this gold had allowed their monetary systems to expand in accordance with gold inflows, all would have been well. Indeed, if they had done so they could not have accumulated so much; the classical price-specie-flow mechanism would have repelled gold. But the recipients sterilized the gold they received. Thus, in some countries such as Britain and Central Europe, the gold outflow exerted a deflationary pressure. This was especially serious in Britain, where tight money could and did affect conditions in the world markets for many primary products. This happened because so much of world trade was financed through London and because British financial institutions held so much overseas paper. But in other countries, especially in France and the United States, gold inflows produced no parallel expansionary pressure. The result was inevitable – a general deflation of the world economy, a profit squeeze, rising unemployment, and looming bankruptcy for the world's primary producers whose incomes were shrinking but whose obligations were not.[2]

It is not very fruitful to search for the origins of the belief that price declines had caused the slump or made it worse.[3] Though such ideas were very unpopular in France and in the smaller "gold bloc" countries of continental Europe, in Britain, the United States, and the overseas Empire they were in the air. The same was true of the attempt to explain price declines by a maldistribution of gold. It is to emphasize that such ideas were linked as much with journalism as with scholarship that we have identified them with the publicist Strakosch. Nevertheless, the ideas had a respectable intellectual pedigree. They had been explored statistically in the work of Joseph Kitchin,[4] whom economists know chiefly because he defined a very short-term cycle in inventories. Sir Josiah Stamp espoused them.[5] So did Keynes, if we are to judge from evidence in his cross-examination for the Macmillan Committee, in his *Treatise on Money*, in his journalism, and in his work for the Economic Advisory Council.[6] The Council Committee reports, indeed, show how widely disseminated these ideas were and themselves provided a channel by which the ideas reached Treasury officials and ministers who could not be expected to read academic treatises.[7] The same ideas can be found in the works of that eminent academic publicist, Professor Gustav Cassel, perhaps the most influential theorist on trade and money during the 1920s and early 1930s. Cassel was deeply attached to the maldistribution explanation of the slump. In 1936, looking backward over the crisis, he wrote:

for the years 1925–31 . . . America had increased her gold reserves by 647 million dollars and France hers by 1585 million dollars. Together these countries had taken not less than 2232 million dollars, a sum roughly corresponding to the world's total gold production in the period. In the same period, some other countries, particularly Holland, Belgium, and Switzerland considerably increased their gold reserves, with the consequence of an actual fall in the total gold reserve of the rest of the world . . . The increasing scarcity of the gold that was actually available for trade purposes could be met for some time by a process of deflation . . . But this process was extremely pernicious and must in the end become intolerable . . . In addition the tendency of strong trade unionism to defend the existing level of nominal wages made the costs of production in many countries so inflexible that further deflation appeared impossible on account of social and political considerations.[8]

What, if anything, did officials read? One supposes they read the daily press, perhaps some specialized weeklies such as the *Economist*, and little more. Within the administrative grade the tempo of professional life would not allow time for broad reading. At the Bank of England, Montagu Norman does not appear to have read widely. Among the Treasury administrators only Sir Frederick Phillips seems to have followed the professional debates of the economists. But insofar as such ideas were in the air the officials could not avoid them, even if the historian cannot trace the routes by which ideas reached the Treasury chambers. Indeed, within the Treasury Ralph Hawtrey, the director of financial inquiries, argued that the credit cycle had caused the price cycle, which in turn had caused the trade cycle.[9] Furthermore, thanks to the initiative of Ramsay MacDonald, since January 1930 there had been a body within the governmental system, a body of economists and experts that regularly produced reports, documents that the responsible officials could hardly have failed to read, if only because Cabinet ministers, who also received them, might ask awkward questions about them. The body was the Economic Advisory Council. It too was "Strakoschite."

In August 1932, Ramsay MacDonald asked the Council to think about the coming conference. Because the Council as such had been in limbo since January 1932, this request was handled by its Committee on Economic Information, whose membership included Keynes; Leith-Ross attended regularly in his capacity as chief economic adviser to the government.[10] In 1930 Keynes had already devised a scheme by which the Bank for International Settlements would create paper money for international use. The new "paper gold" would be lent to governments, so as to strengthen foreign exchange reserves. It would then be possible for the weaker governments to pay off their external obligations or to expand their domestic economies.[11] Prices would then rise, and world trade would be revived. In summer 1932 Keynes and Henderson further developed this idea, and the Keynes-Henderson plan was elaborated by the committee and by the Council's Committee on International Policy; it was also pressed on the Treasury.

As Howson and Winch have explained, the suggestion was taken seriously in the Treasury.[12] We shall trace its reception and development in the next section. Here we should merely observe that the Treasury was readily converted because the committee prescription derived from the same basic diagnosis to which the Treasury had already attached itself: because international reserves were incorrectly distributed and because France and the United States were ignoring the rules of the gold-standard game, the world price level had fallen disastrously, and this fall had either caused the Depression or made it much worse. It was this diagnosis that, in 1931, had led Leith-Ross to press for an international currency conference.

Already in the late 1920s the League of Nations had begun to worry about fluctuations in the price level. In the terminology that had been common since the Genoa Conference, this concern was expressed as "undue fluctuations in the purchasing power of gold."[13] Hence in 1929 the League set up a Gold Delegation.[14] It was told to "examine into and report upon the causes of fluctuations in the purchasing power of gold and their effect on the economic life of the nations." After it produced two interim reports its final report appeared in June 1932. By then events had overtaken it.

Having been appointed before the Depression had become serious, the delegation was not asked to study its causes. But of course it would not ignore the economic blizzard. Nor could its members agree. In the end there was a majority report, a minority report by Albert Janssen, Sir Reginald Mant, and Strakosch, and from Cassel a memorandum of dissent and a refusal to sign either report.[15]

The majority report blamed the crisis on economic maladjustments arising from the war. It also mentioned changes in industrial structure, cartelization, attempts at price control, pools, valorization schemes, tariffs, prohibitions, and bounties. All these things caused maladjustments in "economic factors and processes." Thus they produced general instability, which the gold standard was not able to support, overcome, or digest.

Intellectually the majority report was not impressive. In the Treasury it was not well received. Sir Richard Hopkins wrote: "Nowhere is there any support for the one policy the world needs, viz. immediate *concerted* action on the part of all central banks to operate their affairs in such a manner as to raise the world price level . . . The British Government certainly could not accept the Report as an adequate guide to action."[16] The minority report and Cassel's memorandum were much more impressive, although Hopkins thought they overemphasized monetary factors. The dissenters observed that the majority had provided no evidence; indeed, Mant and Strakosch wrote, the reestablishment of the gold standard was itself proof that by the mid-twenties the wartime and postwar maladjustments had been digested. Further, they observed, because the gold standard had been maintained over a wide area for more than four years while the volume and value of world trade expanded rapidly, by 1930 there must have been still fewer maladjustments than in 1924 or 1925. The maldistribution of gold, they wrote, was the "fundamental cause of the present depression." This had become a serious problem from early 1929. At first it had forced down prices; it had then destroyed the international gold standard itself. Maldistribution, in turn, reflected reparations, war debts, protection, and the refusal to let gold inflow sufficiently expand credit and raise prices. "To put the matter very briefly, we hold that the fall in the general level of prices has been the fundamental cause of the present depression, and that that fall was the result of the obligation to pay reparations and war debts combined with the unwillingness of the receiving countries to accept payments in goods and services, so that payment had to be made in gold."[17]

The majority did not want to do anything to alleviate the Depression by monetary policy. The dissenters, however, wanted vigorous action. Britain should take the lead among the paper-standard countries by stabilizing the sterling price level at a level that would "re-establish a reasonable equilibrium between prices, wages, and debt-charges." Cassel believed that Britain should take the lead in the formation of a sterling group; the other dissenters expected that merely by giving a lead to the other paper-standard countries Britain would find that more and more countries would behave likewise, with splendid effects on the world price level.

Though admitting that it was desirable to restore the gold standard, the dissenters enumerated various conditions that must first be satisfied. The Treasury officials remained skeptical about Britain's power to reflate the world economy either by effort or by example, but they took this list of preconditions to their hearts. War debts and reparations would have to be settled in some way that ensured the payments could be transferred without seriously affecting the gold standard. Tariffs and other protectionist measures must be scaled down. All countries must observe the rules of the gold-standard game, especially by allowing a gold inflow to raise domestic prices via credit expansion. Lest there be an "unnecessary and indeed disastrous rise in the value of gold," the world should decide to economize on gold. In particular, there should be no more stipulations with respect to gold "backing" for currency. Gold mattered only as a way to settle international obligations, and it should be freed for this use. Once all these adjustments had been effected, the world's central banks should be able to devise some way to better distribute world gold reserves. But if they were not effected countries would readily be driven off gold once more. Then the gold standard could not "offer that security for international trade, the establishment of which is the very purpose of that standard."[18]

The Treasury certainly agreed with the diagnosis and prescription. With respect to the impact of monetary expansion, however, the officials were less optimistic than Strakosch. In origin, they thought, the depression was monetary – but not entirely so. They remained distrustful of extreme monetarism, whenever it raised its head – in Keynes's *Treatise*, in Strakosch's popularizations, and in Dominion demands for ever-cheaper money and ever-higher prices.

Strakosch himself thought the delegation had been rather a waste of time. Of the Second Interim Report he wrote:

> The Report, I am afraid, bears all the traces of compromise. This was inevitable in view of the fact that the French – who are, of course, represented on the Delegation – wished at all costs to avoid being shown up as the culprits in the matter of Gold hoarding . . . Having been for ten days immersed is discussions on matters of detail, I frankly lost all sense of perspective, and therefore cannot appreciate whether the document is really going to be of much use. I am, however, encouraged by the view expressed to me by Sir Frederick Leith-Ross (Deputy Controller of Finance at the Treasury), who thinks that it will serve some purpose as it does bring out – it is true in a meek form – many of the faults of commission and omission perpetrated by the French and the Americans.[19]

By 1931, therefore, the Treasury officials had begun to accept the interpretation that traced the world's economic ills to the maldistribution of gold. It followed that the world could not have the gold standard or even stable exchange rates without gold convertibility until it had rid itself of the structural features that had produced the maldistribution. If the nations would cooperate they could do something to reduce the most serious of the distortions that the maldistribution had produced, but the maldistribution would recur if its underlying causes had not been removed. Palliatives would be useful. They might raise prices a little, and they could certainly unfreeze trade and payments in Central Europe at least for a time. But without some changes in the structure of the world economy Britain could not safely commit itself to the gold standard – or even to fixed exchange rates. In the Foreign Office similar views prevailed.

In their preparation for the conference the officials were certainly concerned to devise some palliatives.[20] They were far more eager, however, to press for structural change and to avoid the commitments that would be insupportable without such change.

3. *Treasury policy and the Preparatory Commission*

Before the Lausanne Conference, Whitehall had looked with great favor upon plans for expanding the international stock of reserves. The best scheme, Herbert Henderson wrote, would be a simple one: The Bank for International Settlements should "issue notes which the governments of the world would agree to accept as the equivalent of gold; [thus] an expansion of the international means of payment could be secured to any extent that might be desired." But France, he thought, would almost certainly reject any such inflationary scheme, and the United States would probably not join either. Leith-Ross concluded that at Lausanne Britain should merely "plead for a more liberal policy by creditor countries on the gold standard ... Nothing much may result, but if only as a protection against the expansionist views of certain Dominions at Ottawa who will clamour for sterling inflation, it seems essential not to accept at Lausanne the doctrine that not even *international* action can do anything to raise world prices. Our case at both conferences is that action is very much to be desired." Any novel ideas should be launched "not at Lausanne, but in the milder atmosphere of some expert committee in the course of an exploration of what use, if any, can be made of the machinery of the BIS."[1] Hence, at Lausanne Leith-Ross first moved that in preparing for the coming world conference the experts should consider monetary and credit policy, exchange difficulties, the level of prices, and the movements of capital; he then added that the Lausanne gathering should not "use too great precision in describing the financial and monetary problems to be reviewed; to do so would be merely to embarrass the work of the experts"[2] who would prepare for the later conference.

Within the Treasury, meanwhile, the officials had been developing a policy of their own. To some extent it was simply a reiteration of the "Ottawa policy" – cheap money, low interest rates, and plenty of finance for the legitimate needs of trade. In August 1932, Hopkins and Phillips produced a joint memorandum in cooperation with S. D. Waley.[3] Presumably, they said, Britain should try to get world adherence to the Ottawa policy on money and wholesale prices. But countries differed in monetary matters. Hence, the conference could well impede Anglo-American cooperation with respect to a "regime of cheap and plentiful money," whose effects had not been sufficiently favorable to convince others at once – especially in countries that feared inflation. What Britain would call "reasonable reflation" would elsewhere be called "frankly inflationary." To create such an impression would harm the pound. Hence, "the Conference is not likely to reach international agreement as to raising prices by monetary action." As for the gold standard, Britain could not accept it "now, or in the near future, and we cannot say when conditions will be such that we can safely do so." Nor could Britain make any commitment to de facto stabilization. In this respect as in so many others the interests of Britain and the sterling countries were at odds with those of the gold countries; but Britain could not reflate it the rest of the world was not doing so. Admittedly the depreciation of the pound had given only temporary trading advantages, partly because many countries had imposed restrictions and new duties but also because Japan had left gold. If however, the remaining gold countries should leave the standard "with great suddenness" all the remaining gain would vanish. Wholesale prices must be raised, but there was no one way to achieve this rise. Though monetary cures would not suffice, they were important and must not be neglected.

It was not a hopeful prospect, and when the Preparatory Committee met at Geneva on 31 October the clouds, if anything, grew thicker.

The American government had sent Edwin Day, John Henry Williams, and Herbert Feis. Day and Williams were experts, but neither could commit his government. The two American experts lined up with the Continental gold countries: Britain must peg the pound. If it would not or could not, the conference could remove neither tariffs nor quantitative controls. Thirty years later, Feis commented ironically: "thus began a slide into a strategy for the Conference which caused all the other measures which had figured in the original correspondence to pivot around a stabilisation accord. It was not foreseen that this demand for stabilisation would concentrate upon the dollar."[4]

On 1 November Phillips explained the position of the U.K. government. Drawing on the Ottawa resolutions, he set out the conditions that must exist before Britain could return to gold. He told the other experts that the world could not stand any further price declines. Noting that there were two price problems – the general fall, and the fall in primary prices relative to manufactures – he insisted that if prices fell further there would be defaults, more unemployment, and more labor strife.[5] The others were unmoved. No one shared the British view that cheap money would raise prices. Only Germany joined Britain in arguing that creditor countries must buy and lend more before the gold standard could be reconstructed. The gold countries would accept a lower gold parity for the pound, but a gold pound they were determined to have.[6] Phillips remarked that Charles Rist, the French representative, "continues to produce the economic theories of Sir Robert Peel with a completely maddening logic."[7]

On 9 November the experts adjourned. They decided to postpone the conference. Roosevelt had won the American election; more serious, the experts were so divided that the conference would fail if it met before the disagreements had been resolved.

The Bank and the Treasury began to ask themselves how far they might go toward meeting Franco-American demands. In mid-November the Bank argued that in the ruling uncertainty one could not choose a correct parity, especially when commodity prices were so low. Certainly the Bank blamed tariffs, not monetary contraction, for the slump.[8] But if the gold standard were not rerigged to eliminate internal drains, release sterilized gold, reduce protective tariffs, and abolish quotas, the gold, even if redistributed, would simply flow back to France and the United States. "The present impasse will recur." Even if Britain were to be satisfied on all these structural questions it would first have to stabilize de facto and then to increase its gold reserves.[9] So the Bank argued. Phillips agreed that before joining the gold standard Britain would have to *own* more gold. "We experienced a run of £20 millions in six weeks in 1931 and under no conditions could we agree to return to gold unless assured that a repetition of that experience would not drive us off gold again."[10] But the whole plan would not be practicable if it involved deflation in Britain,[11] and without deflation Britain could not hope to attract more gold.

Eager for stabilization, the Bank of England tried to accommodate the wishes of the Americans and the gold countries. Later in November it said that it could tolerate a British commitment to keep the pound within "certain limits (known only to ourselves) which would not be varied except in deference to a continuing downward trend in our reserves." Because an "artificial redistribution of gold" was "not a necessary prelude to recovery," the Bank now had no interest in redistribution.[12] Phillips praised the Bank for the skill with which it had handled the "very delicate question of what undertakings we could give about sterling."[13] But he and Leith-Ross agreed, "We find it difficult to understand how the British representatives could say all this at the Conference." Hence they opposed the stabilization of the pound "at its present crisis value."[14]

Late in December Leith-Ross described the conference prospects. The experts, he thought, would almost certainly argue that if the conference were to meet in the near future, Britain would have to state the conditions on which it would stabilize sterling. "Now even those, who, like myself, regard the stabilisation of sterling (at the appropriate parity) as an essential step to world recovery would not be prepared to contemplate it unless we can secure the fulfillment of a number of conditions." First, war debts must be settled for good, on the basis of the Lausanne accord. Second, American and French central banks must take wider powers to buy government securities, and they must use these powers to expand credit, thereby securing an increase in the price level. Third, so as to allow the erasure of the existing standstills and exchange controls, there must be some agreement to redistribute gold, to extend credits, or to do both. Fourth, quotas must be abolished – except, perhaps, on agricultural goods. Fifth, there must be "substantial modification of the present tariff policies of the USA and France." Glumly Leith-Ross concluded, "there is no prospect whatever of getting agreement."[15]

Yet in January 1933 the experts reassembled, and early in February they did produce a Draft Annotated Agenda.

As in the autumn, Leith-Ross refused to commit Britain to an unreformed gold standard. After the meetings he wrote, "Determined efforts were made up to the last moment, more particularly by the Americans and Germans, in favour of recommending a policy of *de facto* stabilisation for those currencies, particularly sterling, which are off gold. We naturally raised the strongest objections . . . as regards the general reform of the gold standard very great progress was made." Britain's experts convinced the others to reduce the minimum ratio of gold reserves to paper currency, to concentrate gold in central banks, and to control internal gold drains. The annotations enshrined the Treasury list of preconditions for the restoration of gold. They contained a reference to the possibility of an "international credit institute" which could offer "special assistance . . . to restart the financial machine." But the reference was so phrased that only the cognoscenti could recognize its relationship to the maldistribution of gold.[16] Summarizing the experts' work for the Cabinet, Leith-Ross did not stress this aspect of the Agenda.[17] He did observe, however, that because Britain was a creditor nation, he and Phillips had been concerned to resist any general scaling down of long-term international debts. These, they had successfully argued, "should not be scaled down until it is clear that the existing price structure cannot be altered."[18]

War debts, of course, were another matter. The Agenda did observe that among the many preconditions for a new international gold standard, one was "a settlement of inter-governmental debts."[19] But the Americans had already explained that they would not discuss these at the conference.[20] Another precondition, the Agenda mentioned, was "a return to a reasonable degree of freedom in the movement of goods and services," but the Americans would not allow the conference to discuss tariff rates. One might suppose, therefore, that the conference was doomed to failure at least as far as the gold standard was concerned. Largely at British insistence, the experts had specified preconditions that the conference itself would be powerless to effect.

This was not the opinion of Day and Williams. Not foreseeing the monetary adventures that Roosevelt would begin early in March 1933, they had argued strongly for the stabilization of currencies in general and the pound in particular. Regrettably, Williams had always loved fixed exchange rates.[21] Regrettably, too, the Americans seem to have thought that in the end they would get their way. Reporting to Washington, they did not convey any sense of Britain's attachment to floating rates, and they certainly did not understand the general diagnosis that lay behind the prescriptions of Phillips and Leith-Ross. In December 1932 they reported on the first experts' gathering. The principal need, they said, was "restoration of the gold standard in the Key Countries, England and Germany." This would not happen unless war debts were quickly settled, prices raised, and trade relations improved. On these questions there should be an Anglo-American understanding.[22]

When the Agenda was ready, Day and Williams thought the result "more satisfactory than expected."[23] Their emphasis, however, was still not calculated to transmit the viewpoint of the U.K. Treasury. Four points, they said, were now "essential." First was "the restoration of an effective international standard to which countries off gold can adhere." Second was the use of production or export control to raise commodity prices, and third was the abolition of exchange control. Fourth was greater freedom of international trade. They did note that "many conditions" would have to be satisfied first. They mentioned the possibility of putting "immobilised resources into active circulation." They observed that easy credit would help to raise prices. But they did not present these matters with the force that would have correctly conveyed the importance that Whitehall attached to them.[24] On reaching Washington the American experts went further. Britain, they said, could help by de facto stabilization, "looking toward the ultimate restoration of the gold standard." Germany could help by relaxing exchange control and France by relaxing her quantitative controls on imports. The United States could help by tariff policy and by settling the war debts satisfactorily. Cordell Hull, they suggested, could use the debt question to influence the actions of other governments so as to help the work of economic reconstruction.[25]

Because they believed that Britain and France would use the conference as a weapon in the war-debt dispute, American officials could not think clearly about the gathering itself.[26] In December 1932 France had already defaulted, and everyone knew that Britain had then paid with extreme reluctance. When Ramsay MacDonald came to Washington in April 1933 he would discuss debts as well as the coming conference. The experts had said that debts would have to be settled before economic reconstruction could be begun. They had not explained how or why this was so, though the reason was not far to seek. The United States was still running a current-account surplus. On capital account its foreign lending had virtually ceased. So had external direct investment. If the United States were to insist on collecting the debts that were due to it, the world's gold would drain to that country. Trying to control or prevent this drain, Britain and Europe would be forced to retain or to intensify the various controls by which they tried to restrain imports, encourage exports, and retain gold. In other words, the war debts had helped generate trade restrictions that their continuation would perpetuate.

Meanwhile, in London there was serious discussion of the Keynes-Henderson plan for an international note issue – the plan that had sprung from the Economic Advisory Council's Committee on Economic Information. Howson and Winch have traced the process by which the scheme generated a Treasury counterproposal – the "Kisch plan," which emanated from Sir Cecil Kisch of the India Office and other officials in the Treasury and the Bank. This plan would have redistributed gold from surplus to deficit countries through an International Credit Corporation, which would borrow gold from the former and lend to the latter. In April 1933, however, the Americans rejected both the Keynes-Henderson and the Kisch plans. On 18 May, learning that the Americans disliked both plans, the Cabinet committee on the conference agreed that the Keynes-Henderson plan should not be raised. Though the United Kingdom delegates were willing to put the Kisch plan before the conference, they had no chance to do so.[27] Indeed, after reading the minutes of the delegation's meetings, and of the surrounding conclaves, one must suspect that they really never thought to do so.

4. *Discussions with France and the United States, spring 1933*

The experts had not been able to fix a date for the conference. Everything depended upon the American president-elect, who would not take office until early March 1933. In an effort to smooth the transfer of power, President Hoover had tried to involve his successor in the business of government. Roosevelt, however, had refused. No one knew, therefore, whether he would allow the conference to meet at all or, if it did assemble, what the American line would be. In his campaign Roosevelt had presented himself as an apostle of budget balance and sound money. He might or might not act accordingly. Further, Congress might legislate in unexpected and inconvenient ways. Only one thing was reasonably sure: the new president would not smile upon a renegotiation of war debts.

Roosevelt took office on 4 March. His secretary of state was the eminent internationalist and apostle of tariff reduction, Cordell Hull. Among his assistant secretaries was the politically minded professor of criminology and economic nationalist, Raymond Moley.

In March 1933 Sir Ronald Lindsay gave Moley a memorandum that was meant to begin an Anglo-American conversation on the conference and its objectives. This memorandum gave pride of place to price-raising measures. Bimetalism was impossible. Better to raise commodity prices generally than to raise the price of silver in particular. Various things could be done. The first was "monetary action . . . cheap and abundant short term money . . . [and] well-co-ordinated action between the Central Banks" in the expansion of credit. The second step was "action to restore the purchasing power of debtor countries." This would involve "cooperation between Central Banks, with a view to putting in circulation resources which are at present immobilised." Finally, there were possibilities in trade promotion and in production control. On exchange-rate regimes, there could be no return to an international monetary standard until international cooperation had removed the defects in the old gold standard, and until there was once more "a reasonable degree of equilibrium between prices and costs." On all these matters, and on questions of tariffs and trade barriers, the United Kingdom proposed conversations with the United States.[1]

It was a pity, the ambassador observed, that unless the war-debt question had been satisfactorily settled the conference would not progress. In its response the State Department concentrated only on the rejection of this idea. It gave no words, and seems to have given no thought, to the comments about monetary innovation and exchange regimes.[2] Meanwhile the United States had prohibited the unlicensed export of gold, thereby in effect leaving the gold standard.

Chamberlain was not impressed by these early signs. Early in March he told his sister, "As for USA, they are going from bad to worse. They are practically off gold now and though they say they will be on again next week I hae ma doots."[3] With respect to the Anglo-American discussions on war debts, he had already written, "Once more one is forced to the conclusion that we have the misfortune to be dealing with a nation of cads."[4]

Late in March 1933 the U.K. officials in Washington had their first detailed discussions with the new American administration. Kenneth Bewley, the Treasury official at the embassy, conferred with Hull, Moley, and Feis; later James Warburg saw both Bewley and Emmanuel Monick, the French financial diplomat. As reported by Sir Ronald Lindsay, the first conversations centered upon silver, to which Moley devoted great attention, and upon wheat. Everyone recognized that in the United States the silver question was of great political purport. Nevertheless, Bewley and Lindsay can hardly have been pleased to see it accorded such pride of place.[5] As to the talks with Bewley and Monick, Warburg told Roosevelt on 30 March that they had agreed "the main countries should individually and collectively try to maintain the stability of their currencies," ultimately returning to the gold standard; "whether or not the dollar was to be devalued in terms of gold . . . was left open."[6] Roosevelt is said to have liked Warburg's report. But if Feis has correctly reported the sense of the Warburg memorandum,[7] Warburg had not accurately reported British policy: Although it might be said that the Exchange Equalisation Account was meant to keep the pound stable from day to day, Whitehall certainly was not indifferent to a dollar devaluation.

Meanwhile, in mid-March, the British and French leaders discussed the prospects. To his own surprise Chamberlain found that the two governments were in general agreement – or so it seemed at the time. Chamberlain wrote to his sister: "I had an all day talk with Bonnet yesterday and am glad to say that we found ourselves d'accord all through."[8] The chancellor would soon discover that on one matter – the stabilization of the exchanges – he and the French finance minister still disagreed profoundly.

Leith-Ross had arranged for Georges Bonnet, the new French finance minister, to visit London. In the Foreign Office there was some dismay at the prospect. It was feared that the Americans would suspect some collusion on the war-debt question.[9] Vansittart, however, thought all would be well. Meanwhile Sir Frederick Phillips had prepared a careful brief for the U.K. ministers. It was a most awkward time for a visit, he noted, because no one knew whether the United States would stay on gold. Until Europe knew what the United States thought about a large international credit to debtor countries there was no point in discussing this idea, important though it was. Meanwhile, for the future management of any reconstructed gold standard it was a serious matter that the Bank of France still could not conduct open market operations. Finally, "The greatest evils from which the world is suffering at the present time are the excessively low level of wholesale commodity prices and the vast erratic movements of short term capital from one financial centre to another." Britain was urging the United States to consider some such scheme for credit; "international action in monetary and credit spheres" was "the most vital task of the Conference,"[10] but, of course, the United States might kill or modify such a plan. Meanwhile, if circumstances permitted, Chamberlain should urge the French to liberate some of their gold.[11]

In his memoirs Bonnet claims that when he visited London there was complete accord between him and Chamberlain "to re-establish the stability of the principal currencies."[12] The minutes of the meeting reveal no such agreement.[13] Bonnet did ask Chamberlain whether the conference should exclude questions of currency stabilization. The chancellor did not answer directly, but he did extract from Bonnet an agreement that world prices ought to rise. How might this be done? Production control might, in special cases, be desirable. Chamberlain then argued that there should be simultaneous international action to cheapen money and credit. Central banks should cooperate; perhaps the Bank of France ought to acquire wider powers. Bonnet agreed that he was anxious for the Bank to "associate itself with the action of other central banks on agreed principles." He and Chamberlain agreed that public works would not, of themselves, do much to raise prices. What else could be done? Chamberlain adverted once more to credit expansion; Bonnet spoke of confidence: "The problem was to get people to buy and we always come back to the need of confidence and the monetary problems, including the gold standard." There followed a discussion of the dollar exchange. If America definitively left gold, Bonnet said, he feared that France would lose gold, because it would be the only major country still on a free gold standard. "If the pound had been stabilised," he continued, "there would not be this danger for France." But he did not press Chamberlain to stabilize the pound.[14] Chamberlain explained that the pound would continue to float, returning to gold only after the various conditions, as defined by the Treasury and reproduced by the Draft Annotated Agenda, had been satisfied. There must, he said, be an agreement on the principles, and then the various governments would have to carry them into practice; then Britain could "consider" the question of a return to gold.

Chamberlain did not proffer the British scheme for an international credit institution, but he did suggest that to get rid of exchange controls there might have to be "some system of international loans." Bonnet argued for the "Stresa formula" of a common fund, assembled from a small tax on all imports and exports or from the various countries or from central banks. Leith-Ross said that the Stresa plan was too limited in scope. Britain would want a much larger scheme. This could only be financed, he said, by placing in circulation "the surplus reserves of the central banks." Bonnet, however, did not take the point, and to the British officials his silence must have been eloquent. He was, however, eager for interbank cooperation, suggesting that there should be talks between the two central banks. The Bank of England, he hoped, would approach the Bank of France.[15]

On trade restrictions Chamberlain found Bonnet cooperative. France, Bonnet said, would not oppose some liberalization of quotas.

Three days afterward, Leith-Ross sent a glowing account to the embassy in Paris:

Bonnet's visit passed off very well. The discussion with the Chancellor showed that there was a close approximation in their views on practically all the questions discussed. Bonnet in fact professed to be inspired by very liberal ideas and to favour an expansion of credit by international action as well as a breaking down of trade barriers.[16]

Once the conference had assembled, France's finance minister proved less tractable. By 7 July he was claiming that he had made the stabilization of currencies a precondition for the conference. And by then the schemes for international credit had vanished without trace. Further, long before the conference assembled, American action had made him press much more strongly for exchange stability. As the dollar floated down, and as gold drained from the smaller countries, France became increasingly uneasy, vast though her own hoard was, and increasingly insistent that something must be done.

In Washington Cordell Hull was wondering what Chamberlain and Bonnet had talked about. He asked Ray Atherton to find out. Atherton reported from London that the French believed Britain would soon, perhaps in summer 1933, return to gold.[17] One cannot see how Bonnet could have received any such impression; in the Whitehall records there is no such hint. During the conference itself, however, this impression could have affected French attitudes in various respects – most obviously in the stabilization talks themselves but also, after President Roosevelt's rocket, in the subsequent efforts to enroll Britain within the gold bloc.

The new president decided to let the conference proceed. He invited 53 governments to take part in preliminary bilateral talks. Responding to this invitation, Ramsay MacDonald sailed for Washington, arriving on 21 April. While the prime minister was at sea the president took the United States off the gold standard. Already, on 6 March, he had taken control of gold export. On 18 April he told his associates that he was going a step further: he would license no more gold shipments. His reasons were simple. As the United States was already losing gold, he wanted to end the risk of speculative withdrawals should gold export be freely licensed; he wanted to raise prices and money incomes; he hoped to aid exports, especially of farm products; he intended to put the United States in a better bargaining position vis-à-vis Britain and Europe with respect to relative gold values. Had he given any advance warning to MacDonald and Herriot, already on the Atlantic? No, he had not. The president found this omission amusing, as did his adviser Moley.[18]

When the presidential decision was announced the next day, others were less amused. Aboard the *Berengaria* MacDonald asked his chief economic adviser what he should do; Leith-Ross said they should return to Britain as soon as the ship berthed at New York.[19]

Rejecting this advice, MacDonald proceeded to Washington and talked to Roosevelt, while his advisers met American experts. Meanwhile, before the *Berengaria* docked, he became alarmed about a radio suggestion that America was deliberately depreciating the dollar so as to force the stabilization of the pound. What did Whitehall think?

Hopkins and Phillips replied at once. The United States, they argued, could not force Britain or anyone to agree to anything by injecting new confusion in this way. If the dollar were to fall substantially the result would be serious for Britain's trade and alarming for the gold bloc, especially for Holland and Switzerland, whose currencies were already weak. The more currencies left gold, the more serious for Britain's trade. If the Americans simply left the dollar to float it could not spontaneously fall much because the American payments position was so strong. Britain could live with the result. But if the United States should rejoin gold at a substantial discount from parity, "the effect on the other gold countries is likely to be disastrous, and it is by no means sure that we should not be driven to a series of deliberate measures for reducing value of the pound and procuring rise in sterling prices and other countries might competitively join in."[20] From then on, Treasury policy was to urge the Americans to support the dollar at the old gold parity or very near it.

What of the conference itself? Hopkins at once sent Vansittart a program and a prognosis. If the dollar stayed close to parity and if other countries did not leave gold there was no reason to alter Britain's own plans for the conference. But if the dollar fell a long way or if other countries left gold the conference would have to adjourn. It would be highly desirable if the dollar and sterling could work "roughly together" so as to raise wholesale prices to the 1929 level or higher, but it would be premature to make any agreement about exchange rates, at least for the present. In any case, whatever might later be devised would have to be

entirely informal and elastic. Otherwise the insoluble problem would arise whether London or New York was to be in control . . . The present attitude of US on gold reserves is so preposterous that we do not see how you can altogether avoid referring to it in discussions. Their avowed object is to secure the return of Great Britain to the gold standard, but Britain is not likely to return when 60% of world gold is monopolised by two countries and when every loss of gold by America is treated as a national disaster . . . As compared with even Great Britain the position of debtor countries throughout the world is simply disastrous as they have been almost totally stripped of gold by America and France. In all circumstances we are convinced that to rid the world of the incubus of inter-governmental debt remains the primary need and that in present circumstances any type of a commitment or an early return to gold should be avoided at all costs.

As for the redistribution of gold reserves through governments, central banks, and an international credit institution, the whole idea was in jeopardy, if not altogether otiose, now that the United States seemed totally unwilling to let gold go.[21]

Chamberlain was slightly more charitable than his officials. He believed that Roosevelt had acted not "to defeat British machinations" or to gain bargaining power but to "keep the American coach on the road and save it from the precipice into which it appeared likely to be driven by Congress." Nevertheless, he thought that Roosevelt had done immense mischief. European confidence would be restored if only the president would announce that the dollar would be left free to find its own level, without deliberate depreciation, and that American gold would be spent, if necessary, to steady it. Otherwise the conference could not be held in the reasonable future. As for debts, it was even more necessary for the United States to grant a moratorium because, having "cast this millstone into the pond," it could not expect to get anything on 15 June when the next installments were due.[22]

In Washington, Cordell Hull and his staff did their best to calm the British. They told Sir Ronald Lindsay that Roosevelt had banned gold exports solely for internal reasons. Wanting to raise the internal price level, he would have to contrive a domestic inflation, which would have forced the United States off gold. Billions of dollars would have fled the country. Now there was speculation in commodities, instead of in gold. Hence prices were already rising. And even at the old parity the dollar had been overvalued.[23]

To Whitehall this news was the reverse of calming. They did not believe that the dollar had been overvalued; America's payments were too healthy. Nor did they think the United States should sit upon its gold so as not to lose it. Indeed, they wanted the reverse. An American inflation and a gold outflow might reflate the rest of the world. But this the Americans would not allow.

Roosevelt, meanwhile, was conferring with MacDonald. They were talking partly about the war debts, partly about disarmament, and partly about the conference. What happened at these meetings is still very far from clear. Certainly the president did want a world conference in June at London. He wanted prices to rise.[24] And he did want stable exchange rates. Or so MacDonald concluded. It has been suggested that the prime minister misunderstood the president.[25] This may or may not be so. But Roosevelt's advisers gave every indication that they had presidential approval for stabilization. Further, in early May Roosevelt made a radio speech in which he mentioned that one goal of the conference was to stabilize currencies.[26] If MacDonald was confused he had plenty of reason.

The Continental emissaries, on arrival, were told that the United States had left gold merely in response to "special and urgent circumstances" and that the dollar would be stabilized on gold again as soon as possible.[27] The South African minister was later told the same story.[28] James Warburg and Raymond Moley together with William Bullitt and Herbert Feis were proposing to the British and French officials a series of devices stemming in large part from the presidential desire for higher prices. They suggested an "improved" gold standard, with a 25 percent bullion ratio – a basis that would leave the United States with immense excess reserves. This was precisely the ratio that Britain had put forward at Geneva. However, the Americans would leave countries free to choose when or if they would adhere. The Americans also offered other schemes that were meant to achieve both stable monetary conditions and higher prices.[29] Arthur Schlesinger reports that Roosevelt himself offered the French a tripartite stabilization agreement;[30] Feis explains that while the foreign missions came and went there were talks about dollar stabilization. Though it was hard to tell what the president wanted, his comments and those of his officials led the British and French to infer that it was possible – almost probable – that the dollar would soon be repegged to gold.[31] Nothing was said about Roosevelt's desire to improve America's bargaining position.

Raymond Moley was close to Roosevelt during the confused days of April and May 1933. When he set down his recollections in 1940 he had long since fallen out with the president, and his account may reflect this fact. If we take his record at face value, however, it suggests that Roosevelt was playing a very devious game indeed. Moley tells us that the president was "in no hurry to stabilise until he was sure he was going to get the best bargain there was to get."[32] That is, Roosevelt wanted to get the lowest possible rate for the dollar relative to the pound. In April, Moley explains, four dollars would have been satisfactory; by June, something better was hoped for, and Roosevelt was annoyed with his emissaries because they had become too interested in stabilization; what was needed, he thought, was a good fright, so that the American negotiators would bargain harder.[33] The more frightened and nervous the French and the other Continentals, the better for the Americans.[34]

If Roosevelt really was playing this sort of game he was more Machiavellian than his biographers have thought and more confused than his admirers have been prepared to admit. Whatever the cause, there is no doubt about the pattern.

Many years later Leith-Ross recorded a rather gloomy picture of the Americans' administrative arrangements:

the absence of any settled administrative machinery . . . no one at the Treasury responsible for the exchanges: the Federal Reserve Board . . . practically not functioning . . . the Federal Reserve Bank in New York . . . not favoured by the new administration . . . The Principal of the Brains Trust with whom I had to deal was Professor Moley, who had been a professor of Criminology at a girls' college . . . almost completely lacking in detailed knowledge of many of the questions which we discussed and interested only in the political aspects of any proposal. With him were Dr. Feis . . . Mr. Tugwell and Mr. Taussig, all competent economists but with little practical experience of finance.[35]

It is not an attractive portrait.

MacDonald left Washington on 26 April. For some days Leith-Ross remained behind, reaching London only on 11 May. He was working hard to convince the Americans that they would have to do something about the management of the exchanges. By 24 April he thought they might do something helpful. James Warburg, one of Roosevelt's advisers, came to him with an unexpectedly comprehensive proposal – personal views that Warburg hoped the American authorities might accept. Warburg suggested "*de facto* stabilisation" of the pound, franc, and dollar. The pound would be at $3.50, and the dollar and franc at gold par. There would be equalization funds in all three countries, and these would cooperate closely.[36]

The Treasury was sufficiently perplexed to respond at great length. It did not like the fact that Warburg was an unofficial emissary. What if he came back with the news that his views had been rejected or, "still worse, that his principals accept them heartily subject only to the minor point that the sterling-dollar exchange must be 3.90 or 4 dollars or something of that kind"? It insisted that everything was conditional on a satisfactory debt settlement. It said that no rate over $3.50 could be tolerated given the fact that in spite of depreciation, tariffs, and controls on capital exports Britain's payments were still not balanced. Further, Britain's interest rates were the lowest of all three countries: "If management of the exchanges should require alteration in interest rates you may be certain that in our case it will be an alteration upwards and to the disadvantage of our traders." Nevertheless, the Treasury was so eager to keep the dollar at par with the franc that it was "sympathetic" to the Warburg plan. It also thought that if debts were settled the mere publication of such an agreement would tend to restrain the flow of hot money and might even help raise prices. It therefore suggested that if the war debts were satisfactorily settled Leith-Ross might aim at a de facto stabilization for the term of the conference only. America would keep the dollar at par with the franc; Britain would try to keep the pound in the region $3.40–$3.50. If gold prices should fall, however, each country would be free, after notifying the others, to "modify its parity." [37]

Leith-Ross had thought that the Treasury was so worried by the confusion the United States had caused that it thought

some such arrangement . . . urgently desirable . . . that you wanted the United States if not to return to gold at least to use their resources to keep the dollar as stable as possible . . . the topsy-turvy situation is that until recently the Americans were pressing us to stabilise, they have now given this up and *we* have to press them to support the dollar from speculative fall . . . If we succeed in convincing them that something should be done, I feel it most advisable that we should take similar action and I think you must be prepared for this. Alternative seems a general nose dive of currencies which we must make every effort to avert . . . Difficulty about dealing with principals is that there are none except President.[38]

But by 28 April the Treasury thought a general nose dive much less likely. Though still hoping that the Federal Reserve and the Bank could cooperate and that the Americans would use their enormous resources to support the dollar, London had become a little more confident and a good deal more reluctant to give up "our own independence of action." Conceivably the conference might produce "such general agreement as to liberal monetary policy and raising of prices as to bring into immediate view stabilization *de facto* or otherwise of leading currencies now off gold."[39] But that happy dénouement might or might not occur.

The French representatives learned of Warburg's plan on 26 April. Now, however, Warburg proposed that relative to the old gold parities the dollar stand at a discount of 15 percent. The president, Warburg told Leith-Ross the next day, was "prepared to agree to co-operate to avoid fluctuations between dollars, francs, and pounds." The Americans thought a four-dollar pound about right. Warburg wanted a tripartite stabilization fund, about which the French were less than enthusiastic.[40]

Neither the Treasury nor Leith-Ross was prepared to accept the American proposal. Leith-Ross thought it "impossible for us to co-operate in pegging dollars at wrong level"; either the United States would attract still more gold, repeating French policy and making impossible any reestablishment of the gold standard, or it would pile up immense balances abroad. The Treasury repeated that "without satisfactory settlement of debts and an assured balance of payments no question of stabilisation can arise"; it observed that to depreciate the dollar artificially by 15 percent would drive much of Europe off gold and generate so much ill feeling that the conference would be very hard to manage. Still worried about the risk that other countries would leave gold, the Bank and the Treasury were willing to contemplate a temporary arrangement by which the Americans would prevent the dollar from depreciating further pending the conference while Britain would try to keep the pound above $3.40. Nevertheless, the Treasury reminded Leith-Ross that London might be unable to do so if the large short-term balances left London. In mid-April London's gold reserves covered only one-third of these liabilities.[41] Chamberlain disliked the Warburg plan even more than his officials did. He thought that if the Americans devalued on gold by 15 percent the conference would be not merely difficult but "quite hopeless."[42]

In due course Warburg reported that though Roosevelt did not want to see the dollar fall more than 20 percent he thought that "if every country was going to manage its own operations it was not necessary to commit himself to [any] arrangement at the moment." The Americans, Leith-Ross reported, would take up the question once more through Treasury or Federal Reserve "if and when they have formulated a definite policy."[43]

The Foreign Office found the situation "no less remarkable than disquieting." The Federal Reserve was out of action, and the American Treasury opposed American monetary policy; the president was advised by "two dogmatic and rather overbearing professors (Moley and Tugwell) while along the edge of this constellation there moves the figure of the Banker, Mr. Warburg, who holds no official position but nevertheless seems entrusted with the negotiations . . . the position . . . seems to denote a certain lack of stability and responsibility."[44]

The Americans were certainly inclined to see connections that Whitehall had failed to observe. The American ambassador, for instance, believed that, because of the Ottawa Agreements and the various trade treaties Britain had been devising, with respect to tariffs and quotas the British were in a tactically weak position. Dollar depreciation gave a weapon, he observed, with which the other countries could be frightened into pressing the British toward "mutual stabilisation." The president should grant concessions on war debts as rewards for cooperation in the "broad programme envisaged for the World Economic Conference."[45] What this program might be the ambassador does not say and the historian cannot readily discover. One has the uneasy suspicion that it may be no more than the somewhat abstract resolutions that the American delegation proposed to place before the London assembly.

In January the experts had proposed a "customs truce" – "a preliminary measure, pending the signature of agreements for the reduction of tariffs and other obstacles to trade." In the weeks preceding the conference American diplomacy mightily exerted itself toward such a truce. To Britain and Europe such a truce seemed worse than useless because it did nothing to solve the basic problem, which was America's strong current account. The French in particular disliked the idea. In May Charles Rist, the eminent economic counselor, told the first secretary of the American embassy that the monetary question was much more vital than the tariff question. Deladier, Bonnet, and Moret had just told him that there must soon be a tripartite agreement for provisional stabilization of the dollar and of sterling "at rates which must not differ importantly from those values at which *de jure* stabilisation will subsequently be achieved." Without such an agreement the conference was certain to fail. Further, Rist said, the Bank of France would not undertake open market operations for the sake of expanding credit and shedding gold.[46] So much for the understandings on easy credit and floating currencies that Chamberlain and Bonnet had reached in mid-March.

At once the French government raised the question of currency stabilization with the Americans and the British. The French embassy told the State Department that Paris had been extremely interested in the Washington proposals the U.S. officials had made "in view of establishing a tripartite monetary co-operation . . . The French Government is firmly convinced that the work of the Conference greatly depends upon what will be done in order to remove the uncertainty that exists today as to the future of two currencies as important as the Pound and the Dollar . . . conversations should start immediately between the American, British, and French Governments and . . . Central Banks."[47]

To the Treasury the real trouble was that there was such serious Anglo-American disagreement about the right value for the dollar. Given that, they saw little chance of any cooperation on exchange policy.[48] Roosevelt was saying publicly that it was indispensable to stabilize currencies, and privately Warburg was advocating a meeting of the three central banks. The aim was exchange stabilization. Bonnet tells us that he found these developments reassuring.[49] The Treasury cannot have been equally reassured, and the French did not remain cheerful for very long.

Because Leith-Ross had then left Washington Warburg at once sent for Kenneth Bewley, the embassy financial adviser. The French government, he reported, was now willing and very eager to cooperate in a tripartite scheme for stabilizing the exchanges. Warburg proposed that such arrangements should be made for a succession of three-month periods. Each government could withdraw, or change its exchange rate, on one month's notice. Warburg thought they might begin with the existing rates – the dollar depreciated 15 percent below gold par, the pound at about $3.40 gold or $4.00 paper, and the franc naturally at gold par. The Bank of England and the Bank of France would each be authorized to spend up to $500 million on support operations. Monick, Warburg said, seemed to like the idea; if Britain and France would accept the broad outlines Warburg thought he "could probably get the President to agree to it."[50]

Meanwhile, on 15 May the French had told the British that they cared passionately about stabilization. They wanted "immediate conversations between the three governments."[51] The two central banks had begun to discuss possible plans – among them, the Warburg scheme. But neither bank believed there was any point in discussing technical schemes for exchange management without knowing what monetary and credit policies each government would follow. Everyone knew that the U.K. and U.S. governments agreed on general policy – higher and more stable prices and steady exchange rates. But what steps did the Americans propose to take and when? No one knew. "If exchange stabilisation is attempted by itself without this knowledge or any agreement among the three countries on this subject, it may be defeated by lack of co-ordination of credit policy."[52] There was no point in discussing schemes or giving suggestions to Warburg; what everyone needed was a tripartite discussion on monetary policy, not exchanges. Also, of course, the new Warburg plan still involved an undervalued dollar. On that score alone it was unacceptable.[53]

The Foreign Office warned that "the French will not budge without stabilisation of currencies." The Treasury for its part observed that France was probably worried about "checking fluctuations in the value of currencies pending the World Conference." Britain had successfully kept sterling steady relative to the franc; as the problem was the dollar, the Treasury would agree to talks as long as the Americans also agreed.[54]

Later Leith-Ross wrote of the Warburg plan:

both the Bank of France and Bank of England turned it down as quite impracticable. Our view was that it was ridiculous for the United States to obtain credits to support the dollar and that they had only to make a normal use of their immense gold reserves and allow gold to go out, in order to keep the external value of the dollar up to any point they liked. The French are of course, keen on monetary stabilization, but the Bank of France shared our criticism of Warburg's proposals.[55]

However great the administrative confusion at Washington, the British and French officials can hardly be blamed if they took seriously such concrete proposals as emanated from the American experts. Neither in London nor in Paris would such proposals have been made unless they were meant to be taken seriously; in neither capital would the head of state have announced that it was necessary to stabilize currencies while privately contriving to destabilize as many as possible.

Early in May MacDonald told the Cabinet of his Washington adventures. Roosevelt, he said, thought a gold standard had no political value and was therefore not very keen on it. He was interested, however, in a silver standard, which would be politically useful. He thought the dollar had been overvalued before its departure from gold, but he was most anxious to avoid instability between the dollar, and pound, and the franc. The details of a plan, Roosevelt had said, could be left to experts; the U.S. Treasury, MacDonald reported, did not seem to have worked out these things in any detail, and the United States had no clear policy.[56] Soon thereafter the Cabinet must have seen Leith-Ross's memorandum, in which the Treasury official noticed a broad area of Anglo-American agreement. Both governments agreed that through central-bank action prices should be raised. As to the reestablishment of an international gold standard, the American position "is now almost precisely what ours was last January, viz., that before an international monetary standard can be re-established there must be a radical revision of central bank practices, with a view to ensuring that the gold standard does not depress prices."[57] The Day-Williams view, which had caused so much trouble with the Preparatory Committee of Experts, had been jettisoned. The relief in Whitehall must have been great.

Silver, however, would be a problem. If the Americans were to insist on some measures to raise the silver price there would be monetary disarray in Mexico, China, and India; admittedly the silver countries would automatically gain extra reserves in terms of dollars, but these countries were not the ones where reserves were especially needed. In other words, a silver standard would do nothing to ease the plight of the exchange-control countries in central Europe and Latin America. These were the countries for whose aid the Treasury had devised the schemes to mobilize redundant gold. It still thought that an International Credit Institution, as adumbrated in the Draft Annotated Agenda, was the "main hope of success" as a price-raising device.[58] Would the United States give up gold to such a body? And would it reduce its own trade barriers enough to prevent all redistributed gold from promptly draining back to the United States?

As the dollar continued to fall relative to the pound and the gold currencies, the Treasury again began to worry about its course. Leith-Ross and Phillips agreed that deliberate dollar depreciation would cause trouble for British exports. It would also greatly increase the difficulties of securing any equilibrium on the international exchanges. It might possibly produce a general collapse of the weaker gold currencies as hot money fled from them. "What we should like," they wrote, "is some co-operation to maintain the relations of the three currencies pending the conclusion of the Conference." The French had already begun to press for this.[59] But the Treasury saw little point in discussing such a thing, as they thought the United States would not be willing to help. As for the gold standard, they still maintained that Britain should not discuss any general return thereto or commit itself as to the date on which sterling might return to gold. The gold standard was desirable, but it would not work until prices had risen substantially. Fortunately the United States was not pressing Britain to do anything about gold.[60]

MacDonald had established a Cabinet committee to work out a British policy for the conference. Its members heard about the Treasury worries, though they do not appear to have discussed them.[61] At first, it appears, everyone simply assumed that monetary policy was already settled along Treasury lines. The Dominions and the other sterling countries were never mentioned. The gold countries were not discussed. But on 23 May the prime minister began to insist upon some sort of currency stabilization.

MacDonald reported a trustworthy correspondent had told him that foreign governments would insist on "monetary stabilisation" as an "essential preliminary to tariff reduction and other aids to world trade revival." Hence the conference would fail unless there were some early agreement on stabilization. MacDonald might have reflected that by raising its own tariffs and elaborating its own food quotas his own government was setting rather a poor example to the world, but his thoughts were running along other tracks. Almost certainly he was influenced by his long and disheartening experience with the disarmament talks that had just collapsed in disarray.[62] He must have found it almost impossible to contemplate another conference that would produce merely bitterness and confusion. He must also have been worried, and with good reason, about the French. So often in the early 1930s France had been the stumbling block. Again they were adopting an inflexible position that would probably produce disaster.

Chamberlain did his best to change MacDonald's mind. The chancellor argued that no one knew what Roosevelt would do but that everyone knew Cordell Hull would have no power to fix exchange rates. Leith-Ross explained that the Continental countries would certainly press for de jure stabilization – a full-fledged gold standard. MacDonald retorted that he would urge Roosevelt to disclose his intentions with respect to war debts and stabilization, so that, "if possible, some Anglo-American understanding could be reached before June 2," when the conference would open in London.[63]

The result was a cable that seems to have annoyed Roosevelt's advisers. Whitehall told Washington that unless it was clearly understood beforehand just how far Roosevelt intended to let the dollar plummet the conference could make no progress on monetary agreements. It was suggested that representatives of Britain and France should meet with someone empowered to speak for the United States so as to agree upon a temporary stabilization of the three currencies. MacDonald added a personal plea, hoping that Roosevelt would instruct his representatives as to the rate at which he would be willing to stabilize the dollar,[64] presumably in relation to gold. On 27 May Sir Ronald Lindsay gave Moley an aide-mémoire that put the Treasury view. Moley explained that though Warburg had wanted the president to formulate his exchange policy the president had not been willing to do so.[65]

Bowley was told that the United States would try to keep the dollar from rising or falling "at least until the World Conference opens" but that it could not yet say anything definite about its future credit policy. Warburg's scheme, Bewley gathered, was "now right out of the picture," but the Washington authorities would discuss the matter with Governor George Harrison of the New York Federal Reserve Bank before the governor sailed for Britain. London had asked that the United States should send "a representative or representatives empowered to speak for the United States on matters of credit policy."[66] Although the Americans regarded Harrison as that representative, London would soon learn that he had been given no such powers.

Roosevelt agreed to send O. M. W. Sprague, James Warburg, and George Harrison to London, but he gave them no written instructions. Moley reports that the president told them to shun stabilization like the plague. Feis writes, "as far as is known, President Roosevelt did not give Sprague or Harrison or Warburg any definite or written instructions."[67] When the main American delegation reached London just before the conference, Sprague and his colleagues explained that they had said the American government had only de facto stabilization in mind. The idea was to keep exchange sufficiently stable for the conference to proceed. They were not authorized, they said, to discuss permanent stabilization.[68] But by 10 June, Moley claims, Norman and Moret were making a "peremptory demand for immediate and definite stabilisation."[69] One wonders how Moley, still in the United States and not a member of either official or subsidiary delegation, could have known this. One also wonders whether Moley, whose technical knowledge had not impressed Leith-Ross, understood the difference between a temporary agreement to stabilize exchanges for the term of the conference and a permanent commitment with respect to exchange rates. France was certainly pressing for the former and hoping for the latter; Britain, it is reasonably clear, was prepared to cooperate in the former. If we are to judge by R. S. Sayers's account Norman went no further. Had he done so he would have been going far beyond the policy of the British government.[70]

Before May had ended the Cabinet's policy committee had devised a monetary strategy, and the full Cabinet had approved this strategy as a basis for the conference. Britain should stand by the Ottawa policy of cheap and easy credit for the sake of higher wholesale prices. As for the exchanges, permanent stabilization must "await the restoration of conditions for the satisfactory working of an international standard . . . pending the consideration of these matters by the Conference, every effort should be made to ensure reasonable stability. But each country must separately decide when, or if, to return to gold."[71] These decisions must have formed the basis for the tripartite conversations that shortly began.

The Economic Advisory Council Committee on Economic Information had been pressing for a general de facto devaluation vis-à-vis gold and a stabilization of the dollar-pound exchange rate. It believed that the United States would welcome such an arrangement because it would obviate chaos in the foreign exchanges while putting Britain back on gold, though not at the 1931 parity. By 16 May, when the committee made these suggestions, the Treasury already knew that the Americans were not sufficiently well organized to consider such a complicated proposal, that France would dislike it, that Roosevelt did not like the idea of exchange stabilization at all, and that for a stable dollar-pound rate he would exact an unacceptable price. The committee report, therefore, did not affect the course of events.

The reader may wonder why Britain could not use the Exchange Equalisation Account to hold the set of exchange rates. One might have argued that the speculative movements out of dollars and certain Continental currencies were exactly the sorts of short-run disturbances that the Account existed to offset. In fact, the Account was used in this way: It held the pound steady on the franc for several months prior to the conference. But its resources were limited, and the movements out of the dollar were very large. Susan Howson has discovered that it was because the Account would have had to absorb so many dollars that the Treasury would not support the dollar in this way.[72] Further, such transactions exposed the Account to very severe risks. Dr. Howson believes that the Treasury was not overwhelmingly concerned about these, though it did hope to avoid or control them. What if the franc *were* to leave gold? What if Paris introduced exchange control? The Account might be lumbered with useless accumulations of franc and dollar balances. If exchange rates moved inconveniently these balances would depreciate. There would be capital losses. Holding paper currencies, the Account could not convert paper into gold at a fixed price.

We have already observed that in his magisterial *Age of Roosevelt* Arthur Schlesinger says MacDonald did not understand Roosevelt's intentions with respect to the exchanges. Schlesinger goes on to say that Britain's Cabinet was disunited with respect to the conference.[73] There is something to this charge, though probably not much. Certainly the prime minister hoped for more than the chancellor. We have noticed that Chamberlain saw little point in trying to fix exchange rates or in negotiating with the Americans on this topic. Certainly he expected little of the gathering. In mid-May he wrote of the "awful" World Conference. It was difficult, he observed, to see how "anything valuable can come out of it."[74] But MacDonald was attracted by international conferences, and Chamberlain, especially after his Ottawa adventures, was not.

More important than the question of Cabinet disunity is the question of policy. In this respect Schlesinger is misleading. He writes of Birtain's determination to use the "arsenal of preferential clauses and quotas to protect the sterling bloc."[75] It is certainly true that the more protectionist ministers would have been most unwilling to dismantle the preferential framework so recently erected, but there is absolutely no indication in the documents that in Whitehall anyone connected the preferences and quotas with sterling or with the sterling area. Britain's agricultural quotas were meant to protect its own farmers. In monetary matters, its rulers brooded not about the sterling countries but about the level of commodity prices. Their concern, in other words, was exactly the same as Roosevelt's. Certainly it is most unfortunate that in late May Ramsay MacDonald decided to plague the president about the exchanges. But this question would not have gone away; America's own action had put it on the agenda, and France would have kept it there even if Whitehall had said nothing about it. Rather than castigating Britain's leaders Schlesinger would do better to criticize his own protagonist for adopting a series of tactical gambits that so confused the situation as to make it impossible for this underlying Anglo-American agreement to issue in any positive program for monetary reform.

Freidel offers a more detailed and comprehensive account of the background to Roosevelt's conference policy. He explains how the president tackled sharply in a nationalist direction between the departure of the British ministers and the opening of the conference. Thanks to Freidel's narrative, the reader of the 1970s can understand these developments much more clearly than could the participants during the 1930s. With respect to the purposes of the conference itself, however, Freidel is less helpful. In his account of the preliminary discussions he does not tell his readers that the conference was meant to raise price levels. Indeed, when Roosevelt turned to price-raising measures after he had destroyed the conference, Freidel says that the president had tried to give the gathering "a new main objective,"[76] although we know that this objective had been prefigured explicitly from the beginning. Nevertheless Freidel's remark is illuminating, though in an unintended way. Relying as he does on the American documents, he shows us not only that Roosevelt and his advisers had never learned what the conference was for but also that the permanent officials in Washington had forgotten its original purpose. Further, Freidel reveals how completely official Washington had misunderstood Whitehall's plans and hopes. It is no wonder that the Americans and the British were unable to coordinate their plans.

5. *The Empire, the sterling area, and the conference preparations*

We have seen that in 1931 the Treasury developed a theory of the sterling area in which friendly cooperation was possible, if correctly channeled through central banks, but in which primary responsibility for sterling policy must rest wholly and solely with the United Kingdom. It is therefore not surprising that in the months of conference preparation the other sterling countries were hardly involved. The Dominions were neither consulted with respect to the coming conference nor elaborately informed as to its preparation. As a Dominions Office official explained in April 1933, "we have sent to the Dominions copies of the two reports by Leith-Ross and Phillips . . . but there has been no opportunity, as yet, to take up with the Treasury any of the broad questions of policy connected with the World Economic Conference."[1] The Indian authorities were somewhat better informed. Strakosch and Mant were members of the Council of India, and Sir Cecil Kisch of the India Office helped the Treasury to devise a plan for international credits.[2] In the Dominions Office and the Treasury it might be argued that consultations were unnecessary: The officials already knew that India and the Dominions were at least as eager to raise prices as were Chamberlain and Roosevelt. The newspapers were often loud in their demands for a coordinated sterling policy of monetary reconstruction. In the Treasury such demands were ignored. However, one could not altogether ignore the importunities of the Nordic countries, who were anxious to coordinate their policies with Britain's.

In December 1932 the Foreign Office learned that the Norwegian minister had proposed a preliminary gathering of all the countries that were off gold. This would be a preparation for the general monetary conference. The Swedes also favored such a conference. Minuting was nervous. Everyone thought it premature, and it was uneasily observed that the Dominions would have to come too.[3] In December, also, Britain was informed that the Scandinavian powers, plus Belgium and Holland, would meet early in December to consider the conference; eager to work closely with Britain, they wanted to know what Britain's policy would be.

Only in mid-January 1933 was any reply forthcoming. The Scandinavian countries were then told that as yet nothing could be said about policy but that after the Preparatory Commission had published its report "it may be possible for His Majesty's Government in the United Kingdom to establish contacts with other Governments, and particularly the Governments of those countries whose currencies are largely linked up with sterling." The Swedish government responded that it would receive any information with interest,[4] but it does not appear that anything was told the Scandinavians. In May they asked once more and were told simply that Britain agreed "generally" with the experts' Draft Annotated Agenda and that on monetary questions it adhered to the Ottawa Conference declarations.[5] Meeting with Holland and Belgium at the end of May, the Scandinavians simply announced that the five countries were also in general agreement with the experts, especially the recommendations "which are about the necessity of arriving at a definitive stabilisation of the different moneys."[6] As the belga and guilder were already under stress from the American devaluation, this statement was hardly surprising. Having associated themselves with Belgium and Holland in the Oslo Powers grouping, the Scandinavian states could no longer align their monetary statements purely on British lines, whatever their own desires or intentions may have been.

As for the Dominions, they learned in July 1932 that a conference "to stabilize world commodity prices" would occur. In August 1932 they were told that the League of Nations would act on the Lausanne recommendations.[7] But on monetary affairs they were not consulted, and in the records of the Ottawa Conference (21 July–21 August 1932) the coming World Conference has left no trace. Britain did not devise her "Ottawa policy" of cheap and easy credit with an eye to any subsequent meeting. In part that policy expressed the already-decided commitments of Chamberlain and the Treasury, and in part it was meant to head off the more importunate and inflation-minded Empire leaders.[8] In November 1932 and January 1933 the Dominions received the Treasury accounts of the experts' meetings.[9] They were told of Bonnet's visit to London after that visit had occurred and of Ramsay MacDonald's trip to Washington eight days before he was to set out.[10] They were, however, given a good deal of detail about the Bonnet-Chamberlain talks, when they were told the two men had agreed that higher prices, cheap money, and easy credit were all desirable.[11] Early in May they were sent MacDonald's public statement with respect to the Washington gathering.[12]

It does not appear, however, that the Treasury, the Cabinet, or the Economic Advisory Council asked themselves how the conference might relate to the sterling area. Of course they all knew that their price-raising monetary policies would help the sterling countries, because all these countries specialized in the export of primary products. Perhaps this link was too obvious to be made explicit. Certainly at Ottawa it had been well aired. But thereafter it was rarely mentioned, except in connection with Chamberlain's plans for output restriction. These too were meant to raise prices.

In February 1933, MacDonald and Thomas were told that the Dominions would like to splice a conference of primary producers onto the World Economic Conference. Leith-Ross told the Dominions Office that the plan was not a good one. There was, he thought, some case for a group of such conferences – one for each product. Indeed the government still hoped to arrange the international meat conferences that had been adumbrated at Ottawa. "But regulation of production is at best a palliative and what the world really needs is an increase in production. This largely depends on the solution of outstanding major political problems and on securing international agreement for the relaxation of tariffs, the adoption of more liberal monetary policies, and the abrogation of exchange controls, and so on." A conference or conferences of primary producers would do nothing to assist and "would almost inevitably resolve itself into a series of demands for help."[13] The Foreign Office concurred.

The Empire countries had little by way of domestic money markets. Only South Africa had a proper central bank; Australia had an imperfect approximation; India, New Zealand, and Canada had nothing. Not that these countries were restrictionist in monetary matters. Canada's government was eager to reduce interest rates, both by refinancing its debt and by cajoling the nation's banks and near banks. Late in 1932 the Canadian government used the creaking machinery of "Finance Act rediscounting" to force unwanted excess reserves upon the commercial banks. But before they could take part in any concerted plan of monetary expansion the Empire countries would have to invent a series of central banks. Even if they did so, they were too small to make much impact on the deflation that the Treasury knew to be a worldwide problem. And the overseas capitals had no financial experts – at least, so Whitehall thought. To Chamberlain and his Cabinet colleagues the Empire was involved with the conference almost entirely in relation to quantitative controls – measures that the chancellor wanted but that the Dominions certainly did not.

Late in April S. M. Bruce, Australia's high commissioner, asked Thomas to convene a meeting. On 1 May he and Sir Thomas Wilford of New Zealand met Chamberlain, Walter Runciman, Thomas, and Elliot. Bruce and Wilford pressed for a permanent interimperial committee that could devise a policy for primary products. Chamberlain said that no "monetary manipulation" would raise wholesale prices; there must be "some regulation of supplies." But it was agreed to form a committee, to invite South Africa and Canada, and to meet again on 4 May.[14]

The Treasury thought that the whole thing was rather absurd. In the Dominions Office Sir Edward Harding minuted:

Sir F. Phillips said that he did not think there was any special point in discussing with Dominion representatives at present the question of "monetary manipulation" (to use the phrase used by the Chancellor of the Exchequer this morning) though when the Dominion experts on this question reached London the Treasury would be very glad, and indeed think it essential, to have discussions with them on the line to be taken at the World Economic Conference. It was accordingly agreed that the best plan would be to start on the "economic" side of the Conference.[15]

Hence the committee, which met twice, brooded only on primary products. And it accomplished nothing. The Dominions Office had been wondering whether to tell the Dominions more about the conference. But Sir Geoffrey Whiskard minuted sadly: "I am bound to confess that I am not sure that the United Kingdom has any policy to which we could attempt to get the Dominions to adhere."[16]

The Americans were more forthcoming. When he was arranging his preconference consultations, President Roosevelt invited the Dominions to Washington. From Canada, Prime Minister Bennett actually went. New Zealand regretted that its government had no time to respond. Australia said that it was enormously interested in price restoration, especially for primary products, and that though it would retain complete freedom to fix its exchange rate it would avoid any competitive depreciation of its currency. In London the Dominions Office certainly saw these messages. So did the Foreign Office. And the Treasury? If so, no trace has survived.[17]

7

United Kingdom policy at the World Monetary and Economic Conference

This chapter, like the preceding one, concentrates upon the monetary side of the World Conference that gathered in June 1933. We are chiefly interested in the relations between Britain and the overseas sterling area, especially India and the Dominions. To make sense of these inter-imperial interactions we need to follow certain developments at the conference itself. The first section of the chapter therefore traces the increasingly odd behavior of the Americans and the increasingly vigorous importunities of the French. In the second section we shall see how Empire delegates, ill informed but concerned about Britain's policy, demanded a change of direction and how Chamberlain devised a verbal response for the sake of Empire solidarity.

1. *Problems with the French and the Americans*

The conference assembled on 12 June 1933. There was the usual mixture of plenary sessions, committee and subcommittee work, and informal discussion behind the scenes. Outside the conference proper were the conversations on currency stabilization. These conversations were conducted between treasuries and central banks. Only Britain, France, and the United States were involved. The purpose was not to peg the three moneys permanently to one another, or to gold, but rather to devise a formula for their temporary alignment during the term of the conference only.

The interbank conversations were conducted against a background of gathering gloom. The dollar was depreciating steadily against gold, and speculators were moving funds from the smaller gold-standard countries of Europe. The pound was appreciating relative to the dollar, as the Exchange Equalisation Account was trying to maintain an exchange rate of 88 gold francs to the pound. In April the Treasury had thought that a four-dollar pound would be intolerable; by 16 June it was prepared to accept this rate at least for a short time. To strengthen its power to manage the market, in May the Account's sterling resources had been augmented, rising from £150 million to £200 million. Also, some gold was shed from the Account to the Issue Department of the Bank. But if too much gold crossed the Channel from the Continent life could quickly become very difficult for the Account.

The United States did not honor its promise to steady the dollar during the conference. The American currency sagged, and sometimes lurched, downward, whereas sterling was held at or near 85 francs. Hence the terror of the Continentals and, for opposite reasons, the rage of the sterling countries, especially in the Empire.

The United Kingdom government placed its monetary policy before the conference partly through public statements in plenary and committee sessions and partly through private conversations. In matters of monetary and exchange policy the line was established by Neville Chamberlain when he addressed the conference in plenary session on 14 June. In accord with Treasury and Cabinet policy he spoke with extreme circumspection. There should be immediate measures to avoid the currency fluctuations that capital flows might otherwise cause. Eventually there should be a gold standard but only after prices had risen, debts and tariffs had been adjusted, and tariffs had been reduced. In the future, he said, the gold standard should be so administered as to prevent the price of gold from fluctuating. Later the United Kingdom introduced a resolution calling for cheap, plentiful credit in the interest of higher commodity prices and for central-bank cooperation to this end. Supporting this proposal, Sir Henry Strakosch spoke for India, S. M. Bruce for Australia, and N. C. Havenga for South Africa. R. B. Bennett, for Canada, adopted a more complicated position. He insisted that Britain and the United States must agree on a de facto stabilization of exchange rates; if a common price-raising policy could be adopted, they should also stabilize vis-à-vis the gold franc. Canada, he said, would then try to stabilize its own dollar, which had been off the gold standard since late 1928 and fluctuating vis-à-vis the American and British currencies since September 1931.[1] In private, the Empire delegates told the chancellor that in general they agreed with his statement, though "on some points" they would have been inclined to go farther.[2]

By 20 June Chamberlain thought that the prospects of the conference were gloomy indeed. The United States held the key to the situation, he told the other British delegates, but it declined to play. No one could speak with authority as to President Roosevelt's views. They would have to wait until the president's confidant, Professor Moley, arrived from New York.[3]

By 15 June the central bank and Treasury representatives had almost completed their plan. Although the Foreign Office knew nothing of the details, rumors of their scheme had reached Roosevelt, who cabled Hull, reminding him that the president must approve or disapprove any proposal for currency stabilization. There were "wild reports," he said, "about stabilization at some fixed rate."[4] The next day Hull cabled the representatives' plan "for limiting fluctuation of the exchange during the time that the Conference is endeavouring to lay the foundations for ultimate monetary stability . . . The arrangement is limited to the period of the Conference and is designed solely to facilitate the work of the Conference."

The experts proposed a middle rate of four dollars to the pound, with a 3 percent spread. Each of the three central banks was prepared to spend up to 3 million ounces of gold to control the exchanges. France would remain on the pure gold standard. Britain had agreed to this rate most unwillingly, insisting on the right to ask for a downward adjustment of up to ten cents after a fortnight, even if it had not yet lost 3 million ounces of gold. The agreement would lapse as soon as any of the three central banks had spent this much gold or if any part of the agreement were to become public.[5] The American banker, James Warburg, later explained, "we do not feel that we can propose any suggestions of our own until our attitude toward exchange stability is clear."[6] He and his associates reiterated that the agreement was temporary. They explained that, if Roosevelt wished, the spread could be widened from 3 percent either way, to 5 percent.[7] But the president, though prepared to consider a middle value of $4.15 and a ten-cent spread, preferred to "avoid even a tentative commitment." "Too much importance," he cabled, "is attached to exchange stability by banker-influenced cabinets."[8]

The proposal leaked, apparently causing the exchange to move in favor of the dollar. Concomitantly there was a fall in American commodity prices. Feis suggests that these developments, plus Britain's partial default and France's total default on 15 June, hardened Roosevelt's resolve: he would insist on a better exchange rate, and he would not let France force the United States back onto the gold standard.[9] Moley reports that Roosevelt thought ill of a four-dollar pound in mid-June, when he would have preferred $4.20. If Sprague, James Cox, Warburg, and Harrison could not do better, Moley would have to go to London.[10]

Roosevelt told Hull that he thought "we should avoid even a tentative commitment in regard to any definite program by this government to control fluctuations in the dollar." Hull was to work for the "larger and more permanent program,"[11] presumably the one described in the president's instructions to his delegation. Hull interpreted Roosevelt to mean that the delegation should exert its effort "in the direction alone of permanent and universal stabilization,"[12] because in an earlier message Roosevelt had reminded Hull that "the broad principle we advocated in preliminary discussions in Washington was based on a re-establishment of currencies based on gold or gold and silver by all nations and not by three or four only."[13] Hull claimed that because the American delegation had already introduced the relevant resolutions, calling for the ultimate stabilization of every unstable currency, all was well. But such resolutions, of course, could be of no effect even in the long run. And in the short run they did nothing to restrain speculation against the gold currencies, to stem the fall of the dollar relative to these currencies and to the pound, or to facilitate discussions about tariffs and quotas.

In his instructions Roosevelt had told Hull and the other delegates to work, inter alia, for "the laying of the groundwork for an adequate and enduring international monetary standard." To this end, he provided draft resolutions, which, he said, had been so drawn as to meet the attitudes of other nations as well as the Americans. One resolution related to credit policy: it suggested that central banks should cooperate, that there should be plenty of credit for "sound enterprise," and that synchronized government expenditure would help recovery. Another related to the exchanges.[14]

With respect to the use of gold and the reduction of gold-reserve ratios, the statement embodied the relevant recommendations of the Preparatory Commission and certainly expressed the desires of the United Kingdom Treasury. But it said nothing about redistribution of gold and nothing about the possibility or probability of moving back to gold either in the long run or in the short. It extended no hope to the exchange-control countries. The other American resolutions, on a tariff truce, the removal of exchange controls, and the gradual movement to freer trade, were no more helpful with respect to the reconstruction of a workable gold standard of the sort the United Kingdom Treasury was prepared to contemplate.

It is hardly surprising that James Warburg thought it desirable to ask for sub rosa assistance. Would Roosevelt authorize the Federal Reserve Bank of New York to act in the exchange market so as to limit the fluctuations of the dollar?[15] Eventually Roosevelt said that he thought the Federal Reserve might keep the pound under $4.25,[16] but by then the exchange rate had already moved to $4.42 and the gold countries were both frightened and angry.

Already on 18 June it had been rumored that Roosevelt would reject the central bankers' plan. Though they told him that they would work for a better bargain on the exchange rate, the American negotiators begged Roosevelt to endorse the proposed temporary scheme, "lest the United States he charged with backing down on its implied commitment to stabilise temporarily."[17]

At this point, the president had decided to take a yachting holiday. On 20 June Moley flew from Washington to meet the president at sea. Roosevelt insisted that Moley should go to London, not to negotiate but to act as a conduit between London and the presidency. Roosevelt still opposed any stabilization agreement, even a temporary one, but he was prepared to tolerate some sort of thing that would calm the gold countries and steady the dollar, so long as the United States would not have to ship gold and so long as American prices continued their "magnificent rise." According to Moley, Roosevelt then said, "you know, if nothing else can be worked out, I'd even consider stabilising at a middle point of 4.15, with a high and low of 4.25 and 4.05. I'm not crazy about it but I think I'd go that far."[18] Reading this remark and Moley's surreal comment,[19] one can only conclude that the president was ill-informed.

Meanwhile in London, Ramsay MacDonald was talking to Cordell Hull. The American doubted that even temporary stabilization of exchanges could be achieved. The problem was the domestic situation in the United States, he said. MacDonald explained plaintively that in Washington he had thought Roosevelt had agreed that some temporary exchange stabilization was essential for world recovery.[20] The next day Chamberlain and MacDonald both talked to Hull and James Cox. There was "general agreement that progress with removal of trade restrictions depended upon an agreement for currency-stabilization."[21] On 21 June Cox and Warburg told MacDonald that Roosevelt had rejected the central bankers' plan. Warburg saw no immediate hope of changing the president's mind. He and Cox suggested that MacDonald might send another personal message to Roosevelt, stressing how important was this matter for the future of the conference.[22] If such a message was sent, it was without effect.

Some days later, MacDonald arranged a joint meeting of the American and British delegates – something he had been avoiding for some time. He explained that practically every important representative who came to see him had emphasized the importance of stabilization and of securing equilibrium in the European currency situation. Was it not possible, he asked, for the Americans to move somewhat farther? If nothing were done, there might soon be a grave financial crisis. Various British delegates remarked that there was no point signing a tariff truce with the United States if, at the same time, the United States were depreciating its currency. Senator Key Pittman explained that the United States delegation was not empowered to deal with the question of the exchange. Hull said he saw the point about trade but thought that they should still press on with a long run program of trade liberalization because the "stabilisation question might solve itself." But Chamberlain, Walter Runciman, and MacDonald returned to the attack. Other countries, they observed, simply refused to discuss tariffs, quotas, and so on. Further, Chamberlain said, the European delegates were filled with "fear of what might happen at any moment as a result of excessive speculation and other similar phenomena." The chancellor did not "believe that all countries must stabilise their currencies before embarking on other remedial measures." Was there a chance of a declaration being made that would stop speculation, at least?[23]

Hull and MacDonald then met Bonnet, Bizot, Colijn and Trip of Holland, and Franqui and Gutt of Belgium. Trip described the flight from the Dutch florin, and Colijn said the thing would spread to the Swiss franc, while Bonnet foresaw pressure on the belga and even on the French franc itself. Franqui explained that the resulting chaos would cause revolutions and asked for stabilization of exchanges among the gold bloc, Britain, and the United States. Chamberlain said he would not stabilize the pound for the present though he would help other countries, providing the support that Colijn thought essential. Trip and Colijn thought it was most important to devise some scheme for helping gold countries whose exchanges were imperiled by speculation. MacDonald wondered whether the United States might not at least give some support to the counter-speculation scheme. Bonnet agreed to circulate a draft declaration. Hull would send this to Roosevelt, who was still at sea on an American warship.[24]

Into the situation came Raymond Moley, who reached London on 27 June, just in time to act as midwife in the birth of a counter-speculation statement.[25] He asked Hull to exclude Warburg and Cox, leaving himself and Sprague to carry on the discussions.

Hull told Roosevelt of the 27 June meeting. "Holland, France, Switzerland, and Belgium . . . would be forced off gold in immediate future possibly next week . . . just now this gold standard situation is undoubtedly very acute."[26] The president's response was puzzling. He cabled Washington that he thought France would have to leave gold, that he did not think it very important if she and other Continental countries left gold because he did not expect that their departure would disturb his policy of raising domestic prices, and that "the most important fact is that our London delegation is absolutely right in distinguishing between government action at conference and private action by central banks."[27]

Because the State Department wanted to wait until more information was in hand, it did not send this message on to London. Meanwhile, the gold countries were becoming more desperate and more importunate hour by hour. On 23 June Bonnet urged Chamberlain to cooperate with the gold countries. On 28 June he reported that Daladier attached immense importance to the stabilization of exchanges. Chamberlain wrote: "The alarm . . . reached a crisis yesterday when the French demanded a declaration practically amounting to an announcement that the non-gold countries would support the gold currencies at the existing parities."[28] Bonnet wrote to Chamberlain, explaining that the conference must "give the impression that it recommends the stability of exchanges" at the existing parities. Otherwise there would be a redoubling of speculative pressures. The right impression would be given if "the principal powers . . . mark without delay their wish to restore stability." It would be desirable if the United States could associate itself with such a statement; but it would not do so. Nevertheless, the other powers could and should "mark their intention" to restore monetary order "or adjourn the Conference."[29]

The point had come up before. On 22 June Bonnet and Bizot had told the prime minister that if there were no agreement with the United States it would be up to France, Italy, and especially Britain to cooperate to protect the European exchanges. On 23 June Bonnet had said that if the United States would not agree to stabilization then the other countries should agree among themselves. The pound, he suggested, would then stay with the franc, not "go down with the dollar."[30]

Chamberlain would not stabilize the pound, and he was most reluctant to connect its fate with those of the gold currencies. He told his colleagues,

it became clear that the gold countries wanted the United Kingdom to stand behind and support their currencies. For obvious reasons we were unwilling to undertake any such liability, but . . . were very anxious that . . . America should sign the same document as the rest . . . On his arrival Professor Moley took over responsibility for the conversations with us, and . . . was prepared to go considerably further than had been expected . . . After consultation with representatives of the other gold countries, the French informed us that . . . they would accept [Moley's] redraft subject to two conditions which made the draft wholly unacceptable.[31]

The French wanted the British and Americans to approve of the gold countries' determination to maintain the gold standard and the existing parities; they also wanted the Anglo-American central banks to commit their resources not only to offset exchange speculation but also to avoid "violent fluctuations," whether in their own or other currencies. Neither Chamberlain nor Moley would accept either emendation.[32] After a long discussion between Jung, Moley, and Rist of the Bank of France, and after further conversations between Moley and Chamberlain, on the afternoon of 30 June Moley was able to transmit a proposal to Roosevelt.

The declaration did not commit anybody to anything. Neither Moley nor Chamberlain believed that it involved any commitment as to exchange rates. It did not seem to go beyond the monetary resolutions that Senator Key Pittman had placed before the conference on 19 June. It could make no contribution to tariff bargaining, for it did not tell the gold countries what exchange rates they should expect. But Bonnet and his friends genuinely believed that it would calm speculation. What Moley proposed was a document that spoke of cooperation to limit speculation.[33] It said nothing about exchange stabilization for the time being, though in a general way it did look toward the eventual reestablishment of a "general international gold standard," the time and parities to be decided solely by the "governments concerned." No statement could have more fully safeguarded America's freedom – or that of the United Kingdom.

Moley certainly thought that the president would accept this statement. But a long and distressing wait ensued, chiefly because Roosevelt was on holiday.[34] Bonnet said that if the United States did not accept the declaration, the remaining conferees, including the United Kingdom, should make a statement of their own; otherwise, he said, it would be difficult to continue the conference at all.[35] On 1 July, however, Roosevelt sent Hull a long and obscure message. He rejected the statement on several grounds. It would prevent the United States from stabilizing its domestic price level. It confused the functions of governments, which had "no appropriate means to limit exchange speculation," with those of private banks, and the government could not authorize private action by the Federal Reserve System, which "might morally obligate our Government now or later to approval of export of gold from the United States." Exchange stabilization would not create "permanent stability," because government budgets could remain unbalanced and because "any fixed formula for stabilisation by agreement must necessarily be artificial and speculative." Finally, the president thought, the evil Europeans were trying to put the United States in the wrong.

England left gold standard nearly 2 years ago and only now is seeking stabilisation. Also . . . France did not stabilise for three years or more. If France seeks to break up Conference just because we decline to accept her dictum we should take the sound position that Economic Conference was initiated and called to discuss and agree on permanent solutions of world economics and not to discuss domestic economic policy of one nation out of the 66 present.[36]

The president must have misunderstood. He appears to have thought he was being asked to repeg the dollar and to restrict his freedom of action at home. Neither was suggested. Chamberlain himself would not have agreed to peg the pound or to pursue tight-money policies in the United Kingdom. Roosevelt made matters worse by transmitting a long public statement justifying his decision. He still thought, quite wrongly, that he was being asked to stabilize the dollar. Further, he used the opportunity to inveigh against international bankers, fluctuating purchasing powers, the dissipation of gold reserves, unbalanced budgets, and trade embargoes.[37]

Annoyed by the presidential refusal, Chamberlain at once asked his colleagues what should be done. The gold countries would want support for their currencies in spite of the immense gold reserves they already held. Sir Philip Cunliffe-Lister, the colonial secretary, insisted that the pound could not possibly be linked with the gold currencies, and the meeting agreed that it should not be. However, several ministers foresaw trouble with India and the Dominions, who would shortly have to be told what had been happening.[38] Two days later J. H. Thomas spoke of the risks, to both domestic and Empire politics, of seeming to link up with the gold bloc.[39]

Further, there was a great deal of concern about Britain's own trade, now threatened by a depreciating dollar. To preserve the gains from the Ottawa Agreements, perhaps there should be an agreed Empire-wide surcharge on American goods.[40]

As expected, the French renewed their importunities almost at once. On 2 July Rist asked for a British signature even without an American one. Chamberlain refused. Such action, he said, would disrupt the sterling area and begin a competitive depreciation of the several sterling currencies, because it would appear to ally the United Kingdom with the restrictionist credit policies of the gold bloc. He agreed that he would submit a parallel but independent declaration. Rist, however, found this so vague as to be worthless,[41] and so there was no such statement.

Writing of these events in the 1960s, George Bonnet himself gave an account of the maneuverings. He claims that the conference itself had been called to stabilize currencies and develop exchange.[42] But there had never been any prior commitment to stabilization, and the conference had originally been meant to raise prices. Thirty years on, Bonnet appears to reflect the panic that swept his government and the other governments of what shortly became the gold bloc when the floating of the American dollar provoked a wave of speculation against their currencies. As for Chamberlain's refusal to sign a joint declaration, Bonnet reports that Chamberlain was at first willing to append his signature but withdrew at the last moment in fear of *Canadian* reaction. Bonnet claims that Chamberlain sent a note, saying Prime Minister Bennett had threatened to withdraw the Canadian dollar from the sterling area by pegging it to the dollar and no longer to sterling. "He approved our decision. But the unity of the Empire supervened."[43] The Canadian dollar was not pegged to sterling, however. Hence Bennett could not have made such a threat, and it is hard to believe that Chamberlain could have reported so obvious a falsehood. Doubtless by 2 July the Canadian prime minister was already arguing that Britain should not join the gold bloc. But as we shall see, the Empire pressure was coming chiefly from Smuts of South Africa, whose government could hardly have contemplated another devaluation of its currency vis-à-vis sterling or gold. The political climate of South Africa would not have permitted any such deliberate action; the South African advisers were strongly opposed to it.[44] Chamberlain might have been thinking of Australia and New Zealand, or even of India. He can hardly have mentioned or imagined either South Africa or Canada.

The gold countries went ahead and issued their own declaration on 3 July.[45] Chamberlain later explained that Britain wanted prices to rise and the gold standard to survive within the gold bloc.[46] The French do not appear to have believed him. But if the French were restive so were India and the Dominions. If President Roosevelt had misunderstood so had Bennett and Smuts and Strakosch.

Throughout the proceedings of the Monetary and Financial Commission, Britain had pressed for price increases through credit expansion and cheap money. India, Japan, Argentina, South Africa, and Australia had all agreed. But the gold bloc – Switzerland, Holland, Italy, and France – had thought that prices could best be raised not through monetary policy but through the restoration of confidence, which required a gold standard. Poland, Germany, Romania, and Yugoslavia agreed. According to the American observer H. Merle Cochran, "M. Bonnet of France . . . maintained that monetary stability was at the root of all the problems which had been raised, and that the Conference could yield no definite results unless it reached a conclusion on that subject."[47] The Dominion delegations, especially the Australian and

South African, were especially interested in price raising. So was the government of India.

In fixing their attentions on this matter, the Empire governments were, after all, responding not just to their own local imperatives but to the original plan of the conference, as first proposed by Britain and the United States in the early summer of 1932. At that time and in the planning of the United Kingdom authorities, the World Economic Conference had been directed toward price raising. In Roosevelt's statement of 3 July, also, there was talk of "continuing purchasing power" that would not "greatly vary in terms of the commodities and need of modern civilisation." The Americans, it seemed, also wanted to raise prices to an acceptable level. But the gold bloc? Clearly it did not. If necessary France and its friends would depress internal prices, and thereby world prices, so as to maintain their links with gold and their gold parities, inappropriate though those parities might be. In their joint statement of 3 July the gold countries said:

The undersigned governments, convinced that the maintenance of their currencies is essential for the economic and financial recovery of the world and of credit and for the safeguarding of social progress in their respective countries, confirm their intention to maintain the free functioning of the gold standard in their respective countries at the existing gold parities and within the framework of existing monetary laws. They ask their central banks to keep in close touch to give the maximum efficacy to this declaration.[48]

To the politicians and officials of Australia, India, and South Africa nothing could have been more unsuitable or more frightening than these assertions. Five days later the governors of the six central banks met in Paris to examine measures that could offset exchange speculation and protect the six currencies. The Bank for International Settlements reported, "As a consequence of this gathering and of the conclusions reached, the six exchanges strengthened forthwith, domestic confidence was reassured, and the gold drain which had commenced was not only arrested, but contrary gold movements set in immediately."[49] One only wonders, if the six countries could do so much and so well on their own, why they had thought they needed Anglo-American support. Was Chamberlain right in suspecting that they wanted to spend Anglo-American gold instead of their own?

The French and the Dutch had been urging the United Kingdom to align itself with the gold bloc, stabilize the pound on gold, and lend London's foreign exchange reserves to the fight against speculative capital movements, but at no point was Chamberlain willing to tolerate any such arrangement. He would, if necessary, help with arrangements to offset speculation, but he would not peg the pound to gold or to the gold-standard currencies in any permanent way. On the other hand, both MacDonald and Chamberlain were eager for a temporary de facto stabilization of the pound, dollar, and franc vis-à-vis one another. The reasons were simple. France and the gold-bloc countries had made it clear that if there were no agreement on exchange rates they would not reduce their quotas, tariffs, and other trade impedimenta, all of which were hurting British exports. The depreciation of the American dollar vis-à-vis the pound had already erased most of the gain Britain had attained relative to the United States from its own depreciation in September 1931 and thereafter. If the dollar were to fall farther all the gain might well be lost. Further, if currency speculation should force any Continental country to leave the gold standard Britain's trading advantage would be further eroded. And it would not take much of a capital flight to force any Continental country off gold: Though France and its friends held immense gold stocks, the margins of "free reserves," remaining after the compulsory covers for currency, were far from large. Hence the danger of the speculative flight which dollar depreciation had set off. And to make matters worse, it was to Britain that both American and Continental capital funds were flowing. In Treasury minds and in Chamberlain's, the adverse effect on the exchange rate was sufficiently alarming to swamp the beneficial effect on the reserves. Hence Chamberlain attached enormous importance to American adherence. If the United States would sign the same counter-speculation document as the other countries, and if Roosevelt would assure the world that "the whole resources of the United States would be used if necessary to stop speculation,"[50] all would be tolerable: Although the dollar might continue to depreciate, at least Europe would not leave gold.

2. *Trouble with the Empire*

> I love the Dominions
> They keep me so warm
> I'm in a perpetual
> State of alarm.
> Neville Chamberlain, 4 July 1933[1]

The United Kingdom ministers had made little systematic attempt to inform the Dominion leaders and the Indian delegation of these negotiations. The general questions of monetary policy had been scrutinized on 16 June, but neither the stabilization proposal nor the counter-speculation declaration was discussed with the Empire delegates. Even so, these delegates could hardly fail to know what was in the wind. Chamberlain's secretiveness can hardly have been popular. As the conference proceeded the Empire delegates became more and more restive. To the Indians, South Africans, and Australians in particular, it seemed that the United Kingdom was preparing to join the gold bloc and therefore to operate its monetary policy in the interest of exchange stability rather than price raising. For some time the pound had not fluctuated vis-à-vis gold though it had risen sharply vis-à-vis the American dollar. Roosevelt was trying to raise commodity prices. Should not Britain do likewise? Why was MacDonald so obviously intent on a de facto stabilization agreement even if only for the period of the conference itself?

On 30 June, at the Dominions' request, MacDonald and Chamberlain met Bruce of Australia, Forbes of New Zealand, Smuts of South Africa, Conoly of the Irish Free State, and Strakosch of India. Because there had been little notice the Canadians could not attend, having already made other commitments. Smuts led the attack. The whole Empire wanted credit expansion and higher prices, he said. As these were also Roosevelt's goals, Britain and the Empire should come to some arrangement with the United States. Instead, it seemed, the pound would be "pulled into the gold group." But the gold countries would eventually be forced off the gold standard, and the Empire could not stand more deflation. Britain should not back the wrong horse. Was it doing so? What was British policy?

The chancellor and the officials of Foreign Office and Treasury were sure that Sir Henry Strakosch had put these words into Smuts's mouth. Shortly afterward, Chamberlain told the Cabinet that Strakosch, the only "real expert in the British delegations from overseas," had promoted Smuts's initiatives and also the Dominions' conference resolutions.[2] Indeed. Strakosch had been as vehement as Smuts and in similar terms. The pound, Strakosch told Chamberlain, should be depreciated vis-à-vis gold, keeping in step with the American dollar. Empire price levels should be raised as the United States was raising its prices.

Strakosch, like Smuts, feared that if sterling appreciated vis-à-vis the American dollar the Empire currencies would have to fall vis-à-vis sterling. For both governments, the threat was empty. The South African Cabinet would never have tolerated a downward movement of its money, and the United Kingdom Cabinet would never let the rupee fall. Both battles had been fought too recently for there to be any doubt about the permanence of the outcomes.

What are we to make of Chamberlain's suspicions about a Smuts-Strakosch conspiracy? Certainly the financier had known the South African politician at least since 1920. A South African Reserve Bank had then been a gleam in the eye of the government that Smuts then headed.

And Strakosch had drafted the Reserve Bank bill.[3] Regrettably, however, the Smuts Papers contain no evidence that Smuts and Strakosch actually discussed monetary policy at the World Economic Conference or before it. There was, however, an occasional correspondence stretching well back into the 1920s and dealing largely with questions of money and gold. The terms of this correspondence reflect a certain intimacy. In 1930, for instance, Strakosch sent Smuts his memorandum on economic consequences of changes in the value of gold, a document that was later published in the *Economist*. Smuts must have read the memorandum, for some months later Strakosch thanked him for "appreciative comments . . . which . . . have been a source of comfort and satisfaction."[4] The letters and the memorandum link the gold standard with the declining level of commodity prices – a theme that Strakosch was later to develop at considerable length and that has obvious analogies to the line Smuts was taking in the summer of 1933. In January 1931, again, Strakosch sent Smuts the Second Interim Report of the League Gold Delegation and other materials on gold and monetary policy.[5] Smuts may or may not have been right to call himself "a complete ignoramus in finance."[6] Neither the Smuts Papers themselves nor the available South African Treasury records contain anything to suggest that his own government or its officials had briefed him to follow the line that he took in London. But since 1931 at the latest he had been worried about low commodity prices. It was largely to raise domestic prices for primary producers that he had favored a South African devaluation in 1931–2.[7] In preparation for the conference N. C. Havenga, the finance minister, had asked two South African professors, Robert Leslie and E. H. Arndt, to serve as advisers. They and Dr. J. W. Holloway of the Finance Secretariat produced long memorandums. Organized around the topics of the Draft Annotated Agenda, these memorandums do not point toward the initiative that Smuts later took. It appears that no other formal staff work was attempted.[8]

Whatever Strakosch's contribution may have been, Smuts must also have been influenced by Leo Amery's monetary views. Like Strakosch, Amery corresponded with Smuts from time to time. Some of the letters touch on the monetary matters with which the imperial visionary was so much concerned. Smuts appears to have shared Amery's somewhat overdramatic view of monetary affairs. In March 1932, for instance, he told Amery that he foresaw a "great battle" between the dollar and sterling "for world supremacy as currency." Nevertheless, he said, "I shall not be surprised if sterling wins through."[9] Such predelictions must have contributed to his wish that the conference should contain some concerted Empire effort at monetary reconstruction. Furthermore,

Smuts and Amery were at one in desiring monetary expansion, exchange depreciation,[10] and a program of public works. Thus Amery's influence, though almost certainly more diffuse than that of Strakosch, cannot be ignored.

Smuts himself sent General Hertzog, the South African prime minister, an account of the 30 June meeting with Chamberlain. He wrote: "the Dominion governments gave general expression to the view that they were much more concerned with the relationship of sterling to the dollar and that therefore there should be no linking of sterling to the franc unless the dollar were also brought into some such scheme."[11]

S. M. Bruce joined Smuts in observing that the pound must not be tied to gold, as this would prevent the use of price-raising policies. Britain, Bruce said, should try to agree with the United States on the sterling-dollar exchange rate but should not worry about a general stabilization.

Chamberlain's response was more than a little defensive. Britain's credit policy, he said, had not changed; he still believed in cheap money, easy credit, and higher commodity prices. But the American situation was very dangerous because Roosevelt's actions had set off a speculative fever there. As for Europe, Britain could not stand by and see the Continent cast into "monetary disorder and confusion." Eventually, he agreed, the Continental countries would have to leave the gold standard, but he wanted them to do it in an orderly fashion, not in "chaos while the Conference was actually sitting." He would not peg the pound to gold and he agreed that there had to be "some form of stabilisation," but he could not agree to raise British prices in step with American prices: "by adopting this policy we should hand ourselves over to the United States, who admittedly did not know what they wanted or where they were going." Ending the discussion, MacDonald said that he would welcome further talks with the Dominions and with India.[12]

On 3 July Chamberlain and other United Kingdom ministers met the Empire leaders to discuss Roosevelt's rejection of the "Moley plan" and his note thereon. Smuts said that though he disliked Roosevelt's language he was in general agreement with the president's sentiments. In his dispatch to Prime Minister Hertzog Smuts wrote, "I avail myself of the opportunity to express a fair measure of sympathy with the aim of raising prices . . . it was desirable that the sterling group of countries should state their point of view rather more specifically than had been done hitherto."[13] Smuts then offered a draft resolution that spoke of price raising, cheap and plentiful credit, tax reductions, and public works. The next day the same group discussed this draft. Strakosch and Bruce again argued against any identification with gold or the gold bloc.

Bennett reported that he thought Sweden would adhere to the joint resolution. But Chamberlain "emphasized the difficulty of any useful discussion on the financial side of the Conference if the gold standard countries refused properly to co-operate."[14]

Chamberlain then told his colleagues about these two meetings with the Empire politicians. The atmosphere, he said, had not been satisfactory. It was, for example, ludicrous to suggest that the United Kingdom had no policy when "we were the only Delegation at the Conference which had made specific proposals covering the whole field." General Smuts had put forward proposals that amounted to a thinly disguised attempt to dictate the United Kingdom policy at the conference. Those proposals were "so extravagant that they might almost have emerged from conversations with Mr. Lloyd George and Mr. Keynes." Some of the officials told the ministers that Smuts had in fact been consulting Sir Henry Strakosch. It would be necessary, Chamberlain explained, to examine the question of price-raising measures, as that question "seemed to occupy the minds of the Dominion and Indian delegates to the exclusion of almost everything else."[15] But once again there was general agreement that it would be folly for Britain to connect sterling with the gold bloc; if it were to do so, argued both Sir Frederick Phillips and Sir Philip Cunliffe-Lister, the colonial secretary, it would simply encourage a capital flight from these currencies into the pound. Britain's interest was twofold: It wanted a higher price level, and it also wanted the gold-bloc countries to stay on gold. Chamberlain would see the prime minister and General Smuts; there would then be a meeting with the Dominions and with India.

Smuts then circulated a memorandum that urged the sterling countries to decide several matters.[16] He did not report his initiative to General Hertzog, who was told only that Smuts had pressed Chamberlain to discover the "real intention and objectives of American internal policy. It seemed to me that unless influence were brought to bear on the American President to give some stability to the dollar, it would slide disastrously on its downward depreciation."[17] The memorandum itself was much more specific. How much should prices be raised? How should the pound, the dollar, and gold be related? To facilitate price rises, should there be more public works? reduction of long-term interest rate? reopening of the London capital market for Empire flotations? Finally, could the delegates devise concrete proposals to effect any policy? "The gold bloc has held its meetings and announced its policy. The time has come when the sterling group should do the same."

The Treasury did not much like Smuts's memorandum. Prices were already rising, Sir Frederick Phillips wrote. Although they were still too low nobody could say what the right level should be. Open market operations were certainly desirable to lower the long-term rate of interest, but Britain had been conducting such operations for over a year. The London market was already open to new Dominion long-term loans so long as the proceeds would not be remitted directly or indirectly outside the Empire. And as for sterling, it must "be regarded as an entirely independent currency," not tied to the dollar or to gold.[18]

On 18 July the Empire delegates discussed the Smuts memorandum with Chamberlain. As Chamberlain later wrote, "The Dominions have been troublesome again."[19] Smuts repeated its arguments. Bennett, Bruce, and Strakosch said they were in general agreement with him. So was the New Zealand representative. Smuts said that he wanted prices to rise 40 percent. If his proposals would not work the group must consider alternatives. He himself thought that a large public works program would help to raise prices. If prices did not rise, many primary producing countries might default on their obligations. They might desert sterling, debase or inflate their currencies, or take various other reckless measures. "It had occurred to him, and to others he had consulted, that a sterling group of countries should be formed, with a declared policy on the lines which had been advocated at this Conference by the United Kingdom and the other Commonwealth Delegations."[20]

Chamberlain was annoyed at the talk of tax cuts and public works, redolent as they were of Lloyd George and Keynes. Certainly the Treasury officials were not pleased with such ideas. Chamberlain explained that Britain had tried public works without success[21] and that he could not imagine that any public works programme would be large enough to cope with the problem. He also pointed out that sterling prices had risen and said they would continue to rise. Welcoming the idea of a declaration, he nonetheless doubted that it could contain anything spectacular. He undertook to produce a draft, circulate it, and discuss it privately with the several Empire delegates. Such a declaration might "give an indication, or rather a restatement, of the policy they intended to pursue."[22]

The Chamberlain draft went to a subcommittee and to the United Kingdom delegation on 24 July, then, after amendment, to the Empire delegates at large on 25 July, when they examined it in a drafting session. Strakosch continued to press for a clearer statement on price raising, and Australia and New Zealand wanted a reference to output control. Nevertheless, to Chamberlain the meeting went "much better than I had expected." However, afterward Smuts circulated a much-revised amendment, and Strakosch provided yet more amendments that the chancellor found "quite unacceptable." Chamberlain conferred with

Smuts, saying that if Smuts were going to press his amendment Chamberlain would prefer to have no statement at all. According to the chancellor,

the whole spirit of Ottawa was being attacked and we must vindicate it if we were to save it . . . in the end we found it possible to agree on a redraft which satisfied us both. Later on I met Strakosch with a series of alternative amendments to those proposed by him, and he accepted them, with the result that after an hour and a half's discussion, the final document was signed by all except the Irish Free State representative. All the Dominion representatives appeared in high good humour, and Smuts as he signed it said, "this is a good piece of work; you have done a good piece of work today." [23]

The document was signed on 27 July and published at once.[24]

J. H. Thomas, the Dominions secretary, thought the statement would have a good psychological effect.[25] In fact it did not go beyond the Ottawa monetary declaration of August 1932. But it came to be regarded as a classic expression of the "Ottawa policy," and in later years it was often used as a touchstone for the external monetary policy of the United Kingdom. Prices should be raised, it resolved; credit and money should be easy, though no one should create credit so as to finance government deficits. Eventually the gold standard should be reestablished but only after prices had risen and been stabilized at a higher level. Within the Empire, governments would try to keep exchange rates stable while raising internal prices. If other countries would adhere to the same sort of policy, more exchange rates could be kept stable.[26]

The Commonwealth governments had not changed Britain's policies. Nor had the United Kingdom forced the Empire to form a "sterling bloc." Rather, the Empire had forced Chamberlain to make yet another public statement and yet another forceful clarification of the policies to which he and the Treasury were already attached. But neither in Washington nor in the Continental capitals were things seen in that light.

To Chamberlain himself the statement was of little importance. In his diary he said it was "designed to serve the multiple purpose of (1) diverting the Dominions from the dangerous paths of currency depreciation and public works (2) putting out a joint British declaration which may to some extent distract attention from the failure of the Conference and (3) furbish up the Ottawa agreements which have got a little tarnished by reason of the rather equivocal behaviour of some of the Dominions." Writing to his sister, he added that the declaration would "please the Federation of British Industries and the Monarch and others who say why doesn't the Empire do something," and also "divert the Dominions from subjects they don't understand and on which they can be embarrassing to us."[27] Had Smuts, Strakosch, and Bruce known how the chancellor regarded their opinions, they would have been anything but pleased.

Smuts himself was not satisfied with the outcome. During the conference he had told a South African political ally:

I could only wish that in the Empire and sterling countries we had embarked more resolutely on a policy of price-raising. In the British Empire delegations, we are still urging this policy and before the Conference is over, some definite declaration may yet emerge from our group. It is quite necessary if primary producers are to be saved, and the debt structure of the world is not to collapse, that price levels will have to go up a good deal higher than they are at present.[28]

Once the British Commonwealth Declaration had appeared Smuts received Amery's plaudits:

My congratulations on the statement of Empire monetary policy which appears in the papers today. It is a great thing to have got the British government to announce publicly that it means to proceed independently of gold or dollar. The real question will be whether Chamberlain will act up to the declaration or let himself be pulled back by Montagu Norman all the time.[29]

Smuts responded: "Though I did not carry more than a percentage of my intention in the Declaration it is in the right direction and will I am sure do good."[30]

8

Talking about exchange stabilization, autumn 1933 through June 1936

After the World Economic Conference had collapsed, the question of exchange stabilization did not stay dead. Professor Sayers has explained that Governor Harrison of the New York Federal Reserve Bank pressed for some Anglo-American agreement in summer 1933 and then again in November. Unable to buy gold freely with dollars, the Exchange Equalisation Account operated chiefly in French francs, and from time to time it was able to peg the sterling-franc rate. Between the Bank of England and the Bank of France, understanding and cooperation steadily increased. But the French continued to press for some more formal arrangement, and after the United States had returned the dollar to gold American pressure was not unknown. Though it was interested in the management of sterling, and increasingly willing to envisage some sort of international cooperation in exchange management, the Treasury consistently resisted this pressure. The chancellor of the exchequer was if anything even more determined than his officials. The principal purpose of this chapter is to chronicle the Franco-American initiatives and Whitehall's responses.

1. Franco-American importunities

In the Treasury, the Bank, and the mind of the chancellor, the events of spring and summer 1933 had left a definite deposit of suspicion. As we have seen, Chamberlain was already inclined to distrust the Americans, and, in particular, the president.[1] "Master Roosevelt," as Chamberlain called him, would tack and change course in response to every political breeze. The chancellor observed, "Roosevelt reminded the Governor of Lloyd George which as I told him was the worst thing I had heard about him yet."[2] In Whitehall it was thought that the president had cut himself off from all rational advice in matters of finance. He distrusted the Federal Reserve System because it was a privately owned network of banks, not a government department. Raymond Moley, admittedly, had left the president's entourage, but once William H. Woodin had given up the Treasury, Roosevelt had appointed Henry C. Morgenthau, Jr., a Hudson Valley neighbor who knew little of finance. It was true that Morgenthau rapidly assembled a corps of advisers, drawn chiefly from Taussig's stable of Harvard economists. But few of these advisers were known to Whitehall, and those who were known were not respected. It is just as well that Chamberlain and his advisers did not know precisely how Morgenthau used his staff. In any event, the president did not listen to these experts.

Matters were not helped by the gold-buying experiment on which Roosevelt and Morgenthau embarked in early autumn 1933. In London there was little sympathy for the economic theory on which this price-raising maneuver was based. But there was much criticism of its impact on the distribution of the world's gold and therefore on the difficulties of the Continental gold bloc. Chamberlain told his sister, "Master R. is shoving the dollar down with a vengeance and I expect there is a great deal of anxiety in France and Holland though of course they don't admit it."[3] Was Roosevelt really determined to drain all the world's gold into the United States? If the desperate Continentals became even more protectionist, how would America's farmers gain? Suppose the president or his counselors began again to worry about farm prices, or about overseas competition. Might they not again raise the price of gold?

For the rest of 1933 the gold price was edged steadily upward; the dollar depreciated relative to sterling; the Reconstruction Finance Corporation bought a great deal of gold. The Treasury believed that the Roosevelt plan would speed the dissolution of the gold bloc, because it would depress prices in terms of gold. If the gold bloc were to collapse, Britain's exports would face stiffer competition for some time, until wages and prices adjusted in Continental countries.[4] Nevertheless, for the time being Chamberlain did not want to have any sort of discussion about currency.[5]

When Roosevelt began his gold buying, Sir Frederick Leith-Ross was in Washington to talk about the Anglo-American war debt. He reported that though Roosevelt had not connected debts with currency he had mentioned the "uncertainty of the currency position and the possibility that in six or eight months' time it might be possible to arrive at an agreement on that subject which would help to a general settlement of debts."[6] A few days later, Leith-Ross learned from Dean Acheson, the American Assistant Secretary of State, that Norman had approached Harrison, the governor of the Federal Reserve Bank of New York. Norman had suggested that Roosevelt should say what exchange rate he was aiming at. The central banks would then consider whether that rate could be attained quickly, without upsetting the markets. Harrison had told Roosevelt of the message; the president "agreed that the message was very interesting but refused to commit himself." Leith-Ross believed that as the United Kingdom had made a gesture without result she "should sit back for the time being and wait events . . . if we bide our time, we may expect approaches from here for advice and perhaps for co-ordinated action."[7]

Harrison soon began to discuss exchange matters with Norman. The British authorities thought he did so without authorization or instruction from his government; Stephen Clarke has recently suggested that the initiative really came from the U.S. administration, which hoped for a five-dollar pound. Harrison told Norman he was "simply exploring the ground to see whether the respective central banks could put up agreed recommendations to their governments." The United States, he thought, was politically unable to stabilize the dollar relative to gold, except as a result of an agreement for the "joint stabilization of the dollar and the pound." Norman asked whether, if permanent stabilization was impossible, anything could be done by way of a short-term agreement to "steady the exchanges." Harrison thought that any such arrangement should include France, but the idea did not appeal to him. They would have to begin with present rates, but these were almost certainly not the right ones, and once chosen the rates would be hard to change – especially as it would be necessary to raise the relative value of the dollar in the long run. Hence Harrison thought that a short-term arrangement would break down. It would be much better if the United States and the United Kingdom could both return to gold, having agreed on devaluation in terms of gold so as to achieve a target exchange rate – perhaps \$4.86.[8]

Because neither Roosevelt nor Chamberlain would have considered such a plan, nothing could have come of these talks.

In mid-January 1934 Roosevelt announced that he would no longer raise the price of gold. Vis-à-vis gold the dollar would be stabilized at \$35 per ounce. Part of the "profit" of devaluation would be used to establish an equalization fund of \$2,000 million. This was to manage the exchanges. But what was the fund really for? By returning to gold the Americans had fixed the exchanges between the dollar and the franc, as well as the other gold currencies. In those directions management was neither necessary nor possible. In the American press, however, there had been much criticism of Britain's Exchange Equilisation Account, which was thought to depress the pound artificially and thereby to lower American prices and cheat American industry of export markets. From Washington Sir Ronald Lindsay reported, "Great Britain is of course the country most in mind, and the new fund is a direct answer to the British

Exchange Equalisation Account. I do not believe, however, that the President has the least desire of entering upon a currency 'war' with Great Britain and the creation of the fund may well be intended to lead up to renewed negotiations for holding the two currencies steady in terms of one another." [9]

Having been confirmed as secretary of the treasury, Morgenthau proceeded to talk as if such talks had begun. A confidant of the president's, Morgenthau had been deeply involved in Roosevelt's gold-buying policy. Chamberlain did not like these statements and did not find them impressive. He wrote: "The way they [the Americans] talk over there makes me mad. You would naturally suppose from Mr. Morgenthau's interviews that we were in communication with them over some joint arrangement for stabilisation of the pound-dollar exchange . . . It is quite untrue. Neither we nor the Bank have heard one single word from them." [10]

The Treasury and Foreign Office records confirm the truth of the chancellor's statement. In Washington the embassy financial adviser, T. K. Bewley, studied official statements and wrote reports. But he was not in touch with American officials and certainly not with Morgenthau or Roosevelt. Nor were the Americans either forthcoming or importunate. So matters remained until March 1935, when the ambassador, Sir Ronald Lindsay, made an incautious remark at a Washington dinner party.

The Treasury, of course, thought that Roosevelt's policy had been extremely unwise. The result was an artificially undervalued dollar. Unless the Americans could manage to have a fast and furious inflation, gold would flow to the United States, and things would become much more difficult for the rest of the world. The problems of 1929–33 would be redoubled, as the world's gold stock would become even more maldistributed, and the deflationary pressures in the gold countries would be even more severe. Because American policy was so odd, dangerous, unpredictable, and foolish, the United Kingdom must preserve its independence in matters of credit and exchange. The Treasury was still prepared to contemplate an eventual return to gold, but only when the necessary conditions existed.[11] American action had made that time even more remote .

The French, meanwhile, continued their importunities.

Though the French were not distrusted in Whitehall, their arrangements and their policies were regretted. Increasingly the Bank of England worked with the Bank of France. Whitehall respected French officials, such as Charles Rist, Jacques Rueff, and the omnipresent Emmanuel Monick. But between January 1933 and June 1936 France had nine prime ministers. This endless flux produced political and diplomatic uncertainty. Thus the French were at least as unpredictable as the Americans, though for different reasons. Nor can one ignore the increasingly numerous Anglo-French disagreements over defense and international affairs.

As for France's attachment to the gold standard at the old parity, London was of several minds. The Bank was anxious not to make things more difficult for the French,[12] but eventually, Chamberlain and his officials thought, France would have to devalue. The chancellor wrote, "The franc will eventually be forced off gold but I shouldn't like to say when."[13] Nevertheless, Whitehall hoped that the franc would not fall too soon or too far. An overvalued franc was a help to Britain's export trade, especially given the strength of the pound compared with the dollar. Further, whatever exchange rate the franc might eventually reach, the Treasury hoped that the French would continue to operate a free gold standard. The reasons were partly technical and partly emotional. London disliked exchange control and hoped that France, like Britain, would be able to avoid it. As long as the franc was freely convertible into gold and the American dollar was not, Paris provided an important channel through which the Exchange Equalisation Account could buy gold bullion with foreign exchange. No one could be sure that if France adopted exchange control it would continue to allow the Account to do this; there was every reason to suspect that it would not.

Phillips explained matters as follows. "The future of the gold bloc turns entirely on events in France . . . The French authorities . . . have a fixed idea that if only the United Kingdom and the U.S.A. would stabilise they can get through. But there is no solid basis for this belief . . . stabilisation . . . would do nothing to alter the fact that the franc is greatly overvalued." If Britain were to stabilize the pound first, the events of 1926 might be repeated. Other countries could and perhaps would choose rates that undervalued their moneys relative to sterling. For France, this would occur via a devaluation from the existing overvalued rate.[14]

Leith-Ross agreed. "I am in entire agreement with what Sir F. Phillips has written about the impossibility of attempting stabilisation in the present conditions." It was desirable, but impossible, to arrange a "workable system of stabilisation." Negotiations would fail, or there would be leaks, which would create speculation that would force the gold bloc to leave gold. Hence, he concluded, Britain should not consider any negotiations.[15]

The chancellor of the exchequer, in turn, agreed with Leith-Ross. He minuted, "I wish it were possible to stabilise at a revaluation of currencies but I fear the difficulties of getting a reasonable set of values are at present insuperable."[16]

Worry about the French was thus linked with worry about the competitive position of sterling and with the reason – or unreason – that would dominate in any general conversations about the exchanges. In the negotiations of September 1936, Chamberlain and his advisers would have cause to recall such worries.

In November 1934 the Domergue ministry, a "government of national union" that had endured since February 1934, was replaced by a new ministry under Flandin. In February 1935 Flandin and his colleagues came to London. As a preliminary Leith-Ross received a submission from the French financial attaché, Emmanuel Monick, who presented another proposal. Flandin, he said, would not ask Chamberlain to stabilize the pound, but he badly wanted to know what would happen to it. Already the exchange rate had slipped since the beginning of the year. Would this continue? While the American situation remained so indefinite Britain could not contemplate stabilization; but might Britain not take some definite steps in that direction? Flandin certainly wanted "some provisional linking of the pound with the franc." And "M. Monick," Leith-Ross wrote, "went on to develop his own personal views. He thought that if there could be some provisional stabilisation between the pound and the franc, an agreement might be reached covering the devaluation of the whole gold bloc currencies together and accompanied by a reduction of trade barriers. Any such agreement would have to be subject to revision if the value of the dollar were altered."[17] The franc, Monick thought, should come down by 16 to 20 percent.

As usual Leith-Ross gave little change. Such a devaluation was excessive, and indeed unnecessary, he told Monick. If France would only give up some gold it could manage for a long time, though much would depend on the course of inflation in the United States. Britain had done its best to keep the pound up, but the task was a hard one; France could help by liberalizing its import quotas, thus providing the market with more francs – "the best way of preventing a further fall of sterling." As for stabilization, it was unpopular in the United Kingdom, and no government could safely introduce it for the present.[18]

When Flandin came to London, the Foreign Office later observed, "the time was short and the need for 'solidarity' too great to allow the discussion of such a thorny question as the sterling and franc situation."[19] Chamberlain himself observed,

Flandin had intimated that he wanted to discuss stabilisation but he had had a preliminary talk with Leith-Ross and I think had realised that stabilisation was not possible at present for we did not discuss it at any length and he did not ask for any assurances. I told him that I fully realised the dangers of a disorderly devaluation by the gold bloc and that I would do my best to avoid anything that would facilitate it.[20]

The French, however, returned to the charge. When Leith-Ross was traveling in France and Switzerland, he was interviewed by Jacques Rueff and Emmanuel Monick. Rueff appealed for Britain to consider some provisional stabilization in exchange for some relaxation of quotas and clearings, which he explained Flandin could not abolish unless Britain would do something about stabilization. He had it on good authority, he said, that Roosevelt and Hull were most anxious for some arrangement by which provisional gold parities could be fixed, subject to readjustment if necessary. Monick explained that in Paris people were worried about the fall of the pound. He himself was convinced that Britain was doing all it could, but he found it hard to convince the Parisian critics. Leith-Ross said he did not believe the Americans would contemplate any such arrangement. Chamberlain, he said, believed the United States would stabilize only if it could create a permanently overvalued pound. At present, he said, Britain was certainly not pushing the pound down; rather, "we had used our resources as fully as we could to keep it up." It was the economic disequilibrium that had created the difficulties about stabilization; "so long as France and America pursued their present economic policies stabilisation was obviously impossible... I saw no reason to make any bargain about stabilisation in order to induce France to do what was in her own best interests."[21] The Foreign Office was not pleased with Sir Frederick's forthrightness.[22] As usual, it worried about the alliance, and it hoped that emollient words would flow across the Channel and the Atlantic. But the Treasury officials were adamant, and so was the chancellor.

After the American adventures of 1933 the Treasury could never be sure that Roosevelt would not once more depreciate the dollar relative to gold. Under the legislation of 1934 he retained the power to do so, and neither he nor Morgenthau seemed eager to relinquish this power. In Washington Kenneth Bewley was often preoccupied by this question. In March 1935 he wrote that he did not think the dollar would be depreciated for the moment. However, he observed, "the further the pound falls the greater the demand for countervailing action in this country," whereas "a material fall in internal prices which could with any reasonable probability be attributed to foreign currency movements and particularly weakness of sterling, would be likely to bring matters to a head." As for stabilization, Roosevelt would never make any but the most temporary and qualified commitment, and he would always keep the power to devalue on gold, nor for the present would the Americans contemplate a permanent agreement on exchange rates. The American administration was perturbed by the weakness of sterling and feared that the gold bloc would collapse. Hence the Americans wanted the United Kingdom to support the pound, and they might even help to support it.[23] But nothing more seemed to be in prospect.

There is also some sign that Whitehall was worried by Roosevelt's financial activities. The president had powers to expand the money supply dramatically; his budget obstinately refused to balance; he was unpopular with the financial community on whose confidence so much depended; his financial expedients were dubious at best. Particularly in the Foreign Office, officials worried about these things. Although the point cannot be documented, one may suppose that these worries affected U.K. policy. If American credit and finance were so alarmingly unstable and if Americans were so prone to speculative excess, Britain could not safely attach its currency to the American, however much the Foreign Office staff might yearn for a regime of stable exchange rates.

Sir Ronald Lindsay was especially inclined to think stabilization a Good Thing. Through his inadvertence, the British authorities appeared to give a signal that they were eager to move forward. To trace this comedy of errors, we must now turn to the ambassador's misadventure of March 1935. Over the dinner table Lindsay told the American undersecretary of state that stabilization could not occur until each equalization account knew the actions and intentions of the others. On March 12 the undersecretary called at the embassy. What, if anything, had Britain in mind? Sterling had recently fallen heavily; was there some means by which this might be prevented?[24]

In Whitehall there was consternation. What had Lindsay done? No one had told him to say anything of the sort. The House of Commons did not know, and could not be told, what was happening to the Exchange Equalisation Account. How could the Bank possibly tell a foreigner, especially Morgenthau?

The Treasury promptly cabled Sir Ronald. Britain could not consider stabilization while the United States dollar was undervalued or while the United States was still sucking in the world's gold. The future was uncertain, but unless there was a substantial price rise in the United States the gold bloc would have to devalue or leave gold. Britain, with 2 million unemployed, would not contemplate a renewed deflation for the sake of stabilization. "In any case the British people would have none of it. If challenged on stabilisation, you should make no bones of saying that this country will not contemplate even the risk of having to deflate."[25] Leith-Ross expanded the explanation in a letter:

We have had a good many feelers of different kinds and until the [U.S.] Administration comes out into the open it does not seem to me that we need take such feelers very seriously ... It is very trying that we cannot get either the Americans or the French to understand the fundamental difficulties about stabilisation, but there seems equal dreaminess on other points of American policy.[26]

Lindsay's response was wistful. The undersecretary, he reported, "was disappointed," and the Americans probably felt snubbed. "I dare say the idea I broached ... that the two funds should keep each other informed of their respective operations, is sheer nonsense, but the Americans would, I believe, welcome it."[27] Indeed they would; for the rest of the decade it was one of their consistent demands.

Once more the Foreign Office thought the Treasury unduly abrupt and coarse grained, but it had to transmit a Treasury instruction that was meant to stiffen the ambassador's nerve. Only if the United States would allow a substantial inflation, cut its tariffs dramatically, restart its foreign lending, and/or appreciate the dollar relative to gold would exchange matters improve. The Treasury went on to summarize its reservations about the political domination of American monetary policy:

Our feeling is that so far as possible any further talk about stabilisation had better be avoided ... You should of course continue to report such information as reaches you about US Treasury views, but we feel that in the long run these are of limited value, since the actual course of events will turn on the President's decisions which depend on internal political considerations as they develop from week to week. The only object on their side in conversations would be to get some half promise or commitment out of us while reserving their position for the President to decide.[28]

Leith-Ross himself would not have objected to "quiet conversations" with the French, the Americans, or both, but Chamberlain would not accept even this modest suggestion. Such conversations, the chancellor thought, would be futile and would cause a great deal of political misunderstanding. Fearing that the gold countries would over-devalue in the near future, Leith-Ross wrote, "I think we must continue for the time being to paddle our own canoe as well as we can into the rapids which lie ahead."[29]

Lindsay did not expect that Roosevelt would let him off so easily. Hence Leith-Ross wrote again. Because everything would depend on Roosevelt, he said, in the nature of the case any American emissaries would have nothing definite to tell the ambassador, and so "conversations develop into a fishing expedition on their part in which they try to obtain some commitment on our part, while the essence of our position is that at the moment we are not in a position to tie ourselves up by any commitment at all." And Roosevelt of course would tack by the moment's political breezes.[30]

On the American side, however, Professor Jacob Viner and his fellow advisers in the American Treasury were urging Morgenthau to stabilize exchange rates. Morgenthau himself wished to do so, though he and Roosevelt were determined not to talk of a "return to the gold standard." Further, they insisted that governments, not central banks, be responsible for any such development.

Early in March 1935, Jerome Blum tells us, France asked Morgenthau to offer Britain a joint credit. The pound was falling, and the French were alarmed. Because the British had not asked for the credit, Morgenthau refused, but he did tell the French that he would be happy to see a Franco-British agreement, "assuming that what is presently aimed at is an exchange relation among the pound, franc, and dollar at a level substantially where it has been in the past year,"[31] that is to say, at the five-dollar mark. In April 1935 he told the French ambassador that he favored stabilization at the current exchange rates and that Roosevelt was not opposed. But the State Department was hostile. Cordell Hull thought that the British would have to let the pound depreciate further and that the United States should cooperate in this. If necessary they should work back to the sort of exchange rate that had existed before the adventures of 1933. Roosevelt and Morgenthau overruled Hull, however.

Rebuffed in private, the United States would continue its pressure in public. In mid-April Morgenthau and his advisers began to draft a public statement. Though they worked on it for a month, Morgenthau began to contrive to leak his convictions.[32] Satisfied with the present level of prices, the American authorities were willing to see the dollar at its existing level. If someone were to call an international monetary conference, they would at once attend, but as long as Chamberlain refused to stabilize the pound the United States itself could not call such a conference.

The rumors reached Paris. Flandin wrote personally to Chamberlain, saying he had heard the "American government seemed anxious to negotiate on monetary and economic questions." He asked whether Chamberlain was "still on the same line we spoke of in February."[33] Though the chancellor's answer does not seem to have survived, he must have said yes.

Morgenthau shortly announced that the United States was "not unwilling to stabilise." On 13 May he made a radio broadcast. "The world should know," he said, "that when it is ready to seek foreign exchange stabilisation Washington will not be an obstacle." Of course he said nothing about rates. But he did proceed to put his money behind his announcement: He lent $150 million to the Bank of France.[34]

The Foreign Office was not impressed by the broadcast. Officials minuted, "The United States as a creditor nation are still determined to carry out a 'debtor nation' policy. They have learned nothing and forgotten nothing . . . this speech should be framed."[35]

In Paris and Rome the Morgenthau statement caused immense excitement. Soon Emmanuel Monick was interrogating Leith-Ross. The Americans, Monick said, would contemplate an exchange rate of $4.60 or so, if necessary; France was swinging toward a devaluation of 30 percent. What did Leith-Ross think of Morgenthau's proposal? What were the prospects of a stabilized pound? Leith-Ross was not encouraging. While the United States continued to absorb gold there was nothing to be said for Morgenthau's offer – to restabilize the dollar if all other countries agreed on suitable rates. "I rather doubt," he told the French attaché, "whether the offer was seriously intended . . . I told M. Monick frankly that I had reported to the authorities here the suggestions made to me in Paris and Geneva for a discussion of these questions but that the view here was very definitely that any such discussion would only lead to misunderstandings, which it would be well to avoid."[36]

Sir Frederick Phillips was of like mind. "What would be required," he wrote, "would be a complete reversal of American commercial policy," through which the United States was swallowing the world's gold reserves and its gold production.[37] The Treasury officials saw little or no hope of the French actually moving. "In aptitude for regarding devaluation in a not too unfavorable light Monick is well ahead of Rueff, Rueff well ahead of Baumgartner, and Baumgartner well ahead of Tannery. Tannery is in fact still rigidly opposed, on the ground that 60 per cent of the population look forward to an old age supported by pension or income from savings."[38] By 4 June Norman, Hopkins, Fisher, and Phillips had agreed that it would be pointless to talk stabilization with the French or with the Americans; they also decided that they could not tell the American Treasury what the Exchange Equalisation Account was doing in the market. Chamberlain minuted, "I have read the papers and with every desire to promote stabilisation I see no reasonable prospect of any success in conversations with the French much less the Americans."[39]

May 1935 saw further visits and yet more conversations. Sir Josiah Stamp visited Washington unofficially. He talked to Cordell Hull, Roosevelt, and Morgenthau. Hull definitely wanted some continuing conversations with the British, but neither Roosevelt nor Morgenthau cared very much. Nevertheless, the secretary of the American treasury suggested that there might be an informal meeting on neutral ground – perhaps in Canada.[40]

Meanwhile, in London, Harry Dexter White was taking his first faltering steps as a financial diplomat. On 7 May he turned up in Leith-Ross's office. Later he saw Phillips and also Emmanuel Monick of the French embassy. To the Treasury White argued the case for immediate de facto stabilization of sterling; to Monick he mentioned a rate of $4.60. Monick was pressing the Treasury to begin informal talks about the Anglo-French exchange rate.[41]

The Whitehall officials were not impressed by White.[42] Neither was Monick.[43] The officials had treated him politely, but they saw no reason to be interested in him or his views. They regarded him as a person of no political weight, another of Viner's boys, a meaningless emissary sent without their invitation and without preparation to urge on the United Kingdom a policy the chancellor had publicly and repeatedly rejected. On his return to Washington, however, White succeeded in misleading himself or Morgenthau – or at least Professor Blum, who writes that White "succeeded . . . in winning the confidence of economists and bankers." Further, he says, "although British Treasury officials considered the pound overvalued at the existing rate, their desire for some kind of stabilisation encouraged White, as it encouraged Morgenthau."[44] It would seem that White had misunderstood the Treasury position.

These visits and perturbations led Phillips to set his thoughts in order once again. Should there be stabilization? And could there be talks about it?

As to the first question, Phillips wrote, "Why should we not aim at exchange stability of a temporary or provisional character while definitely refusing to commit ourselves to any change in our existing credit policy?" He found three answers. First of all, it would be senseless to stabilize when rates were so seriously out of equilibrium; the United States would certainly not accept rates that were not disequilibrium rates. Second, a named figure would have a psychological effect on the tightness of credit, especially at the Bank of England, which would inevitably tend to defend the stabilized rate no matter how tentative its stability might theoretically be. Third, to name a figure would be to encourage destructive speculation. Hence there was no hope for a temporary stabilization except on terms that France and the United States were unlikely to accept – especially if the initiative were to come from Britain.[45]

As to the second question, Phillips was prepared to contemplate informal talks with the French as long as the United Kingdom could retain its freedom to manage credit without regard to the exchanges. But he concluded that "unless there is some real assurance that the talks could really be kept informal it might be too dangerous, and we should have to back out at once if it became clear that the French were still harping on our immediate stabilization."[46]

The officials continued to record their reservations about a regime of fixed exchange rates. Though British recovery was well underway, it would not stand the "shocks caused by alterations of credit policy necessitated by difficulties connected with foreign exchange." Britain dare not use credit conditions to manage the exchanges; it did not have enough gold to take shocks on the reserves; even when sterling was strong, there was still considerable risk of losing gold to the United States because the dollar was still undervalued.[47] The Americans could not be expected to remove this undervaluation by agreeing to stabilize at a more suitable rate. In September the Economic Advisory Council observed that the government must keep the power to loosen credit and must not adopt an exchange policy that would restrict this power. Phillips minuted his approval.[48]

The Flandin government fell late in May 1935. After a brief interlude, on 7 June a new government was formed under Pierre Laval. Georges Bonnet was minister of commerce. The new government was, if anything, more eager for a stabilized pound than its predecessor had been. The League of Nations provided a new forum. In August Chamberlain told Anthony Eden that he thought France would drag the question of stabilization before the League Assembly. "This is a matter," he wrote, "on which we definitely do not want public debate if it can be avoided. I shall be very grateful to you for anything you can do to ensure that stabilisation is not discussed."[49] On 17 September, however, Bonnet told the Second Committee of the League that France would negotiate wide-ranging trade agreements with any countries that would stabilize their exchanges – either at the existing parities or perhaps plus or minus 10 percent. This proposal the U.K. delegation thought wholly unacceptable. France, however, continued to talk as if it would promptly reduce its trade barriers in a world of more stabilized exchanges.[50]

At his Mansion House speech on 1 October, Chamberlain mentioned Bonnet's proposal and went on to explain why Britain could not accept it. Until the international skies had cleared and until the dollar and the franc could "look one another in the face without a squint," the pound could not safely be stabilized; the country could not run the risk of tight credit and deflation, which would "be even more disastrous to the Dominions and Colonies."[51]

Thus in autumn 1935 Britain's exchange policy and the reasons for it

were enunciated in public once more. In the winter of 1935–6 no one
was given any reason to believe that policy had changed. Certainly the
international scene was, if anything, more obscure than ever, and with
the advent of the French Popular Front the world was even less likely
to believe in the general equilibrium that was a precondition for exchange commitments. Also, Roosevelt and the Americans were as mer-
curial as ever.

Morgenthau had no reason to think that British policy had changed.
In May 1936 a Whitehall official wrote:

We have, of course, been very successful in keeping stable for some months past
and there is no reason to anticipate any change in general policy. But if we
were to make some agreement about stabilisation we should really be committing ourselves to deflate to any extent that might be necessary to keep the
pound stable. There could be no question of this since the overriding consideration is that we should continue the policy of cheap money so long as we
have so grave a problem of unemployment to face.[52]

Yet by May 1936 Morgenthau had come to believe that he had discovered
a new weapon in his battle to alter that policy.

Britain, Morgenthau was told, had nearly $1,000 million in earmarked
gold at the Bank of France. In Paris, disorder was likely. What would
happen to the gold? Britain would not dare to withdraw it; to do so
would be to put the match to the powder keg. But the U.S. Treasury
would not sell gold to Britain. Some of his advisers were urging Morgenthau to let the Bank of England buy. He would not surrender so
great a weapon. If there were to be riots in Paris or if France were to
embargo gold export, Britain would have to come to the United States
for gold (Morgenthau had forgotten about South African gold). Morgenthau would then have Chamberlain at his mercy. Roosevelt and
Morgenthau were agreed that this was desirable. Indeed, why not prompt
the French to apply an embargo? On 11 May President Roosevelt did so.

The President saw the French Ambassador who is leaving tomorrow for France.
He talked stabilisation with him – gave Laboulaye a definite hint that the
French should embargo gold in order that the British would have to come to
us and that if they did so, we would drive a bargain with them which would
take care of the French interests.[53]

Morgenthau had already told the President what sort of bargain he
had in mind. He did not care if the pound rose relative to the dollar.
But he would worry if it fell.[54]

On 29 April Morgenthau asked Roosevelt for permission to discuss
stabilization with the British. But Roosevelt, who, Morgenthau noted,
thoroughly distrusted Chamberlain and the British, resisted the idea.

The president thought the idea should come first from the London side. Nevertheless, the president did allow Morgenthau to bring the matter up. The British, Morgenthau thought, would do anything to prevent the French from devaluing.[55] Why he thought this is not apparent.

In May 1936, therefore, Morgenthau had returned to the charge. For the time being he did not want to know about the Exchange Equalisation Account. But on 5 May, meeting Bewley at dinner, he implied that it would be useful to have a better channel of communication with London. This proposal was repeated in stronger terms on 18 May, when Morgenthau said that it was up to the United Kingdom to "make the next move." He was clearly annoyed that Chamberlain had been so unforthcoming.[56]

The Treasury thought this matter very important indeed. So did Sir Ronald Lindsay. The ambassador, noting that American monetary policy had become "much more responsible," thought that Morgenthau wanted a new statement of British policy in light of the current French difficulties. Chamberlain minuted, "The Americans seem to have some chronic grievance against us, but I confess I do not know what it is all about." Nevertheless, after Chamberlain and the foreign secretary had discussed the problem the ambassador was instructed to tell Morgenthau that Chamberlain welcomed the American desire to use Bewley. He was also told to explain the chancellor's monetary policy. There would be cheap money and no deflation; eventually there would be a new gold standard, but the Exchange Equalisation Account was used to smooth fluctuations, not to depreciate the pound. If the franc were to be devalued, there might be a drain of refugee funds from London, but the pound-dollar rate would probably not change very much. Finally, Lindsay was to ask for some assurance that Britain would be able to buy gold with dollars.[57]

Lindsay himself, and the Foreign Office officials, strongly favored such Anglo-American cooperation. In London Lord Cranborne observed, "The Treasury have shown themselves unresponsive to earlier advances by the United States and it is difficult to see what we can hope to gain by administering a series of snubs." Chamberlain's position, however, was simple and logical enough. There was really very little that could be discussed with the United States. Britain's monetary policy was well known; the Accounts' operations would not be disclosed; "on questions such as the source of currency raids we have little or no information beyond the gossip of the Exchange market which is reproduced in the daily press." American monetary policy remained irresponsible. Having swallowed masses of gold in the past 24 months, it still would not say whether it would ever disgorge. "Until that position is cleared up,"

Chamberlain cabled Lindsay, "it is altogether premature to be thinking about re-establishment of an international monetary system on a permanent basis. This is a matter which may be distasteful for Mr. Morgenthau to discuss. You might refer to it indirectly if a suitable opportunity offered, but you should use the greatest tact in doing so." [58]

Bewley passed all this to Morgenthau on 1 June. Each country, he said, must make up its own mind as to the time for returning to gold. Blum reports that Morgenthau found the news encouraging: "obviously the British were reconciled to the American decision of 1933 to avoid stabilisation until the dollar was adjusted to domestic conditions. Obviously also they were prepared to work with the United States to sustain the existing dollar-pound ratio." [59] It is very hard to see how Blum could reach this conclusion on the basis of the Morgenthau Diaries, or how the secretary of the treasury could believe such things on the basis of Bewley's report. Nothing had been said about the exchange rate, or about 1933; Britain had not opposed the American decision about stabilization in 1933 but had objected instead to the confusion that President Roosevelt had spread through his complex dealings and changes of mind. One also wonders what Morgenthau thought new in the statement; it merely reiterated what Chamberlain had been saying since 1932. Nevertheless, Lindsay reported that Morgenthau was delighted: the statement had removed all his suspicions with respect to British monetary policy.[60]

Almost at once Morgenthau began to use the "Bewley channel." On 4 June he asked Bewley to ask the Treasury about a joint Anglo-American statement to the effect that if the French were to devalue by not more than 30 percent the pound and the dollar would continue to be held at their previous levels. This is a perplexing statement; one wonders just what this level relates to. One supposes that the secretary meant the Americans would not reduce the gold value of the dollar and the British would not reduce the pound relative to the dollar. If Morgenthau could ask such a question or make such a proposal he had certainly not understood Bewley's statement of 1 June. Morgenthau wished to propose this to the French who, he said, had told him that they would devalue if international agreement were possible. What did London think?[61]

Bewley believed Morgenthau had activated the channel simply to put this suggestion forward. Whitehall knew as well as Morgenthau that Léon Blum, whose Cabinet was about to assume office, was pledged to avoid devaluation. The American had asked his Paris representative to approach Vincent Auriol, Blum's finance minister, for any indication as to policies on exchange rates or gold embargoes. However, there is

no indication in the Morgenthau Diaries that he had got any word before he talked with Bewley on 4 June. On 5 June Merle Cochran cabled:
Auriol did not have any faith in a large monetary conference, and he
planned no immediate monetary actions. On 6 June Morgenthau again
telephoned Cochran in Paris. He was to see Auriol and to find out if it
"would be helpful to the French if they could devalue knowing that the
United States and England would not devalue further." The same day
Cochran reported that Auriol did not find the suggestion appealing. He
was unwilling to "enter into a separate tripartite agreement on these
terms," though he would like some more all-enveloping "monetary truce
at agreed rates" that the United States would informally arrange. It was
especially important to include the Dutch and the Swiss. Auriol could
not approach Britain, he said; the United States must do so. It was
important not to upset Germany, Italy, or even Russia, whose ruble was
pegged to the franc. Bewley learned of this message on the same day.
American emissaries, Morgenthau said, would approach the Dutch and
the Swiss.[62]

The Foreign Office thought Morgenthau's behavior "unwise and
precipitate." Lord Cranborne observed:

Evidently the French Government, undecided as to what they will do, are reluctant to take the first step in approaching us. The Chancellor of the Exchequer, on the other hand, declines to move unless approached by the French.
Meanwhile Mr. Morgenthau wrings his hands and says that if matters are left
to drift the French will do something silly, such as the imposition of drastic
exchange restrictions.[63]

The Treasury disliked Morgenthau's initiative just as violently as
did France and the Foreign Office. As yet, the French had not approached
the British; the Bank of England had no reason to suppose that France
would do anything decisive at once, and the Treasury knew that officially France was still tied to gold.[64] Chamberlain had the strongest
possible objections to Morgenthau's proposal. He could not fix an exchange rate without new legislation, and he did not want to do so. He
did not want France to devalue by more than 20 percent, though Morgenthau seemed willing to tolerate 25 percent to 30 percent. Further,
there was the risk that France might stabilize on sterling. "Morgenthau
would no doubt dislike this intensely," but Britain could not prevent
it, though Britain would rather see France stay with gold at a lower
parity. Finally, Morgenthau could not be allowed to state Britain's
policy as he proposed, "since he could not be expected to put the matter
in the words we should use ourselves, or to give proper weight to our
qualifications."[65] Chamberlain quickly agreed with Phillips and Norman that "it is most unwise to be drawn into all this." Their reason was

semipolitical. "It is impossible to say how France would react to advice. If the French ask for our opinion, or for our assistance, it would be a different matter."[66] Chamberlain later explained why it would be dangerous to suggest any particular course of action to the French: "If they act accordingly, all the blame for any subsequent mismanagement would be laid upon ourselves."[67] A prescient remark, given the rough waters through which the French monetary authorities would have to steer the franc.

According to Dr. Clarke and Professor Blum, "neither the French nor the British were ready to act."[68] The French perhaps were not ready; the British certainly had good reason for not acting.

Lindsay was instructed accordingly. Chamberlain was not inclined to take any initiative, though he would talk to the French if they approached him. The law did not allow him to keep the pound at any particular level, and he thought public opinion would not tolerate the legislation that such a commitment would require. He was legally prevented from using the Exchange Equalisation Account in this way. On the other hand, he saw no reason to expect any considerable changes in the dollar-sterling rate. As for the French problem, he had nothing to suggest.[69]

The next day Bewley explained London's position to Morgenthau, who concluded that "as things stood they could only wait for a while and see what happened."[70] London agreed. On 8 June Léon Blum had made a speech that committed France to stability at the existing rate. "Until that idea breaks down there is nothing to be done – and there would be no point in Anglo-American conversations.[71]

Roosevelt had agreed that Morgenthau could sell gold from the American stabilization fund, with or without a public announcement. The documents had been drafted, and the president had signed them.[72] However, the secretary did not tell Bewley this for many, many weeks.

Morgenthau's advisers had become very excited about his splendid initiative with respect to exchange rates and its enormous value. Like the secretary himself, they believed that only London was standing in the way of a franc devaluation and a tripartite agreement on rates. The important thing now was to "break that London ice so that they should show their hand to some extent so that the world would know where it is."[73] The secretary, meanwhile, continued to explore the matter, even though neither Britain nor France had welcomed his initiative. On 8 June he met with Harrison and Williams of the Federal Reserve Bank of New York and with several eminent private bankers. What should exchange rates be, and how wide should be the spreads? The consensus was that if the Blum government embarked on a program of government spending and monetary inflation France would have to devalue. The bankers thought that the United States should agree to stabilize exchange rates with a French devaluation of 20 to 25 percent and with the pound between $4.75 and $4.90. It was then hovering around $5.00.[74] Cordell Hull had already reported that if France would devalue by 20 percent it would be "satisfactory." What a pity that the French did not want to.[75]

In mid-June Bewley left Washington, remaining in London until the end of July. For the time being, therefore, Ray Atherton of the American embassy was to be the link between the two treasuries. He spoke to Chamberlain on 15 June at the chancellor's request.[76] Chamberlain explained that there were risks of misunderstanding because the two governments worked on different principles. No American could make a binding commitment because Congress might always overrule the executive branch. Chamberlain explained that as in London the day-to-day management of exchange was in the hands of the Bank there would be little point in a direct transatlantic link between treasuries. In any case, he observed, Britain would not peg the exchange, and it was still dangerous to suggest any particular line of action to the French.[77]

Atherton asked for fortnightly meetings. Almost at once, however, he went home on leave. Also, the State Department was slow to give its permission. Hence these regular meetings began only late in 1936, after the Tripartite Declarations of September 1936 had been devised.

Morgenthau, hoping to save French democracy and to pacify Europe by a grand international monetary coup, was not alive to the danger that the French would object to advice or use it against the givers. The British had told him that they would not approach the French though they would not rebuff any French approach. The French said that they could not approach the British though they would not say why.[78] From Paris Merle Cochran shortly urged Morgenthau to let him tell Auriol that the British wanted to hear directly from the French. Morgenthau at first demurred but then gave way: Cochran would tell Auriol and also the Dutch. Speculating on the reasons for Britain's insistence on a French approach, Morgenthau concluded that Britain wanted to put France under some obligation so as to extract trade concessions.[79]

It is true that in the conversations of September 1936 the Treasury and the Board of Trade did try to extract some such concessions. But in June 1936, such matters do not appear to have been mentioned. Chamberlain was reluctant to act, but his reasons were very different.

In their public statements, Léon Blum and Vincent Auriol continued to decry devaluation. According to Blum, socialists could not devalue because speculators had long been working to that end. According to

Auriol, devaluation would not work because workers would at once demand corresponding wage increases. Prices would soar; the government would have to inflate. On the other hand, from Paris Ernest Rowe-Dutton was telling Treasury and Foreign Office that the Blum government would be obliged to do something: devalue the franc, float it while prohibiting the export of gold, or control the exchanges.[80] But none of this was new. Ever since 1933 Whitehall had been expecting that sooner or later the franc would fall. Blum's Front populaire had affected the timetable but not the prediction itself; sooner rather than later, it would have to swallow its words and bring the franc down.

The French leaders had begun to lay the foundations for a change in policy. In the Senate on 16 June Blum said that no one contemplates devaluation "except as part of international arrangements . . . and of a contractual and general alignment." On 19 June Auriol said that unilateral devaluation was a danger and an illusion because other countries might simply do likewise or might impose trade barriers. Hence one could not be sure that devaluation would revive the export trade. Also, wage levels might rise. An agreed monetary realignment would be a different matter, but it was "difficult." Rowe-Dutton suggested,

It looks as if the aim of the Government would be . . . to secure international assurances as a preliminary to a devaluation which may prove less politically dangerous after labour has received the first-fruits of the accession to power of the *front populaire* . . . The present measures of the government in the monetary sphere may be designed to enable them to proclaim that they have done everything in their power to avoid devaluation, so that, if it comes, it can be represented as due to the power of events (including malevolent influences) and not to deliberate choice.[81]

While Rowe-Dutton was writing, however, Emmanuel Monick was already in Washington.[82]

9

The Tripartite Agreement of 1936

In the last chapter, we saw that the years 1933–6 were littered with Franco-American initiatives in the matter of exchange rates. Throughout these years, Chamberlain's position was consistent: The pound would not be artificially devalued, but neither would it be pegged to gold or to the dollar until the world had been freed of the trading and financial barriers that had made the old gold standard unworkable. In public and in private he and his officials put forward this view. Behind the scenes British policy makers were more divided. Leith-Ross and the Bank continued to hanker after a fixed exchange rate, whereas Phillips and the chancellor were persuaded that it was unsafe to imperil the domestic cheap-money policy by committing the country to a fixed rate. Further, it is possible to assert that through the Exchange Equalisation Account the pound *was* being kept below its market value. Certainly the Account and the Bank were accumulating gold. On the other hand, the authorities knew that sterling balances were also accumulating, and they were aware that hot money was flowing into the London market. In these conditions, it may be argued, they were right to strengthen their gold reserves. If this claim is granted, Chamberlain and his officials were correct in stating that the pound was not being depreciated artificially. As for the internal disputes about a fixed rate, neither the French officials nor the Americans were made aware of these differences, though perhaps they were known to American and French central bankers.

It is widely believed that in 1936 British policy changed. This belief derives from a further belief that in September 1936 the British government joined with the American and French governments in something called a Tripartite Stabilisation Agreement. Other countries, we are told, then adhered thereto. Leith-Ross tells us that the Tripartite Agreement was aimed at "limiting the fluctuations of the dollar, pound, and franc, and gradually restoring stable exchanges." It was, he writes, "the basis of our currency policy until the Second World War."[1] According to W. Arthur Lewis,

When in 1936 France decided to leave the Gold Standard, Britain, France and the United States signed a tripartite agreement not to alter exchange rates without consultation. The gold standard had not been restored, but the intentions and the practical consequences of the new arrangements were similar . . . The gay unilateral abandonment of the Gold Standard gave way to . . . stability by agreement, starting with the tripartite agreement of 1936.[2]

More recently, Charles Kindleberger has written, "The Tripartite Monetary Agreement committed the major powers to almost nothing, but constituted a significant step in rebuilding the international economic system . . . For the first time after June 1933, exchange rates were discussed, technical arrangements made, and international co-operation built in the monetary area . . . the statement in the Tripartite Declaration that the constant object of policy is to maintain equilibrium in international exchange and to avoid utmost disturbance there by monetary action represented a fundamental change."[3]

Finally, in Susan Strange's recent work we are told that the agreement was partly "to maintain the parity of the newly devalued franc by means of an exchange equalisation account" and partly to "regulate the dollar-sterling rate in the common interest of the two leaders and of the currency areas group around them."[4]

There was, strictly speaking, no agreement at all. On 26 September His Majesty's government in the United Kingdom published a declaration about its attitude to the French devaluation and about its own exchange policy as affected thereby. France and the United States issued their own declarations. But the terms of the three declarations had been harmonized among the three governments and were, in all matters of substance, identical. This harmonization, in turn, was the end of an exercise in financial diplomacy – an exercise that may be said to have begun formally late in June 1936. Behind this exercise lie the various initiatives and conversations that we have traced in the last two chapters. Now we shall see how Chamberlain maintained his position, and his freedom of action, when faced with unacceptable demands or suggestions – now from the Americans, and now from the French.

Stephen Clarke has recently traced the steps of this exercise in financial diplomacy.[5] The present chapter parallels Clarke's work, which is based on some though not all of the same documentary materials. With respect to the actual course of the negotiation we will not add much to Clarke's account. Indeed, we might well have referred the reader to that account, thereby shortening this chapter dramatically. But if we had done so, there would have been an awkward break in the narrative. Further, our questions are not quite the same as Clarke's. He is interested partly in the actual process of negotiation itself and partly in the declarations as representing "the first step . . . toward the rebuilding of an international monetary system."[6] We are more interested in other matters: how British policy was presented and defended in the course of the negotiations; what Britain wanted of the French and feared about the Americans; whether the declaration does mark any sort of turning point in the management of sterling; what Whitehall meant by the declarations, and what it thought they would produce. In Chapter 10 we shall see how great was the gap between expectation and reality.

As Kindleberger points out, in September 1936 Britain did not agree to stabilize the pound.[7] But as we shall see in Chapter 10 the declarations did quickly produce a rigidity of the sterling-dollar rate that the United Kingdom had certainly not intended. On the other hand, that rate did change, and change considerably, after the declarations appeared on 26 September. Further, thereafter the franc was devalued several times and was, intermittently, a freely floating currency. We shall trace these developments in Chapter 10. They are interesting because they show how three parallel declarations, which were not meant to constrain British policy, were transmuted into an arrangement that certainly did constrain it.

1. *The events of late June and July*

In June 1936 Emmanuel Monick had come to Washington. Normally based in London, where he was France's financial attaché, Monick was a convinced devaluationist. He also believed that France could devalue only with the cooperation of Britain and the United States. At this time British officials did not know that he was in Washington. But by October 1936 he had told the Treasury that he had been sent on a secret mission to prepare for the devaluation of the franc in an internationally acceptable way. He also reported that the Franco-American discussions had assumed a tripartite stabilization rate of 100 francs = \$4.86 = 1 pound.[1] Leith-Ross later wrote that for years Monick had worked toward a realignment of currencies.[2] In Washington Monick conferred with Morgenthau, Roosevelt, and various officials.[3]

Roosevelt insisted that France would have to approach Britain directly, lest the British *amour propre* be wounded. Monick agreed to do this. France would definitely devalue, Monick explained, but for this it needed the support of Britain and France. Morgenthau assured Monick that so long as American prices did not fall, and so long as there was no large flight of capital from the United States to France, America would not retaliate against French devaluation. He explained, "We feel that if France would devalue, it's the one barrier for the moment which is

keeping the world from getting together on stabilisation of currencies."
The real problem, in Monick's opinion, was the United Kingdom.
Chamberlain and the rest "wanted to keep the pound independent and
refuse to come to any agreement." Morgenthau agreed that Britain was
the stumbling block. Fortunately, France would not have to consult
Switzerland, Holland, or even Russia. Nor need there be multilateral
discussions or even a large number of bilateral conversations. Monick
had been empowered to negotiate with the United States and with
Britain. The pound, Monick said, should be in the range $4.75 to $4.97.
"We have got to limit the fluctuations of the pound, and . . . it is awfully
important to make these definite rates." France, he said, would have gold
and fix the franc at 100 to the pound. Morgenthau refused to endorse
these rates or ranges; "it is too early," he said.

When Monick had arrived in Washington, the French authorities had
been eager for quick action. When he left on 30 June, they were not so
pressing. Monick and Morgenthau agreed that the next approach should
be left to the British. Monick, however, did not call at the Treasury
until 22 July. He then reported to the officials that France wished to
devalue by one-third but only in the context of some tripartite agreement. If Britain would agree to keep the pound between $4.75 and $4.97,
France would fix an exchange rate of 100 to the pound, with gold points
of plus and minus 2½ percent.[4]

For three years the Treasury had expected and hoped for a French
devaluation. But now France was proposing to join the sterling area!
It would be much better, the officials argued, for France to devalue and
stay on the gold standard. Already the Exchange Equalisation Account
was unable to buy gold with its American dollars. So far as Whitehall
knew, it would never be able to do so. In fact Morgenthau already had
the presidential approval for gold sales.[5] Further, on 22 July he told
Bewley that in the context of a tripartite agreement and with the pound
stabilized between $4.90 and $5.00 he would sell gold at $5.00 and buy
it at $4.90.[6] Whitehall did not know about the former arrangement
and had not yet heard about the latter statement. But the French proposal was offensive in more critical ways. First, it would commit the
British to support the franc. Second, it would oblige the British to peg
the pound vis-à-vis the dollar.

The French, with malice or in confusion, were proposing gold points
such that when the franc was weak Britain would lose gold, and when it
was strong gold would flow to Paris, not to London. Sir Frederick Phillips quickly detected the flaw.[7]

Much more serious was the stabilization that France clearly meant to force on the pound. Phillips remarked that the proposals would put the United Kingdom back on the gold standard. Waley wrote on 22 July,

we cannot, I take it, give any assurances of this kind . . . Our policy is to manage sterling so as to suit our own economy . . . The French idea of co-operation is as usual one-sided. In return for France doing what she needs to do to save her from disaster and for America doing what she in any case intends to do, we are asked to alter our whole monetary policy, and to receive nothing in return except the satisfaction of helping France to overcome internal political difficulties.[8]

Monick told Waley that he realized the British position. He assured the Treasury official, "The manner in which we receive the French proposal is really more importan than the formula which we agree to adopt." But as Britain could not risk offending Roosevelt and Blum, Waley thought it would have to agree to a formula, even if it would mean very little.[9]

Monick spoke to Chamberlain, who agreed to meet Blum at lunch on 27 July.[10] Then began an attempt to find a form of words by which the United Kingdom could bless a French devaluation. At first Monick pressed for the stabilization of sterling. Chamberlain insisted that he was not prepared to stabilize sterling on gold, the dollar, or anything else. But when the French offered a draft declaration, he wrote, "I am afraid this shows that the French want to do exactly what I told M. Blum I could not agree to, viz., find a formula which will mean one thing to them and another to us."[11]

2. The events of September

In London, by late August, it was thought that the French would not act soon. The chancellor had gone off on holiday. Monick, Washington learned, no longer had his government behind him.[1] If France did eventually devalue, there need be no Anglo-American retribution, but Britain would still refuse to "hold the pound between certain gold points." Phillips wrote early in September, "The letter, now in draft, which the Chancellor of the Exchequer expressed himself willing to send to the French Government, if asked, is not of course in any way dependent on USA co-operation nor on the other hand will it need alteration should USA-French co-operation prove to be a fact."[2] But the Whitehall officials were not to be let off so lightly.

Through August nothing was heard from Paris. Until early September the French still had not decided what, if anything, to do.[3] But on 4 September Vincent Auriol, the French finance minister, saw Cochran.

He had prepared a "prestabilization" agreement for submission to Britain and the United States. Would the secretary prefer to see it first, or should it go simultaneously to London and to Washington? After conferring with Feis and Viner, Morgenthau decided that it should be simultaneously submitted, and he reported as much to the British embassy;[4] Whitehall, he told the embassy, would shortly be made aware of the French proposals, which would, he said, "deal solely with the subject of stabilisation."[5]

On 9 September both capitals received a quite remarkable text.[6] France proposed to propose that Britain, France, and the United States should conclude a prestabilization agreement, which would fix limits for the values of the three currencies relative to one another. "These limits shall not be modified except by common agreement or subject to notifying the contracting powers in case of exceptional and unforeseen circumstances, the final objective of the contracting parties being the general return to the international gold standard when the conditions necessary are found to be realised." The limits would be specified only after the Anglo-Saxons had approved the text in principle.

"In pursuance of the policy of the closest contact with the British Treasury," Morgenthau at once told the embassy of Auriol's sounding "regarding stabilisation." It was planned, he said, to deliver a note simultaneously to Britain and the United States on 8 September. That note "will deal solely with the subject of stabilisation."[7]

Distressed and worried, Sir Frederick Phillips wrote:

If the French put forward the plan previously mentioned, viz. devaluation to about 100 francs, we will promise warm sympathy etc. and undertake not to retaliate either by lowering the pound or by imposing countervailing duties on French goods. But I fear from Morgenthau's telegram that he thinks he can get us into a tripartite talk on stabilisation all round. This the Chancellor will certainly refuse; the draft letter mentioned above made it explicitly clear that he was not prepared to keep the pound between fixed gold points.[8]

To Washington, Vincent Auriol said that if the franc were attacked once more there would be exchange control. Jacques Rueff added that there was need for haste lest France be forced to act unilaterally. In London Monick conveyed a similar impression of urgency when he delivered the prestabilization proposal, though from Paris Ernest Rowe-Dutton had just reported that the French Cabinet still had not decided what, if anything, to do.[9]

In Scotland Chamberlain minuted despairingly: "At almost a moment's notice they bring up what are practically the old [unacceptable] proposals and try to rush us into them by saying they have communicated them to the USA. The procedure makes a very bad impression on

my mind."[10] Phillips observed that the "French documents are even
more hopeless than we could have expected. They represent in fact a
proposal for a stabilisation agreement."[11] Further, they were supported
by threats either of exchange control or of a unilateral linking of the
franc to the pound. What to do? Britain must adhere to Chamberlain's
draft statement, which simply asserted that Britain would not *retaliate*
against a French devaluation. Prepared in July at France's urging, it
had been transmitted to Paris, but it had not been made public.

To Phillips the new French proposal was objectionable for several reasons, old and new. Briton would lose its liberty of action with respect to
the control of credit. Once the limits for the pound were known, there
would be risk of speculation. It would be hard to agree with the Americans just before their presidential election. If the French were to link
to the pound, on the other hand, by choosing the gold points they could
ensure that

the practical control of the exchange between London and Paris will have
passed from our hands to those of the French. Moreover it would be much more
difficult for us to control the value of sterling in terms of gold when it is no
longer possible for us to purchase francs in Paris with the certainty of being
able to convert them as we please into gold bullion . . . our efforts to control the
external value of sterling would be practically limited to operations in the
London gold market, in the absence of any arrangements with the Americans
similar to those we have had hitherto with the French.[12]

Without consulting the Americans, Phillips and Chamberlain devised
a chilly response. Monick received it on 14 September, and the chancellor cabled its purport to Washington. The note reiterated the July
promise not to retaliate by devaluing the pound or by imposing dis-
criminating duties as long as France chose a rate of 100 francs to the
pound. But it emphasized that Britain had made no commitment as
to the dollar rate, nor would it do so.[13] To Morgenthau, the Treasury reported that the chancellor would not make such a commitment because
he had to allow for "the credit policy needed for domestic recovery
and the prospects of stable international relations." Finally, the chancellor wanted "no formal convention" on exchanges.[14]

Thanks to Professor Blum and the Morgenthau Diaries themselves,
we know something of the terms in which Washington received the
French proposal. Naturally enough, neither Morgenthau nor Roosevelt
liked the reference to the gold standard. But they and their advisers
wanted to know what exchange rates the French had in mind and what
to do about the pound. Among Morgenthau's advisers, Herbert Feis
thought the proposal "fantastic." The French, he said, "had apparently
not learned much in the past three years."[15] Meeting with Harry Dexter

White and other officials, Morgenthau thought that a 25 percent devaluation would be inappropriate given American prices. For France, 15 to 20 percent should be enough. Taylor pointed out that for the United States England mattered more: "so far as France alone is concerned we could afford to be generous providing sterling and the sterling group did not drop in relation to the dollar." Lochhead urged the case for a five-cent franc and a five-dollar pound.[16] Roosevelt also found this attractive. Neither Morgenthau nor Hull was inclined to press at once for a written agreement; until after the American elections, a gentlemen's agreement would suffice.[17]

To a casual reader, the American response closely resembles the British. Professor Blum, finding both in the Morgenthau Diaries, concludes that Chamberlain and Morgenthau had rejected the French proposal for the same reason: fear of rigid exchange rates and desire to remain "on a day-to-day basis, to avoid any declaration that resembled a treaty, and to rely instead upon informal co-operation and international good will." Blum writes that the proposal "failed to permit the flexibility which both England and the United States had consistently demanded."[18] If he means flexibility in exchange rates, Blum is clearly wrong: While it wanted the right to manipulate the dollar vis-à-vis *gold*, the American government certainly did not want to leave Britain a similar power over the sterling-dollar rate. Morgenthau himself was of the same opinion: On 14 September he told Cochran that the "British reply is in main substance the same as our reply."[19] In fact, as Dr. Clarke has detected,[20] the two responses could hardly be more different.

With Roosevelt's approval, Morgenthau cabled an anodyne response that could mean almost anything and that committed the United States to nothing.[21] Understandably, this message provoked from the French an anguished inquiry: Just what, in fact, did Morgenthau propose to *do*?[22] As Cochran reported, France wanted to "get at something concrete," preferably through an American counterproposal.

Through the British embassy, Morgenthau received an account of the French initiative and Chamberlain's response.[23] If there were a "reasonable" devaluation of the franc, Britain would not retaliate by depreciating the pound or imposing discriminatory duties. Indeed, it would try to ensure that the price of sterling would not undergo "undue fluctuations." But the chancellor would not "give a guarantee that the pound should be linked to gold within points that were fixed." He would have to guide himself not only by the disadvantages of international monetary instability but also "by the opinion he may form from time to time of the credit policy which stable international relations and domestic recovery might make necessary."

The chancellor's response was a good deal more definite than the American. Britain would not peg the pound; it would not retaliate; it would continue its efforts to prevent undue day-to-day fluctuations in exchange rates; it did not want a formal agreement. Only the most charitable reader could discover any such concrete meaning in the Morgenthau text. Nor did it surprise the French. When Monick received the British reply, Sir Frederick Phillips observed that the attaché had "scarcely tried to hide the fact that the latest approach was really a try-on to which they did not really expect any answer other than the one we gave."[24]

Discussions now proceeded in Paris, with Leith-Ross representing Britain and Cochran the United States. The French continued to press for a joint declaration that they could publish. It seems they had not realized that Chamberlain's original letter was meant for publication;[25] perhaps they continued to hope that the chancellor would eventually agree to peg the pound. From Washington Morgenthau was telling Cochran, "It is our understanding that statements by the three Governments will be made only when the specific limits of a mutually acceptable alignment of the three currencies have been determined. If I read the British reply to the French note correctly, the British Treasury has the same expectation."[26] Of course Morgenthau was wrong. Britain cared about the franc-pound rate but would give no undertakings as to the dollar-pound rate. It is hard to see how Morgenthau and his advisers, having been told the truth so often, could cling to this illusion. But Vincent Auriol, the French finance minister, wanted preambles and declarations that would place the declaration in a wider context. It was to be a demonstration of monetary amity and a step toward the solidarity of the freedom-loving world. As Cochran reported, the trouble was to convince Auriol that the British and American proposals would achieve this end. If the French public did not perceive the declaration as "international monetary peace," Auriol believed there might be communist riots and the fall of the French government.[27] In response to Anglo-American pressure Auriol gradually yielded some ground. At the joint insistence of London and Washington he purged the draft of all reference to the gold standard and to fixed exchange rates and ranges of variation. At American insistence he abandoned the idea of a single declaration. Instead he accepted Morgenthau's proposal for three cognate statements. He had wanted a version that spoke of freedom and harmony and other absolutes, thereby embarrassing the U.K. Treasury immensely. As Hopkins wrote, "The French draft of a joint declaration . . . to speak as kindly as possible, strikes me as inconceivably French."[28]

Once the joint draft had gone, each government could work on its own version, subject to the approval of the other two. But it was irritating to observe that the French still had not definitely said how much they proposed to devalue or exactly how. Leith-Ross thought they would move the rate farther than anyone had previously expected. Certainly they would go beyond 100 francs to the pound, the rate envisaged in Chamberlain's July letter. Further, they now thought of an almost inconvertible franc. It seemed the paper franc would buy gold only if it were presented by the central bank of a country that was on the gold standard. Thus Britain would not qualify, nor, in all likelihood, would the United States.

On 17 September Vincent Auriol sent Chamberlain a new draft declaration. Chamberlain saw it on 22 September when he returned to London after his holidays. The new draft was so vague that it might mean anything. Like its predecessors, it spoke of peace, liberty, and international order. It mentioned an eventual return to gold, "when necessary conditions have been realised." But it did not say what France was actually proposing to do. As the French schemes seemed to change from day to day, Chamberlain insisted that before issuing any declaration he must have a written statement of France's intentions. Accordingly, Monick visited Sir Richard Hopkins on the evening of 22 September. He explained that the plan was to fix 43 and 49 milligrams of gold as the upper and lower limits for the franc. As long as the pound was about $4.84, France would aim at 105 francs to the pound. The three equalization funds would agree from day to day on the exchange rates to be aimed at and would sell gold to each other at such rates. Because the pound was overvalued, Monick observed, the French authorities had to retain a wide spread; for French trade, it was the pound that mattered, and only a rate of 105 or more would justify the French authorities in removing or relaxing trade quotas. The Bank of France in fact wanted a rate between 110 and 124.[29]

Meanwhile, from Washington the embassy reported that Morgenthau thought a statement would be made only "when specific limits on a mutually acceptable alignment of the three currencies have been determined."[30] It would seem that neither Morgenthau nor his advisers had yet noticed Chamberlain's unwillingness to make any such commitment. Monick, however, maintained that the current French proposals left the United Kingdom in control of the pound – "so long as we did not use this liberty to depreciate or appreciate the pound in terms of gold beyond the limits fixed for the franc."[31]

In Paris, Blum was becoming restless. On 23 September he sent Monick to beg Leith-Ross for a quick decision. Leith-Ross took the opportunity to point out how unsatisfactory the French behavior had been. Chamberlain had only had the French proposals for 24 hours. These proposals differed from those of July, from Monick's suggestions of 9 September, and from the remarks that Vincent Auriol had made when Leith-Ross had been in Paris. At that time it had seemed that France planned to devalue but stay on gold, as Belgium had done. Now it appeared France would leave gold while trying to tie the United Kingdom to gold, although Chamberlain had repeatedly said that he would not make any such promise. Was there a lack of candor? No, Monick asserted, merely inexperience. He tried to convince Leith-Ross that the French were really not trying to fasten Britain to a gold standard, and he explained that if the tripartite conversations did not succeed there would be exchange control or a gold embargo in any event.[32]

By 23 September the Whitehall officials had already agreed that they could accept a rate of 110 francs to the pound, or a central rate of 105. As Hopkins wrote, the right exchange rate was unknowable. What was important was that devaluation succeed. That is, it must go far enough to convince the speculators to return their funds to France. But the officials were still uneasy about the arrangements for the purchase of gold. Phillips argued that before committing itself to anything Britain should ask for details of the proposed gold arrangements.[33] Further, they were increasingly determined to extract some sort of promise about the relaxation of French quotas, a major impediment to Anglo-French trade. Finally, as in 1933, they worried about the control of the exchange rates in the new dispensation. Who would fix the price of the franc in terms of pounds? The British Equalisation Account? Or the French?

On the evening of 23 September, after Monick had left, Leith-Ross and Hopkins talked to Chamberlain. It had been intended that Leith-Ross should transmit through Monick a very stiff note for Vincent Auriol. This would have urged France to stick to a free gold standard, urged the finance minister to wait a week or ten days if he could not do so, and suggested that if France could neither stick with gold nor wait Britain could not make any declaration of encouragement.[34] But Leith-Ross had agreed, in light of Blum's appeal, that Monick need not transmit this to Vincent Auriol. He then argued to Chamberlain that France could not be expected to go back to a free gold standard; this must have been a French Treasury proposal, and the French authorities must have definitively rejected it. Nor would it be safe to wait for a week or ten days. Agreeing, Chamberlain then began to consider what sort of declaration he might make. Monick received this new draft at 11:00 P.M.[35]

The declaration committed Britain so to manage its monetary policy as to "avoid so far as possible any disturbance of the basis of international exchanges arising out of the proposed realignment." Monick explained that Paris now proposed that the exchange authorities' currency balances could be converted into gold each day. Thus the Treasury and the Bank of England had got their way. Paris also wanted the British to agree that the franc could be further devalued in future, if necessary.

On the other hand, Chamberlain had begun to press the French to remove their quotas and exchange controls. It will be recalled that Morgenthau had believed the British would apply such pressure. Within the circle of officials, it had been suggested for some time that this be done. France's quota system was a serious impediment to world trade. So were its high protective duties. The franc once devalued, the excuse for these devices would be gone. So Whitehall argued. But it began to do so only at the last minute, and its success was slight.

On the morning of 24 September, having consulted Paris, Monick proposed a counter-draft. Later Waley wrote that it "went some way to meet our views, but still would have committed us too far in the direction of an attempt definitely to stabilise the pound."[36] Chamberlain later devised a new version. Transmitting it to Morgenthau, he remarked on his disappointment that France was not remaining on a free gold standard, because a managed currency would not restore French confidence. He would have liked, he said, to spend more time in examination and in consulting Morgenthau. But Blum's appeal had moved him to act at once.[37] In the evening of 25 September, the French government accepted, with minor alterations, Chamberlain's most recent revision. It appeared that the declaration could be issued at nine o'clock that very evening. Unfortunately, at that point Morgenthau intervened. By raising at the last minute the awkward question of the dollar-sterling rate, Roosevelt and Morgenthau almost disrupted the conversations.

To trace the force and origin of this awkward intervention, we must go back and observe how Washington was dealing with the negotiations in Paris.

On receiving Auriol's second draft proposal, Morgenthau closeted himself with his advisers – Feis, White, Bullitt, and the rest. Feis argued that so as to stave off French exchange controls, and a fall in the pound relative to the dollar, the problem of the franc would have to be solved. But everyone was dismayed to observe that France was still not saying how much it would devalue.[38] Viner urged the secretary to keep the Federal Reserve informed of the discussions, but Morgenthau refused;[39] this was a matter for governments, not banks. At last Cochran reported that the French would set up a stabilization fund, and that they proposed to devalue by 24 to 32 percent. Morgenthau and Hull concluded that this devaluation was "not impossible."[40]

Learning that Paris was eager to consider American phraseology, the American Treasury prepared a draft,[41] which, after approval by Morgenthau and Roosevelt, reached Paris on 19 September.

The American officials were trying to produce a version incorporating the common elements in the positions of all three governments. The final Tripartite Declarations are rather similar to it. It is in this respect that Morgenthau may claim some special credit for the declarations. It is also possible that by agreeing to sell gold he brought both European governments closer together. By 23 September the matter was of importance not just to Britain but to France; having decided to leave gold and set up a stabilization fund, the French authorities like the British were wondering whether Roosevelt would sell them gold.[42] Had the secretary said he would not, perhaps the French would have devalued within the framework of the gold standard, as Whitehall had originally expected and hoped. But America's gold did not create the devaluation. Nor was Morgenthau successful in forcing Britain to peg the pound in exchange for access thereto.

On 23 September Morgenthau reminded Cochran that "the issue of a simultaneous declaration can only take place when mutually acceptable range of rates has been determined. We have nothing as yet definitive regarding dollar sterling exchange rate contemplated."[43] On 24 September he told the British chargé that America wanted a five-dollar pound, plus or minus ten cents. The message went to London at once.[44]

This extraordinary demand reflects the fact that Roosevelt's mind had been turning to the foreign exchanges. The president, Morgenthau learned, insisted on a five-dollar pound as a sine qua non. He himself believed that the British must have had a five-dollar pound in mind all along because "nothing has been said to the contrary."[45] Certainly his staff had been thinking of a pound in this range, and so had the secretary himself. On 24 September he said, "I think we might just as well say right now to the French and the British that as far as we are concerned we want a $5 pound. We ought to do this before this thing goes too far."[46] The next day, John Henry Williams and Harry Dexter White agreed that Morgenthau was wise to wait until he got his five-dollar pound.[47] Early in the morning of 25 September, therefore, the Treasury received telegrams stating that, because the United States thought the existing dollar exchange rate was satisfactory to both Britain and itself, if the United States proceeded with the proposed scheme it was because it assumed that a five-dollar pound was proposed. There could be some leeway – ten cents in either direction. But both governments were to keep the exchange rate within those limits. Reporting that he had the full approval of President Roosevelt, Morgenthau asked Chamberlain to send a confirmation at once – perhaps by long-distance telephone.[48]

One cannot find the origins of this intervention in sophisticated calculations, whether of purchasing-power parity or of anything else. Of course, for more than a year the dollar-sterling rate had been hovering around the five-dollar mark. As Britain's Exchange Equalisation Account was managing the rate, the Americans might be excused for believing that Whitehall found it satisfactory. Morgenthau's advisers certainly thought that Britain deliberately manipulated the rate. Certainly they knew that the Account was absorbing gold. They might easily have supposed that if Britain had wanted a lower rate, it would have absorbed still more gold, thereby making such a rate effective. If the advisers did think this way, the documents do not reveal the fact. But the thought was, in any event, inaccurate.

Since 1933 Britain's exchange management had been conditioned first by the desire to help the French stay on gold and second by the fear that the United States would further devalue relative to gold. Whitehall had long suspected that if the pound fell relative to the franc, France would have to devalue, while the United States might very well choose to do so. The British also knew that whenever the pound fell, especially to $4.86 or below, Washington became very agitated indeed. Hence it was quite wrong to conclude that because London had acquiesced in a five-dollar pound it was satisfied with it. Nor would London necessarily defend that rate if pressure became acute. Throughout the negotiations Chamberlain had been fighting for his freedom not to do so.

Reading the minutes of Morgenthau's staff discussions, one can only conclude that the American experts were confused. Knowing that the French were aiming to price the franc at 1/105 of a pound, they alarmed themselves with the thought that the cross-rate would have to be $4.86. On the eve of the American elections, neither Roosevelt nor Morgenthau was prepared to accept such a rate,[49] and London almost certainly knew this. But the pound was floating vis-à-vis the dollar, and the French were about to peg the franc to the pound, not to the dollar or to gold. Because within a certain range the franc could move, one could not deduce the rate between the pound and the dollar merely by knowing the rate between the pound and the franc. Morgenthau and his advisers were shying at shadows. To make matters worse, the secretary believed that London and Paris were somehow *conniving* to create a $4.86 pound.[50]

Professor Blum has solemnly reproduced these confusions, but sensibly he has concluded that Morgenthau and the president were responding to political instinct, not to expert advice. Of course this is precisely what Chamberlain and his advisers had expected of Roosevelt, and feared about him, ever since the disasters of summer 1933. They had long been convinced that if the president could make political capital by irresponsible or foolish actions one could not rely on him to do the responsible or sensible thing. This last-minute intervention can only have confirmed these convictions.

In Whitehall Morgenthau's message was received with incredulity. Neither Chamberlain nor his officials could believe that Morgenthau had not perceived their repeated statements about the floating pound. Though he had hoped to go fishing, the chancellor was obliged to stay at his post. Neither he nor his staff yet knew for certain whether Morgenthau would accept the form of declaration on which London and Paris had now agreed.[51] Fearing leaks, and also nervous about the transatlantic telephone itself, Chamberlain hastened to send the Americans a reply by cable. He did not agree that he would use resources to hold the pound at or very close to five dollars. He had no legal power to stabilize the pound, nor would he do so. Instead, in the future as in the past, he would refrain from competitive depreciation. Regrettably, Britain's trade balance was weakening, and funds might well flow back from Britain to France in the wake of the French devaluation. Hence, he expected that if anything the pound would weaken, though not enough to distress the United States. "The future," he insisted, "must be entirely reserved by His Majesty's Government, as by the United States Government in the interests of national prosperity."[52]

Meanwhile there was an alarming message from Paris. On 25 September the ambassador reported that Blum and Auriol believed "everything had been settled satisfactorily between the British and American authorities regarding the rate of the pound against the dollar." The Treasury responded abruptly: "We do not understand at all M. Vincent Auriol's statement . . . there is no foundation for this statement . . . no agreement has been reached between His Majesty's Government and the United States Government. Please disabuse the French Government at once."[53]

In Chamberlain's opinion the French were devaluing "by a method that was not at all agreeable to us." The limits, 43 and 49 milligrams of gold, were too wide apart, and the mean point, 46 milligrams, represented a devaluation that was probably excessive. In the circumstances he had not pressed these objections, though he did report them to Morgenthau.[54]

On receiving the chancellor's message about the exchange rate, Morgenthau at once telephoned the president, who dictated the response that was promptly relayed to London. Though still believing that a five-dollar pound was "appropriate" and "reserving every right to state our position as it develops in the future," Roosevelt did not think that the disagreement need prevent the two governments from making a statement to help the French. That objective remained "broad, useful, and, indeed, essential." In the Foreign Office Gladwyn Jebb observed, "Mr. Morgenthau has not pressed his point, but the question is one which will probably give trouble in the future."[55] The sequel proved Jebb correct.

The message having gone, Cordell Hull called on Morgenthau. What did Chamberlain mean? According to the stenographic record, Morgenthau responded, "I just feel that he doesn't want to commit himself, and on the other hand I don't feel that he doesn't want to commit himself, and on the other hand I don't feel that he is going to try to drive it down . . . And what the President said is, that this thing has gone so far now that he doesn't feel he wants to stop it. He thinks there is too much at stake." In any event, the secretary continued, if the British should push the pound down too far he could and would cut them off from the American gold. The secretary of state remarked, "This looks good to me."[56] But neither man had really understood the British reservations or the inwardness of Chamberlain's position.

Meanwhile, the three governments continued to exchange drafts and last-minute emendations in the statement. Eventually they were able to agree on a text. Chamberlain and the Americans having agreed to disagree about the five-dollar pound and its future, it was possible for all three governments to publish the declarations almost at once. Britain released its declaration at 12:30 A.M. on 26 September.[57]

Some material was included only because France insisted on flowery phrases about truth, beauty, and goodness. Strangely, the Americans seem to have taken them seriously. Certainly the embassy reported that Morgenthau thought the declaration was "a great step in improvement of peaceful world conditions."[58] As for the U.K. Treasury, it expected nothing. In particular, it did not expect that other nations would take up the invitation to cooperate in realizing the policy of the declaration. When smaller states inquired how they might do this, there was consternation in Whitehall.

The declaration contained the commitments on relaxation of quotas and exchange controls that Britain had extracted from France with considerable difficulty. There was of course no way to enforce these, especially because the declaration makes no mention of France in connection therewith. On this score, not surprisingly, France did not perform very well.

Though Britain promised not to retaliate against the French devaluation and not to disturb equilibrium by its own monetary actions, it did not promise anything about exchange rates – levels, stability, or anything else. Instead, Britain reaffirmed "the purpose to continue the policy which they have pursued in the course of recent years." That policy had involved smoothing, giving way in face of strong downward pressures, and preventing undue increases in the value of sterling; it had also involved a basic commitment to cheap money at home and a refusal to let the exchanges affect domestic monetary policy at all. Hence the significance of the assertion that Britain would "take into full account the requirements of internal prosperity of the countries of the Empire." Ever since 1932 it had been thought that this prosperity required easy credit and cheap money; the Treasury was still of the same mind.

The declaration spoke of "consultation" between "approved agencies." These words were meant to cover cooperation between the central banks and equalization funds. The Banks of England and France were already cooperating; the Federal Reserve Bank of New York would soon do so. France was about to set up an equalization fund; for the rest of the decade this would work with the British and American funds in the day-to-day and hour-to-hour management of the foreign exchanges. Regrettably, the phrases also could be thought to justify Morgenthau's importunities, his demands for information, and his yearning for consultation on matters small as well as great. In later years Treasury officials must have often regretted that they had left so large an opening for American inquisitiveness.

The account in this section is at odds with that of Benjamin Rowland,[59] who argues that "Britain dropped her objections to a measure of stabilisation." That is precisely what Chamberlain did *not* do. So that the French might adjust their exchange rate, he was prepared to issue an anodyne statement that committed him to nothing. There is no sign that this decision was connected with any failure of the imperial system, any desire to conciliate the United States, or any diplomatic failure. The issue presented itself, and was discussed, in the most pragmatic terms. Chamberlain did not consult the Foreign Office, and he showed a quite remarkable lack of interest in the larger political questions within which the stabilization declarations might seem to be embedded.

Nor does Rowland correctly describe the actual content of the declarations. He writes, "In theory the franc could devalue between 25.19 percent and 34.35 percent of its former parity; the dollar between 50 and 60 percent of its earlier gold parity; while the pound remained completely free."[60] But the declarations said nothing about any particular exchange rate or rates. The Americans had promised nothing about the gold dollar, and Whitehall certainly did not believe Roosevelt could not be trusted to maintain any particular value or range for the dollar relative to gold. At most one might say that though Chamberlain had promised nothing about sterling, both Paris and Washington seem to have expected a five-dollar pound.

3. Other currencies follow the franc

The franc had previously been worth 65.5 milligrams of gold. Now it was to float within the range 43–49 milligrams. The Equalisation Fund was meant to keep it within that range. Eventually, perhaps, a more definite value might be fixed; for the time being the Treasury believed the French authorities were aiming to follow the pound at a rate of about 106 – a devaluation of about 35 percent relative to sterling and 42 percent relative to gold. Like the Scandinavian countries, France had joined the sterling area, at least in the sense that its authorities would henceforth govern their behavior on the basis of the sterling exchange rate. It is far from certain that the United States authorities had realized this fact.

Late on 26 September the Swiss and Dutch governments decided that they too would devalue. When the London market reopened on Monday, 28 September, there were no dealings in French or Swiss francs, or in Dutch currency. Gold however rose, and sterling fell from $5.03 1/8 on Friday to $4.95. That day Greece decided to peg the drachma to sterling and to devalue it a little. Turkey and Latvia also moved from the franc to sterling. The Turks devalued slightly, and the Latvians devalued substantially. Shortly Uruguay also pegged to sterling. On 29 September the London market again began to deal in guilders and Swiss francs. When trading resumed, relative to sterling the guilder was 22 percent lower than it had been on Friday, 25 September; the Swiss franc had fallen by 45 percent. Soon thereafter the Italians adjusted the lira, and the Czechoslovak crown was further devalued relative to gold.[1]

For British trade these developments were of course extremely serious, at least potentially; they may deserve some of the blame for the worsening of Britain's trading account in the succeeding months and years. Then and later, however, the Foreign Office inclined to see the declarations as a significant step in democratic cooperation, consultation, and solidarity. Chamberlain, as usual, derived some satisfaction merely from the fact that negotiations had not broken down. Actually he thought that he had managed things rather well. To his sister he wrote:

The reception of the devaluation has been pretty good – almost too good in fact – for I fear that in their anxiety to get it across the French have described it and its effect in over-glowing terms. As for Morgenthau, he has made an ass of himself over the alleged attempt at sabotage by the Soviet. But it is clear that he has just been concerned to get something out of it for the presidential election campaign. He wanted to get on the telephone to me but I wasn't having any. I prefer to use a long spoon in supping with the Americans.[2]

In his diary he recorded: "The common declarations by France, United Kingdom, and USA on currency were duly agreed and issued and had an excellent reception. All has since proceeded in orderly fashion on exchange markets.[3]

Leith-Ross was less happy. Writing to Rowe-Dutton in Paris, he regretted that the French officials had not been willing to fix a definite value for the franc; further, he thought it a pity that Holland and Switzerland had also opted on the French example for managed currencies. "The only effect of this will be to increase speculation and to make it more difficult to resist pressure here for extra tariffs or other protective measures."[4] Rowe-Dutton agreed that it had been a "major error" not to refix the franc to gold: France must draw its fugitive capital from abroad, and only a gold franc would be sufficient attraction.[5] Morgenthau also feared that a floating franc would encourage speculation.[6]

This evidence is enough to cast some doubt upon Stephen Clarke's contention that Britain wanted France to stay on gold so that the Exchange Equalisation Account could continue to control the sterling exchange rate.[7] Clarke ignores Britain's other interest in a free French gold standard. The authorities in London wanted to produce a reflux of hot money across the Channel to France, and they believed that only if the franc were firmly pegged to gold could such a reflux occur. Admittedly, in the winter of 1936–7 Whitehall changed its position – but only when it realized that because Paris was defending an untenable rate it was creating a one-way option for speculators. Certainly the British authorities were concerned about the question of control. Where two or more currencies are floating, the question naturally arises. However, as long as the partners can agree on procedures by which dealing rates are to be announced or negotiated this question will solve itself. Moreover, as recent experience ought to show, this question has no logical connection with the question of convertibility *into gold*. If the various authorities are willing to hold foreign exchange, they can manage the exchanges perfectly well without any guaranteed convertibility, with or without a fixed price. Admittedly the British authorities were concerned to ensure that their foreign exchange balances could be converted. But if they had been denied this right it is reasonable to suppose that they would have quickly begun to manage the exchanges simply by dealing in and holding exchange – accepting the potential for capital loss that such dealings created. Also, of course, they could deal in the London gold market, using that market to convert exchange holdings.

British officials were also uneasy about French commercial policy. Admittedly the French government had accepted the British phrase about progressive relaxation of quotas and exchange controls. In autumn 1936 British officials applied some pressure to the French, urging more rapid and extensive action. On 20 October the French government did reduce duties, but only on the few goods not subject to quota. It also suppressed one-third of the quotas. But an official later observed, "they are by far the least important," corresponding to only 10 percent of import values.[8] Having devalued, France was as protectionist as before.

4. *Morgenthau agrees to sell gold*

With respect to American gold sales, things went rather better.

The three central banks and exchange funds had already begun to coordinate their interventions. As soon as the three declarations were made, Morgenthau set his officials to work on the documents that would be needed if he decided to sell gold to Britain and France.[1] Morgenthau knew that the French, like the British, were anxious to be assured that their stabilization fund could buy gold with dollars.[2] He had already sent Cochran a proposal under which he would sell gold to exchange funds that would sell gold to the United States. The arrangement, he proposed, should be revocable on 24 hours' notice.[3] He suggested:

In connection with the announcements made by him on January 31 and February 1, 1934, to the effect that the Treasury would buy gold, and supplementing the announcement on January 31, 1934, referring to the sale of gold for export, the Secretary of the Treasury states that, hereafter, and until, on 24 hours notice, this statement of intention may be revoked or altered, he will also sell gold for immediate export to, or earmark for the account of, the exchange equalization or stabilization funds of those countries whose funds likewise are offering to sell gold to the United States.

Cochran thought the proposal offensive and believed that the United States should at once agree to sell gold. He cabled, "I have always doubted the efficacy of our gold as a weapon to force the British to stabilise."[4]

On 5 October Morgenthau told the British chargé in Washington that the French were pressing him hard. Clarke reports that the French were pressing because the British had asked them to. Recalling his July conversations with Bewley, when he thought he had expressed hope for a tripartite arrangement, Morgenthau now told the chargé that as the French were so persistent he would agree to a "day-to-day reciprocal arrangement" between the French stabilization fund and the American government. He now proposed a similar plan for the Bank of England and the Federal Reserve. "I want to have the word of His Majesty's Government that I can get gold," he said. And he wanted a response by the next day.[5] He said nothing about the pegging of the pound. But we have already seen that if the pound should depreciate inconveniently he was prepared to cancel the arrangement. Fortunately he seemed to be happy with the way in which the tripartite program was working. The embassy reported that he thought both parties were working in complete accord with the spirit of the agreement. The pound had admittedly fallen, but the secretary said he knew the pressure on it was genuine and that the British authorities had spent a great deal in its support. From Washington Bewley reported, "Morgenthau is of course delighted with the tripartite agreements and is at present bubbling over with peace and good will."[6] When so disposed, the secretary was not inclined to be sticky about gold.

In London the Treasury and the Bank quickly agreed on their response. Hopkins regretted that Morgenthau wanted to publish his declaration. "It is much better," he wrote, "that arrangements of this kind should be understood to exist than that they should be promulgated. But it cannot be helped." On 7 October the Treasury agreed to Morgenthau's plan.[7] The arrangement, it suggested, would be of an indefinite period, subject to review or suspension. Morgenthau, however, was attached to the 24-hour principle, and after informing Cochran and Chamberlain on 8 October he proceeded on 13 October to issue a statement substantially identical with the proposal he had sent to Cochran in late September. He would sell gold to the stabilization funds of countries that allowed the United States to buy gold from such funds. The price would be $35.0875 per ounce.

Morgenthau's statement of 13 October was a unilateral declaration, not an international agreement. It remained in force from day to day and could be revoked at any time. It was not part of the tripartite declarations, but it followed directly from them. If the Americans had not been satisfied that they had brought some order into the system of exchanges they would not have agreed to sell gold. In the event, they were not often asked to do so. Admittedly, from time to time the exchange funds must have presented dollars for conversion. But from October

1936 until the outbreak of war the United States remained a consistent importer of monetary gold. Nevertheless, central bankers who managed the stabilization funds still thought in terms of gold. To them the right to buy gold was important, even though they might seldom be able to buy any. The Morgenthau declaration must have increased their willingness to buy dollars in circumstances where their own currencies were strong but where they might otherwise have been deterred by the prospect of a capital loss in terms of gold. In this sense the U.S. declaration increased the ease and efficiency of market management from autumn 1936 until late summer 1939. Certainly it helped the three funds to cooperate in managing the exchanges, and it encouraged other governments to "join" the tripartite "agreement." Nations seem to have believed that by adhering to the agreement they could get on Morgenthau's list. But because sterling and the European currencies were so often weak relative to the dollar, markets were managed more efficiently only in the shortest of short-run senses. Taking one year with another or even one month with another, the European stabilization funds did not support the dollar by accumulating dollar balances; rather, they supported their own currencies by shedding gold to the United States.

To the American secretary, the "commitment to consult" was a serious matter; in Whitehall it was at first little more than a nuisance as far as the United States was concerned. The Treasury still could not tell the Americans what was happening to the Exchange Equalisation Account. It could rarely answer Morgenthau's more abstruse queries: Why does Bulgaria want to buy a little gold? Why is the franc weak, and what are its prospects? [8]

The Tripartite Declarations of 26 September had spoken of other governments that might "co-operate to realise the policy" – presumably the principles of orderly exchanges and nonretaliation. This phrase was included solely to keep the French happy. No one in London hoped or expected that other countries would sign on. But by 29 September the Czechs were already wondering in what form they might associate themselves with the declarations. By mid-October Switzerland and Denmark had applied to join. At this time, the question of adherence became entangled with the question of gold buying. Holland and Belgium soon joined the queue. On each occasion Morgenthau consulted London, and presumably Paris as well. Leith-Ross wrote in some annoyance that the Czechs, and their demands for financial help, would soon appear in London. "We can scarcely explain to them that the high-sounding terms of the Declaration were simply put in to help the French Government with their domestic political troubles and mean nothing." [9]

10

Intergovernmental conversations and the management of sterling, 1936-1939

The Tripartite Agreement brought a shadow of international monetary cooperation but not its substance. Admittedly, in the day-to-day management of the exchanges there was regular contact between the central banks of Britain, France, and the United States. Admittedly, too, in principle the British and American treasuries now stood rather nearer to one another and to the French than they had done before. From Washington, Morgenthau loved to send cables, and he rejoiced in the transatlantic telephone, a device that London still treated with suspicion. Emmanuel Monick still perambulated the English-speaking world to interpret the most recent developments in Paris – usually somewhat after they had occurred. T. K. Bewley in Washington, Ernest Rowe-Dutton in Paris, and W. W. Butterworth in London all had more work than before. Although the Bank for International Settlements has not left many traces in the Treasury records of the late thirties, perhaps in addition there were new sorts of contact at Basel. But none of this made any fundamental difference. I have argued elsewhere that with respect to the management of the franc after September 1936 there was little tripartite consultation and less cooperation,[1] although London certainly gave advice and help to Paris while Washington agonized. Most of the time Paris simply did what it wanted, telling London and Washington after the fact. As far as France was concerned the tripartite understanding remained in existence only because Britain and the United States were prepared to ignore the way in which France ignored it.

The present chapter marshals parallel evidence and tells a similar story with respect to the pound. Little need be said about central bank cooperation, important though this may have been in giving the general public a new impression of orderliness. It is more important to observe how incomplete, spasmodic, and perfunctory were the intergovernmental discussions on more fundamental matters – the trend of sterling and the price of gold.

Our attention must be focused on London and Washington because it was between these two capitals that discussions about the gold price and the sterling-dollar rate would most naturally arise. As far as the documents reveal, Paris did not get involved in either question, nor were the sterling area governments consulted in any systematic way, although, as we shall see, the gold question did come up at the Imperial Conference of 1937. Questions of credit do not often arise in this chapter because in these years the British did not ask for credits from the Americans, nor did Washington actually ever offer any, although the possibility was considered. It should be remembered that the Tripartite Agreement had not said anything about credit and that the three central banks almost always settled their accounts daily, in gold. During the two years of difficulty that followed the September 1936 devaluation of the franc, Paris could and did ask for credits, and London was sometimes able to oblige, whereas Washington blew hot and cold and actually did nothing helpful. In any event, because both Britain and France were in default of their war debts to the United States, American law would have made it difficult for Morgenthau to do anything useful with respect to stabilization credits even if he had been inclined to be helpful.

1. Sterling's dirty float, 1936–1939

In January 1937 Walter Runciman, the president of the Board of Trade, visited Washington where he talked with President Roosevelt. Describing his visit he wrote:

The President expressed pleasure at the tripartite currency agreement. He said it enabled the three governments to act together in closer union and accord, and adopting the phraseology of Mr. Morgenthau, he said that we could talk now freely on subjects which formerly they would have been reluctant to discuss with us. I asked the President if we could now count on easier co-operation to which he replied, "Yes."[1]

In the years to come the Americans would certainly talk freely. Morgenthau developed a penchant for consultation that infuriated Chamberlain and annoyed the Treasury. When exchanges moved unexpectedly or when sterling was weak, there were inquiries from Washington. The central banks were in close contact, but between the two treasuries or governments discussion, though freer than before September 1936, was spasmodic. There is nothing in the documents to suggest any close coordination of currency policy between 1936 and 1939. Thanks to the agreement each government expected to be consulted, informed, and asked. In London embassy staff called now and then upon the Treasury;

in Washington Kenneth Bewley saw Morgenthau and his advisers from time to time. As yet there was nothing more dramatic by way of integration or consultation.

The Tripartite Declarations had committed the United Kingdom to abstain from competitive depreciations or deliberate devaluations. After September 1936 the British authorities honored this commitment asymmetrically. When sterling was weak the reserves were used to defend it; though sterling was allowed to depreciate that decline was controlled. There was no deliberate depreciation. But when the pound was strong, as in 1937, it was not allowed to rise; instead the authorities built up their reserves. At such times, it might be argued, the authorities were trying to achieve a deliberate undervaluation though not a devaluation as such. In pursuing this objective they could count on the acquiescence of Morgenthau and Roosevelt who, they already knew, desired and expected a five-dollar pound.

A strong pound and a gold problem. In the first 18 months the problem for the authorities was to digest an avalanche of gold.[2] They need not worry about Morgenthau. In the last 17 months they worried instead about the problems of allowing the pound to descend while keeping the Americans happy without imposing a disastrous strain on the reserves or provoking an even more rapid flight of capital funds.

After September 1936 the pound was much more stable relative to the dollar than the franc relative either to dollar or to pound. But the dollar-sterling exchange rate was very far from fixed. Immediately after the declarations the pound dropped a little, as capital funds began to drift toward France. Thereafter, however, sterling strengthened, drifting upward and quickly reaching the five-dollar mark at which it had stood in July and August 1936. It hovered around this level until summer 1938. Then began a downward dribble to $4.68. But for eighteen months or more Morgenthau had, or nearly had, the five-dollar pound he had wanted. Until spring 1938 the Tripartite Agreement deserves none of the credit for this. Sterling was strong, though the current account deficit was increasing. Capital funds flowed in from several sources: repayment of old sterling debt, accumulation of new sterling balances as primary-product prices revived, and inflows of refugee capital funds from France and other European countries. The Exchange Equalisation Account was seldom obliged to support the pound; rather, it swallowed enormous quantities of gold to prevent sterling from rising relative to the dollar. As the authorities were content to prevent the pound from appreciating relative to the dollar, sterling was stable and gold flowed in; though Morgenthau may have rejoiced in the skill with which he had convinced the British to stabilize the pound, in fact he had done nothing of the sort. Although the current account was weak,[3] Britain's capital account was strong and would remain so until early 1938.[4] Hence sterling was strong, and no thanks were due either to the United States or to the tripartite agreement.

Recently scholars have directed our attention to the "gold glut" of 1937.[5] Our account relies heavily on their work, which spares us from explaining the glut in great detail. In a physical sense its origins were obvious enough. India was still disgorging gold from its hoards; in South Africa and other lesser gold producers the price changes of the early 1930s still stimulated gold mining; from Europe gold was flowing across the Channel and across the Atlantic. In 1933–6 a great deal of the newly mined gold had been hoarded in western countries, but in the autumn and winter of 1936–7 most of these new private hoards were dishoarded. In Britain, unless the Exchange Equalisation Account were given more resources it could not indefinitely absorb gold. The Americans too were buying gold and sterilizing it. But they might not do so forever. In April 1937 there were nasty rumors that Roosevelt planned to cut the price. Already in autumn 1936 the Bank of England and the Treasury had agreed that the Bank would buy gold from the Account but that the fiduciary issue would be reduced. The Treasury had then successfully opposed the Bank's proposal – that the pound should appreciate. Tight money would help prevent inflation; a more costly pound would cause unemployment. The Bank did not give up: In April and May the governor was still canvassing a cut in the gold price, which should be agreed with the United States.[6] In the Treasury other ideas were being examined.

Throughout the world the rumor of a price cut had disturbed the stock markets and distressed the gold producers and hoarders, who had promptly shipped even more gold to the United States. How had the rumor begun? In Washington the embassy believed that Marriner Eccles, the governor of the Federal Reserve System, had done the damage. He had spoken of the possibility of adjusting the price of gold so as to check "excessive expansion at home." Hence, he thought, the president should retain executive discretion in matters that could affect the exchange rate. On 5 April Reuter's had picked this up.[7]

Journalists believed that Eccles had been floating a trial balloon. So did the City. So did the embassy, whose staff thought it ill judged. From Washington it reported:

The recent rumor that the Secretary of the Treasury was likely to decrease the price paid for gold, which was clearly a piece of kite-flying on the part of the administration, was not a very well-planned move, quite apart from its serious effect on world markets. Even supposing that, as it was understood Mr. Morgenthau had in mind, the United Kingdom Government might have supported the United States by lifting the value of sterling simultaneously with the dollar, France might very well have been considerably embarrassed, and the Tripartite Agreement would, to say the least, have been difficult to maintain. Internally the effect of the move was to accelerate the flow of gold into the country, instead of decreasing it as the intention was, in the hope that it might be landed before the decrease in price took place . . . it is understood that Mr. Morgenthau is not at present particularly dissatisfied with the situation although the amount of gold in the inactive fund is now about $600 million and will inevitably increase.[8]

Whatever Eccles had in mind, the American secretary of the treasury was floating trial balloons of his own. Early in April he asked Bewley what he thought of a drop in the price of gold. The Tripartite Agreement, he suggested, did not appear to require any signatory to consult any member before doing such a thing. Nevertheless, Morgenthau explained, he thought they should consult. Why might gold be cheapened? The problem as Morgenthau saw it was that in some countries internal price levels might be rising too rapidly relative to the rest of the world. Morgenthau explained that these were just ideas, not yet crystallized in his mind and not to be passed on to Whitehall. The American was aware that the Bank of England had already sounded Butterworth on this subject, but he did not tell Bewley, who seems to have known nothing of the Bank's approaches. Bewley's response predictably was not enthusiastic.[9]

Later in April Sir Frederick Phillips told Butterworth that Britain was ready to exchange views about gold with the United States at any time. As for the price of the precious metal, eventually the powers might have to reduce it but that time was not yet. Morgenthau was not prepared to consult about gold by cable. Reminding Butterworth of the previous approach by the Bank of England he explained, "If Mr. Phillips wants to come over, all right." Butterworth agreed to put this proposition to Phillips, who, he admitted, seemed to feel no urgency about the gold price.[10]

Meanwhile, in London the Treasury brooded upon the gold problem. On 31 May Leith-Ross wrote to Hopkins and Phillips. He urged that "an effort to stabilise currencies, accompanied by arrangements for the relaxation of trade barriers, would do more than anything else to spread and strengthen the present trade revival . . . The time seems to me to have come when we ought to reconsider our general attitude toward stabilisation and work for a general agreement." It should include a general fixing of all main currencies to gold; exchange rates should vary only "in cases of proved necessity"; if the gold inflow threatened to raise prices, *all* currencies should raise their gold content, and the agreement should provide for this; the free-exchange countries should grant credits to any exchange-control countries that are willing to free their exchanges. Thus the world demand for monetary gold would be increased, reducing the inflationary potential of South African production; exchange control would fade; the world would be back on the gold standard.[11]

Sir Frederick Phillips had already developed his ideas at length in a semiacademic memorandum on the present and future of gold.[12] He argued as follows: If a long-run and serious inflation were to be avoided, the world must find ways to absorb the flow of gold, unless somehow production could be cut back. Governor Montagu Norman favored an approach to the United States so that the two great sterilizers could jointly and simultaneously depreciate gold. If the United States were to act unilaterally Britain could thwart her by refusing to cooperate, thus forcing up the value of the dollar relative to the pound. Such a change in the exchange rate was "anathema to the Americans." But in the United States there would soon be internal political pressures both to reduce the gold price and to maintain it. Many observers, and even Morgenthau himself, resented the cost of the sterilization, and they had noticed that under the present system the main beneficiary was the British Empire, which produced most of the new gold and some of the dishoarded gold. The real risk was the strain on the Americans' will to sterilize. If sterilization ended the gold price might fall dramatically, because neither Britain nor France could absorb the flow. Gold might even fall out of use as a monetary metal. For South Africa and other Empire countries the effect would be disastrous. It would be equally serious for the United Kingdom, where gold mining had been an important outlet for investment activity during the Depression. Further, the currency club would collapse in chaos. The British Account would not want to hold dollars, and the United States Fund would not want to hold sterling; the tripartite arrangements had only worked "because there is a fourth money, gold, which United States, France, and ourselves are willing to buy and sell from each other."

"*It is reasonably certain*," Phillips wrote, "that in the end there must be a reduction in the price of gold." Admittedly there would be no problem if gold could flow back to France and the other Continental economies. But it would not do so without international credits, which were politically impossible in 1937 as in 1933. To avoid exchange chaos and deflation, when the change came it would have to be worked jointly and simultaneously throughout the currency club. Credit in Britain and the United States would have to be adjusted so as to avoid any deflationary repercussions, and the public would have to be assured about this adjustment. When the time came, Britain should insist on these conditions and on the payoff from a restoration of European purchasing power. The problem was urgent because markets were already nervous and because it was known that South Africa would raise the matter at the coming Imperial Conference. Perhaps Britain should not press the United States to act at once, but it could hardly refuse to discuss the matter if Morgenthau should raise it, as he certainly would.

Leith-Ross's scheme did not impress Phillips. The exchange-control countries, he pointed out, did not really want to hold gold. Further, Holland and Switzerland were shedding gold as fast as they could; even France might not want to add to its gold hoard. If Leith-Ross's ideas were to be adopted, little would change in the short run: Stabilization on gold at the existing Anglo-American exchange rate "would mean that the USA and the United Kingdom would go on buying gold as at present and the rest of the world would be very happy to keep *their* store of value in the form of dollar and sterling deposits and securities, also as at present." In any event, Phillips believed, the superfluity of gold would end; Leith-Ross had ignored the longer-run adjustment processes. The inflow would certainly raise prices, reducing the profitability of mining. In any case, the world would not be able to stabilize its exchange rates on a gold basis; the basis must be the dollar. Hence progress would depend upon Anglo-American agreement; unilaterally Britain could do nothing. In the interim Britain could extend the Tripartite Declaration so as to fix "fairly narrow limits" that could be changed only on six months' notice "to the world." But this could be done only if the two nations could reconcile their ideas about monetary policy. Britain would tolerate some further price increase but not an inflationary boom; no one knew what American price policy might be, but Phillips feared that it might be unduly expansionary. If these ideas could be reconciled, France and perhaps Germany could be brought into the agreement with respect to limits. No one should consult the smaller countries, however: "they are merely a nuisance in monetary negotiations and they are always quite content to do what they are told if only the big powers agree." [13]

Sir Richard Hopkins was inclined to agree with Phillips but thought that little could be done. For an exchange agreement the United States would demand a double price in terms of the trade agreement then under negotiation and of the actual exchange rate. These would exceed "any which we are prepared to pay." Also, in Europe it would be immensely difficult to negotiate any agreement. Hence the Leith-Ross strategy would not reduce the "difficulties which will face us in the immediate future in relation to the gold question." Sir Warren Fisher agreed with Hopkins.[14]

Late in June Bewley reported that the American Treasury no longer thought that the right way to handle excess gold was to lower its price. Morgenthau himself reported in exactly the same sense. At the same time the new chancellor, Sir John Simon, transmitted his own reservations and those of his staff. Britain would deal with the gold flow by augmenting the Exchange Equalisation Account, which would continue to buy gold. As for a price cut, Simon said,

I am convinced that the most important matter [for economic revival] is that there should be no setback in the process toward reviving confidence . . . Whether a simultaneous reduction in the price of gold by all the leading financial powers would have deflationary results is a matter on which I have not yet come to any definite conclusion. At the present moment, however, a large section of the public seem to have formed the opinion that deflation would be the result of any change in the gold price, however universal. Even if it were wrong, the existence of this opinion would have to be taken seriously into account, since what the public think is going to happen is itself an important factor in bringing events about. For these reasons I think that in the absence of a demonstrable crisis we should work to prevent the early stirring up of this matter at any rate until recovery is better assured than at present.[15]

In the longer run some changes might be needed, but nothing should be done at once. During September Sir Frederick Phillips was to be in Canada on family business. Morgenthau had told Simon that he was ready to discuss the question of gold whenever the world was ready. Might Phillips come to Washington? He could then discuss "the gold question and generally problems of mutual interest." Apparently because he himself had made a similar suggestion not long before, at first Morgenthau thought the suggestion "perfectly ridiculous." But the message, he thought, showed that "Simon wants to play ball just as much as Chamberlain did." Accordingly he decided to welcome Phillips.[16]

The Empire and the gold problem. During the summer the United States tried to prevent three small countries from dumping gold. But the flow continued. In London the Account still absorbed gold. By lowering its offer price London could have diverted gold to the United States. But in so doing the United Kingdom would have forced up the pound on the foreign exchanges and would have annoyed the Empire, especially the South Africans. As the international scene became more gloomy the question of Empire solidarity became more important. No one could be confident that South Africa would follow Britain into war.

In May 1937, at the Imperial Conference that decorated the coronation, the gold question reared its head. South Africa and Australia were both anxious that there should be some sort of monetary resolution. So were Strakosch and Kisch of the Indian delegation. All these governments, and Canada as well, had been dismayed by the rumors about American policy. All were determined that commodity prices should go on up, and all hoped that the price of gold would not go down. The United States and the Continental countries expected that the conference would have to discuss gold. Britain's ministers and officials, however, had not brooded upon the Empire's determinations and desires in advance of the conference itself.[17]

One could not have a monetary resolution at the Imperial Conference without saying something about gold; public opinion would expect something. If there had been no gold crisis, the Treasury would have favored some sort of statement on monetary policy. But gold was a matter for Britain and the United States, perhaps also for France. Simon was doing his best to consult the Americans before saying anything about gold. Yet one could not ask an Imperial Conference to consider a declaration that must then be submitted for American approval. Hence the Treasury and the governor agreed that nothing could be said about the gold price, and "on the whole no declaration may be preferable to a declaration which of necessity omits reference to the price of gold." The Treasury worked out a draft resolution. This spoke cheerfully about the relative stability of exchange and the rise in price levels since 1933 and repeated the 1933 affirmations on money, credit, and exchanges, which it said were still "appropriate." The Americans were told to expect some such declaration.[18]

Nicholaas Havenga, the South African finance minister, led the onslaught. On 27 May he pleaded for the gold standard, disparaged managed currencies, and congratulated the "statesmen" who had devised the Tripartite Agreement. Prime Minister Lyons of Australia had earlier suggested that "it would be reassuring to know that the great increase in the production and valuation of the world's gold supplies will not be allowed to become a disturbing factor" in exchange rates. Chamberlain responded by suggesting that ultimately the United Kingdom must return to gold, that the Commonwealth could not act alone, but that "it might be very desirable to have some further discussion" on monetary matters at the conference.[19] In private conversations the South Africans then proposed that the conference might issue a statement on monetary policy. The Treasury draft was the result. On 14 June the principal delegates agreed that Canada, South Africa, and the United Kingdom would devise a joint statement. Shortly thereafter Chamberlain and Simon discussed the Treasury draft with Havenga of South Africa and Charles Dunning of Canada. It was agreed to circulate the draft and to consider it at a meeting of principal delegates later that day.[20]

When the delegates assembled at 4:00 P.M. on 14 June to consider the draft, the result was a fiasco. Dunning explained that the Canadians had not had time to consider it. M. J. Savage of New Zealand disagreed with every reference to the gold standard and refused to let the document go forward. Havenga, on the other hand, regretted that nothing more definite could be said about gold and its price. New Zealand would not accept a statement that contained the passages South Africa thought essential; without such passages South Africa thought any statement worse than useless. Deadlocked, the delegates decided to say nothing about gold or monetary policy.[21] The South Africans presumably went away discontented but not surprised.

From the imperial viewpoint 1937 would have been an awkward time to contrive an appreciation of the pound. Empire statesmen were in London for the coronation and for the Imperial Conference, at which they would be told various unpleasant things about defense, foreign affairs, and the future of the preferential system. It would hardly have been politic to reduce their domestic price levels at the same time. The South Africans, having adjusted their economy to a sterling basis and enjoyed a gold-mining boom, would be told that this boom was to be curtailed. Indian finances were now in the hands of P. J. Grigg, a vigorous defender of the 1/6 rupee.[22] He would not complain. But if sterling were to rise relative to the dollar, the "question of the ratio" would once again be debated in Indian politics, and for the government of India the remittance problem might reappear once the rupee price of gold had been reduced. New Zealand would hardly suffer, as it sold little except to Australia and Britain. But for Australian and South African pastoralists a heavy pound would be no light matter.

Similarly, within the Empire several countries would have suffered if the gold price had been reduced. Canada, Australia, Kenya, Southern Rhodesia, and especially South Africa all produced gold; Indian hoards had not been exhausted. If the gold price had been lowered Britain's politicians would have been hard put to contain the political reverberations – especially at a time when they were trying once more to orchestrate an imperial approach to the looming problems of defense. In South Africa the regime was most delicately balanced, as the events of September 1939 were to show. But in Canada too, the forces of isolationism and Anglophobia were strong within the Department of External Affairs, and no one could be sure which way Prime Minister King would scurry. It was by no means obvious that India could be persuaded to fight vigorously on Britain's side.

Anglo-American gold talks. In mid-July 1937 Morgenthau told Butterworth that he would be delighted to see Sir Frederick Phillips in the week of 13 September. Because of Phillips's family obligations in Canada the visit was eventually fixed for the week of 20 September.

Before he left for Washington Phillips expected that the Americans would be far more interested in sterling than in gold. He foresaw that Morgenthau would press for the stabilization of sterling on gold – not that there was any question of Britain agreeing to such a demand. If America really wanted to speed progress toward a general stabilization, Phillips wrote, it had better come to some sort of agreement with Britain on the management of money and credit. In 1937 as in 1933, Phillips and the Treasury were insisting that Britain could not commit itself, through the compulsions of the gold standard, to follow American credit policy if that policy was to be "entirely isolationist." As for gold, no single country could undertake to lower the price without at once appreciating its money and imposing deflation on itself. Britain need not rule out a simultaneous parallel reduction by the currency club, but this step would be a very long-run remedy, and it need be applied only if prices were getting out of hand. So far Phillips observed no such tendency; indeed, the Treasury hoped that prices would go on rising "within reasonable limits."[23]

In Washington all questions of exchange rates were interwoven with questions of trade negotiations. The former questions belonged to Morgenthau in the Treasury; the latter belonged to Cordell Hull in the Department of State. The two men and the two departments were by no means perfectly coordinated, though Hull usually sent Herbert Feis to sit in on any discussion of the exchanges. In addition Morgenthau generally consulted Hull whenever he perceived a connection between trade and exchanges. In autumn 1937 there was already a good prospect of an Anglo-American trade agreement. Hence Hull and Morgenthau agreed that with respect to the Phillips visit they should coordinate their schemes. American gold buying and silver buying, they decided, should be used as a lever to force Britain to adopt the appropriate line with respect to the trade agreement.[24] Fortunately for Britain this resolution seems to have been ignored. Certainly there is no sign that Morgenthau kept it in mind – or even recalled it.

The Washington officials worked hard to prepare for the Phillips visit.

They suggested that Morgenthau should discuss silver, hot money, measures against Japan, development of the tripartite understanding, and gold – its production and use. They wanted more exchange of information about capital movements, tax data, Japan's sterling and dollar balances, and hoarded gold. They wondered what Britain would do about the £40 million credit to French railways, which was to expire in December 1937. They wondered how much the franc could slip without discommoding the British and whether French exchange control would take France out of the tripartite understanding. They hoped that Britain would cooperate in an embargo of Japanese imports, exports, and gold. But most of all they wondered about gold. Did Britain want to curtail world gold production? If so, how? Had the Imperial Conference discussed the matter? What of Russian gold production and sale? Might Russian gold be restricted? With respect to gold supplies, what were the advantages and disadvantages of output restriction compared with price declines? What might be done to increase the monetary use of gold? Would Indian residents begin to hoard or dishoard more gold? As for the tripartite understanding, was Whitehall satisfied with its working?[25]

Phillips visited Morgenthau on 20 September 1937. The serious discussions occurred on the following three days.

In the event, Morgenthau surprised Phillips. Neither the secretary nor anyone else mentioned sterling stabilization. The price of gold was mentioned only because Phillips asked Morgenthau about it. Meeting the secretary in the company of Viner and the other advisers and officials, Phillips was amazed to find that conversation centered on the control of supply. Morgenthau admittedly was a little annoyed that the Empire produced so much gold and held relatively little. He wondered about gold reserves in South Africa and India; he asked about hoarding and dishoarding; he announced that the Russians had said they were willing to cooperate in international controls over gold sales. Phillips reported that Britain was not worried by the current level of gold production. The Treasury, he said, believed that outside the East the private hoards were already sufficiently small so that one could see an end to private dishoarding. As for controlling the flow of gold, Phillips could see no way to manage production. Neither the Soviet Union nor the smaller countries, he thought, would cooperate. Phillips became convinced that if the gold problem became more serious the American government would try to control output and marketing, not cut the price. As for the price, Morgenthau told Phillips that Roosevelt and he were agreed that "whatever course of action might be required in connection with gold imports a lowering of the price of gold was definitely not part of it."[26] Phillips was "gratified" by Morgenthau's assurances.

Until spring 1938 the Bank and the Account continued to ingest gold, but compared with the increases of spring and early summer 1937 the increases were small.[27] The Treasury was still worried about inflation, however. Hopkins observed:

The prospect of our currency if pinned to gold being led on a great inflationary dance with soaring wages and cost of living until the inevitable collapse later is quite different to our experience in the postwar period of depression, but I do not know that it is any less terrifying in its probable social effects.

Leith-Ross still pressed for stabilization on gold, but Phillips and Hopkins still thought little of this policy. Early in December 1937 Chamberlain ended the debate by announcing that with respect to a renewed gold standard he agreed with Hopkins.[28]

By midwinter of 1937–8 it was clear that the trade cycle had turned down once more and that the economic problem was contraction, not inflation. Morgenthau soon modified his arrangements for gold sterilization so that more of America's new gold would affect the monetary system and swell the reserves of the banks. From the United States there would soon be rumors of an even higher price for gold. In Britain, too, other forces would soon be at work. From December 1937 to March 1938 Britain's gold hoard grew extremely slowly. It then dwindled almost as rapidly as it had once accumulated.

The pound weakens and the Americans complain. By March 1938 gold reserves were 119,389 ounces, and this gold was worth £836 million. In December 1931 reserves had been valued at £121 million. From March 1938 until the outbreak of war, however, the pressure on sterling was almost continuous. The pound and the gold reserves declined. By late November 1938 the former was worth only $4.62, and the latter had fallen to £615 million.[29]

The British authorities believed that the problem was political, and in this they were largely right. But Britain's current-account deficit was still rising, and sterling balances were rapidly falling. Some of the withdrawals were motivated by political fears; some reflected the inconvenient things that the renewed recession was doing to the earnings of the overseas sterling countries.[30]

Ever since 1931 the authorities had been worried about Britain's sterling liabilities.[31] When the gold reserves began to fall they blamed these liabilities, which, they said, were affected by political circumstances. In August 1939 Phillips wrote an account of the gold drain that was almost entirely political. When the franc was devalued in May 1938, he observed, there was a £50 million fall in the reserves. From midautumn there was a repatriation of capital to France. The reflux to France continued in the first half of 1939. Such developments were determined chiefly by French politics: A center-right government had replaced the Bloc populaire, and there was little chance of a further devaluation. The annexation of Austria, Phillips believed, had produced no visible effect, but "from the summer of 1938 it became apparent that international politics were the dominant influence on the exchanges and on sterling in particular." The autumn Czechoslovak crisis had caused a net loss of £100 million. When Germany invaded Bohemia in spring 1939 there was a further sharp deterioration. And it was to the United States that the gold was chiefly flowing. From January to July 1939 Britain received £54 million in gold from South Africa, £5 million from Russia, £8 million from India, and £30 million from Holland. It gave up gold to the value of £188.5 million, of which £43.5 million went to France, £103 million directly to the United States, and £42 million to the exchange market whence, Phillips thought, it went indirectly to the United States.[32]

In July 1938 Morgenthau discussed the monetary aspects of the pending Anglo-American trade agreement with his officials. Britain had asked for the elimination of a provision by which each government should be free to terminate the agreement if the exchange rate should vary considerably from the rate that prevailed on the day of signature. London had suggested that this clause was acceptable only if there were "an informal understanding that the rate would be permitted to vary 10% from the old parity of $4.86." The British preferred a clause that would simply say that, if a wide variation should occur and if either party believed that it had been injured thereby, the agreement might be renegotiated. Morgenthau was surprised to find that the British seemed to be suggesting that they would keep the exchange rate within a 10 percent range around $4.86. In 1936, he observed, Chamberlain had refused to accept any such limits. Actually the British negotiators were safeguarding their right to manage sterling. The American wording involved a commitment to a particular exchange rate whereas the British proposals involved a 20 percent band around $4.86 or no commitment at all. Neither Morgenthau nor his advisers seem to have understood the British position. Morgenthau decided to keep the original clause and to say nothing about the question of the exchange rate until after the trade agreement had been signed. Thereafter, he suggested, one could discuss the sterling-dollar rate under the umbrella of the Tripartite Agreement.[33]

Already sterling was weakening. In June William Butterfield had remarked on Britain's passive current-account balance and on the size of the sterling balances. By August, from Paris, Merle Cochran was reporting that, because the Continent believed that sterling was over-valued and because people expected an international discussion that would fix new parities, sterling was weak. Meeting Phillips at Rouen, Morgenthau expressed his anxiety. If the old par of $4.86 were to be passed, surely there would be considerable pressure upon sterling, which might make it go much lower. Phillips then thought the pound could be held around $4.80. He told Morgenthau that he did not share the general worry about breaching $4.86. Butterworth was less sanguine. He thought that in the face of a real European crisis the British authorities would quickly let sterling fall, before supporting it at a new and much lower level. But even without a war scare he feared that $4.86 might prove to be a critical figure. London's sterling balances were so large and Britain's budget and trade positions were so weak that the pound was very exposed. Confidence was all. Finally Butterworth reminded Morgenthau that because so much British gold could flow to the United States it was in America's interest to forestall a flight from the pound.[34]

By late August the pressure on sterling had become too strong for the authorities in London to resist. On 30 August the pound fell below $4.86 for the first time since late 1933. Morgenthau promptly reported the fact to President Roosevelt. The secretary and the president at once devised a demand for an exchange control, and they pooled their anxieties with respect to the deluge of gold that America might expect to receive. Meanwhile Harry Dexter White was preparing an unpleasant memorandum. He argued that there was no justification for the fall in the pound. A cheaper pound would unsettle monetary arrangements throughout the world, and it would cause troubles for American trade. The Equalisation Account, he wrote, was now losing a mere £8 million per month on current transactions. There was plenty of British gold to cover such an outflow. As for capital outflow these could best be stemmed by showing a determination to support the pound. On purchasing power parity grounds Britain was more competitive than it had been. If the pound continued to fall, American pressure groups might call for a revision of the trade agreement. Since February the pound had fallen from $5.02 to $4.86. Enough, White thought, was enough.[35]

As sterling continued its descent Morgenthau became ever more agitated. His staff had told him that American trade would not suffer until the pound had descended to $4.50 or $4.60. Nevertheless the slippage worried him. He knew that the British authorities had spent gold lavishly to defend the pound. But the draft trade treaty in effect assumed a $4.90 pound, whereas by late October the pound stood at $4.75. Late in October he summoned a gathering of professors and asked them whether the United States should worry about the fall in the pound and whether it should propose a sterling floor in the trade treaty. Was there not some risk that as soon as the treaty was concluded Britain might withdraw all support from the pound?[36]

From Harry Dexter White came a most profound distrust of Britain. He believed that the United Kingdom was trying to see how low it could go without provoking the Americans. Pointing out that if the British authorities were deliberately forcing down the pound so as to extract a competitive advantage, he reminded Morgenthau and the other discussants that thanks to the tripartite accords Britain was not allowed to do any such thing. Britain should tell the Americans what its criteria were. Thanks to the Tripartite Agreement, America was entitled to ask. Herbert Feis, also, thought that consultation would be in order.[37] So did the other economists. However, they did not think that the trade treaty should include any floor or ceiling for sterling. On the other hand, they argued that through the tripartite accord the United States could and should try to establish a range of variation of the exchange rate; if the rate should move outside that range there would be automatic consultation.[38]

Fortunately for Whitehall Morgenthau decided, "I wouldn't dream of making this move until I had at least 2 or three weeks' time to work out a very careful agenda across the table."[39] But the documents make it clear that he was concerned. Without consulting the United States, Britain had allowed the pound to decline. No one had told the Americans why this was happening or how far it might go. Knowing what we know about Britain's payments position, especially the current-account deficit and the capital outflow that began early in 1938, we can see why sterling was declining. But of the former the Americans had unsatisfactory estimates only, and of the latter they knew little. Though Whitehall had begun to publish the state of the Exchange Equalisation Account, the figures appeared after a three-month delay and said nothing about sterling balances.

By late October Bewley had become aware of Morgenthau's concern. He reported that the secretary of the treasury had told him Washington could accept the descent of sterling to $4.76. Nevertheless, he thought the Americans were worried both by this descent and by the conjoint descent of agricultural prices. He feared that if sterling were to fall to $4.50 or $4.60 the president would face strong political pressure to devalue the dollar vis-à-vis gold. He also reported that the American Treasury was suspicious about sterling. Morgenthau himself said the British had always done what he asked them, but some of his officials believed that the pound could and should have been held at $4.86.[40] They badly wanted to know how much gold was in the Exchange Equalisation Account.

Early in November Morgenthau convened another academic conference on sterling. The membership was much the same as in October. White prepared an agenda and background paper, which asked the members to consider "the feasibility of consultation with Britain . . . with respect to the course of the sterling-dollar rate and related matters, and the form such consultation should take." Once more White functioned as rapporteur and as the articulator of anti-British sentiment. He wanted to know how the British Treasury chose the sterling price of gold; he also hoped for a great deal of information about gold losses, hoards, sterling balances, external short assets, forward exchange positions, transactions in London on foreign account, and an estimated balance of payments for 1939. White and Viner voiced special alarm because so many currencies were pegged to the pound. Thus, when sterling fell relative to the dollar it was almost, they said, as if the dollar were moving up against the world. The academic advisers reported that the secretary was right to worry about the exchange rate, that the depreciation of sterling was a threat to the United States, and that Britain should be called to account for its actions.[41]

Morgenthau, however, decided to wait. More concerned about the franc than the pound and deeply involved with the secret mission he had entrusted to Jean Monnet,[42] he would do nothing until after 15 November. Then he would see Bewley.[43]

In preparation for this confrontation Morgenthau consulted President Roosevelt. The president was anxious to sign the trade treaty not because of the prospective Anglo-American possibilities but because a Canadian-American treaty was part of the package. He asked Morgenthau how low the pound could go without upsetting American industry. The secretary responded that his staff told him the critical range was $4.50 to $4.60. Roosevelt said, "If you'll tell me that the Canadian dollar is all right, let's let this thing go . . . but when we sign it, we'll put the British on notice."[44]

After Morgenthau's departure the president at once called a State Department official and asked about the sterling exchange. That official at once called the American Treasury, which told him that except in the face of a really massive capital flight Britain could certainly hold the exchange rate if it chose. The official then went to see Sir Ronald Lindsay, the British ambassador, to whom he delivered an alarming message. Having transmitted the president's dismay at the decline of sterling, he said, "I suggested that he might want to cable at once to London to see what steps could not be taken to sustain the pound, particularly during the coming few days." He also proposed, and Sir Ronald agreed, that someone should deny the rumor about the coming trade agreement. Though the agreement did not specify any particular exchange rate, it was widely believed in the American Treasury that the market expected the treaty to specify a $4.50 pound. Such a rumor would of course generate speculation against sterling, causing some of its current weakness. But the State Department official had not correctly transmitted Morgenthau's own concerns. He was not particularly interested in the course of sterling during the coming few days, before the trade agreement had been signed, but he was very much interested in its course thereafter. If sterling continued downward, he told White, he would have to do something. At least he would certainly have to talk to the British – whether sterling fell or not. White certainly hoped and expected that his chief would do so.[45]

Whitehall promptly sent Morgenthau an explanation of recent developments. Up to 30 September Britain had spent a great deal of gold to support sterling. The weakness was due in small part to a weak balance of payments on current accounts but chiefly to "withdrawal of sterling balances from London by citizens of neutral countries aided at times by withdrawal of French balances." The loss of gold had been accompanied by a reduction in Britain's short-term liabilities, but these were still very large. If Britain "were to adopt any rigid policy of pegging the current losses of gold might become so great as to imperil the position ... On any recovery of confidence His Majesty's Government see no reason why an improvement should not take place in sterling."[46]

This response was more than a little disingenuous. Since 1931 the Bank of England had been gathering data on foreign funds in London. But it did not give the results to the Treasury. Hence, an official wrote, "we are not in a position easily to estimate how far sales of sterling are due to capital movements and how far to an adverse balance of payments on current account." This lacuna was especially embarrassing as the Americans were again pressing for more information about short-term capital movements and about the gold position.[47]

On 22 November Bewley met with Morgenthau and his advisers, who had already received Whitehall's response. White handed Bewley a one-page memorandum headed, *"We are concerned by the decline in sterling,"* and giving four reasons for this concern. First, the decline raised a question about the "meaning and usefulness of the Tripartite Accord." Second, it might not be in Britain's own interests to let the pound decline. Third, the decline might "seriously endanger the world economic situation." Fourth, it was not justified by the trading position of the United States [*sic*]. Also, the memorandum asked for much more data about Britain's gold and short-term capital position. Morgenthau reminded Bewley that as yet there had been none of the consultation that the tripartite accord might be thought to have foreshadowed. He explained that though he had nothing concrete to suggest, he was worried, especially about commodity prices. Once Bewley had withdrawn, White told Morgenthau, "That was perfect. He knows you are concerned." Meanwhile Bewley at once informed London that Morgenthau, still distressed by the fall of the pound, felt "somewhat handicapped" by the lack of data. He wanted frequent consultations and some "remedy" for the weak pound.[48]

On the American side there was a good deal of confusion. Morgenthau himself was afraid that the fall of sterling would prompt Congress to force him into some foolish course of action, such as devaluation of the dollar relative to gold.[49] He was also concerned about commodity prices, and he feared that the exchange-control countries of Central Europe would mount a competitive campaign that would bring back depression in the United States. Britain and America, he thought, should surely be able to devise countermeasures.[50] But he had not forgotten that the Tripartite Agreement did not commit Britain to any particular exchange rate.

From W. W. Butterworth, who was in Washington on leave, Morgenthau got good advice. Just before sailing from Britain Butterworth had seen Phillips and Norman. They explained that the exodus of funds, which they compared to the 1931 exodus, was caused by the market's evaluation of political prospects. They thought it impossible to peg sterling or even to fix limits within which it could fluctuate. Norman had explained that if Britain had stabilized the pound in 1936 the position in 1938 would have been hopeless. But Britain had no long-run policy, Butterworth said. There was simply pessimism and improvisation from day to day. It was the loss of gold, not the weakness of sterling, that worried the Bank and the Treasury, neither of whom had any idea of depreciating the pound for the sake of a trade advantage.[51]

Regrettably Morgenthau's resident advisers, especially White, did a good deal to muddy the waters. White told the secretary that he doubted Norman's statement about the impossibility of pegging the pound, and he believed there had been "no real attempt to see how much gold would hold it." He then did his best to confuse the secretary with respect to the distinction between a devaluation that is aimed at competitive advantage and a depreciation that is produced by market forces. White and the other advisers were also less than helpful with respect to the realities of Britain's position. By emphasizing the size of Britain's gold reserves relative to its current-account deficit and by saying little about the relationship between gold reserves and capital outflow, they did little to instruct the secretary about the underlying reasons for the falling pound. White, in particular, repeatedly told Morgenthau that Britain could easily hold the pound if it wanted to; he also argued that if capital flight were the problem the authorities could stem the tide and turn it by demonstrating their determination to hold the rate. He thought they had not tried.[52] Implicitly, therefore, the advisers were assuming that capital was going because the pound was tending to fall; they showed remarkably little interest in or knowledge of the world political pressures that were moving gold from Europe to the United States.

Whatever his hopes, White could not entirely control the volatile mind of Morgenthau, let alone that of Roosevelt. By late November White and Morgenthau expected that Britain would need exchange control within a few days.[53] The idea did not distress them. But both secretary and president were worried about the problem of hot money and the westward flow of gold that it produced. Ever since 1936 the Treasury had been investigating the problem, having considered various ways in which hot money could be repelled or shut out. Morgenthau drew on these schemes in his broodings on the franc. By late November 1938 Roosevelt was actively considering the question, and Morgenthau thought the president might tell him to stop the gold inflow. In effect the American Treasury would stop buying gold; presumably, too, gold imports would be prohibited. In Britain, the secretary observed, speculators were buying gold and exporting it. Might not America help Britain by means of gold embargo? He observed, "If the fellow owns sterling and sells sterling and he can't get gold out, what the hell is he going to do with it?"[54]

Morgenthau's advisers were quick to point out that if America refused gold the pound would fall even farther and faster because the British authorities would not be able to use gold to support it. They had, however, another suggestion. The manager of the American Stabilization Fund told Morgenthau that the time had come for the Fund to support sterling by accumulating sterling balances and holding them for twelve to eighteen months.[55] Morgenthau's response was predictable. Because he might lose money on sterling or be unable to unload it, he would not countenance any such purchases.[56] Further, we may suppose that White would have opposed any such device if only because it would have made things easier for the British.

The Treasury sent Bewley detailed instructions. He was to tell Morgenthau that sterling was weak for psychological reasons. The world was anxious about the international situation; there was fear that

British rearmament might damage its financial resources. He was authorized to explain that since 30 September the Treasury had spent £60 million in gold and also supplied forward dollars in an amount equal to £40 million. "We have done far more than we were called on to do by the Tripartite Agreement and further . . . in face of withdrawals of capital on an even greater scale than in 1931 we have been successful in preventing a serious break in the exchange rate." As for the secret consultations that Morgenthau had requested, these could occur as long as only Britain and France took part in them.[57]

This was not enough to satisfy the American secretary of the treasury, who "did not think he could sit quiet and just watch a long continued fall of the pound." He wanted to know whether the British authorities were really convinced that neither government could do anything more.[58]

On 28 November sterling rose. On 29 November the Bank of England told the Federal Reserve of some new defensive measures. The British banks had agreed not to finance forward exchange transactions or gold purchases. The Bank would close out its own short position in dollars by the end of December, thus causing a shortage of sterling in London and squeezing the speculators who had gone short on sterling. The Federal Reserve, as usual, at once transmitted the news to Morgenthau, who believed that the British actions and the rise in sterling were the result of his representations.[59]

But neither White nor the secretary was satisfied. Morgenthau reconvened his officials and his academic panel – Viner and others. White prepared a memorandum in which he argued that by spending more gold, by announcing that sterling was not overvalued, and by asking for American cooperation Britain could do a good deal to strengthen sterling. The United States, White suggested, "might consider" using up to $200 million of its Stabilisation Fund to support sterling as long as Britain would promise to spend at least as much from its own reserves. Britain must promise that "any loss we might sustain . . . be limited in amount by British guarantee to supply gold to us at a pre-agreed-upon rate." White also thought the Americans might consult with the British so as to secure "an informal agreement to stabilise the sterling dollar rate." Why he thought it worthwhile to seek such an agreement, given Britain's repeated refusal to consider stabilization, the documents do not reveal. If there could be an agreement it might be supported, he thought, by measures against hot money, controls on unwanted capital flows, and an exchange of information "to facilitate such control." Here is an echo of a proposal that Morgenthau had thrust on the French, but not on the British, earlier that same autumn. White reminded the secretary that if Britain proved uncooperative there were numerous weapons in the Americans' hands. The secretary could read Britain out of the Tripartite Agreement, raise the price of gold, invoke the exchange clause in the new trade agreement, and force the export of some foreign capital funds from the United States. The academic visitors considered White's suggestions and debated these and other ideas with one another and with Morgenthau and his staff. Although they did not agree fully, they tended to think that Britain should sell more gold and that the two exchange funds should operate "for joint account, without conversion into gold." Their advice tended to encourage Secretary Morgenthau.[60] Though he did not expect to get any results, he would continue to press the British.[61]

In early December the pound was somewhat stronger, and things became quieter in Washington. On 30 November Bewley had explained the technique of the Bank's squeeze – "a palliative not a panacea." He also explained that even if the world political situation had not worsened sterling would have tended to fall, because the United States was buying much less in 1938 than in 1937. With respect to the exchange rate Morgenthau was not obstreperous, but he did observe that he hoped Britain's authorities would not let their anxiety to rebuild reserves prevent them from letting the pound rise. On 3 December Bewley gave Morgenthau such information about liabilities and gold flows as London had managed to assemble. He informed the secretary that between April and December 1938, the Exchange Equalisation Account's gold reserves had fallen from £290 million to £60 million. This news may have had a chastening effect. No longer could White or Lochhead argue that Britain was not trying to defend the pound. Besides official reserves, Bewley reported that there was perhaps £200 million in private gold hoards. The Americans had asked about this because of their own attempts to nationalize such private hoards.[62]

Morgenthau was still anxious to learn more about Britain's plans and intentions. On 9 December he asked Bewley to obtain a general "appreciation" of developments since the upturn at the end of November. He had no particular reason, he said; he simply wanted to stay in close, friendly touch. Bewley told Morgenthau that the embassy had heard of dissatisfaction in the American Treasury. If the Americans were not completely satisfied with the way in which the pound had been handled they should, he said, be completely frank. Morgenthau appears to have told Bewley that he *would* be completely frank and that the British should be the same.[63]

The Treasury and the Bank agreed to tell Morgenthau that the pound had strengthened, first, because of technical pressure against bear speculators, and, second, because in France things were much better. The outlook for the pound, however, remained obscure. Political considerations remained dominant, and "there are no encouraging factors at present in view."[64]

These interventions had reminded Whitehall that the Americans might still devalue against gold. The president still had power to reduce the dollar's gold content. Both Morgenthau and Roosevelt wanted to retain that power. Arguing for its extension in March 1939, Morgenthau said that it should be "retained as a weapon in case other great commercial countries should at any time start a race in currency depreciation." Reading the above, a Foreign Office official observed, "They have a standing fear of further foreign devaluation."[65] Kenneth Bewley, the financial adviser in Washington, did not think devaluation was likely. Morgenthau and his staff, he observed, were no longer enamored of monetary experimentation. But if sterling went on down while agricultural prices were still depressed there would certainly be pressure from Congress, and one could not be sure about the president; he might overrule the Treasury. Morgenthau himself had said that he thought of dollar devaluation only as a weapon for a great emergency, which he did not envisage. But he continued to talk of devaluation – partly, Bewley thought, to keep Britain up to the mark in the defense of sterling.

The Foreign Office was not amused. One official minuted, "The Americans once found it expedient to devalue themselves, but they have forgotten that now. Meanwhile, we in all good faith are losing a lot of gold supporting the pound, the weakness of which is due to international political pressure which the Americans largely escape."[66]

The Treasury was horrified at the thought of another gold manipulation. In February 1938 Sir Frederick Phillips had thought it "mad." In the autumn the Treasury officials observed that one could not devalue the dollar against itself. If the Americans raised the dollar price of gold the only gainers would be the gold producers and hoarders; other moneys would follow the dollar. Bewley was urged to wean the Americans from this course. He responded by explaining the political realities. Although the two treasuries agreed, Congress might not be equally sensible. And neither might a politically sensitive president.[67]

By December 1938 Norman was extremely pessimistic about the pound. According to Phillips, by year-end he believed that all Europe thought sterling was too high and would have to go lower. Gold was to be shifted from the Bank to the Exchange Equalisation Account, which by the end of the year would be down to £40 million, and it would be necessary to replenish it far more amply than anyone had foreseen only a fortnight earlier. Norman thought that in January the pound would be $4.61 or thereabouts and would then go lower. He wanted to pass this dismal prognosis at once to Morgenthau. Phillips agreed, and so Bewley was asked to arrange through Morgenthau for oral discussions in London.[68]

Morgenthau was not pleased at the news. A sharp fall in sterling just when Congress was convening would, he reported, make things very difficult. Though pessimistic about the pound he had nothing to suggest, but he asked Butterworth to meet with the Treasury officials.

Butterworth met Phillips, Waley, and Catterns, the deputy governor of the Bank, on 28 December. The American was told that the British authorities would check the fall as long as they could, fighting, the deputy governor said, "while there is a shot in our locker." But beyond this they had no proposals to make. When he had received Butterworth's report Morgenthau told Bewley that he hoped the United Kingdom would not "adopt too defeatist an attitude or give way too easily at the outset."[69]

At the beginning of 1939 the British authorties asked the cooperation of authorities in Paris, Brussels, Zurich, and Amsterdam to limit speculation against sterling "by way of gold." They also decided to transfer gold worth £350 million at current prices from the Bank of England to the Exchange Equalisation Account. Morgenthau was told on 6 January. He welcomed the decision, which he said "should have a good effect." Encouraged, the Treasury asked if Morgenthau could suggest to American banks that they too might refrain from speculation against sterling through gold. Morgenthau agreed to make the necessary arrangements through the Federal Reserve Bank of New York.[70]

These technical arrangements and the Bank's successful "bear squeeze"[71] contributed to the strength of sterling during the first ten weeks of 1939 when Britain added a little to its gold reserves while holding the exchange rate just below $4.70. From mid-March to mid-July, however, it could hold the rate at this level only at heavy cost to the reserves.

This was in part the cost of keeping Morgenthau quiet. As long as the pound was reasonably stable at around $4.68 little was heard from Washington. But even if the Americans had not cared so passionately about the exchange rate the authorities in London might still have wanted to support sterling or at least to slow its descent. Though steadily declining, the sterling balances were still immense. If the pound were to fall below $4.65, some Continental authorities would be very unhappy,[72] and at any marked decline the South African authorities might be expected to complain. As for private sterling balances, these might be withdrawn more quickly if sterling were to fall relatively far or fast.

The authorities held the exchange at $4.68 from early 1939 until August.[73] Until mid-March 1939, when Germany occupied Prague, they were able to do this at little net cost to the reserves. Then began a pressure that continued without remission until war broke out. By 21 August the gold stock was down to £470 million.[74] It is hardly surprising that on 24 August the authorities removed the peg. The pound then fell sharply toward the level of $4.03, where it was pegged at the outbreak of war.[75] In June 1939 both reserves and external liabilities had been £542 million. In summer 1939 the current-account deficit continued, and so did the export of capital. Thus by August 1939 liabilities must have been larger than reserves. In itself this was not an unusual situation. It had been the case before 1914, in the late twenties, and from 1931 through 1936. Only in 1937–8 had reserves stood a little higher than net external liabilities. But in the Treasury these liabilities were seen as responsibilities.

In August 1939 the Treasury saw three alternatives. The Bank might be told to cease defending the pound at $4.68. Both Treasury and Bank favored this course. Admittedly, "We could not contemplate the market being allowed to drive sterling say below four dollars, and if it got to such a figure whether we wanted to or not we should be forced to come back to its support." But "there are no economic data which would enable anyone to announce from an armchair what is the proper rate of exchange between sterling and the dollar." Hence there was no point in trying to predetermine some rate to which sterling might properly fall. There remained exchange control. But this was extremely undesirable, and it could not be imposed lightly because once imposed it could not be quickly removed. Though a free float "runs counter to the hopes of the Tripartite Agreement," Britain could not possibly consult France or the United States in advance. But Bewley, or someone, had better tell Morgenthau beforehand.[76]

On 24 August, when support was withdrawn from the pound, France and the United States were given a small amount of advance warning. Butterworth, from the American embassy, and Le Norcy, from the French, called at the Treasury. They were told that the U.K. authorities were not prepared to lose more reserves for the sake of maintaining the exchange rate. There was no question of seeking a trade advantage; the point was to protect the reserves, pending the outcome of the political crisis. In the current week, Britain had been spending £10 million per day to support the pound. "We had hitherto, in accord with the hopes expressed in the Tripartite Agreement, held the rate firm, but in existing circumstances we feel that this is no longer practicable."[77]

Thus Britain ended the Tripartite Agreement in everything but name. Admittedly, in Paris Paul Reynaud maintained that it and its "technical dispositions" were alive and well. Admittedly, too, the three central banks continued to cooperate. But Reynaud now claimed, "Given the repercussions that may occur, the French Government must preserve the same liberty of action as regards the franc."[78]

2. Some conclusions

Since 1933 it had been clear that the American authorities would not let the United Kingdom fix the sterling-dollar rate. From mid–1933 until mid-August 1939 the U.K. authorities managed the exchanges with an eye to American desires insofar as they could understand these or learn about them. Washington wanted a strong pound, and that is what it got. The Tripartite Agreement really involved no extra commitment on Britain's part. It would consult when and if it wished. When the pound became weak it did not do so, until the United States made threatening noises. And when Britain had to float the pound just before the outbreak of war France and the United States received a little advance warning, but no one asked what Paris or Washington thought. In deciding to support the pound so long and at such cost, London may have been influenced, at least a little, by the "spirit of the Tripartite Agreement." But surely it was more concerned to prevent a flight from sterling or a dollar devaluation against gold.

As long as the franc was weak the Tripartite Agreement provided a wonderful club with which Whitehall could beat the French. The agreement licensed Washington to ask questions in London; it also licensed London to give Paris unsought advice – or so the British officials seem to have believed. France's policies were deplorable in 1936–8 because they so closely paralleled Britain's own policies of 1930–1. The cure that had worked in Britain would work in France. A budget deficit and an expensive social program had destroyed confidence and weakened the currency; by balancing the budget and by reducing one's programs of social improvement one could produce a reflux of capital, thereby strengthening the currency. When Paris finally swallowed the medicine late in 1938, its condition rapidly improved just as Whitehall had expected.

Though the gold standard had been abandoned, gold still mattered. The French held it and dishoarded it; the Empire produced and dishoarded it; the United States absorbed it. Whatever their effects on ordinary trade, exchange rates certainly affected gold production and gold distribution. In Britain, excess gold could be an embarrassment, and the price of gold was important to Empire solidarity. In the American capital, the gold price was a weapon that could be wielded for domestic political advantage and for international leverage as well.

However fine the phrases of the Tripartite Agreement, in the management of its currency each country was still very much on its own. With respect to the gold price, the Americans left the British guessing. The French consulted spasmodically and incompletely; the British record was equally bad. Although the British authorities did help the French to borrow in London, the authorities themselves did not finance one another on any regular basis. Thus there was no pooling of reserves and very little mutual assistance. Like many other such emanations, the spirit of the Tripartite Agreement was not much help in a time of trouble. But for Morgenthau and his officials, the agreement provided an opportunity to ask questions and exert pressure.

The monetary regimes of the 1930s are often described in terms of blocs – sterling, franc, dollar, gold, and exchange-control zones. David Calleo has recently argued that the Tripartite Declarations provided "a new degree of consciously organised cooperation" for the bloc system. He believes that this cooperation "appeared to lead toward a resumption of liberalism." Harold Cleveland, too, has recently maintained that after the Declarations of September 1936 there was "relative harmony in relationships among monetary authorities and consistency of monetary policies . . . due to . . . the rise of Nazi Germany, which caused France and Britain to turn to the United States for political support." The evidence of this chapter suggests that Calleo and Cleveland have produced a perplexing mixture of truth and error.[1]

First of all, it is hard to see either consciously organized cooperation in matters of substance or harmony and consistency in monetary policy. Certainly the central banks of the three countries were in regular contact; but as we saw in Chapters 8 and 9, well before September 1936 there had been intermittent contact between treasuries, and after that date the intergovernmental contacts were spasmodic at best. Nor did these contacts produce any coordination of monetary policy. At best, one might say that each government had a somewhat better idea of what the other governments were up to.

As for a "resumption of liberalism," the record of the late 1930s has precious little to show and less that can be connected with the agreement. Admittedly, there were some new trade agreements and some relaxations of quotas. It is also true that Britain and France set the Belgian prime minister to produce a report on the dismantling of trade and exchange controls. But this effort was part of "appeasement," and of course nothing came of it, while precious little came of the new trade agreements. Indeed, some tariffs went up, and some new quotas were imposed, not least by Britain herself.

On the other hand, both Calleo and Cleveland are right to stress the political side of the monetary conversations. It was not for political or military reasons that the French turned to the British in summer 1936; Paris simply wanted to make sure that it would actually be allowed to devalue – that sterling would not follow the franc down. But as the world scene darkened politics mingled with economics in the working of the tripartite monetary relationships. Britain was concerned to prop up France and to conciliate Washington; its exchange policy, like its tariff policy, was influenced by these desires. Washington was concerned to save European democracy at no cost to itself and to protect the French New Deal, while some American officials already hoped to make Britain more dependent by stripping it of gold. As for the French governments, it is hard to see any consistency or direction in the helter-skelter of the various popular-front regimes. On the other hand, in working for a larger gold hoard and a stable franc in 1938–39 France obviously was not forgetting defense. Also, it is plausible to argue that the French were attached to the rhetoric of monetary cooperation because they believed that this rhetoric would somehow strengthen the democracies.

Cleveland also suggests that by 1939 the system of franc, sterling, and dollar blocs had evolved into an "unrecognised form of dollar standard," with the three blocs linked closely together.[2] He thinks this because, though the French authorities managed the franc in relation to the pound, the British managed the pound in relation to the dollar. But in two crucial respects the "tripartite system" differs from the world of Bretton Woods. First, the exchange rates were anything but stable. Second, in the fixing of rates the American authorities were active, not passive. After the Second World War, the United States allowed other countries to choose the exchange rates they wished; only in the 1960s and 1970s did Washington become less complaisant. But from 1933 until 1939 the American authorities cared passionately about the rates – especially the dollar price of sterling – and they did everything they could to ensure that Britain would acquiesce in the rate the Americans wanted. Nor did Washington ignore the price of the franc.

Some observers have suggested that in the years between 1936 and 1939 we see foreshadowed the American monetary "hegemony" of the postwar years. Though it is hard to be sure what hegemony means in relation to monetary affairs, the evidence does not suggest that the United States ran monetary or exchange policy either in the sterling area or in France. In neither bloc did domestic credit expansion necessarily parallel American. As war came nearer, both Britain and France became more concerned to conciliate the Americans, but neither government was willing to let Washington dictate monetary or exchange policy, and both governments wanted gold, not dollars, for their exchange reserves.

Between 1936 and 1939 the intergovernmental relations were too complicated to be accurately subsumed under such labels as dollar standard or American hegemony, and it is really not correct to see this short and confused period as a "bridge to Bretton Woods."

11
Conclusion: the significance of sterling

This final chapter is not a summary of material from the preceding ten chapters. Rather, it offers some reflections on the place of sterling and the sterling area in the world monetary system of the 1930s. Sterling mattered because the sterling area was a vast zone of fixed exchange rates, because sterling was one of the two great reserve currencies, and because the world suspected that the clever British were manipulating sterling and the sterling area for their own advantage.

To the suspicious Americans and the nervous French, the sterling area resembled Gulliver's Laputa:

The reader can hardly conceive my Astonishment, to behold an Island in the Air, inhabited by Men, who were able (as it should seem) to raise, or sink, or put into a Progressive Motion, as they pleased . . . I . . . chose to observe what course the Island would take; because it seemed for a while to stand still . . . In the lowest Gallery, I beheld some People fishing . . . I called and shouted with the utmost strength of my voice . . . I found by their pointing towards me and to each other, that they plainly discovered me, although they made no return to my shouting.[1]

In reality things were by no means so simple. The "island" was not nearly so solid as it seemed, nor were its monetary affairs under a single management, however diligently Montagu Norman cultivated his ties with the central banks inside the Empire and outside it. The Dominions would follow sterling as far as they could and insofar as it suited them to do so; though India could be coerced, politics imposed limits on the burdens that India could be asked to bear as a result of its adherence.

In the 1930s the sterling area was a zone within which exchange rates were kept absolutely stable for very extended periods. For the currency-board areas in the Dependent Empire, this stability was automatic and thoughtless. In the course of the decade automaticity and thoughtlessness became more common, as Hong Kong and the West Indies adopted variants of the currency-board system. For India, stability was dictated from Whitehall, over the opposition of some expatriate officials and, eventually, of the Reserve Bank board. For Australia, New

Zealand, and South Africa, stability grew out of commercial-banking practice but was eventually imposed by central bank or government. For non-Empire sterling countries, too, it was government policy to follow sterling.

There can be no doubt that the U.K. authorities were glad to find that sterling provided so large an area of exchange stability. In 1931–2 the Treasury officials had hoped that countries would peg to sterling, and they had encouraged the Bank of England to extend modest credits to that end. Throughout the decade London's new-issue controls were used to the same end, and special arrangements might be made, as for New Zealand in 1939–40. The idea was not to encourage the buildup of sterling balances. Useful though these might be in external finance, they were also extremely risky, and that riskiness was well understood in London. It had been exposed by the Macmillan Committee, but the Bank had long been aware of it, and in summer 1931 it had been revealed most painfully in the capital flight that pushed sterling off gold. As long as sterling was freely convertible into other moneys, one might almost say that sterling balances were a necessary evil – evil because they might be withdrawn at awkward moments, though necessary for exchange management within the sterling area. But stable exchange rates were good, because they reduced the risks of trade. Forward cover was available in London, but in the uncertain world of the 1930s its cost could be considerable, and neither Empire traders nor imperial banks were accustomed to it. In any case, if rates changed countries might retaliate with higher basic tariffs or with exchange-dumping duties. The Empire countries had demonstrated in 1931–2 that in the use of these weapons they were adepts.

Because from late 1933 until 1938 sterling varied little relative to the dollar while the currencies of the sterling area remained locked together, for five years a very large part of the trading world enjoyed a reasonable degree of exchange stability while suffering insofar as the actual rates were wrong. Over the same period the currencies of the "gold bloc" were pegged either to gold or to sterling and therefore to the system, though with occasional changes in rate. The area of stability was therefore extremely large, and it endured for a large part of that troubled decade. Only from September 1931 until late autumn 1933, in autumn 1938, and in summer 1939 might one really speak of disorder in the foreign exchanges. It was in those periods that sterling fluctuated or fell relative to the dollar. Admittedly, in 1936–8 the franc fell jerkily relative to both Anglo-Saxon moneys. But relative to the pound and the dollar, the franc and the franc zone counted for little in world trade and payments. It is therefore quite wrong to see the 1930s only as a decade of disorder. If anything, that decade was no more disorderly than the 1920s – and a great deal less disorderly than the 1970s. To that relative order and stability the sterling area and the management of sterling made their separate and immensely important contributions.

The United Kingdom authorities were interested primarily in their power to keep credit easy and cheap at home. This desire determined their choice of exchange-rate regime. As for the target rate, they were more concerned about stability than about level. Their reasons were at first economic: Sterling should be kept steady, and market forces would cause it to float below $4.86. Later the reasons were political: It was necessary to keep the Americans sweet. Washington could impose a higher exchange rate on the British; Roosevelt and Morgenthau could impede the financing of the war effort that Britain was increasingly obliged to anticipate. The authorities knew that gold reserves and sterling balances had a depressing tendency to rise and fall together. This knowledge conditioned their management both of reserves and of exchange rates, if only in that they knew their net reserves were always far smaller than the gross figures might suggest. If they could have brought themselves to share this insight with the Americans, the path of monetary cooperation would have been far smoother, both before the Tripartite Agreement and afterward.

The outside world could hardly be expected to know that at first the "Ottawa policy" of cheap credit, easy money for legitimate commercial purposes, and extensive intraimperial stabilization of exchange, was in part a formula to keep the Dominions and India quiet.[2] It would have been natural to assume that there actually was a concerted imperial policy on money and exchanges. This impression was strengthened when, after the collapse of the London Economic Conference in summer 1933, the Commonwealth delegates issued their declaration, reiterating their common commitment to expansionary monetary measures and their common abhorrence of a premature return to gold. In Chapter 7 we saw how this declaration came to be issued. The story reveals neither a common purpose nor a guiding hand from Britain. But the French, who thought Albion perfidious, and the Americans, who thought Norman and the Treasury too clever by half, can hardly have known this. Finally, as the outer Empire countries equipped themselves with central banks and as those new institutions were staffed so extensively from London, it was natural to suspect that Britain was equipping the Empire with monetary institutions that the Bank of England could somehow control.

With respect to the flow of information London was as closemouthed inside the sterling area and inside the Empire as outside. Especially in

1931–2 this reticence was not without its costs. The South Africans were infuriated because they could not discover what was to happen to sterling. Admittedly, in autumn 1931, when the high commissioner first asked, London did not have an answer. But by spring 1932, when a definite policy was taking shape, the British authorities were no more forthcoming. Similarly, if the Canadian officials had been assured in spring 1932 that Britain was embarking on a policy that guaranteed cheap money, easy credit, and a controlled, rather modest depreciation of sterling, it is not impossible that they would have convinced Prime Minister Bennett to take the Canadian dollar into the sterling area. It is true that Bennett had other reasons for following the American dollar, not the pound. The point is that until the Ottawa gathering the Canadians received no clear lead from Whitehall. Finally, in India Sir George Schuster found life unnecessarily difficult because he had no idea what sort of monetary policy or what sort of exchange policy his masters in London might choose. The Ottawa declaration may be viewed as an attempt to tell the Empire and any non-Empire sterling countries what Britain's monetary policy was to be. For the rest of the decade Britain certainly used it in that way. But it does not seem to have been conceived with that end in view. In any event, such a declaration is a singularly roundabout way for signaling one's intentions to one's junior partners. Perhaps matters were different once central banking had spread to New Zealand, India, and Canada. If so, the difference has left remarkably little trace in government records or official papers.

There is very little evidence that the Bank of England directly affected policy in the new institutions. Admittedly, all the new central banks revealed by their actions an attachment to stable exchange rates – in Canada, vis-à-vis the American dollar; elsewhere, vis-à-vis sterling. This attachment can hardly have displeased Norman; but in the histories of the several banks one finds no hint that he had produced it. If he attempted to influence their reserves policies, or succeeded in doing so, the historians have not told us about attempts or successes. In the Dominions, there were plentiful domestic reasons for a commitment to fixed exchange rates. As for India, neither the government nor the British authorities were prepared to allow a change in the rupee exchange rate. It was these attitudes, not subtle consultations among friendly central bankers or resolutions at imperial conferences, that kept exchange rates so stable within the Empire. Similarly, there were good commercial, financial, administrative, and legal reasons for so many Empire banks and trading entities to hold sterling. In 1923, the Imperial Economic Conference had urged that Empire countries should build up sterling reserves so as to stabilize intraimperial exchange rates. The Ottawa

Conference, by emphasizing the desirability of intraimperial exchange stabilization, might be thought to imply the same action. But there is absolutely no sign that such resolutions ever affected anyone's behavior.

Nor did Britain have total control over the "rising," the "sinking," or the "progressive motion" of sterling. As to the rising, Britain could not force the pound to rise; as to the sinking, American importunities imposed an equally stringent limit, and so from time to time did the troubles of the French. Indeed, it would appear that in each successive year the authorities had less freedom to choose a target rate and work toward it. In 1931–2 the authorities had power to prevent sterling from rising, though they lacked reserves to prevent it from falling. The commitment to cheap money and easy credit, enshrined in the Ottawa Conference proceedings, may be seen as a reflection of this fact: If cheap money kept sterling well below $4.86, so much the better. But in 1933 the Americans in effect took control of the dollar-sterling rate. For the rest of the decade the British were free only to prevent sterling from falling below the Americans' target level. And in 1938–9, when capital flows turned against the pound, the British authorities were free only to support their currency, at enormous cost to their gold reserves; they were not free to let sterling freely depreciate.

We are often told that in the 1930s there was a great deal of "competitive devaluation." The literature suggests that country after country deliberately depreciated its currency so as to win a competitive advantage. It is never clear, however, which countries are supposed to have done this evil thing. Clearly neither Britain nor the Empire countries did so. Devaluations, when they occurred, were imposed by market forces; at worst, one might say that from time to time both Britain and other Empire countries resisted pressures that would otherwise have floated their exchange rates upward. New Zealand is an exception, but surely not an acutely important one, except to New Zealanders. There is no doubt that sterling floated dirtily; but it was not devalued competitively. Neither was the franc, at least before 1937 and probably not even then. Neither was the mark. Though the system of multiple rates and exchange controls that Germany evolved in the 1930s was sometimes manipulated to encourage German exports, fundamentally the system was a response to the weakness of Germany's external payments and to the policies of fiscal and monetary expansion that Germany's government pursued after 1933. As for the currencies of the smaller European countries, market pressures forced devaluations on some while others protected theoretical parities by means of exchange control. As for the yen, it left gold and fluctuated for the same reasons as the pound. What remains? Only the United States.

It was the Roosevelt administration, alone among major powers and almost alone in the world, that deliberately depreciated its currency against gold, thus winning an advantage in world trade even though its balance of payments was already in surplus on current account and even though it had virtually ceased to lend abroad. Further, it was the Roosevelt administration that insisted on retaining the right to make further devaluations, not just in 1934 but for the rest of the decade. When we are told that the 1930s was a decade of competitive devaluation, in large part we are hearing an echo of American economists' guilt: It was their country, not Britain, that deliberately destabilized the set of exchange rates.

In 1933 Roosevelt demonstrated that he would not allow Britain to manage sterling in its own interest. Washington would not tolerate a really cheap pound. In summer and autumn 1936 and again in late autumn 1938 London was reminded of that fact. Fortunately for the British, from mid-1933 until mid-1938 their balance-of-payments position was sufficiently strong that they could accommodate the Americans without affecting the pace of their domestic recovery. Short-term balances were building up in London, and long-term loans were being repaid. These inflows more than sufficed to cover new overseas direct investment and to finance the current-account deficit.

In 1931–2 it was recognized by all that there could be no collective control of Britain's own monetary policy. Other countries (India always excepted) were free to follow sterling or to depart from it; if a country adhered to the pound, it must accept British monetary policy as one of the things to which its own economy would have to adjust. Therefore, its own monetary policy must be consistent with the commitment to a fixed exchange rate. Fortunately, in Britain credit was easy and cheap. Thus the sterling system could readily accommodate the cheap-money policies of Scandinavia, Australia, and South Africa. Fortunately, too, London stood ready to supply some new long-term credit, to refinance old debt on better terms, and from time to time to offer emergency short-term assistance. By supplying the sterling-area countries with the sterling they needed to balance their international accounts, London helped to make the system work.

Sterling balances were freely convertible into other currencies. Through the London gold market, sterling was also convertible into gold. This market was plentifully supplied by the regular shipments from South Africa. Because of this double convertibility the British authorities could not force sterling on reluctant holders. Hence, before 1939 the sterling system did not give Britain any sort of hegemony within the sterling area.

Much of world trade was still invoiced in sterling and financed through London; the City still provided substantial sterling credit, both long-term and short. Many overseas banks, businesses, and governments still found it helpful to hold transactions balances in London. The British authorities, by holding sterling relatively stable vis-à-vis the dollar from late 1933 to 1938, must have rendered sterling balances more attractive than they would have been if sterling had continued to fluctuate as it had done in 1931–2. Given confidence about the exchange rate, the sterling balances reflected the continuing importance of sterling invoicing and the continuing weight of Britain as supplier, customer, and financier. But besides the transactions demand, sterling was of use as a store of value and as a secure sort of asset. The overseas banks of the Empire still based their operations in London and held their liquid assets in sterling; so did new central banks and other currency authorities. The London market was active and well organized; sterling assets could be easily acquired and quickly liquidated. In fiscal and monetary policy Britain had eschewed inflationary experiment. There was no risk of a socialist government, or even of a social democratic one. And so long as peace endured there was no risk of comprehensive exchange control. Further, though sterling was managed it was managed "sanely." No Roosevelt was likely to disturb Britain's monetary order. The authorities would act to offset the wilder day-to-day fluctuations, and over longer periods they would steady the rate as far as possible. There were, in any event, few alternatives. Holland and Switzerland could provide shelter for some. As for France, its polity was unstable and its policies were worse. And many people distrusted the Roosevelt administration.

Foreign demand for short-term sterling assets made its contribution to the survival of the discount houses, and until mid-1938 it helped the authorities in the management of the public debt. The authorities must have been inconvenienced by the rundown of sterling balances in 1938–9, just when, for the first time in a decade, they wanted to sell new bonds on a significant scale. But they do not seem to have connected the growing debt with the weakness of sterling, as they did in 1931 or as they argued relative to the franc in 1936–8.

Because the world was still willing to hold sterling balances, Britain was not obliged to deplete its overseas assets as rapidly as it would otherwise have had to do, given the weakness of its current account. Wherever the interest cost fell short of the yield on the corresponding overseas assets, Britain certainly gained. This kind of gain is properly called "seigniorage," because it results from the creation of a money that people are willing and eager to hold. In the 1930s the margins were not insignificant. After the conversion of mid-1932 and the introduction of cheap money, sterling balances yielded very little. In 1938, for instance, the average yield on treasury bills was 0.611 percent and on consols, 3.38 percent. New overseas direct investments were presumably yielding 5 percent or more; during much of the 1930s, new mining investments did rather better than that, though for overseas governments the London market charged rather less. At the end of 1938 the sterling balances were £598 million. Against these should be set the cost of the extra gold the authorities wanted to hold because of the balances. Regrettably, we cannot know what this figure might be, and though the documents tell us that there was some connection they also warn us against assuming any simple numerical ratio. But if we ignore the extra gold reserves and assume that new foreign investment yields 5 percent while sterling balances cost 0.611 percent, we can calculate a sort of measure that we shall call the "gross yield on the sterling area." The figure is £26,246,220. This is 2.8 percent of Britain's export receipts in 1938, and 0.5 percent of its gross national product – not without value, certainly, but hardly a large item in the national economy.

The authorities were able to manage the pound partly because the world believed that sterling was managed "skillfully," partly because the United Kingdom eschewed exchange control, and partly because history had endowed Britain with a vast heap of long-term external assets that could be depleted and transformed under the stressful conditions of the 1930s. Britain could accumulate gold partly because some European countries were still shedding the yellow metal but chiefly because Indians were dishoarding and because South Africans were mining with vigor and success. The dishoarding and mining at first reflected the depreciation of sterling vis-à-vis the dollar and then, after mid-1933, the depreciation of the dollar relative to gold; they also reflected the price declines of the early 1930s.

To study and explain the processes that connect prices and balances of payments in the various countries of the world economy, economists construct models in which gold flows back and forth from one country to another, but the stuff does not get produced; it just *is*. Perhaps because economists' theoretical constructs condition their thinking, they frequently tell the monetary history of the 1930s without mentioning that South African gold production increased dramatically or that Indian private holders disgorged a great deal of the gold that they had been steadily hoarding for decades or centuries. In addition, there were relatively small but helpful increases in gold production both in Australia and in Canada. It follows that the Empire supplied almost all the world's new monetary gold, whether this came from current production or from dishoarding. Thanks to Roosevelt's manipulations, by 1937 the world was awash in monetary gold, and the recovery of the 1930s was lubricated thereby. Further, when this new gold first reached the London gold market, almost all of it was "sterling area gold." Of the world's important gold producers only Canada and the USSR stood outside the sterling area. Though the newly mined gold was marketed in London it would remain there only insofar as Britain's balance of payments was strong enough. The Empire authorities could help this balance only by accumulating sterling claims. Their policy in this respect was entirely their own affair. Nevertheless, whenever Britain's authorities were willing and able to increase their holdings of gold the London gold market was a considerable advantage. Through it the authorities could buy what they wanted without having to pull gold from some other monetary center in Europe or in the United States. In the 1930s the gold flows were so large that they must often though not always have been able to do exactly this.

In the world economy Britain was no longer sufficiently large, central, or secure for its monetary sanity to produce a world recovery. Within the Empire cheap money and easy credit could have their beneficent effect as long as Britain eschewed exchange controls. But Britain could not offset the monetary absurdities of other countries. When other countries absorbed gold and sterilized it, allowed their banking systems to collapse, contracted their money supplies either deliberately or absentmindedly, and mindlessly protected overvalued exchange rates, there was by 1930 little or nothing that the United Kingdom could do. During the period 1930–3, its authorities had some hope that international negotiation and discussion might produce a return to sanity. That hope evaporated, dispelled as much by French intransigence and by the spread of exchange controls as by President Roosevelt's bombshells of 1933. Thereafter, at best the authorities could try to operate a monetary policy and an exchange policy that would assist Britain's own recovery and that of the Empire. In so doing they had to protect their own freedom to manage the exchanges while recognizing that other countries – especially France and the United States – were not indifferent to the international value of the pound. If they had wished, the Empire countries could have manipulated their exchange rates without worrying about foreign reactions; Britain could not – especially after Franklin D. Roosevelt had attained power in Washington.

Empire primary producers, like American, regularly demanded devaluation as a price-raising device. We have seen that in India and South Africa governments resisted this demand, whereas in New Zealand, as in the United States, governments acquiesced. Australia did not deliberately devalue for this reason, but its primary producers reaped a convenient harvest from the depreciation of the Australian pound. In Canada such manipulation was considered but rejected, though the authorities were not sorry to see the Canadian dollar floating a little below the American. Fortunately for everyone the United States provided a floor price for gold. But other primary producers were not so well looked after. And if we are to judge by the adventures of Australia, New Zealand, and South Africa in the early thirties, for such products as butter and meat the output response could be very large and the price declines very disappointing. We know that in 1932–7 the United Kingdom authorities spent much time and labor on the quantitative control of such products. They hoped to regulate production in their principal suppliers or, failing that, imports therefrom. It is possible to see their labors as a necessary response to the avalanche of output that the Empire devaluations of 1930–2 had generated. We also know that from time to time the Bank of England provided lines of credit to support the two Australasian pounds. It would be amusing if we could see these credits as an indirect means of protecting British pig growers, cattle raisers, and butter and cheese makers. But surely even Montagu Norman cannot have been quite so devious, or quite so far-seeing.

Notes

A note on primary documentation

The following primary materials are cited in the notes. Where abbreviations have been used, they appear in parentheses in the list, which also gives the location of each collection.

Public Record Office, London: Cabinet Papers (CAB); Foreign Office Papers (FO): Dominions Office Papers (DO); and Treasury Papers (T).

India Office Library, London: India Office Records (IOR).

University of Birmingham Library: Neville Chamberlain Papers (NC).

University of Cambridge Library: Stanley Baldwin Papers.

Public Archives of Canada, Ottawa: Department of Finance Papers (RG 19); R. B. Bennett Papers (microfilms of originals in Harriet Irving Library, University of New Brunswick, Fredericton): W. L. M. King Papers; Department of External Affairs Papers (RG 25), Norman Robertson Papers.

Public Archives of Nova Scotia, Halifax: E. N. Rhodes Papers.

Central Archives Depot, Pretoria: Charles te Water Papers; Finance Department Files: J. C. Smuts Papers.

Jagger Library, University of Cape Town: Sir Patrick Duncan Papers.

Cullen Library, University of the Witwatersrand: J. H. Hofmeyr Papers.

Roosevelt Library, Hyde Park: F. D. Roosevelt Papers; Henry C. Morgenthau Papers (MD).

Chapter 1. The sterling area in the 1930s

1. What was the sterling area?

1 Peter H. Lindert, *Key Currencies and Gold, 1900–1913*, Princeton Studies in International Finance, no. 24 (International Finance Section, Department of Economics, Princeton University, 1969), Table 2.

2 On this background see David Williams, "The Evolution of the Sterling System," in J. S. G. Wilson et al., *Essays in Money and Banking in Honour of R. S. Sayers* (Oxford: Clarendon Press, 1968).

3 G. R. Hawke, *Between Governments and Banks: A History of the Reserve Bank of New Zealand* (Wellington: A. R. Shearer, Government Printer, 1974), chapter 2, esp. pp. 16–18.

4   *Parliamentary Papers*, vol. 13 (1930–), Cmd. 3897, p. 301.

5   Treasury Papers 160/807/F. 11935/1 (hereafter cited as T): Sir Frederick Phillips to Sir Richard Hopkins, 2 February 1930.

6   See L. F. Giblin, *The Growth of a Central Bank* (Melbourne: At the University Press, 1951) pp. 126–9; and R. F. Holder, *Bank of New South Wales* (Sydney: Angus Robertson, 1970), 2: 736.

7   See Hawke, *Governments and Banks*, p. 24.

8   See G. H. de Kock, *A History of the South African Reserve Bank* (Pretoria: J. L. van Schaik, 1954), pp. 161–2, 192–6.

9   Foreign Office Papers 371/15754, pp. 46, 47, 96 (hereafter cited as FO).

10   FO 371/15682, p. 294; FO 371/15561, pp. 52, 63, 70, 94, 97.

11   FO 371/15627, pp. 298, 310–12, 317; FO 371/15566, pp. 18–19, 22–4; FO 371/15556, p. 9.

12   T 175/56, pp. 229–30.

13   FO 371/19600, pp. 168–9.

14   T 175/56, pp. 136–7: memorandum, Hopkins to Neville Chamberlain, 8 December 1931.

15   R. S. Sayers, *The Bank of England, 1891–1944* (Cambridge: Cambridge University Press, 1976), p. 449.

16   Sir Henry Clay, *Lord Norman* (London: Macmillan, 1957), p. 368: and T/160/807/F. 11935/1.

17   Giblin, *Growth of Central Bank*, pp. 128, 142–3, 236–41, 242.

18   Sayers, *Bank of England*, pp. 449–50.

19   Clay, *Lord Norman*, pp. 416–17.

20   T 160/627/F. 14377: Treasury memorandum, 14 October 1935.

21   These contents are discussed in Chapter 5.

22   T 160/683/F. 14659: memorandum, Sir Frederick Phillips, 18 July 1936.

23   T 160/627/F. 14377; T 160/F. 13427/3: C. F. Cobbold to S. D. Waley, 9 April 1936.

24   T 160/683/F. 14659: memorandums, Phillips, 7 July 1936, and anon., 7 July 1936.

25   Clay, *Lord Norman*, p. 413.

26   Sayers, *Bank of England*, pp. 512–27.

2. *Empire money and the sterling bloc*

1   Sayers, *Bank of England*, pp. 416–30; Susan Howson, "The Managed Floating Pound, 1932–39," *Banker*, March 1976, pp. 259–65; idem, *Domestic Monetary Management in Britain, 1919–1938* (Cambridge: Cambridge University Press, 1975), pp. 79–86 and App. 4; Susan Howson and Donald Winch, *The Economic Advisory Council, 1930–1939* (Cambridge: Cambridge University Press, 1977), pp. 100–5, 254–63.

2   FO 371/15681, pp. 121–4: memorandum, Sir Frederick Leith-Ross, 2 October 1931.

3   I must thank Professor Susan Howson for the attributions and for telling me about the relationship between the drafts and the missing memorandum. See also T 175/56: Chamberlain to Hopkins, 26 December 1931.

4   T 175/56, pp. 229–30: memorandum, n.d., apparently January 1932; pp. 227–8: memorandum, n.d., apparently January 1932.

5   Ibid., pp. 238–41: memorandum, n.d., probably January 1932.
6   T 175/57, pp. 87–8: Treasury memorandum, Hopkins, spring 1932.
7   Cabinet Papers 58/169 EAC (H) 147, 9 March 1932 (hereafter cited as CAB); reprinted in Howson and Winch, *Economic Advisory Council*, pp. 254–63; see also pp. 100–5.
8   T 175/45, p. 194.
9   T 172/1738: Thomas to Chamberlain, 4 January 1932.
10 Ibid.: Thomas to Chamberlain and vice versa, 3 and 4 March 1932. Professor Howson's suggestions have improved the argument of this paragraph.
11 Sayers, *Bank of England*, pp. 448–50.
12 Neville Chamberlain Papers (hereafter cited as NC): Chamberlain to Amery, 10 March 1933.
13 Cf. Keynes in CAB 58/169, EAC [(SI) 31]2, 16 November 1931, and EAC (H)147, 9 March 1932, as reprinted in Howson and Winch, *Economic Advisory Council*, pp. 254–63.
14 Sayers, *Bank of England*, pp. 536–43.
15 FO 371/17318, pp. 116–24: memorandum, January 1933.
16 Ibid., p. 115: minute on January memorandum, A. W. A. Leeper.
17 Ibid., pp. 133–4.
18 Ibid., pp. 130–1: minute, 6 February 1933.
19 Ibid., pp. 131–2: minute, 11 February 1933.
20 CAB 58/169, EAC [(SI) 31]2, 16 November 1931.
21 Ibid.
22 Ibid., EAC(H)147, 9 March 1932, reprinted in Howson and Winch, *Economic Advisory Council*, pp. 254–63.

3. Empire money at the Ottawa Conference

1   R. B. Bennett Papers, Harriet Irving Library, University of New Brunswick, Fredericton, p. 115,190: Amery to Bennett, 23 January 1932.
2   Dominions Office Papers 114/42 (hereafter cited as DO): telegram Clark to Dominions Office, 12 March 1932.
3   T 172/1738: D. Ferguson (Treasury) to C. G. Syers (Dominions Office), 16 March 1932.
4   T 160/550/F. 7219/; DO 114/42: telegram, Thomas to Clark, 23 March 1932.
5   T 160/550/7219/1: Clark to Sir Ernest Harding, 13 April 1932.
6   T 160/550/F. 7219/1: telegram, Government of India to secretary of state for India, 16 April 1932. For a description of the Bank's nervousness about such ideas, see Sayers, *Bank of England*, pp. 449–52.
7   T 160/550/F. 7219/1: memorandum, unsigned, 29 April 1932.
8   Bennett Papers, p. 105,686.
9   DO 114/42: telegram, Canadian Government to Dominions Office, 24 May 1932.
10 Bennett Papers, p. 105,689: telegram, New Zealand Government to Canadian Government, n.d.
11 DO 114/42: telegram, Dominions Office to Canadian Government, 30 May 1932. See also Bennett Papers, pp. 105,897–900.
12 Bennett Papers, pp. 105,875–6.

13   T 172/1738: undated and unsigned Treasury memorandum, with penciled note thereon.

14   CAB 32/114, IEC(32)/84(CD). Chamberlain might have added that the Account was already supporting sterling. See Sayers, *Bank of England*, p. 452.

15   CAB 32/114, IEC(32)/136(CD)(4A). On the Bank's contribution to this careful phrasing, see Sayers, *Bank of England*, p. 451.

16   CAB 32/101, O(UK)(32), 40th meeting. Earlier Chamberlain had been less sanguine. For his earlier reservations, see ibid., O(UK)(932), 21st meeting. Before addressing the committee, Chamberlain discussed his text with the rest of the British delegation. See also Ian M. Drummond, *Imperial Economic Policy, 1917–1939* (London: Allan & Unwin, 1974), pp. 228–30.

17   Drummond, *Imperial Policy*, p. 228.

18   *Parliamentary Papers*, vol. 10 (1931–2), Cmd. 4175, p. 167.

19   Ibid., pp. 30–2.

Chapter 2. Sterling and the rupee

1   B. R. Tomlinson, "Britain and the Indian Currency Crisis, 1930–1932," *Economic History Review*, 2d ser. 32 (February 1979): 88–99.

1. The crisis of 1931

1   Oscar Wilde, *The Importance of Being Ernest.*

2   On the prewar arrangements, see J. M. Keynes, *Indian Currency and Finance* (London; P. S. King, 1912), Report of the Chamberlain Royal Commission, *Parliamentary Papers*, vol. 10 (1914), Cd. 7236.

3   These developments are traced by the official *History of the Reserve Bank of India (1935–1951)* (Bombay: Reserve Bank, 1970), pp. 47–53.

4   Ibid., pp. 28–35.

5   For the pre-1914 situation and its importance to Britain, see S. B. Saul, *Studies in British Overseas Trade, 1870–1914* (Liverpool: Liverpool University Press, 1960).

6   Tomlinson, "Britain," p. 90.

7   India Office Records L/F/7/474, file 22 (hereafter cited as IOR): telegrams, Government of India to Secretary of state for India, 24 April and 5 May 1931.

8   IOR L/F/6/1177/3693/31: Norman to Kisch, 5 May 1931; telegram, secretary of state to Government of India, 6 May 1931, reporting a conversation with Norman.

9   IOR L/F/6/474, file 22: telegram, controller of currency to secretary of state, 10 May 1931.

10   Ibid.: telegram, Finance Department to secretary of state, 9 May 1931.

11   IOR L/F/7/1177/3693/31: dispatch, Lord Willingdon, Sir George Schuster, and others to secretary of state, 8 June 1931 (airmail): and telegram, Schuster to secretary of state, 10 June 1931.

12   CAB 27/471, BDG(F)(31)5, 11 June 1931.

13   CAB 27/469, RTC(31)5, 18 September 1931.

14 IOR L/F/6/1177/3693/31: memorandum, R. Mant, H. Strakosch, L. Kershaw, C. Kisch, and C. Rhodes, 2 June 1931; circulated to the Cabinet subcommittee as BDG (F)(3)2.

15 CAB 27/470, BDG(31)6, 19 June 1931; CAB 27/471, BDG(F) 2d Councls., 3d Concls.

16 CAB 27/370, BDG(31) 6th Cons., 22 June 1931, 7th Cons., 25 June 1931.

17 IOR L/F/7/1177/3693/31: minute, Kisch, 15 June 1931, on dispatch from viceroy and others, 8 June 1931.

18 CAB 27/470, BDG(31)5, dispatch, Finance Department to secretary of state for India, 8 June 1931.

19 In January 1931 the government had proposed to say that there would have to be "such immediate provisions as may be necessary to guarantee, during a period of transition, the observance of certain obligations and to meet the special circumstances that may be agreed upon." When the Cabinet discussed this form of words, some members thought it might be an insufficient safeguard. The Cabinet resolved that the words be brought into accordance with the report of Lord Sankey's Federal Structure Subcommittee and that the chancellor of the exchequer should be consulted before the report was finally approved. CAB 23/66, 14 January 1931.

20 CAB 27/470, BDG(31) 7th Cons., 25 June 1931 (Snowden's additions italicized).

21 IOR L/F/6/1177/3693/31: Leith-Ross to Sir Findlater Steward, 26 June 1931; L/F/7/474, file 22: Hopkins to undersecretary of state, India Office, 4 July. The drafts are attached to the Leith-Ross letter.

22 IOR L/F/7/474, file 22: telegrams, secretary of state to Government of India, 9 July 1921, and Government of India Finance Department to secretary of state, 13 July 1931.

23 Ibid.: minutes by and to G. H. Baxter, 26 August 1931.

24 Ibid.; telegram, secretary of state to Government of India, 28 August 1931.

25 Ibid.: telegram, Government of India Finance Department to secretary of state, 31 August 1931.

26 Ibid.: minute, Baxter, 2 September 1931.

27 Ibid.: telegram, secretary of state to Government of India, 10 and 18 September 1931. On 23 September the secretary telegraphed, "most anxious not to add to your anxieties at the present moment and am accordingly postponing decision regarding gold shipments"; telegram, secretary of state to Government of India, 23 September 1931.

28 IOR L/F/6/1177/3693/31: telegram, Government of India Finance Department to Secretary of state, 1 August 1931.

29 Ibid.: minute, Kisch, on above telegram.

30 Ibid.: telegram, secretary of state to Government of India, 15 August 1931.

31 IOR L/F/7/474, file 22: telegram, Government of India Finance Department to Secretary of state, 9 May 1931.

32 CAB 23/68, 17 September 1931. This question came before the Cabinet because to balance the budget India would almost certainly have to raise the duties on cotton textiles.

33 CAB 27/469, RTC(31) 2d Cons., 21 September 1931.

34 T 160/434/F. 12471/06/1: telegram, secretary of state to Government of

India, 20 September 1931; IOR L/F/6/1181/6195/31: telegram, secretary of state to Government of India, 20 September 1931. The former telegram is also in CAB 23/68, 23 September 1931.

35 T 160/474/F. 12471/06/1: telegram, Government of India Finance Department to secretary of state, 21 September 1931.

36 CAB 23/68, 23 September 1931: telegram, Government of India Finance Department to secretary of state, 21 September 1931.

37 T 160/474/F. 12471/06/1: minute, Hopkins, on 21 September telegram, 22 September 1931.

38 CAB 27/469, RTC(31)5, 18 September 1931.

39 CAB 23/68, 22 September 1931.

40 T 160/474/F. 12471/06/1: memorandum, Waley, 23 September 1931; unsigned memorandum for Hopkins and Ferguson, probably also by Waley, 23 September 1931.

41 Ibid.: memorandum, Leith-Ross for chancellor of the exchequer, 28 September 1931.

42 CAB 23/68, 23 September 1931: telegram, Government of India to secretary of state, 23 September 1931.

43 Ibid.: telegram, secretary of state to Government of India, 23 September 1931.

44 Ibid.: telegrams, Government of India to secretary of state, 24 and 28 September 1931.

2. *Later developments*

1 T/175/84; memorandums, Phillips, 27 November 1933, and Hopkins, 22 December 1933.

2 IOR L/F/7/474, file 22: telegrams, Government of India to secretary of state, 24 April and 5 May 1931; minute, G. H. Baxter, 26 August 1931, on telegram, Government of India Finance Department to secretary of state, 13 July 1931.

3 T 175/57, pt. 2, p. 1: Phillips to H. Henderson, 26 February 1932.

4 On private account exports, see IOR L/F/7/474, file 22: minute, G. W. Martin, 8 March 1932, on telegram, secretary of state for India to Government of India, 2 December 1931; on the resumption of remittances, see ibid.: telegram, Government of India Finance Department to secretary of state for India, 19 November 1931.

5 T 188/18: memorandum, Phillips to Leith-Ross, 31 March 1932.

6 IOR L/F/6/1162, file 3427, F193 of 1934.

7 T 160/474/F. 12471/06/2: telegram, Government of India Finance Department to secretary of state for India, 18 January 1932.

8 T 160/474/F. 12471/06/1: telegram, Government of India Finance Department to secretary of state for India, 3 October 1931.

9 Ibid.: minute, Leith-Ross to Hopkins and Waley, 11 October 1931; telegram, secretary of state for India to Government of India, 14 October 1931.

10 T 160/474/F. 12471/06/2: telegram, Government of India to secretary of state for India, c. 5 January 1932.

11 Ibid.: minutes, Waley, 5 January 1932, Leith-Ross, 6 January 1932; minute from chancellor of exchequer, 11 January 1932, and Chamberlain's undated minute, "Agreed"; Hopkins to India Office, 13 January 1932.

12 T 160/474/F. 12471/06/2: telegrams, Government of India Finance Department to secretary of state for India, 9 March 1932, vice versa, 26 March 1932, with minutes thereon by Leith-Ross and others.

13 T 177/18: memorandum, "Sterling and the Gold Price Level," 7 January 1933.

14 T 177/39: memorandum, 11 March 1937.

15 Ibid.: minute, Chamberlain, on memorandum by Hopkins for Fisher and Chamberlain, 25 May 1937.

16 The interested reader may pursue the question in CAB 27/470, BDG(30)2, BDG(30)8, 19 November 1930, BDG(30)14, December 1930, BDG(30)17, 10 December 1930; CAB 23/68, 11 September 1931; CAB 27/469, RTC (31) 3, 18 September 1931, and addendum, 28 September 1931; CAB 27/521, CI(32)7 and CI(32)23: memorandums, Mant, Kershaw, Waley, and Kisch, on financial safeguards, 2 August 1932 and n.d., CI(25), CI(26), CI(27); CAB 27/520, CI(32) 9th meeting, 11 October 1932, 21st meeting, 12 October 1932.

17 CAB 23/73, 7 December 1932.

18 Government of India Act, 1935. For fiscal and exchange provisions, see section 12(1)(*b*), 12(2), 14, 15, 33, 34, 37, 44, 152, 153, 161, 183.

19 See R. S. Sayers, *The Bank of England, 1891–1944* (Cambridge: Cambridge University Press, 1976), pp. 318–19; and *History of Reserve Bank*, pp. 98 ff., 121.

20 P. J. Grigg, *Prejudice and Judgement*(London: Cape, 1948), pp. 258, 296.

21 *History of Reserve Bank*, pp. 162, 222–3.

22 Ibid., pp. 172–5.

23 Ibid., p. 60.

24 Ibid., pp. 58–9, 169.

25 Ibid., p. 59.

26 Balance of Payments, from *Bank of England Quarterly Bulletin*, March 1974, p. 49.

27 Tomlinson, "Britain," p. 97.

Chapter 3 The Canadian debate over money and exchanges, 1930–1934

1. The financial system

1 The following paragraphs are based on the information in R. Craig McIvor, *Canadian Monetary, Banking, and Fiscal Development* (Toronto: Macmillan, 1958), esp. chaps. 6, 7 (pp. 101–58), where other secondary works are fully cited.

2 Public Archives of Canada, Records Division, RG 19/825/725–5: memorandums, 9 January and 29 April 1925.

3 Ibid.: Robb to Sir Vincent Merideth, 13 February 1926, C. E. Neill to Robb, 25 March 1926.

4 Ibid.: Jackson to Robb, 16 April 1926, and attached memorandum.

5 Ibid.: memorandum "for Mr. Robb," 21 May 1926. The author was probably J. C. Saunders, the deputy minister of finance.

6 This paragraph draws on the as-yet-unpublished work of Dr. Derek Chisholm.

7 Public Archives of Canada, RG 19/594/155–32NY reports these negotiations.

8 As explained in ibid., RG 19/594/155–60NY.

9 One example among many may be found in ibid., RG 19/3380/03185a: Charles Batchelder to Sellars, 23 October 1931.

10 R. B. Bennett Papers, Harriet Irving Library, University of New Brunswick, Fredericton, vol. 301, file F102: letter and attached memorandum, Macaulay to Bennett, 14 August 1931.

11 Ibid.: Bennett to G. Digby, 26 September 1931.

2. *The departure from gold and a policy for the dollar*

1 Bennett Papers, vol. 301, file F102: letter and memorandum, Noble to Bennett, 26 September 1931.

2 Ibid.: undated and unsigned comment on Noble's memorandum of 26 September. The comment may be the work of Norman Robertson, who had recently joined the Department of External Affairs. It is hard to think of any other Canadian official who could have written such a comment in September or early October 1931. However, the comment might have come from an outside adviser, or perhaps from O. D. Skelton, the deputy minister for external affairs.

3 Ibid.: undated and unsigned memorandum.

4 Ibid., vol. 293: two memorandums. Noble, 4 October 1931 and February 1932.

5 Ibid., vol. 301, file F102: memorandum, Watson Sellars to Bennett, 9 October 1931, reporting a telephone call from White.

6 Ibid.: report from Currency Branch. Between 5 September and 5 October, free gold shrank from $2.4 million to $0.9 million, and $6.9 million in gold was paid out in redemption of notes, of which only $0.4 million was drawn by individuals and the rest by banks.

7 Ibid.: Gregory, "Memorandum on Canadian Currency Policy," London, 10 October 1931.

8 DO 35/253/9099/3: dispatch, U.K. high commissioner in Canada to Dominions Office, 8 October 1931.

9 Bennett Papers, vol. 293: Bennett to James Hunter, 30 December 1931; president of Canadian Bankers' Association to Bennett, 21 December 1931.

10 Ibid., p. 115,292: rejoinder by Canadian cotton manufacturers, June 1932.

11 Ibid., vol. 297 (pp. 199,783–92): letter and memorandum, Amery to Bennett, 13 August 1932.

12 Ibid., vol. 293 (pp. 197,035, 197,093): Bennett to Charles A. McRea, 27 February and 4 April 1932.

13 Ibid.: C. S. Tompkins (inspector general of banks) to Bennett, 15 April 1932, covering Towers's memorandum (pp. 197,121–25).

14 Ibid., p. 197,126: Bennett to Tompkins, 19 April 1932.

15 Public Archives of Canada, RG 25/D1/769/332: Clark to Bennett, 28 March 1932.
16 Bennett Papers, pp. 112,587–98.
17 Ibid., Clark later produced another and very similar memorandum on monetary reconstruction, which was also circulated to university economists. See ibid., pp. 111,100–288, 112,711.
18 Ibid., vol. 297 (pp. 199, 778–82): memorandum, Sellars to Bennett, 5 July 1932.
19 Norman Robertson Papers, Public Archives of Canada, vol. 10, file 103: "Imperial Economic Conference 1932: Matters of Government Policy." Much of this memorandum embodies Clark's earlier memorandum, which may be found inter alia in Public Archives of Canada, RG 25/D1/769/332, on "action possible in the monetary field during the conference."
20 Robertson Papers, vol. 2, file 119: memorandum, "The Gold Standard."
21 Bennett Papers, pp. 112, 714–5: Bennett to Dafoe, 18 July, 1932.
22 Public Archives of Canada, RG 25/D1/804/562: Skelton to Clark, 25 May 1932.
23 Bennett Papers, vol. 293 (pp. 197, 310–11): H. T. Ross to R. J. Manion, 23 July 1932.
24 Ibid., vol. 297, p. 199,863): Bennett to H. F. Skeg (Toronto manager of the Bank of Montreal), 27 January 1933.
25 Robertson Papers, vol. 10, file 86: memorandum, Robertson, "Some Phases of the Present Economic Depression in Canada," prepared late in 1930 for the League of Nations.
26 Bennett Papers, (pp. 115,575–604: undated memorandum. Though unsigned, the memorandum is almost certainly by Skelton. It is certainly not by Clark.
27 E. N. Rhodes Papers, Public Archives of Nova Scotia, MG 2, file folder 2B01: White to Bennett, 31 October 1933; file folder C07: White to Rhodes, 19 May and 29 December 1932; memorandum on artificial currency inflation and artificial depreciation, White, 30 December 1932. This reference, and the other references to the Rhodes Papers, I owe to Derek Chisholm of the University of Western Ontario.
28 Ibid., file folder C07: Clark, "Memorandum on Sir Thomas White's Discussion of Inflation," 5 January 1933.
29 Ibid.
30 Ibid.: Rhodes to W. M. Southam, 2 April 1932.
31 Ibid.: Rhodes to Robert Weir, 18 August 1932; Rhodes to A. N. McLean, 2 November 1932, Rhodes to F. W. Ransom, 24 January 1933.
32 Ibid.: Rhodes to White, 29 December 1932.
33 Ibid.: H. H. Stevens to Rhodes, 8 November 1932; Rhodes to Charles A. Huntley, 9 November 1932; Rhodes to Southam, 29 December 1932.

3. Later developments

1 Public Archives of Canada, RG /19/476/ "CMF documents": manuscript notes, apparently by W. C. Clark, on the proceedings of the First Subcommission of the Monetary and Financial Commission, World Monetary and Economic Conference. See also Bennett Papers, vol. 175, file C518, vol.

2: O. D. Skelton to Bennett, 29 June 1933. Skelton did not attend the London Conference, where Bennett's advisers were Clark, L. D. Wilgress, N. A. Robertson, and C. P. Vanier. Bennett Papers, vol. 179, file C518, vol. 3: Bennett to Sir George Perley, 22 and 29 June 1933.

2 In the Bennett Papers there are many letters in which outsiders criticize the proposal and Bennett defends it in just these terms.

3 McIvor, *Canadian Monetary Development*, p. 134.

4 Public Archives of Canada, RG 25/G1/1609/125: telegram, Canadian Government to chancellor of the exchequer, 10 January 1934. Neither the Finance Department records nor the Bennett Papers tell us anything about the Canadian background to this inquiry.

5 Ibid.: telegram, chancellor of the exchequer via Dominions Office to Canadian Government, 17 January 1934. The Dominions Office file has been destroyed, but a record remains as D03/60 entry for file 8399, and some comment survives in the Treasury papers.

6 The parliamentary discussion and the evidence before the Royal Commission are summarized and discussed in Linda Grayson, "The Founding of the Bank of Canada" (Ph.D. thesis, University of Toronto, 1975). On the Bank's later adventures, see E. P. Neufeld, *Bank of Canada Operations and Policy* (Toronto: University of Toronto Press, 1959).

7 McIvor, *Canadian Monetary Development*, 135.

8 Rhodes Papers, MG 2, file folder 4C07; Currency: memorandum, "Some Comments on an Article by E. S. Bates . . . ," undated and unsigned; probable date, autumn 1933; probable author, W. C. Clark or C. S. Tompkins.

Chapter 4. South Africa, sterling, and the gold standard, 1931 and thereafter

1. The confusions of 1931

1 Charles te Water Papers, Central Archives Depot, Pretoria, vol. 37, file IV(a): te Water diary, 13 October 1931.

2 For accounts of the South African financial system, and of the gold standard controversy, see E. H. Arndt, *Banking and Currency Developments in South Africa, 1652–1927* (Cape Town and Johannesburg: Juta 1928); G. H. Kock, *A History of the South African Reserve Bank* (Pretoria: J. L. van Schaik, 1954); J. A. Henry and H. A. Siepmann, *The First Hundred Years of the Standard Bank* (London: Oxford University Press, 1963); Sir Julian Crossley and John Blandford, *The DCO Story* (London: Barclay's Bank International, 1975); *A Banking Centenary* (London: for private circulation by Barclay's Bank (DCO), 1937); and R. S. Sayers, ed., *Banking in the British Commonwealth* (Oxford: Clarendon Press, 1952).

3 te Water Papers, vol. 13: te Water to J. B. M. Hertzog, 18 November and 29 October 1931.

4 Ibid.: te Water to Hertzog, 11 November 1931.

5 Ibid.: te Water to Hertzog, 18 November 1931.

6 Ibid.: vol. 14: Louw to te Water, 23 November 1931.

7 DO 35/251/9059/20: telegram, U.K. high commissioner to Dominions Office, 31 October 1931 (circulated to Treasury; see T 160/850/F. 12612/1).

For the pessimism of the South African financial press as to the reality of the gold standard, see T 160/F. 12612/1: telegram, U.K. high commissioner to Dominions Office, 11 November 1931.

8   T 160/850/F. 12612/1: telegram, U.K. high commissioner to Dominions Office, 6 November 1931.

9   Ibid.: memorandum, Leith-Ross, 30 September 1931.

10   Ibid.: memorandum, Leith-Ross, on copy of South African Government telegram, 29 September 1931.

11   Ibid.: memorandum of meeting, 30 September 1931. For te Water's report, see te Water Papers, vol. 13: te Water to Hertzog, 18 November 1931.

12   T 160/850/F. 12612/1: telegram, U.K. high commissioner to Dominions Office, 6 November 1931.

13   Ibid.: Leith-Ross to Sir Henry Batterbee, 9 November 1931.

14   Ibid.: Dominions Office to U.K. high commissioner, 16 November 1931.

15   te Water Papers, vol. 13: te Water to Hertzog, 18 November 1931.

16   South African House of Assembly, *Debates*, 20 November 1931, cols. 29–31, 24 November 1931, cols. 268–9.

17   Ibid., cols 36–38; Select Committee on the Gold Standard, *Report* (Cape Town: Cape Times, 1932), p. 7.

18   E. W. Kemmerer and G. Vissering, *Report on the Resumption of Gold Payments by the Union of South Africa*, UG no. 12, 1925 (Pretoria: Government Printing Office, 1925).

19   Ibid., p. xix.

20   Kemmerer-Vissering, *Report . . . with Minutes of Evidence, Appendices, and Index*, UG no. 13, 1925 (Pretoria: Government Printing Office, 1925), qns. 2997–9. Clegg's 1925 evidence is so sensible that one wonders why, in 1931, he supported the government's attachment to gold – or whether he really did so.

21   Apart from the evidence in the House of Assembly *Debates*, for proof of Smuts's sincerity, see Sir Patrick Duncan Papers, Jagger Library, University of Cape Town, BC 294, DI.35.28; Smuts to Duncan, 4 November 1931.

22   For the inquiry, and the way that Thomas handled it, see te Water Papers, vol. 13: te Water to Hertzog, 18 November 1931.

23   de Kock, *History*, pp. 214, 231–3.

24   Duncan Papers, BC 294, D5.23.2 and 5.23.3: Duncan to Lady Selborne, 14 and 21 October 1931.

25   Ibid., BC 294, D17.1.1: Duncan to C. J. Krige, 15 October 1931; see also BC 294, E10.15.32: Duncan to Lady Duncan, 10 October 1931.

26   House of Assembly, *Debates*, 20 November 1931, col. 31.

27   Ibid., 24 November 1931, cols. 268–9.

28   On the relations between Smuts and Strakosch, see Chapter 7.

29   Duncan Papers, BC 294, E10.15.32: Duncan to Lady Duncan, 1 November 1931 et seq. (*a diary letter*).

30   Ibid., BC 294, D1.35.28: Smuts to Duncan, 4 November 1931. For Smuts's earlier forebodings about sterling, see ibid., BC 294, DI.35.37: Smuts to Duncan, 17 September 1931.

31   For these arguments and their circulation, see DO 35/251/9059/20: telegram, U.K. high commissioner to Dominions Office, 31 October 1931.

32 J. H. Hofmeyr Papers, Cullen Library, University of the Witwatersrand, Box D1-Dj, file k: Hofmeyr to W. A. Martin, 11 January 1932.

33 House of Assembly, *Debates*, 20 November 1931, cols. 19–38, 54.

34 Ibid., 25 November 1931, cols. 276, 272–3.

35 Ibid., 24 November 1931, cols. 179–80.

36 The issues have been sketched, not very fully, in W. K. Hancock, *Smuts: The Fields of Force, 1919–1950* (Cambridge: Cambridge University Press, 1968), pp. 242–3.

2. *The Select Committee*

1 House of Assembly, *Debates*, vol. 18, 28 January 1932, cols. 423–4, 430: 1 February 1932, cols. 505–16.

2 Duncan Papers, BC 294, D5.24.7: Duncan to Lady Selborne, 18 February 1932.

3 House of Assembly, *Debates*, vol. 18, 28 January 1932, cols. 429–30.

4 Ibid., cols. 724–33.

5 DO 35/251/9059/20: Sir H. Stanley to Sir E. Harding, 8 December 1931. de Kock (*History*, p. 140) claims that Clegg was at one with the government; Stanley, however, bases his report on "really good authority."

6 Select Committee, *Report*, pp. 814 ff., esp. 828, 836–7.

7 Ibid., pp. 818, 821.

8 Robert Leslie and E. H. Arndt, professors of economics at Cape Town and Pretoria respectively.

9 Select Committee, *Report*, pp. 707–8.

10 Ibid., pp. 605, 607.

11 Ibid., p. 755.

12 Ibid., p. 617.

13 Ibid., p. 613.

14 Ibid., pp. 7–20, 904–18, esp. 14, 20, 913–14.

15 From South African Reserve Bank, *Reports and Annual Accounts*.

16 T 160/850/F. 12612/3: memorandum, Hopkins, 10 February 1932.

17 South African Reserve Bank, *Reports of the Ordinary General Meetings*, 6 July 1932 and 28 June 1933.

18 J. C. Smuts Papers, Central Archives Depot, Pretoria, vol. 49: Smuts to L. S. Amery, 3 February and 9 March 1932.

3. *A forced devaluation*

1 T 160/651/F. 12612/4: telegrams, U.K. high commissioner to Dominions Office, 22 and 24 December 1932.

2 de Kock, *History*, pp. 161–2; Crossley and Blandford, *DCO Story*, p. 61; House of Assembly, *Debates*, vol. 20, col. 579.

3 Duncan Papers, BC 294, D5.24.31 and D5.25.1: Duncan to Lady Selborne, 28 December 1932 and 4 January 1933.

4 DO 35/252/9059/174: telegram, U.K. high commissioner to Dominions Office, 28 December 1932; DO 35/252/9059/178: dispatch, U.K. high commissioner to Dominions Office, 30 December 1932.

5   T 160/651/F. 12612/4: telegram, U.K. high commissioner to Dominions Office, 29 December 1932.
6   Henry and Siepman, *First Hundred Years*, p. 248.
7   de Kock, *History*, p. 194.
8   T 160/651/F. 12612/4: telegram, U.K. high commissioner to Dominions Office, 24 January 1933.
9   de Kock, *History*, p. 192.
10 House of Assembly, *Debates*, vol. 20, cols. 578–83; T 160/651/F. 12612/4: telegram, U.K. high commissioner to Dominions Office, 8 February 1933, and dispatches, 10 and 17 February 1933.

4. Later developments, 1933–1939

1   From South African Reserve Bank, *Reports and Annual Accounts*.
2   South Africa, Bureau of Census and Statistics, *Union Statistics for 50 Years* (Pretoria, 1961): A. F. W. Plumptre, *Central Banking in the British Dominions* (Toronto: University of Toronto Press, 1940), Appendix.
3   de Kock, *History*, pp. 206–7.
4   South African Reserve Bank, *Reports and Annual Accounts*.
5   Kemmerer-Vissering, *Report*, UG no. 13, 1925, qns. 1367, 1375. Holloway was then professor of economics at the Transvaal University College.
6   T 160/651/F. 12612/5: telegram, U.K. high commissioner to Dominions Office, 2 March 1935.
7   Ibid.: Clark to Sir Eric Machtig, 27 January 1937.
8   Ibid.: Kershaw to S. D. Waley, 23 February 1937.
9   T 160/967/F. 15036/1, 2.
10 Total reserve assets: gold plus balance with Bank of England plus balance employed under Bank of England guarantee plus foreign bills.
11 Data from South African Reserve Bank, *Reports and Annual Accounts*, at 31 March.

Chapter 5. Australia and New Zealand, 1930–1939

1   L. F. Giblin, *The Growth of a Central Bank* (Melbourne: Melbourne University Press, 1951, pp. 46–7.
2   G. R. Hawke, *Between Governments and Banks: A History of the Reserve Bank of New Zealand* (Wellington: A. R. Shearer, Government Printer, 1974), pp. 20–1.
3   Giblin, *Growth of Central Bank*, p. 63.
4   Ibid., pp. 73–77, 128. See also Reserve Bank of Australia Occasional Paper no. 4A, *Australasian Banking and Monetary Statistics, 1817–1945* (Sydney, 1971), Table 52, which omits some of the steps that Professor Giblin details and which does not always agree as to dates.
5   See Chapter 1.
6   Hawke, *Governments and Banks*, p. 19; see also S. B. Sutch, *The Quest for Security in New Zealand* (Wellington: Oxford University Press, 1966), p. 167.

1. New Zealand's Troubles

1 R. B. Bennett Papers, Harriet Irving Library, University of New Brunswick, pp. 112, 731–3.

2 As New Zealand had refused to receive a high commissioner from the United Kingdom, the governor-general still served as the channel of intergovernmental communication.

3 T 175/70: telegram, governor-general of New Zealand to Dominions Office, 21 November 1932.

4 Stanley Baldwin Papers, University of Cambridge Library, vol. 97 (p. 143–4): Stewart to Baldwin, 27 December 1935.

5 T 175/84, pt. 1: Phillips to Sir Geoffrey Whiskard, 28 December 1933.

6 Hawke, *Governments and Banks*, pp. 202–4.

7 Ibid., pp. 41–44, 52–54.

8 Keith Sinclair, *Walter Nash* (Auckland: Auckland and Oxford University Presses, 1976), p. 112.

9 Baldwin Papers, vol. 97 (p. 160): Lord Galway to Baldwin, 27 December 1935.

10 Hawke, *Governments and Banks*, p. 110.

11 Reserve Bank Amendment Act. 1936, no. 1, cited in ibid., pp. 61–62.

12 For an account from the viewpoint of Nash's principal adviser, see Sutch, *Quest*, pp. 206–12. See also Hawke, *Governments and Banks*. The discussions are examined in the context of United Kingdom meat policy by Ian M. Drummond, *Imperial Economic Policy, 1917–1939* (London: Allan & Unwin, 1974), and by Sinclair, *Nash*, pp. 132–51.

13 T 160/965/F. 14687/1: Bennett to Chamberlain, 17 October 1936.

14 Ibid.: Lord Hartlington to MacDonald, 6 November 1936.

15 Ibid.: memorandum, S. D. Waley for Sir Frederick Phillips, 12 November 1936.

16 T 160/965/F. 14687/2: memorandum, Hopkins, 3 December 1936.

17 Ibid.: memorandum, Phillips, 14 December 1936.

18 Ibid.: memorandum, Waley, 13 January 1937.

19 T 160/965/F. 14687/5: telegram, governor-general of New Zealand to Dominions Office, 16 October 1937; Sinclair, *Nash*, p. 154.

20 T 160/965/F. 14687/5: minute, Waley, 19 October 1937.

21 Sinclair, *Nash*, pp. 171–5; Hawke, *Governments and Banks*, pp. 102–11.

22 Hawke, *Governments and Banks*, p. 103.

23 Sinclair, *Nash*, pp. 171–2.

24 T 160/965/F. 14687/5: R. Kershaw (Bank of England) to Waley, 16 November 1938. Hawke, *Governments and Banks*, p. 110, reports contemporary controversy as to the size and significance of capital flight. He concludes that though we cannot be sure about the magnitudes, private capital movements were probably greater in 1936–7 than in 1937–8.

25 T 160/965/F. 14687/5: telegram, United Kingdom trade commissioner in New Zealand to Board of Trade, 9 November 1938.

26 Ibid.: minute, Phillips, 16 November 1938.

27 Ibid.: memorandums, Hopkins to Waley, 18 November 1938, and Waley to Phillips, 22 November 1938.

28 Ibid.: minute, Waley, 16 November 1938.
29 Ibid.: "Note of Interdepartmental Meeting," 25 November 1938; T 160/965/F. 14687/6: telegram, Dominions Office to governor-general of New Zealand for Government of New Zealand, 2 December 1938.
30 T 160/965/F. 14687/6: telegram, Department of Overseas Trade to United Kingdom senior trade commissioner in New Zealand, 2 December 1938.
31 Ibid.: telegram, Government of New Zealand to Dominions Office, 6 December 1938, with minute by Hopkins: dispatch, United Kingdom senior trade commissioner in New Zealand to Department of Overseas Trade, 8 December 1938.
32 Baldwin Papers, vol. 97 (p. 60): Lord Galway (governor-general of New Zealand) to Baldwin, 27 December 1935.
33 T 160/965/F. 14687/6: telegram, governor-general of New Zealand to Dominions Office, 7 December 1938.
34 Ibid.: telegram, United Kingdom high commissioner in New Zealand to Dominions Office, 30 April 1939. The high commissioner, Sir Henry Fagg Batterbee, was the first that New Zealand had agreed to receive.
35 Sutch, *Quest*, pp. 234–8; Sinclair, *Nash*, pp. 177–8.
36 Sutch, *Quest*, pp. 228–30; CAB 21/504: telegram, Batterbee to Dominions Office, 30 May 1939.
37 For France, Ian M. Drummond, *London, Washington, and the Management of the Franc 1936–1939* (Princeton University, International Finance Section, 1979), pp. 39–42.
38 CAB 21/504: Treasury memorandum on New Zealand, 24 May 1939; meeting of officials, 15 May 1939.
39 Ibid.: NZ Minutes 1/39, 5 June 1939.
40 CAB 21/506: NZ 7/39, 8 June 1939, pp. 207–9; NZ Minutes 2/39, 7 June 1939.
41 CAB 21/504: note of meeting between Nash and Sir Thomas Inskip, 15 June 1939.
42 Ibid.: note of meeting between Inskip and Norman, 14 June 1939.
43 CAB 21/505: note of meeting between Nash and Inskip, 23 June 1939; CAB 21/506: p. 85, "Presentation of the Plan," 29 June 1939; CAB 23/100: 21 June 1939.
44 CAB 21/506: NZ Minutes 5/39, 26 June 1939.
45 CAB 21/505: note on meeting of ministers, 27 June 1939.
46 CAB 21/506: pp. 91–2, and NZ Minutes 8/39, 5 July 1939. See also Sinclair, *Nash*, pp. 181–3.
47 *Parliamentary Papers*, vol. 20 (1938–9), Cmd. 6059, 12 July 1939, pp. 1077–80.
48 Sinclair, *Nash*, p. 186, citing Sir Henry Clay, *Lord Norman* (London: Macmillan, 1957), pp. 413–14.
49 See Sutch, *Quest*, pp. 229–35.

2. Australia's adventures with the London capital market

1 T 160/516/F. 11935/05: Hopkins to Sir Maurice Gwyer, 3 March 1933.
2 Ibid.: Hopkins's memorandum of a conversation, 24 March 1933.

3 Ibid.

4 Ibid.: memorandum, Hopkins, 14 April 1933.

5 Ibid.: memorandum, Hopkins, 4 July 1933.

6 R. S. Gilbert, *The Australian Loan Council in Federal Fiscal Adjustments, 1890–1965* (Canberra: Australian National University Press, 1975), pp. 188–90.

Chapter 6. Monetary preparations for the World Economic Conference

1. Why a world conference?

1 FO 371/15641, p. 197: Leith-Ross to C. Howard Smith, 16 January 1931. See also Sir Henry Clay, *Lord Norman* (London: Macmillan, 1957), pp. 370–1, and D. E. Moggridge, *British Monetary Policy, 1924–1931* (Cambridge: Cambridge University Press, 1972), pp. 240–1.

2 FO 371/15641, p. 192: Leith-Ross to Smith, 14 January 1931.

3 FO 371/15640, pp. 135–6: memorandum, Leith-Ross, December 1930; pp. 169–73.

4 Ibid., pp. 156–66: memorandum, Leith-Ross, on officials' conversations, 2–3 January 1931.

5 Ibid., pp. 192–4: Leith-Ross to Smith, 14 January 1931; p. 220 ff.: notes on officials' conversations, 14–15 January 1931; pp. 302–12: memorandum on officials' conversations, 20–21 February 1931.

6 FO 371/15080, p. 351: Foreign Office to U.K. embassy in Paris, 24 September 1931.

7 Ibid., p. 356: telegram, Lord Reading to Foreign Office, 24 September 1931; FO 371/15682, pp. 233–4: Lindsay to Smith, 28 October 1931.

8 FO 371/15682, pp. 218–19: memorandum, Leith-Ross, on conversations with French officials, 8 October 1931; FO 371/15681, pp. 121–4: memorandum, Leith-Ross, 20 October 1931.

9 FO 371/15862, pp. 310–12: memorandum, Leith-Ross, on conversation with Jacques Rueff, 1 December 1931.

10 FO 371/15680, pp. 342–3: telegram, Lord Tyrrell to Foreign Office, 24 September 1931.

11 FO 371/16382, pp. 311–14: telegram, Foreign Office to Lindsay, 11 May 1932.

12 Ibid., pp. 319, 322: telegrams, Lindsay to Foreign Office, 11 and 14 May 1932.

13 Ibid., p. 342: minute, Sir John Simon, 24 May 1932.

14 Ibid., pp. 340–2: minutes, including Vansittart, 20–34 May 1932; see also FO 371/16383: Vansittart to Tyrrell, 2 June 1932.

15 The investigation began in 1930. The report appeared in *Parliamentary Papers*, vol. 10 (1930–1), Cmd. 3932, p. 981 ff.

16 For Indian silver policy, see *Parliamentary Papers*, vol. 12 (1926), Cmd. 2687, p. 501 ff.

17 Herbert Feis, *1933: Characters in Crisis* (Boston: Little, Brown, 1966), esp. pp. 21–6. Herbert Hoover, *The Memoirs of Herbert Hoover, 1929–1941* (New York: Macmillan, 1952), corroborates other accounts and docu-

ments to some extent but is neither complete nor altogether accurate. See also FO 433/1: Simon to Lindsay, 30 May 1932; and R. B. Bennett Papers, Harriet Irving Library, University of New Brunswick, vol. 175, file C-518: H. H. Wrong of the Canadian legation to Bennett, 15 June 1932.

18   See inter alia Hoover, *Memoirs*, p. 99, and M. Friedman and Anna Schwartz, *The Great Contraction* (Princeton, N.J.: Princeton University Press, 1965), pp. 51–3, 88–93.

19   An account from the American side appears in *Foreign Relations of the United States (FRUS)*, 1932, 1: 808–16, esp. telegram, Stimson to Ambassador in United Kingdom, 26 May 1932.

20   Ibid., p. 809.

21   Susan Howson, *Domestic Monetary Management in Britain, 1919–1938* (Cambridge: Cambridge University Press, 1975), pp. 90–9; R. S. Sayers, *The Bank of England, 1891–1944* (Cambridge: Cambridge University Press, 1976), pp. 436–9.

22   FO 371/16383, pp. 15–16: Vansittart to Tyrrell, 2 June 1933.

23   DO 114/39: circular telegram, J. H. Thomas to the several Dominions, 3 June 1932. See also T 160/486/F. 13017/1, and *FRUS*, 1932, 1: 811: telegram, Mellon to Stimson, 31 May 1932.

24   FO 433/1: Simon to Tyrrell (in Paris), 2 June 1932.

25   *Parliamentary Papers*, vol. 27, Cmd. 4126, Cmd. 4129, 1931–2, pp. 931 ff., 947 ff.

26   CAB 23/72, 45 (32), 4 August 1932.

27   FO 433/1: Simon to R. H. Campbell, 13 September 1932.

28   Bennett Papers, vol. 175, file C-518: W. Riddell to Bennett, 8 November 1932; dispatch, Riddell to Bennett, 20 January 1933.

2. Some of the background

1   Charles P. Kindleberger, *The World in Depression, 1929–1939* (London: Allan Lane, Penguin Press, 1973), p. 145; W. Arthur Lewis, *Economic Survey, 1919–1939* (London: Allen & Unwin, 1949), pp. 138–201.

2   See the *Economist* throughout 1931–3 for examples.

3   Lewis, *Economic Survey*, is a classical citation for this attitude, though Lewis's position is more complex than this. See Don Patinkin, *Money, Interest, and Prices*, 2d ed. (Evanston, Ill.: Row Peterson, 1956), for the classic formulation of the real balance effect, which suggests the reverse.

4   See "The World's Gold Reserves and Commodity Prices," supplement to the *Economist*, 21 January 1933.

5   See Macmillan Committee, *Evidence*, qq 3722, 3728, 3795–801.

6   See *Nation and Athenaeum* 48 (27 December 1930): 427–8; J. M. Keynes, *A Treatise on Money* (London: Macmillan, 1930).

7   See Susan Howson and Donald Winch, *The Economic Advisory Council, 1930–1939* (Cambridge: Cambridge University Press, 1977).

8   Gustav Cassel, *The Downfall of the Gold Standard* (Oxford: Clarendon Press, 1936), pp. 60, 67–8.

9   Macmillan Committee, *Evidence*, qq 3906, 3909.

10   Howson and Winch, *Economic Advisory Council*, pp. 107–8, 117.

11 Ibid., pp. 114–15.
12 Ibid., pp. 116–21.
13 Cassel, *Downfall*, p. 56. See Sayers, *Bank of England*, 1: 346–51.
14 The members were Professor M. J. Bonn of Berlin; comte de Chandar of Compagnie d'assurances générales sur la vie; G. Juna of the Instituto nationale per l'esportazione; Professor Feliks Mlynarski, formerly vice-governor of the Bank of Poland but now a professor of commerce; Dr. Vilim Pospisil, governor of the National Bank of Czechoslovakia; G. E. Roberts of the National City Bank of New York; L. J. A. Trip, governor of the Nederlandsche Bank; Professor Albert Janssen of the University of Louvain; Sir Reginald Mant and Sir Henry Strakosch of the Council of India; and Professor Gustav Cassel of Sweden.
15 Report of the Gold Delegation of the Financial Committee of the League of Nations, no. C.502.M243.1932.II.a, Geneva, June 1932.
16 T 175/70, n.d.
17 Ibid., pp. 64–6, 67.
18 Ibid., pp. 71–5.
19 J. C. Smuts Papers, Central Archives Depot, Pretoria, vol. 48: Strakosch to Smuts, 29 January 1931.
20 Howson and Winch, *Economic Advisory Council*, pp. 116–21.

3. Treasury policy and the Preparatory Commission

1 T 160/488/F. 13017/01: unsigned memorandum, 7 June 1932. I must thank Professor Howson for the attributions.
2 T 160/488/F. 13017/01/1.
3 T 160/447/F. 13017/06: "Monetary Policy and the Level of Prices" (Hopkins's revise), 18 August 1932, and "The Level of Prices as Affected by Monetary Policy" (Phillips's preface to Hopkins's memorandum), 1 September 1932.
4 Feis, *1933*, p. 113.
5 T 177/12, pt. 3: unofficial minute of meetings, Preparatory Commission.
6 CAB 58/183, EAC(S2)(32), Annex 11: report, Leith-Ross and Phillips, 10 November 1932.
7 T 177/12, pt. 3: Phillips to Hopkins, 4 November 1932; see also Phillips to Hopkins, 2 November 1932; T 160/489/F. 13017/013: telegram, Leith-Ross and Phillips to Hopkins, 6 November 1932 – "It is very difficult to get progress on the side of prices, but we have explained our position thoroughly."
8 T 177/12, pt. 2: memorandum, Henry Clay, 14 December 1932.
9 Ibid., pt. 2: memorandum, Bank of England, 15 November 1932.
10 T 188/56: memorandum, Phillips to Leith-Ross, 17 November 1932.
11 T 177/12, pt. 1: Phillips's comments on the Bank memorandum of 15 November 1932.
12 T 188/56: memorandum, Bank of England, 25 November 1932.
13 Ibid.: minute, Phillips, on Bank memorandum of 25 November 1932.
14 Ibid.: memorandum, Phillips and Leith-Ross, n.d.
15 T 177/12, pt. 2: memorandum, Leith-Ross, 20 December 1932.

16 Draft Annotated Agenda, pt. II, sec. II.3 (League of Nations official no. C.48.H.18.1933.II [Conf. H.E. I]; also in *Economist*, 28 January 1933).
17 On this point Howson and Winch, *Economic Advisory Council*, may mislead the unwary, though their account is wholly accurate.
18 CAB 58/183, EAC(S2) (32)15: report, Leith-Ross, on the second experts' meeting.
19 Agenda, pt. II, sec. I.1.
20 As explained in many places, among them T 160/488/F. 13017/13: U.K. minister in Washington to Henry L. Stimson, 28 July 1932.
21 J. H. Williams, *Argentine International Trade under Inconvertible Paper* (Cambridge: Harvard University Press, 1920).
22 *FRUS*, 1932, 1:839–40: report, Day and Williams, 1 December 1932.
23 *FRUS*, 1933, 1: 453: telegram, Day and Williams, 19 January 1933.
24 Ibid., pp. 456–7: telegram, Day and Williams to secretary of state, 20 January 1933.
25 Ibid., pp. 463–4: Day and Williams to Hull, 24 February 1933.
26 A striking example is ibid.: telegram, Ray Atherton (in London) to Hull, 9 May 1933.
27 Howson and Winch, *Economic Advisory Council*, pp. 116–21.

4. Discussions with France and the United States, spring 1933

1 *FRUS*, 1933, 1: 465–71: memorandum, British embassy, apparently delivered just before 4 March 1933.
2 Ibid., pp. 472–3, 24 March 1933.
3 NC 18/1/815: Chamberlain to Hilda Chamberlain, 4 February 1933.
4 NC 18/1/819: Chamberlain to Hilda Chamberlain, 4 March 1933.
5 FO 433/1: dispatch. Lindsay to Sir John Simon, 30 March 1933.
6 Feis, *1933*, pp. 121–2: Frank Freidel, *Franklin D. Roosevelt: Launching the New Deal* (Boston: Little, Brown, 1973), pp. 326–31.
7 I have been unable to locate this memorandum in the voluminous Roosevelt papers.
8 NC 18/1/820: Chamberlain to Hilda Chamberlain, 18 March 1933.
9 FO 371/17304, pp. 137–8: Foreign Office minutes.
10 T 160/487/F. 13017/3: Treasury memorandum for Lindsay, 4 April 1933. See also FO 371/17304, p. 230.
11 T 188/64: Treasury brief for chancellor of exchequer, March 1933. See also FO 371/17304, pp. 189–206.
12 Georges Bonnet, *Vingt ans de la vie politique*, 1918–1938 (Paris: Fayard, 1969), p. 162.
13 FO 371/17304, pp. 180–4: "Notes of Meetings . . . March 17, 1933."
14 T 188/63: minute, Leith-Ross to Chamberlain, 7 July 1933.
15 T 160/487/F. 13017/3: memorandum of conversations; telegram, Treasury to Lindsay, 5 April 1933; CAB 29/140, MEC(33)4; T 175/59: Hopkins to Norman, 28 March 1933, asking Norman to begin interbank discussion.
16 T 188/64: Leith-Ross to Tyrrell, 20 March 1933.
17 *FRUS*, 1933, 1: 471–2: telegrams, Hull to Atherton and Atherton to Hull, 17 March 1933.

18 Feis, *1933*, pp. 124–6; Freidel, *Roosevelt*, pp. 328–33.
19 Sir Frederick Leith-Ross, *Money Talks* (London: Hutchinson, 1968), p. 160.
20 FO 371/16604, pp. 269–70: radiograms, Vansittart to Treasury and vice versa, 19 and 19/20 April 1933.
21 Ibid., pp. 287–9: telegram, Hopkins to Vansittart, 21 April 1933.
22 Ibid., pp. 301–2: telegram, Chamberlain to MacDonald, 22 April 1933.
23 Ibid., pp. 304–5: telegram, Lindsay to Foreign Office, 23 April 1933.
24 For the published communiqués, see *FRUS*, 1933, 1: 491–3, 26 and 29 April 1933. For details on the conversations, see Freidel, *Roosevelt*, pp. 380–9.
25 Arthur M. Schlesinger, Jr., *The Age of Roosevelt: The Coming of the New Deal* (Boston: Houghton Mifflin, 1959), p. 206. Freidel, *Roosevelt*, p. 386, explains that though on 24 April Warburg thought the president wanted stable exchange rates Roosevelt later believed that even then he had not committed himself.
26 Cordell Hull, *Memoirs* (London: Hodder & Stoughton, 1948), 1: 246.
27 Feis, *1933*, p. 131.
28 Treasury Files, vol. 7476, file 95/36, Annex II, Central Archives Depot, Pretoria: memorandum of conversations in Washington, 23 May 1933.
29 Raymond Moley, *After Seven Years* (New York: Harper, 1940), pp. 203–4. Schlesinger appears to have read Moley carelessly or not at all.
30 Schlesinger, *Age of Roosevelt*, p. 206.
31 Feis, *1933*, pp. 144–6.
32 Moley, *After Seven Years*, p. 216.
33 Ibid., p. 228. It is far from clear why Schlesinger ignores this line of thought.
34 Feis, *1933*, pp. 144–6. Freidel, *Roosevelt*, p. 387, suggests, instead, that Roosevelt was simply unable to make up his mind about exchange stabilization.
35 Leith-Ross, *Money Talks*, pp. 164–5.
36 FO 371/16604, pp. 309–11: telegram, Leith-Ross to Hopkins, 24 April 1933. Warburg's April plan is also discussed in Sayers, *Bank of England*, 3: 276–7, and by Feis, *1933*, p. 102, whose account is too brief to be altogether clear. See also Freidel, *Roosevelt*, pp. 386–7.
37 FO 371/16604, pp. 312–18: telegram, Treasury to Leith-Ross, 26 April 1933.
38 Ibid., pp. 343–4: telegram, Leith-Ross to Treasury, 26 April 1933.
39 Ibid., pp. 346–7.
40 Ibid., pp. 364–6: telegram, Leith-Ross to Treasury, 27 April 1933.
41 Ibid., pp. 364–6: telegram, Leith-Ross to Treasury, 27 April 1933; pp. 369–70: telegram, Leith-Ross to Treasury, 28 April 1933; pp. 371–5: telegram, Treasury to Leith-Ross, 28 April 1933.
42 Ibid., p. 383: telegram, Treasury to Leith-Ross, 29 April 1933.
43 FO 371/16605, pp. 401–2: telegram, Leith-Ross to Treasury, 2 May 1933.
44 Ibid., pp. 306–7: Foreign Office minutes, 2 May 1933.
45 *FRUS*, 1933, 1: 597–600: telegram, Norman Davis to Cordell Hull, 9 May 1933.
46 Ibid., pp. 601–7: telegram, chargé in France to Hull, 15 May 1933.

47 Ibid., pp. 608–9: memorandum, French embassy to secretary of state, 16 May 1933. See also Sayers, *Bank of England*, 3: 277, and Bonnet, *Vingt ans*, p. 162.
48 FO 371/16605, p. 403: telegram, Treasury to Leith-Ross, 3 May 1933.
49 Bonnet, *Vingt ans*, p. 163; Feis, *1933*, pp. 148–9
50 FO 371/16606, pp. 36A–38: telegram, Bewley to Treasury, 16 May 1933; see also Sayers, *Bank of England*, 3: 277–9.
51 FO 371/17316, p. 346: French ambassador to Simon, 15 May 1933.
52 FO 371/16605, pp. 45–8: telegram, Treasury to Bewley, 25 May 1933.
53 Ibid., pp. 43–4: telegram, Bewley to Treasury, 16 May 1933.
54 FO 371/17316, pp. 348–9: Treasury response, 18 May 1933; p. 353: Foreign Office minute, n.d.; see also FO 371/17305, p. 118: Foreign Office minute.
55 FO 371/16606, p. 200: Leith-Ross to F. A. Gwatkin, 13 June 1933.
56 CAB 23/76, 5 May 1933.
57 CAB 29/142, ME(B)1: memorandum, Leith-Ross, drafted 1 May 1933.
58 T 160/487/F. 13017/3: telegram, Treasury to Lindsay, 4 April 1933.
59 See Schlesinger, *Age of Roosevelt*, p. 210, for the French approach to the United States.
60 CAB 29/140, MEC(33)4: memorandum on money and prices, Leith-Ross and Phillips, 15 May 1933.
61 For the proceedings, see CAB 29/140. The members were MacDonald, Baldwin, Hailsham, Hoare, Cunliffe-Lister, Elliot, Chamberlain, Simon, Thomas, and Runciman. Hankey, Phillips, Leith-Ross, and Henderson were regularly in attendance.
62 For the background, see David Marquand, *Ramsay MacDonald* (London: Cape, 1977). Marquand does not treat the Economic Conference as such.
63 CAB 29/140, MEC(33) 6th Cons., 23 May 1933.
64 Moley, *After Seven Years*, p. 216.
65 FO 371/16605, p. 115: telegram, Lindsay to Foreign Office, 27 May 1933.
66 Ibid., p. 108: telegram, Lindsay to Foreign Office, 25 May 1933; pp. 138–9, Bewley to Treasury, 30 May 1933; p. 184: telegram, Foreign Office to Lindsay, 26 May 1933; see also Sayers, *Bank of England*, 3: 279.
67 Moley, *After Seven Years*, p. 216; Feis, *1933*, p. 151; Freidel, *Roosevelt*, pp. 462–5.
68 Feis, *1933*, p. 179.
69 Moley, *After Seven Years*, p. 228.
70 Sayers, *Bank of England*, pp. 455–7.
71 CAB 29/140, MEC(33) 7th Cons., 26 May 1933; CAB 23/176, 31 May 1933; CAB 29/140, MEC (33) 7: Report of the Committee on Economic Information EAC (50)7; see also Howson and Winch, *Economic Advisory Council*, p. 120.
72 Susan Howson, "The Managed Floating Pound, 1932–39," *Banker*, March 1976, p. 251.
73 Schlesinger, *Age of Roosevelt*, pp. 209–10.
74 NC 1/18/827: Chamberlain to Hilda Chamberlain, 14 May 1933.
75 Schlesinger, *Age of Roosevelt*, pp. 209–10.
76 Freidel, *Roosevelt*, p. 490.

5. *The Empire, the sterling area, and the conference preparations*

1 FO 371/17305: letter, Sir Ernest Harding to Sir V. Wellesley, 20 April 1933.

2 See section 2 to this chapter, and Howson and Winch, *Economic Advisory Council*, pp. 117, 120, for the "Kisch plan."

3 FO 371/15682, pp. 344–5: Foreign Office minutes, December 1932; FO 371/15683, p. 373; Foreign Office minutes, December 1932.

4 FO 371/17304, pp. 5, 9–10, 135.

5 FO 371/17305, p. 253: telegram, Foreign Office to U.K. embassy, Stockholm, 27 May 1933.

6 FO 371/17306, p. 173.

7 DO 114/40: telegram, Dominions Office to the several Dominions, 9 August 1932.

8 Ian M. Drummond, *Imperial Economic Policy, 1917–1939* (London: Allan & Unwin, 1974) pp. 208–16.

9 DO 114/40: dispatch, Dominions Office to four Dominions, 15 December 1932; and DO 114/47: telegram, J. H. Thomas to Dominions, 9 February 1933.

10 DO 114/47, pp. 151–2: telegram, Thomas to Dominions, 25 March 1933; DO 35/265/9223/100: minute, S. L. Holmes, 10 May 1933, and memorandum, 18 May 1933.

11 DO 35/266/9223/78: telegram, Dominions Office to Dominions, 25 March 1933, drawing on materials the Treasury had supplied.

12 DO 114/47, p. 153: telegram, Dominions Office to Dominions, 4 May 1933.

13 DO 35/266/9223F/1: Leith-Ross to E. H. Marsh (Dominions Office), 28 February 1933.

14 DO 35/266/9223F/3: note of a meeting, 1 May 1933.

15 DO 35/266/9223F/2: minute, Harding, 1 May 1933.

16 DO 35/266/9223/82: minute, Whiskard, 19 April 1933.

17 For the American messages to and from the Antipodes, see DO 114/47.

Chapter 7. *United Kingdom policy at the World Monetary and Economic Conference*

1. *Problems with the French and the Americans*

1 CAB 29/141, pp. 46, 51, 70. See also *Parliamentary Papers*, vol. 21 (1932–3), Cmd. 4357, p. 487.

2 CAB 29/143, MEC (BC) (33), 2d meeting, 16 June 1933.

3 CAB 29/142, ME (UK), 4th meeting, 20 June 1933.

4 *FRUS*, 1933, 1: 641: telegram, Roosevelt through State to Hull, 15 June 1933. See also Frank Freidel, *Franklin D. Roosevelt: Launching the New Deal* (Boston: Little, Brown, 1973), pp. 467–9.

5 *FRUS*, 1933, 1: 642–4: telegram, O. M. W. Sprague to W. H. Woodin, 16 June 1933.

6 Ibid., pp. 646–7: telegram, Warburg to Roosevelt, 18 June 1933.

7   Ibid., pp. 647–8: telegram, Warburg, Cox, and Sprague to Roosevelt, 18 June 1933.

8   Ibid., pp. 649, 650: telegram, Roosevelt to Phillips, 19 June 1933; telegram, Roosevelt through State to Hull, 20 June 1933. These developments are reported in Raymond Moley, *After Seven Years* (New York: Harper, 1940), 229, and Herbert Feis, *1933: Characters in Crisis* (Boston: Little, Brown, 1966), p. 182.

9   Feis, *1933*, p. 182.

10 Moley, *After Seven Years*, pp. 230–2.

11 *FRUS*, 1933, 1:650: telegram, Roosevelt through State to Hull, 20 June 1933.

12 Ibid., p. 651: telegram, Hull to Roosevelt, 21 June 1933.

13 Ibid., p. 646: telegram, Roosevelt through State to Hull, 17 June 1933.

14 Ibid., pp. 626–7: memorandum on policy for American delegation, transmitted to Hull by Roosevelt 30 May 1933. A copy of the memorandum is in the Roosevelt Papers in Hyde Park (PSF file on London Economic Conference), but there is no information by which we can discover anything about the background to it.

15 Ibid., p. 653: telegram, Warburg to Roosevelt, 22 June 1933.

16 When the pound reached $4.42, Sprague urged that the Federal Reserve should at once start selling gold, until the dollar had fallen to $4.30. Ibid., p. 664: telegram, Sprague to Woodin and Baruch, 29 June 1933. Roosevelt's permission, when it came, was too late to save the conference.

17 Moley, *After Seven Years*, p. 232.

18 Ibid., p. 236.

19 Ibid., p. 235: "I also felt, with him, that the sort of agreement which Cox, Sprague, and Warburg wanted would cause a chaotic decline. If we were ingenious, there was scope for action that would permit our recovery to proceed but, at the same time check speculative excesses. Did that represent his beliefs? It did, he answered."

20 CAB 29/142, ME(Conv)3, 19 June 1933.

21 CAB 29/142, ME (Conv)7, 6.

22 CAB 29/145, entry for 21 June 1933; CAB 29/142, ME(Conv)7, 21 June 1933.

23 29/142, ME (UK), 12th meeting, 27 June 1933.

24 CAB 29/142, ME (Conv)14, 27 June 1933.

25 For Moley's activities, see Moley, *After Seven Years*, p. 245 ff.; Feis, *1933*, pp. 198–212; Sir Frederick Leith-Ross, *Money Talks* (London: Hutchison, 1968), p. 168 ff., Freidel, *Roosevelt*, pp. 472–89.

26 *FRUS*, 1933, 1: 658: telegram, Hull to Roosevelt, 27 June 1933.

27 Ibid., pp. 660–61: Roosevelt to the acting secretary of state in Washington, 28 June 1933. Note that the president was still on the seas.

28 NC 2/22: diary entry for 29 June 1933.

29 NC 7/11/26/5: Bonnet to Chamberlain, 28 June 1933.

30 CAB 29/142, ME(Conv)10, 22 June and 12, 23 June 1933.

31 CAB 29/142, ME (UK), 18th meeting, 2 July 1933, and ME (Conv)18, 28 June 1933, for conversations with the gold representatives.

32 *FRUS*, 1933, 1: 665–6: telegram, Moley to Woodin and Baruch, 30 June 1933. On Moley's opposition to the statements, see CAB 29/142, ME(Conv) 2A, 30 June 1933.

33 *FRUS*, 1933, 1: 665, 667: telegrams, Moley to Woodin and Baruch, 30 June 1933, and acting secretary of state to Roosevelt, 30 June 1933. On 1 July Moley transmitted an additional sentence for S.2: "They are convinced of the importance from the point of view of the restoration of world economy and finance of the maintenance by their respective countries of the gold standard on the basis of the present gold parities." Ibid., p. 670: telegram, Moley to Roosevelt, 1 July 1933. By then, however, the presidential decision had been taken.

34 For a detailed account of the comedy of errors that surrounded the receipt and transmission of Roosevelt's refusal, see CAB 29/142, ME(Conv)29A: "The Negotiations for Temporary Stabilization: events of Saturday and Sunday First and Second July 1933" (a "Most Secret" memorandum by Hankey). Moley records his surprise in *After Seven Years*, p. 250 ff., where he argues that Roosevelt had not understood the proposal. Moley claims that because Roosevelt argued against the scheme with passages from Swope's antistabilization memorandum, the president must have thought it involved exchange stabilization. See Freidel, *Roosevelt*, 35, pp. 477–80.

35 CAB 29/142 ME(Conv)27, 30, June 1933.

36 *FRUS*, 1: 669: telegram, Roosevelt to Hull, 1 July 1933.

37 Ibid., pp. 673–4: public statement by President Roosevelt, cabled to Hull 2 July 1933.

38 CAB 29/142, ME(UK), 18th meeting, 2 July 1933.

39 Ibid., 20th meeting, 4 July 1933.

40 Ibid., 19th meeting, 3 July 1933; T 177/18: Leith-Ross to Sir H. Hamilton, 2 July 1933.

41 CAB 29/142, ME(Conv)27, 2 July 1933.

42 Georges Bonnet, *Quai d'Orsay*, trans. (Douglas, Isle of Man: Times Press and Anthony Gibbs & Phipps, 1965), pp. 110–1.

43 Georges Bonnet, *Vingt ans de la vie politique, 1918–1938* (Paris: Fayard, 1969), p. 176.

44 Treasury Files, vol. 7575, file 95/36: Annex II, Central Archives Depot, Pretoria, contains the relevant advice from Professors R. Leslie and E. Arndt and Dr. J. W. Holloway, N. C. Havenga's advisers.

45 The text appeared in the annual report of the Bank for International Settlements.

46 CAB 29/142, ME(UK), 21st meeting, 5 July 1933.

47 Roosevelt Papers, PSF London Economic Conference: "Memorandum on the work of the First Subcommittee of the Monetary and Financial Commission" by H. Merle Cochran, 20 July 1933.

48 As reported in Bank for International Settlements, *Fourth Annual Report*, 1933–4, p. 13.

49 Ibid.

50 CAB 29/142, ME(UK), 12th meeting, 27 June 1933: 18th meeting, 2 July 1933; 19th meeting, 3 July 1933.

2. Trouble with the Empire

1. T 160/516/F. 11935/05.
2. CAB 23/76, 7 July 1933; FO 371/17307, p. 273: Foreign Office minute, 19 July 1933.
3. G. H. de Kock, *A History of the South African Reserve Bank* (Pretoria: J. L. van Schaik, 1954), p. 13.
4. J. C. Smuts Papers, Central Archives Depot, Pretoria, vol. 45, items 149 and 150: "confidential" letters, Strakosch to Smuts, 3 June and 6 August 1930.
5. Ibid., vol. 48, item 65: "private and confidential" letter, Strakosch to Smuts, 29 January 1931.
6. Ibid., vol. 213, item 153: Smuts to Gilbert Murray, 2 May 1933.
7. See Chapter 4.
8. Treasury Files, vol. 7575, file 95/36, and vol. 7576, file 95/36, Annex II, contains the conference materials. The memorandums are in Annex II.
9. Smuts Papers. vol. 49: Smuts to Amery, 9 March 1932.
10. Ibid., vol. 52: Smuts to Amery, 1 February 1934.
11. Treasury Files, vol. 7576, file 95/36, Annex II: dispatch, Smuts to Hertzog, 7 July 1933; Smuts says that the meeting happened on 29 June.
12. CAB 29/142, ME(Conv)23, 30 June 1933.
13. Treasury Files, vol. 7576, file 95/36, Annex II: dispatch, Smuts to Hertzog, 7 July 1933. Smuts dates this meeting as 4 July.
14. CAB 29/143, ME (BC) (33), 5th meeting, 3 July; 6th meeting, 4 July 1933. Also described by Chamberlain in his diary, NC 2/22: entries for 4 and 5 July 1933.
15. CAB 29/142, ME(UK), 21st meeting, 5 July 1933.
16. Smuts Papers, vol. 116: dispatch, Smuts to Hertzog, 14 July 1933.
17. CAB 29/143, ME(BC)(33)22.
18. T 177/12, pt. 1: memorandum, Phillips, 20 July 1933.
19. NC 2/23a: diary entry for 24 July 1933.
20. CAB 29/143, ME(BC)(33), 10th meeting, 18 July 1933.
21. Late in 1932 Phillips had written a memorandum on public works. He explained that the Treasury believed the problem to be a shortage of savings, not a deficiency of investment or of new issues. The Treasury agreed, he wrote, more with Gregory, Hayek, Plant, and Robbins than with MacGregor, Pigou, Keynes, Layton, Salter, and Stamp. T 175/70: memorandum, Phillips, 19 October 1932.
22. CAB 29/143, ME(BC)(33), 10th meeting, 18 July 1933.
23. NC 2/23a: diary entry for 27 July 1933.
24. On its formal passage through the meetings of delegates, see CAB 23/76, 26 July 1933, and CAB 29/143, 11th, 11Ath, and 12th meetings, 24, 25, and 27 July 1933.
25. CAB 23/76, 26 July 1933.
26. As printed in Bank for International Settlements, *Fourth Report*, pp. 13–15; also, *Parliamentary Papers*, vol. 21 (1932–3), Cmd. 4403, p. 499.
27. NC 1/18/837: Chamberlain to Hilda Chamberlain, 23 July 1933; and NC 2/23a: diary entry for 24 July 1933.
28. Smuts Papers, vol. 213, item 166A: Smuts to M. Kentridge, 19 July 1933.

29 Ibid., vol. 50; Amery to Smuts, 29 July 1933.
30 Ibid., item 165: Smuts to Amery, 29 July 1933 (misdated "29 May" in type-
    script and corrected in error by archivist to "29 June?").

Chapter 8. Talking about exchange stabilization,
autumn 1933 through June 1936

1 R. S. Sayers, *The Bank of England, 1891–1944* (Cambridge: Cambridge
   University Press, 1976), pp. 463–7.

1. Franco-American importunities

1 T 177/18: memorandum, Phillips, on the dangers of an undervalued U.S.
   dollar.
2 NC 18/1/843: Chamberlain to Ida Chamberlain, 17 September 1933.
3 Ibid., NC 18/1849: Chamberlain to Ida Chamberlain, 4 November 1933.
4 FO 371/16607, pp. 203–4: telegram, Treasury to Leith-Ross, 25 October
   1933.
5 FO 371/16608, p. 283: telegram, Fisher to Leith-Ross, 1 November 1933.
6 Ibid., p. 286: telegram, Leith-Ross to Fisher, 1 November 1933.
7 Ibid., p. 17: telegram, Leith-Ross to Fisher, 8 November 1933. For an
   account that suggests a larger degree of U.S. government initiative and
   commitment, see Stephen V. O. Clarke, *Exchange-Rate Stabilization in
   the Mid-1930s: Negotiating the Tripartite Agreement* (Princeton University, International Finance Section 1977), p. 3.
8 FO 371/17567: memorandum, Bewley, 16 December 1933, of a conversation with Harrison on 13 December 1933; for the transatlantic view, see
   Clarke, *Exchange-Rate*, p. 3.
9 T 160/949/F. 13672/1: dispatch, Lindsay to Foreign Office, 8 February 1934.
10 NC 18/1/859: Chamberlain to Hilda Chamberlain, 3 February 1934.
11 T 160/949/F. 13672/1: Waley to G. H. S. Pinsent, 8 February 1934.
12 Sayers, *Bank of England*, pp. 466–8.
13 NC 18/1/887: Chamberlain to Ida Chamberlain, 4 September 1934; T
    175/84, pt. 2: memorandum, Phillips to Hopkins, 27 July 1934.
14 T 160/840/F. 13427/1: memorandum, Phillips, 12 April 1934.
15 Ibid.: memorandum, Leith-Ross, 13 April 1934.
16 Ibid.: minute, Chamberlain, 15 April 1934.
17 FO 371/18795, pp. 66–9: memorandum, Leith-Ross, 23 January 1935.
18 Ibid.
19 FO 371/19601, p. 82: Foreign Office Minute, 10 February 1935.
20 NC 2/23a: diary entry for 3 February 1935. On the Flandin visit, Clarke,
    Exchange-Rate, p. 8, is misleading.
21 T 188/116: Leith-Ross to Bewley, 11 March 1935, and note of interview,
    6 March 1935. Clarke, *Exchange-Rate*, p. 8, reports this interchange but
    suggests, incorrectly, that it *preceded* Flandin's visit.
22 FO 371/19601, pp. 87–95: Foreign Office minutes on Leith-Ross's note of
    interview, 6 March 1935.

23 T 188/116: Bewley to Leith-Ross, 29 March 1935; and FO 371/18757, pp. 201–5: Bewley to Leith-Ross, 7 March 1935.
24 FO 371/19600, pp. 104–5: telegram, Lindsay to Foreign Office, 13 March 1935.
25 T 160/845/F. 13640/1: telegram, Treasury to Lindsay, 23 March 1935.
26 Ibid.: Leith-Ross to Lindsay, 30 March 1935.
27 FO 371/19600, pp. 139, 157–9: dispatch, Lindsay to Foreign Office, 28 March 1935, and Lindsay to Leith-Ross, 29 March 1935.
28 T 160/845/F. 13640/1: telegram, Treasury to Lindsay, 13 April 1935, with minute by Chamberlain.
29 T 188/116: Leith-Ross to Bewley, 14 May 1935.
30 T 160/845/F. 13640/1: Leith-Ross to Lindsay, 29 March 1935.
31 John Morton Blum, *From the Morgenthau Diaries* (Boston: Houghton Mifflin, 1959–67), 1: 131.
32 T 188/116: Bewley to Leith-Ross, 17 April 1935.
33 NC 7/11/28/14: handwritten letter, Flandin to Chamberlain, 19 April 1935 (in English).
34 Clarke, *Exchange-Rate*, p. 13.
35 FO 371/19600, pp. 189–90.
36 FO 371/19600, pp. 249–52: memorandum of an interview between Leith-Ross and Monick, 10 May 1935. "Paris and Geneva" refers apparently to the discussions of early March 1935.
37 T 160/840/F. 13427/2: memorandum, Phillips, 15 May 1935.
38 Ibid.: Phillips to Hopkins, 19 May 1935.
39 Ibid.: minute, Chamberlain, 21 May 1935.
40 T 160/845/F. 13640/1: memorandum, Stamp, May 1935.
41 Ibid.: memorandums, Leith-Ross, 7 May 1935, and Phillips, 15 May 1935.
42 See ibid.: Leith-Ross's memorandum of 7 May 1935: "A Mr. White, who described himself as belonging to the US Treasury, called . . . I would not place much confidence in him." Also see T 188/116: memorandum, Phillips to Hopkins, 18 April [May] 1935: "As White was perfectly explicit in disclaiming any authority to negotiate, and as he gave no hint to anyone here of wanting to discuss exchange rates, I doubt if any importance attaches to his remark to Monick about a $4.60 rate."
43 T 188/116: memorandum of conversations between Leith-Ross and Monick, 17 April 1935.
44 Blum, *Morgenthau Diaries*, 1: 139–40. Blum tells us, wrongly, that White's visit occurred in May 1936.
45 T 160/845/F. 13640/: memorandum, Phillips, 30 May 1935.
46 T 160/840/F. 13427/2: memorandum, Phillips, 19 May 1935.
47 Ibid.: memorandum, Phillips, 18 May 1935.
48 T 160/840/F. 13427/3: memorandum, Phillips, on 18th report of Economic Advisory Committee, 14 September 1935.
49 FO 371/19601, pp. 413–4: Chamberlain to Eden, 23 August 1935.
50 Ibid., pp. 427–9, 433, 436.
51 Ibid., p. 456.
52 T 160/840/F. 13427/3: Waley to Pinsent, 28 May 1936.
53 Henry C. Morgenthau Papers, Roosevelt Library, Hyde Park: Diaries

(hereafter cited as MD), 24:2, 11 May 1936. The so-called Diaries consist partly of memorandums and position papers and partly of stenographic transcripts. For Morgenthau's determination to use gold as a weapon to bring the United Kingdom to heel, see MD 26:117A (Morgenthau talks to Bewley, 4 June 1936), 26:151–151F (minutes of a meeting, 8 June 1936); for Bewley's statement of June 1, see MD 26:2–2E, 1 June 1936. Professor Blum, *Morgenthau Diaries*, has omitted all mention of this dimension to Morgenthau's strategy.

54 MD 24:70, 5 May 1936: telephone conversation between Morgenthau and Roosevelt.

55 Blum, *Morgenthau Diaries*, 1: 141–2; MD, 23:5, 1 May 1936: report from Morgenthau to Roosevelt, based on a transatlantic telephone conversation between Morgenthau and Merle Cochran in Paris.

56 MD 23:70, 5 May 1936, and 24:192, 18 May 1936; T 160/845/F. 13650/2: Bewley to Waley, 7 May 1936; FO 371/19831, pp. 345, 358.

57 T 160/845/F. 13640/2: minute by Chamberlain, 29 May 1936, and telegram, Treasury to Lindsay, 28 May 1936; FO 371/19831, pp. 374–6. Clarke, *Exchange-Rate*, p. 24, wrongly interprets this statement as a "pledge" that the dollar-sterling rate would remain unaltered.

58 FO 371/19831, p. 377: telegram, Chamberlain to Lindsay, 28 May 1936.

59 Blum, *Morgenthau Diaries*, 1: 143. For transcript of the meeting, see MD 26:2–2E, 1 June 1936.

60 T 160/845/F. 13640/2: telegrams, Lindsay to Foreign Office, 8 June 1936.

61 Ibid.: telegram, Lindsay to Foreign Office, 6 June 1936. See also Blum, *Morgenthau Diaries*, 1: 146; Clarke, *Exchange-Rate*, pp. 24–5.

62 MD 26:116C, 4 June 1936: transcript of transatlantic telephone call; 26:141–141B, telegram, Cochran to Morgenthau, 5 June 1936 (printed in *FRUS*, 1936, 1: 535–6): 26:148, 6 June 1936, and 26:149, 6 June 1936: transcripts of transatlantic telephone call; 26:150, 6 June 1936: transcript of Morgenthau-Bewley conversation; FO 371/19831, pp. 380–1, 407–8: telegrams, Lindsay to Foreign Office, 4 and 6 June 1936.

63 FO 371/19831, pp. 406, 410: minutes, Lord Cranborne, 8 and 9 June 1936.

64 Ibid., pp. 382, 384–5: telegrams, Chamberlain to Lindsay and to Morgenthau through Lindsay, 5 and 7 June 1936.

65 Ibid., pp. 386–7: telegram, Chamberlain to Lindsay, 7 June 1936.

66 T 160/845/F. 13640/2: memorandum, Phillips, and minute, Chamberlain, 5 and 6 June 1936.

67 Ibid.: note, Hopkins, 17 June 1936.

68 Blum, *Morgenthau Diaries*, 1: 146.

69 T 160/845/F. 13640/2: telegram, Treasury to Lindsay, 7 June 1936; FO 371/19831, p. 409: telegram, Treasury to Lindsay, 8 June 1936.

70 T 160/845/F. 13640/2: telegram, Lindsay to Foreign Office, 9 June 1936.

71 Ibid.: memorandum, Phillips for Chamberlain, 8 June 1936.

72 MD 26:152.

73 MD 26:2–2E.

74 MD 26:151–151F. The minutes were taken by Harry Dexter White, not by Mrs. Klotz, Morgenthau's usual stenographer.

75 For Hull's opinion, see MD 26:142A, 5 June 1936.

76 His account of the meeting is in *FRUS*, 1936, 1: 537 ff.

77 T 160/845/F. 13640/1: note, Hopkins, 17 June 1936.

78 MD 26:153–153J, 8 June 1936.

79 MD 27:219 (memorandum reporting telephone conversation with Cochran), 15 June 1936; 26:160D, 8 June 1936. See also Blum, *Morgenthau Diaries*, 1: 146–8.

80 FO 432/2, V, nos. 77, 91, 98, 102.

81 Ibid., Annex V, nos. 104, 112, with enclosures.

82 Clarke, *Exchange-Rate*, p. 15.

Chapter 9. The Tripartite Agreement of 1936

1 Sir Frederick Leith-Ross, *Money Talks* (London: Hutchinson, 1968), p. 170.

2 W. Arthur Lewis, *Economic Survey, 1919–1939* (London: Allen & Unwin, 1949), pp. 71, 157.

3 Charles P. Kindleberger, *The World in Depression, 1929–1939* (London, Allan Lane, Penguin Press, 1973), pp. 257, 260, 261.

4 In Andrew Schonfield, *International Economic Relations of the Western World, 1959–1971* (Oxford: Oxford University Press for Royal Institute of International Affairs, 1976), 2: 54, citing League of Nations, *International Currency Experience* (Geneva, 1944), the apparent origin of the confusion about the declarations.

5 Stephen V. O. Clarke, *Exchange-Rate Stabilization in the Mid-1930s: Negotiating the Tripartite Agreement* (Princeton University, International Finance Section, 1977).

6 Ibid., p. 55.

7 Kindleberger, *World*, p. 260.

1. The events of late June and July

1 FO 371/20458, p. 339: memorandum, Waley, 2 October 1936.

2 Leith-Ross, *Money Talks*, p. 228.

3 For the conference with Roosevelt, see *FRUS*, 1936, 1: 539–41: memorandum, William Phillips. See also MD 27:148, 20 June 1936; 148C, 20 June 1936; 26:176 ff, 23 June 1936; 178 ff, 23 June 1936; 201–201B, 30 June 1936. See also John Morton Blum, *From the Morgenthau Diaries* (Boston: Houghton Mifflin, 1959–67), 1: 159, and Clarke, *Exchange-Rate*, pp. 27–9.

4 T 160/840/F. 13427/4: memorandum, Waley, 22 July 1936.

5 See Chapter 8.

6 MD 28:110–110B, 22 July 1936; see also Blum, *Morgenthau Diaries*, 1: 159.

7 T 160/840/F. 13427/4: memorandum, Phillips, 25 July 1936.

8 Ibid.: memorandums, Waley, 22 July 1936, and Phillips, 25 July 1936.

9 Ibid.: memorandum, Waley, 22 July 1936.

10 Writing to his sister, Chamberlain mentioned that he had seen Blum

about "various financial matters." NC 18/1/971: Chamberlain to Hilda Chamberlain, 25 July 1936. The Chamberlain Papers contain no other mention of the July discussion.

11 T 160/840/F. 13427/4: minute, Chamberlain, 26 July 1936.

2. *The events of September*

1 MD 30:356F, G: dispatch, Cochran to State Department, 27 August 1936.
2 T 160/840/F. 13427/4: memorandum, Phillips, 7 September 1936.
3 T 160/685/F. 14741/1: Rowe-Dutton to Phillips, 8 September 1936.
4 MD 31:101: telegram, Cochran to Morgenthau, 4 September 1936, and associated discussions. The telegram appears in *FRUS*, 1936, 1: 541–3. Professor Blum *Morgenthau Diaries*, 1: 160) says that Cochran was handed the draft on 4 September, but Cochran cabled, "I have not seen the document."
5 FO 371/20458, p. 256: telegram, U.K. embassy in Washington to Foreign Office, 5 September 1936.
6 As printed in *FRUS*, 1936, 1: 544–5. See also Clarke, *Exchange-Rate*, pp. 33–7.
7 FO 371/20458, p. 108: telegram, Morgenthau through U.K. embassy to Foreign Office, 5 September 1936.
8 Ibid., pp. 106–7: "very secret" minute, Phillips, 7 September 1936.
9 *FRUS*, 1936, 1: 543–5: telegram, Cochran to State Department, 9 September 1936; T 160/685/F. 14741/1: Rowe-Dutton to Leith-Ross, 8 September 1936.
10 T 160/840/F. 13427/4: minute, Chamberlain, 12 September 1936.
11 Ibid.: memorandum, Phillips, 10 September 1936.
12 Ibid.
13 Ibid.: draft and final notes, 12 September 1936; see also FO 371/20458, pp. 187–90.
14 FO 371/20458, p. 256: telegram, Sir Warren Fisher to Mongenthau, 14 September 1936.
15 MD 32:65–68.
16 MD 32:74–75: minutes of evening meeting, 9 September 1936.
17 Blum, *Morgenthau Diaries*, 1: 162.
18 Ibid., pp. 160, 163.
19 *FRUS*, 1936, 1:546–7: telegram, Morgenthau to Cochran, 14 September 1936; See also FO 371/20458, pp. 116–17: telegram, U.K. embassy to Foreign Office, 14 September 1936.
20 Clarke, *Exchange-Rate*, p. 35.
21 *FRUS*, 1936, 1: 545–6: telegram, Morgenthau to Cochran for Auriol, 9 September 1936.
22 MD 32:88: memorandum of telephone conversation, Cochran and Morgenthau, 10 September 1936.
23 As printed in *FRUS*, 1936, 1: 547.
24 T 188/167: Phillips to Leith-Ross, 14 September 1936.
25 T 160/840/F. 13427/4: Leith-Ross to Phillips, 16 September 1936.

26 *FRUS*, 1936, 1: 553: telegram, Morgenthau to Cochran, 19 September 1936.
27 MD 32:219: telegram, Cochran to Morgenthau, 15 September 1936.
28 T 160/840/F. 13427/4: memorandum, Hopkins for chancellor of the exchequer, 18 September 1936.
29 FO 371/20458, p. 339, Annex VI.
30 Ibid., pp. 256/5: telegram, U.K. embassy to Foreign Office, 21 September 1936.
31 Ibid., p. 339, Annex VI.
32 Ibid., pp. 339/3–4.
33 T 160/840/F. 13427/5: memorandums, Hopkins, 21 and 23 September 1936; Phillips to Hopkins, 21 September 1936. Clarke (*Exchange Rate*, p. 45) appears to place excessive emphasis on this matter.
34 FO 371/20458, p. 339/3.
35 T 160/840/F. 13427/5: memorandum, Waley, 23 September 1936.
36 FO 371/20458, p. 339/4.
37 FO 371/20458, p. 256/8: telegram, Treasury for Morgenthau, 24 September 1936.
38 MD 32:289–306.
39 MD 33:8P-Q.
40 MD 33:8X and 8GG. See also Blum, *Morgenthau Diaries*, 1: 163 ff.
41 As printed in *FRUS*, 1936, 1: 554: drafted by Morgenthau, Feis, Taylor, Haas, White, and Viner on 18 September 1936. See MD 33:18A-N. See also Clarke, *Exchange-Rate*, pp. 34–40.
42 *FRUS*, 1936, 1: 554 ff.: telegram, Cochran to Morgenthau, 33 September 1936.
43 Ibid., p. 557: telegram, Morgenthau to Cochran, 23 September 1936.
44 MD 33:250.
45 MD 33:250: conversation with the president; 33:194: telephone conversation, Morgenthau and Cochran, 24 September 1936.
46 MD 33:222 ff., 24 September 1936: minutes of staff discussion; 33:232, 24 September 1936; 33:153: minutes of staff discussion, 24 September 1936.
47 MD 34:7–8, 25 September 1936.
48 FO 371/20458, p. 256/4–5: telegram, U.K. embassy in Washington to Foreign Office, 11:45 P.M., 24 September 1936.
49 MD 33:153: 24 September 1936. See also Blum, *Morgenthau Diaries*, 1: 169.
50 MD 33:158.
51 NC 2/23a: diary entry for 25 September 1936; see also NC 18/1/978: Chamberlain to Ida Chamberlain, 28 September 1936.
52 FO 371/20458, p. 256/10: telegram, Chamberlain through Foreign Office to embassy for Morgenthau, 3:05 P.M., 25 September 1936. See also Clarke, *Exchange-Rate*, pp. 49–51.
53 FO 371/20458, pp. 199–200, 211: telegrams, Sir George Clark to Foreign Office and vice versa, 25 September 1936.
54 NC 2/23a: diary entry for September 1936; FO 371/20458, p. 256/10: telegram, Chamberlain through Foreign Office to embassy for Morgenthau, 3:05 P.M., 25 September 1936.

55 T 160/840/F. 13427/6: telegram, Morgenthau to Chamberlain, received 11:00 P.M., 25 September 1936; MD, 34:10,43. See also Blum, *Morgenthau Diaries*, 1: 169–70; FO 371/20458, p. 223: minute, 28 September 1936.

56 MD 34:46.

57 As in FO 371/20458, p. 339, Annex X; printed in Bank for International Settlements, *Seventh Report*, 1936.

58 FO 371/20458, p. 256/6: telegram, U.K. embassy to Foreign Office, 26 September 1936.

59 Benjamin M. Rowland, ed., *Balance of Power or Hegemony: The Interwar Monetary System* (New York: New York University Press, 1976), p. 209.

60 Ibid., p. 210.

3. Other currencies follow the franc

1 The details may be found in Bank for International Settlements, *Seventh Report*, and in "Chronicle of the Past Week," *Economist*, 3 October 1936, pp. 3–5.

2. NC 18/1/978: Chamberlain to Ida Chamberlain, 28 August 1936. On the Soviet "sabotage," see Kindleberger, *World*, p. 258; Morgenthau thought that on 26 September the USSR had sold dollars merely to drive the dollar down.

3 NC 2/23: diary entry for 7 October 1936.

4 T 188/167: Leith-Ross to Rowe-Dutton, 29 September 1936.

5 T 160/685/F. 14741/1: Rowe-Dutton to Waley, 6 October 1936.

6 MD 34:255: telephone conversation, Morgenthau and Harrison, 25 September 1936.

7 Clarke, *Exchange-Rate*, pp. 36–7.

8 T 160/685/F. 14741/2: memorandum, Foreign Office commercial counselor, Paris, 15 January 1937.

4. Morgenthau agrees to sell gold

1 MD 34:380–1: 26 September 1936.

2 *FRUS*, 1936 1: 555: telegram, Cochran to Morgenthau, 1:00 P.M., 23 September 1936.

3 Ibid., pp. 557–58: telegram, Morgenthau to Cochran, midnight, 23 September 1936.

4 Ibid., pp. 562–3: telegram, Cochran to Morgenthau, 6 October 1936.

5 T 160/885/F. 17657/09/1: telegram, U.K. embassy in Washington to Foreign Office, 5 and 6 October 1936; Clarke, *Exchange-Rate*, pp. 51–4.

6 T 160/885/F. 17657/09/1: telegram, embassy to Foreign Office, 8 October 1936; Bewley to Waley, 12 October 1936.

7 T 177/33: telegram, Chamberlain to Morgenthau, 7 October 1936; T 160/885/F. 17657/09/1: memorandum, Hopkins, 6 October 1936.

8 T 160/885/F. 17657/09/1: telegrams, U.K. embassy to Treasury, 16 and 30 October 1936. On Swiss and Japanese adherence to the declarations, see material in T 160/840/F. 13427/8.

9 T 177/31: minute, Leith-Ross to Phillips and Hopkins, 29 September 1936.

Chapter 10. Intergovernmental conversations and the management of sterling, 1936–1939

1 See Ian M. Drummond, *London, Washington, and the Management of the Franc* (Princeton University, International Finance Section, 1979).

1. Sterling's dirty float, 1936–1939

1 FO 371/20656, p. 33.
2 This subdivision follows R. S. Sayers, *The Bank of England, 1891–1944* (Cambridge: Cambridge University Press, 1976), p. 481.
3 *Bank of England Quarterly Bulletin*, March 1974, p. 49.
4 From *Parliamentary Papers*, vol. 18 (1950–1), Cmd. 8354, p. 553. External liabilities were counted only in June and in December.
5 Sayers, *Bank of England*, pp. 483–5; Susan Howson, *Domestic Monetary Management in Britain, 1919–1938* (Cambridge: Cambridge University Press, 1975), pp. 126, 136; Susan Howson and Donald Winch, *The Economic Advisory Council, 1930–1939* (Cambridge: Cambridge University Press, 1977), pp. 145–6.
6 Sayers, *Bank of England*, pp. 484–5; Howson, *Domestic Monetary Policy*, pp. 126–7; Sir Henry Clay, *Lord Norman* (London: Macmillan, 1957), p. 429.
7 FO 371/20656, p. 292.
8 FO 371/20657, pp. 2–21: memorandum, E. Trentham, financial adviser, 18 May 1937.
9 MD 61:155A: 1 April 1937.
10 MD 65:114–17: telegram, Butterworth to Morgenthau, 16 April 1937; 65: 195–9: telephone conversation, Morgenthau and Butterworth, 19 April 1937.
11 T 160/840/F. 13427/8: memorandum, Leith-Ross, 31 May 1937.
12 T 175/94, pt. 1: memorandum, Phillips, "The Present and Future of Gold," 1937.
13 T 160/840/F. 13427/8: memorandum, Phillips, 7 June 1937.
14 Ibid.: memorandum, Hopkins, 9 June 7937, and minute thereon by Fisher.
15 FO 371/20689, pp. 17–19: Foreign Office minute, 24 June 1937; p. 52: telegram, Morgenthau to Treasury; pp. 47–50: telegram, Simon to Morgenthau, 23 June 1937; MD 74:11–17, 40, 48.
16 MD 74: 11–17, 40, 48.
17 See CAB 32/127 for the preparations. For American and Continental opinion, see MD 72:50.
18 T 175/94, pt. 1: Treasury minute for Hopkins, n.d.; pt. 3: text of draft resolution; *Parliamentary Papers*, vol. 21 (1932–3), Cmd. 4403, p. 499, for the 1933 Commonwealth statement. For Simon's requests for American comments on gold, see MD 71:252–73; MD 74:11–17; MD 72:286, for notification to Americans.
19 CAB 32/128, E(PD), 8th meeting, 27 May 1937.

20   CAB 27/130, E(MP), 1st meeting, 14 June 1937; CAB 32/128, E(PD), 19th meeting, 14 June 1937.
21   CAB 32/128, E(PD), 20th meeting, 20 June 1937.
22   See P. J. Grigg, *Prejudice and Judgment* (London: Cape. 1948), p. 296; W. K. Hancock, *Survey of Commonwealth Affairs, II: Problems of Economic Policy* (Oxford: Oxford University Press for RIIA, 1940), vol. 1; and Ian M. Drummond, *Imperial Economic Policy, 1917–1939* (London: Allen & Unwin, 1974).
23   T 175/94, pt. 1: note, Phillips, preceding his visit to Washington; see also MD 73:345; telegram, Cochran to Morgenthau, 21 June 1937.
24   MD 88:253: memorandum, Morgenthau, 17 September 1937.
25   MD 88:125–8: memorandums, Haas and others, n.d.
26   T 175/94, pt. 3: memorandum, Phillips, "Talk with Mr. Morgenthau on Gold," 25 September 1937.
27   Sayers, *Bank of England*; Cmd. 8354, *Parliamentary Papers*, vol. 18, 1950–1), p. 553, shows the authorities' gold holdings rising by 12 percent from March to June 1937, by 3.6 percent from June to September, by 1.4 percent September to December, and by 0.9 percent from December 1937 to March 1938.
28   T 160/770/F. 15583: minute, Hopkins, 25 November 1937; minute, Chamberlain, 2 December 1937. See also Howson and Winch, *Economic Advisory Council*, pp. 146–7.
29   *Parliamentary Papers*, vol. 18 (1951–2), Cmd. 8354, p. 553.
30   Ibid. In addition, the Exchange Equalisation Account held about £25 million in foreign exchange.
31   See, for instance, T 175/94, pt. 1: untitled anonymous memorandum, 1936.
32   T 160/877/F. 16003.
33   MD 134:199–207: 14 July 1937. The participants were Morgenthau, Taylor, Oliphant, Lockhead, Bernstein, and White.
34   MD 131:316 ff.: memorandum, Butterworth to Morgenthau, June 1938; 135:31–4: Cochran to Morgenthau, 5 August 1938; 135:51: telegram, Cochran to State, 9 August 1938; 135:283–4: memorandum, Cochran, 25 August 1938; 135:326.32: telegram, Butterworth to Morgenthau, 26 August 1938.
35   MD 137:87, 90, 166, 241–53.
36   MD 147:74–129: conference on sterling, 21 October 1938. Participants were Taylor, White, Lochhead, Viner, Riefler, Goldenweiser, Burgess, Stewart, Warren, and Feis. See, in particular, pp. 74, 76, 91–2.
37   MD 147:93, 118, 124.
38   MD 147:146–69.
39   MD 147:156.
40   T 160/871/F. 15777: Bewley to Waley, 27 October and 2 November 1938.
41   MD 150:97–111, 10 November 1938. For White's agenda, see MD, 150: 118–21.
42   See Drummond, *London, Washington* .
43   MD 150:98.
44   MD 151:2–4: memorandum, Morgenthau, 15 November 1938.

45 MD 151:2–4, 10, 12–13, 93–8: esp. memorandum, Morgenthau, 15 November 1938, on the conversations and events of 14 November.
46 T 160/871/F. 15777: telegram, Lindsay to Foreign Office, 14 November 1938; memorandum, Hopkins, and telegram, Foreign Office to Lindsay, 16 November 1938 (drafted by Hopkins and approved by Siepmann on behalf of the Bank). See also MD 152:355–6.
47 T 160/871/F. 15777: memorandum to R. G. Hawtrey, n.d.
48 MD 152:316–22, 357; T 160/871/F. 15777: telegram, Bewley to Treasury, 22 November 1938.
49 MD 153:183.
50 MD 153:184.
51 MD 153:187, 193–4.
52 MD 153:199.
53 MD 153:198.
54 MD 152:364–7, 153:218. For a U.S. Treasury attempt to dissuade Roosevelt, see MD, 153:253–4.
55 MD 152:369–70: memorandum, Lochhead, 22 November 1938.
56 MD 153:243.
57 Ibid.: telegram and instructions by bag to Bewley, n.d., certainly written between 22 and 28 November 1938.
58 T 160/871/F. 15777: telegrams and dispatches, Bewley to Treasury, 28 and 30 November and 1 December 1938; MD 153:64–70.
59 MD 153:177–9, 181–221, 182.
60 MD 153:221–4 (White's memorandum), 153:255–6 (agreed statement by visitors).
61 MD 153:181–221, 226–52, esp. 237.
62 MD 153:375–6; 154:232: memorandum, Cochran, 3 December 1938.
63 MD 155:218: memorandum, Taylor for Morgenthau, 9 December 1938; T 160/871/F. 15777: telegram, Bewley to Treasury, 9 December 1938.
64 T 160/871/F. 15777: Bewley to Waley, 8 December 1938; telegram, Treasury to Bewley, c. 13 December 1938. See also Sayers, *Bank of England*, pp. 563–4.
65 FO 371/22810, p. 240: dispatch, U.K. embassy in Washington to Foreign Office, 3 March 1939; p. 239.
66 FO 371/21540, p. 361: minute, 17 November 1938, on Bewley to Waley, 2 November 1938.
67 FO 371/22810, pp. 256–7: memorandum, Phillips, 12 February 1938; T 160/871/F. 15777: telegrams and dispatches between Bewley and Treasury, 22 November to 1 December 1938. See also MD 157:217, 223–4, 268, 282–3.
68 T 160/871/F. 15777: memorandum, Phillips, 21 December 1938; minute, Hopkins, 22 December 1938; telegram, Treasury to Bewley, 22 December 1938. See also Sayers, *Bank of England*, pp. 564–5.
69 T 160/871/F. 15777: telegrams, Bewley to Treasury, 22 December and 30 December 1938; Bewley to Waley, 23 December 1938; memorandum of meeting, 28 December 1938; Sayers, *Bank of England*, p. 565; MD 158: p. 66–73: telegram, Butterworth to Morgenthau, 28 December 1938.
70 MD 158:66–73; see also T 188/232.
71 Sayers, *Bank of England*, pp. 563–4.

72 Clay, *Lord Norman*, p. 433; Sayers, *Bank of England*, p. 565.
73 For their struggles, see Sayers, *Bank of England*, pp. 563–7, and Susan Howson, "The Managed Floating Pound, 1932–39," *Banker*, March 1976, p. 255.
74 T 160/877/F. 16003: brief, apparently by Phillips for chancellor of the exchequer, 21 August 1939. Sayers (*Bank of England*, p. 571) gives August reserves as below £450 million.
75 For developments in the last days of August, see Sayers, *Bank of England*, pp. 571–2, and idem, *Financial Policy, 1939–1945* (London: HMSO, 1956), pp. 226–35.
76 T 160/877/F. 16003: brief for chancellor, 21 August 1939.
77 Ibid.: Treasury brief for talk with Franco-American diplomats.
78 Ibid.: memorandum, Bewley (now in London) for Phillips, 25 August 1939.

2. *Some conclusions*

1 Benjamin M. Rowland, ed., *Balance of Power or Hegemony: The Interwar Monetary System* (New York: New York University Press, 1976), pp. 251, 51.
2 Ibid., p. 56.

Chapter 11. Conclusion: the significance of sterling

1 Jonathan Swift, *Gulliver's Travels*, pt. 3, chap. 1.
2 See Chapter 1; and R. S. Sayers, *The Bank of England, 1891–1944* (Cambridge: Cambridge University Press, 1976), pp. 447–53.

Index

absence of consultation under Tri-
partite Agreement, 223, 247–9
Acheson, Dean (U.S. official), 182
Amery, Leo (U.K. politician), 19, 23,
64–5, 94, 175–6, 180
Anglo-American trade agreement, 229,
233–8, 259–60
Anglophobia, 7, 53, 233
Angus, H. F. (Canadian political
scientist), 66
Argentina, 171
Arndt, E.H.D. (South African economist), 175
Ashton Gwatkin, F. (U.K. Foreign
Office official), 9, 21
Atherton, Ray (U.S. diplomat), 125–6,
143, 199
Auriol, Vincent (French politician),
196–7, 199–200, 205–6, 209–10, 215
Australia, 1, 3, 5–7, 10–12, 26, 34, 36,
70, 99–104, 112, 115–8, 159,
161, 163, 171, 174, 231, 252, 257,
259–61
  contrasts with New Zealand and
  South Africa, 99, 102–4
  refunding operations in 1930s,
  115–19
  risk of default on overseas obligations, 11, 34, 36, 115–19

Babington Smith Committee, 29
Bank for International Settlements
and "paper gold," 62, 67, 130,
133–9, 142, 172, 223
Bank of Canada, 13, 72–3
Bank of England, 6–7, 9, 11–15, 17–18,
20, 22–3, 33, 50–2, 81–2, 102–5,
107–15, 125, 130, 137, 141, 148,

151, 163, 181, 184–5, 192, 194, 197,
199, 201, 212, 217, 220, 222,
226–7, 235, 240, 243–4, 246, 254–5,
261
credit to Australasia, 10, 104, 109,
261
credit to India, 34–43
credit to Nordic countries, 10
Bank of Finland, 8
Bank of France, 121–3, 141, 150–2,
169, 181, 184, 190, 194, 210, 217,
222
Bank of Sweden, 8
Barclay's Bank, 76–8, 91, 92, 94–5
Batchelder, Charles, (U.S. banker)
59–60
Baumgartner, Wilfred (French Treasury official and banker), 191
bear squeeze, 243–4, 246
belga, 167
Belgium, 126, 128–9, 158, 167, 211,
222, 249
Benn, Wedgewood (U.K. politician),
33–4, 36–7
Bennett, R. B. (Prime Minister of
Canada), 12, 19, 23, 52–4, 57–8,
60–1, 64–7, 71–5, 106–7, 160, 163,
171, 177–8, 255
Bewley, T. K. (U.K. diplomat), 140,
151, 154, 184, 187, 195–6, 198–9,
204, 221, 223, 225, 227, 230,
238–42, 244–5
bilateral trading arrangements and
New Zealand, 104–14
Bizot, Henry (French Treasury official), 167–8
Blum, John Morton (U.S. historian),
190, 192, 196, 198, 207–8, 214